POSTMODERN SPIRITUALITY
IN THE AGE OF
ENTITLEMENT

DAVID JOHN ROBSON

Bibles Used

NRSV   New Revised Standard Version Bible © 1989 - the Division of Christian Education of the National Council of the Churches of Christ in the United States of America

CEB   Common English Bible © 2011 - The United Methodist Publishing House, Nashville TN

Tellwell Talent
www.tellwell.ca

ISBN
978-0-2288-5570-5 (Hardcover)
978-0-2288-5571-2 (Paperback)
978-0-2288-5569-9 (eBook)

CONTENTS

Preface v

Introduction ix

Chapter 1   Postmodernism and Western Society 1

Chapter 2   Postmodernism and Western Christianity 24

Chapter 3   Postmodern Spirituality 50

Chapter 4   Spiritual but Not Religious 73

Chapter 5   Spirituality and the Brain 120

Chapter 6   Spirituality and Mindfulness 140

Chapter 7   Spirituality and Issues of Loneliness 152

Chapter 8   Spirituality and Education 167

Chapter 9   The Future 199

Appendix A: A Practical Model of "Spirituality and Learning:"
            Rooted in Adult Learning Principles 245

Appendix B: A Partial List of Topics that Examine Spirituality in
            Postmodernism 259

Appendix C: Some Tools and Models Used To "Measure"
            Spirituality 261

Appendix D: Some Tools and Models Used To "Measure"
            Mindfulness 268

Appendix E: Mindfulness in Education Research Highlights 271

Notes 277

Bibliography 323

About the Author 353

PREFACE

The great global crisis of the early 1940s greatly disrupted my parents' lives. One sailed off to war, while the other, at 14, began work in a factory. When World War II ended, thoughts of ongoing education ended. Dad immigrated to Canada and resumed his banking career. When they raised sufficient funds, the young woman he'd dated for six weeks "crossed the pond" and became his bride. Their practice of reading, learning, and "churchmanship" remained. They passed this gift on to their three sons. From an early age, my twin and I, and later my younger brother, saw our parents actively model reading.

In recent years, perhaps because it was to be demolished and replaced by a more modern and adaptable building, I began to reflect on my days in high school. Social media connections with people unseen for decades also developed. In my reflections, I began to realize how I was inspired by the late Marnie McVeigh, Nora Guthrie, Don Baxter, and Art Brown, among others. In my pondering, I realized they didn't so much teach as stimulate me to learn. What was your experience like? Many decades later, I still thirst for much learning—but as high school proved, not for math or science!

As a child, I read the cereal box almost every morning! I loved comics, magazines, and books. Through the years, I continued to find reading invigorating and stimulating. Writing, however, was another matter! To resolve this deficiency, my practice was to write, rewrite, and rewrite. In time, I learned discipline! Reading and writing remain great passions. Ironically, my career path, while requiring much reading and writing, greatly depended on the spoken word. First, an illustration to explain postmodernism.

Without question, I am a product of postmodernism. When I was baptized, the liturgy was from the 1918 Church of England in *Canada Book of Common Prayer*. From a young child until ordination, I used the 1962 *Book of Common Prayer*. It was the first Canadian worship book for the newly renamed Anglican Church of Canada. I still have my presentation copy from 1966! While I don't appreciate the medieval theology often expressed by Thomas Cranmer's writing of the first *Book of Common Prayer*, its poetic cadence still soothes me. I was ordained and married using draft versions of the 1985 *Canadian Anglican Book of Alternative Services*. Thus, in less than three decades, I was the product of three diverse books of worship. This news is radical, especially considering that the previous revision of Anglican liturgy took place in 1662! As an aside, the few updates after 1662 remained, in my view, fundamentally similar to the original. Postmodernism, or the New Reformation, oozes broader, deeper, and faster social and personal change than the rest of history combined.

I was fortunate to live my dream as an Anglican/Episcopalian priest. Half of my career was in my native Ontario, the other half in Pennsylvania. While in full-time parish work, I was able, because of disciplined early morning routines (who doesn't love 5:30 a.m.?) to read, write, and reflect. In that productive quiet time, and throughout the day, I valued the opportunity of exploring and understanding spirituality. In turn, I often contemplated concerns and issues about various societal developments. This practice led me to the joy of researching, writing, and reflecting upon postmodern spirituality.

A small grant from the Congregational Development Committee of the Episcopal Diocese of Central Pennsylvania allowed me to contract a typist to transcribe pages of outlined quotes from dozens of books, countless journal articles, news clippings, various graduate theses, and some doctoral dissertations. I was fortunate that Ms. Paula Beever proved an awesome help in this undertaking. For the grant and Paula, I am so very thankful. Likewise, I am grateful to my American Episcopalian congregations for their patience as I sometimes "road tested" ideas or models of spiritual practices with them.

Many thanks to Mark Wilkins of Verona, Ontario, who volunteered to proofread. His insights and recommendations helped reshape this effort. When I was frustrated, he helped revive my enthusiasm.

Also, my thanks to all the folk at Tellwell for guiding me through this self-publication. I chose these fine people over traditional publishers because mainstream publishers often symbolize a long and arduous path. Given that my zip is sometimes zapped, I wasn't sure I would have the energy to invest in that lengthy process.

As noted, this effort is the product of continuous involvement of research, writing, reflection, rewriting, etc. My lifelong partner, Lynn, was gracious and patient (sainthood application is pending) with me while I was on this incredible journey.

This work took over a decade to create, given the priority of full-time parish obligations. However, its roots go back to my earliest days in ordained ministry. Shortly after ordination, I started reflecting on the society changing around me. Likewise, I took notice of church attendance trends across denominations and local churches. Too often, I saw clergy in emotional and spiritual pain as they bore the brunt of the changing reality of smaller congregations. I saw the introduction and rise of the big box churches and societal shift to evangelical theology as part of the mainstream decline. In some cases, it seemed easier for congregations and management to blame clergy for declining attendance and income than to address evolving (devolving) societal issues. In the year I was born, Pete Seeger wrote about flowers disappearing. Both he, the folk group, Peter, Paul, and Mary, and others made the song popular. Throughout my ministry and other life situations I used Seeger's words, and often wondered, "When will we ever learn?" As one who passionately enjoys learning about adult learning, many years ago that as a society we tend to give much attention to "what" we learn and little to "how" we learn. We need understand both context and process before can dare explore content. Good context and process filter out poor content, whereas little or no exploration of issues or questions without dealing with process or context does not! In time, I was able to weave many threads of adult learning, practical experiences, and spiritual practices and began to see and cull emerging trends in new societal changes taking place in postmodernism.

Early in my ruminations, I realized that many authors of non-fiction books typically write with the dominant message of, "This is what I think!" When I began this effort, I was motivated to offer a variation of this theme.

While there is much of David within this effort, I felt that the thoughts of many fine scholars should be included. In other words, I had a strong desire to expose the reader to the powerful insights and labours of others. This means there are some long quotes. I hope that readers might say, "Oh, that author's thoughts are fascinating, I think I will look for that book!"

In another unique turn, I constantly ask the reader questions on the theme, "What do you think?" It's a call for readers to stop, to be still for a moment, and to reflect. We might say these questions invite readers to take time from horizontal or progressive reading to practice vertical pondering, or to take time to go deeper—to listen to what one's spirit is saying!

While the majority of the quotations are in American English, those written in the Queen's English appear in that form. While I grew up using the Queen's English, I also grew up when many publications in Canada, perhaps to broader their appeal, began using American spellings. For example, "colour" in the Queen's English, began being printed as "color," the American form, in books, magazines, and newspapers, etc. While a Canadian, and one who enjoyed almost two decades in Pennsylvania, American English is used for continuity except as just noted.

The journey was long with many hills, valleys, twists, and turns. Some of these hills, valleys, twists, and turns were exciting. However, others caused me to rethink and ponder anew. The journey saw sunlight and rain, dark days, and some long, clear pathways. The printing of this book is the destination that shows the long, winding journey was an awesome and fruitful ride! I hope readers glean a few insights into life, postmodernism, and spirituality in this, the Age of Entitlement.

David John Robson
Belleville, Ontario
Christmas Season 2021

INTRODUCTION

"I t was the best of times, it was the worst of times, it was the age of wisdom, it was the age of foolishness, it was the epoch of belief, it was the epoch of incredulity ... " So begins Charles Dickens' iconic 1859 novel, *A Tale of Two Cities*. These famous and oft-quoted words truly describe our society! I'd like to suggest that we can co-opt this famous introduction of Dickens to the joys and struggles we encounter.

We live a world of greatness and a time of despair. We live in a global village, yet how many people can we truly call "my friend?" Similarly, in our topsy-turvy postmodern world, we may have sex with strangers yet not know the names of our neighbors! We sacrifice intimacy and friendship for fleeting "hook-ups." We desire physical release and satisfaction without any mental, emotional, or spiritual connection. Instead of whole connectedness, we may consider sex as merely a fleeting and momentary physical release. This is reflective of much in postmodernism. We are drawn to the fleeting over the foundational, to instant gratification over long-term obligations, to self-satisfaction ahead of meeting the needs of others. We want, expect, and desire our wants and needs to be met (often instantly) while often feeling no obligation to respond in kind.

In turn, we often sacrifice a sense of community, of knowing and living with those around us, because our needs (and perhaps only our needs) are of primary concern. In other words, in looking after #1, we may afford only shallow commitment to others. Have we lost, or are we losing, our souls? Have we as social creatures lost our sense of true and affirming communities? These questions are relevant for all in the vast global village. Where is our spirituality in the postmodern world? Where is spirituality in the postmodern world? These questions beg our attention.

Postmodernism provides countless benefits. Even so, postmodernism, with its many centers, options, and varied views and vastness, can leave people floundering with indecisiveness. We seem to be looking for direction and purpose in life but may find the number of choices overwhelming, too complex, and, consequently, confusing. We wonder how we can choose, and what we choose. Unlike past societies, solutions and decisions that fit and worked on Monday may not apply on Friday. Consider that Western Society existed for centuries on ideals rooted in the ten Mosaic codes that, for many, were "carved in stone." Today, our codes are "stored on smartphones." They're also likely time-stamped because of constant updates and revisions!

In postmodernism, global religions are sailing in unknown and uncharted waters. Solutions of the past seem neutered. Religions seem confused and confounded on how to address issues where changes move at accelerated rates. Specifically, it's difficult for religious institutions in Western Society, which adjust slowly and with carefully measured actions, to move at any rate near those of societal shifts. Richard Hamm, in *Recreating the Church: Leadership for the Post-Modern Age*, explains this well:

> ... Unfortunately, it is also true that most institutions (including church institutions) tend to favor homeostasis— "staying the same"—no matter what happens in their cultural context. This should not come as a great surprise since institutions are created in the first place to conserve particular values and ways of doing things. And, institutions are created by human beings, who themselves have a distaste for change even when it is required to avoid disaster or to respond to a captivating vision ...[1]

Today in the postmodern world it's clear that Western Christianity is in rapid and unprecedented decline. Denial is not an option! Despite this decline, it's also a time of remarkable interest in spirituality! The SBNRs (Spiritual But Not Religious) is the largest group in Western Society.

Likewise, fields of education, medicine, and business have also entered the field of studying spirituality.

In this work, we limit our attention to some thoughts on postmodernism, the effects of postmodernism on Western Society, and some important trends taking place in Western Christianity. In the context of these topics, we consider how postmodernism weaves itself with Western spirituality. This effort is not exhaustive, but it is comprehensive. Postmodernism replaced modernism.

Modernism was marked by the rise of capitalism and science around the end of the seventeenth century. Rational ideas, the acceptance of scientific ideas, and knowledge were key elements. This period marked a slow, subtle shift from the sacred to the secular. Postmodernism moved from knowledge to opinions and, specifically, to honoring "my opinions." The role of community was replaced by the rise of individualism. "Me-ism" and fragmented compartmentalized lives became the normal benchmark of Western Society.

Postmodernism is like the 1939 classic movie *The Wizard of Oz*. At the beginning of the movie, a tornado takes young, naïve Dorothy and transports her to the strange land of Oz. Postmodernism has metaphorically lifted and moved the world, including Western Society, Western Christianity, and Western spirituality, to a strange, unknown land. Dorothy learned to adapt to her new environment. Compared to her staid, rural Kansas farm background, the land of Oz, like the postmodern landscape, was full of countless new realities. Like Dorothy, we too learned to assimilate ourselves to our new surroundings. Dorothy and her companions were enlightened when they pulled back the curtain exposing The Great Oz as an ordinary man pulling levers to create a façade. In postmodernism, we need to pull back the curtain or the blinders that prevent us from looking at and dealing with the evolving world, society, community, and spirituality around us. We must be bold and look in the mirror to see who we are and how we are spiritual beings in this greatest reformation in history.

After World War II, Western Society began a slow societal change. In the 1960s, this change, or evolution, picked up speed. Perhaps we might say that the comfortable family sedan gave way to a wave of fast, powerful, muscle cars! The rapid change and growth of the 1960s is still speeding up. Great change is swirling around us. At times, it seems that as soon as we begin to adjust to our environment, a bold new direction emerges and transports us once more. Moreover, if we're always in the process of moving, we must wonder, "What has happened to our rootedness?"

Postmodernism and Oz are places offering great benefits, yet in both, people need to utilize "heart, bravery, and smart thinking." In the movie, Dorothy's goal was to return to Kansas because "There's no place like home." She naturally desired to return to her familiar life and roots. We are like Dorothy. We live in a world so complex that we yearn to return to what we perceive were simpler and better times. At best, we yearn for a world we can put our arms around and hold. Unlike Dorothy, we can't go back. We can't return to what was. Today, our world knowledge is so vast we can at best barely hold or grasp a few small parts. In our frustration to try to grasp everything, and in a time of much disruption, we often fall into confrontation instead of collaborative or conversational actions. We act as if wounded, and we lash out. Some may say this is reflective of a stratified and dysfunctional *Brave New World*.

In 1932, Aldous Huxley wrote this epic work, in which the underlying theme explored futuristic realities. Huxley wrote of the rise of technology. Specifically, he noted how it moves humanity away from a sense of the transcendent. Huxley described that with the removal of God, the removal of a sense of community, a fixed class system, and a corresponding sense of limited connectedness, people develop grim, sad lives. We can't help but wonder if Huxley's literary projections and marvellous satire depict our postmodern world?

In *The Wizard of Oz*, Dorothy Gale suddenly finds herself in a strange world. Our transition, which began in the 1960s, was slow and incremental. Our transition is like the classic frog in the kettle analogy. When we apply high heat to the kettle, the frog reacts and jumps out of the kettle. However, if we slowly raise the heat, the frog is unaware of the changes. In other words, we cook the frog—literally.

In the last few decades, however, these slow and incremental changes gave way to faster and more intensive changes. Given human adaptability, we began to accept these faster shifts as our new normal! These shifts affected our social, religious, political, and environmental environments.

Somehow, we seem to take many of these paradigm-changing realities of a brave new world in stride. However, at some point we realized, "We were not in Kansas anymore!" The "Kansas" (insert your location here) that we used to live in was gone. It will never return. We then recognized our need to try to make sense of our new postmodern environment, and if not embrace it, to at least live in it.

In our brave new world, where we are not in "Kansas," we see the best and worst of everything. Instead of living and delving into the middle ground of issues, perceptions, and opinions, we now accommodate the edges. It's easier to consider hard-line or extreme conservative or liberal views than to seek and wrestle with a common middle ground. We no longer embrace the middle of the bell curve. A bell curve is a chart where the distribution of data forms a bell shape. This means that most of the data tends to be near the center of the chart. Some may suggest that in postmodernism, we embrace an inverted bell curve, where the weight is at the edges, not the middle. This means we listen to polarized views!

In turn, we easily accept and embrace like-minded thinking and reject other views. Consequently, we cradle one view and reject others, often without merit. Therefore, we adopt what we perceive is "the best" and label other views as "the worst." We might even call the other views fake. In other words, the bell curve is ever-increasing, becoming flat and polarized as people embrace the edges. A good read on how past and present polarization emerged, and an overview of postmodernism, can be found in Robert D. Putnam's book, *The Upswing: How America Came Together a Century Ago and How We Can Do It Again.*

With so much change, evolution, and expansion surrounding us, we may feel overwhelmed. We may not even realize that we're overwhelmed. We may find it hard to grasp what is transpiring around us. Inevitably, we can't juggle all the changes swirling around us. To illustrate the fantastic growth taking place in our postmodern reality, we need to look at the model developed in 1973 by the French economist Georgeś Anderla.

Anderla postulated a statistical model centred on the accumulation of human knowledge. He began by defining the known technology around the time of Jesus and assigned it the value "1." He suggested human knowledge doubled by 1500. It doubled again by 1750. Thus, in 1750, human knowledge was four times the amount at the time of Jesus. Anderla said it doubled again by 1900.[2] His research, which ended in 1973, stated that human knowledge, at that point, was 128 times greater than in the year 1 AD. In 1973, the personal computer, the Internet, smartphones, etc. were unknown. Today, various articles on the world's largest library, the Internet, indicate that in recent decades, human knowledge seemed to be doubling every few years. While researchers vary on actual rate and speed of growth, and periods tied to that rate, they typically agree that growth compared to the previous generation is incredible. Paul Chamberlain offers a clear, balanced view of this:

> In his book, *Critical Path*, Buckminster Fuller (Fuller 1981), American architect, systems theorist, author, designer, inventor, and futurist, created the "knowledge doubling curve". He noticed that until 1900 human knowledge doubled approximately every century and by the end of World War II knowledge was doubling every 25 years. Some years later a report published by IBM anecdotally added to Fuller's theory and predicted by 2020 knowledge would double every 12 hours fuelled by the Internet of Things (Schilling 2013). Different types of knowledge have different rates of growth but it is generally acknowledged that human knowledge is increasing at an extraordinary rate. Arguably we may have reached a point where relevant knowledge is increasing faster and in greater quantities than we can absorb. However, while knowledge is increasing, the useful lifespan of knowledge is decreasing. Consequently, we need to be constantly replacing out-of-date knowledge with new knowledge in a continuous process of unlearning and learning. Knowledge alone however is not sufficient and as important is the ability to apply good judgment based on knowledge …what we know as wisdom. It is knowledge and wisdom put into action that gives us insight. The creation of relevant up-to-date knowledge is critical to inform the creation of better

products, environments and services to support health and enhance wellbeing.[3]

Definitely we have more information constantly confronting us than we can ever comprehend. This is postmodernism. As Craig Detweiler wrote in *iGods: How Technology Shapes Our Spiritual and Social Lives*:

> … From the beginning of time until 2003 we generated 5 billion gigabytes of data (5 exabytes)—all the books and news and movies and information in history. We now generate five exabytes of data every ten minutes.[70] We should wonder what kind of brain could possibly track all of the data swirling around the universe. And how does that Search Engine in the Sky know where I am and what I care about? It recognizes me amid a sea of swirling TMI. *(DJR—Too Much Information)* But by reserving the big picture for themselves, Google makes Big Data the real, elusive omniscience. For techno-enthusiasts like Kelly, Big Data *(DJR—Big Data is a recent field within the computer world. It deals with data that is either too large or complex, or both to be embraced by traditional software applications)* of is close to Big Daddy, the uber-lord of the clouds, who curates our daily dose of information every single day.[4]

We might be so bold to declare that in the last five years we have accumulated more knowledge than in all of recorded history combined. Moreover, while we're swimming in knowledge and information overload, we must ask, Where is wisdom? To borrow a first-century comment from Matthew 16:26: "What will you gain, if you own the whole world but destroy yourself? What would you give to get back your soul?" (CEB). Yes, we have the whole world before us, but what about our souls, and what about our spiritual lives and that of others? These are deeply personal issues. These are questions for Western Society, Western Christianity, and Western spirituality.

We live in a postmodern world. It's a time of profound and unprecedented change, evolution, information overload, and paradigm shifts. While we may know that we live in the postmodern world, do we know what it is? We need to explore this. We will build arguments. We will provide a lot of information (isn't that ironic?). Additionally, we will pose questions, some of which we will explore, and some of which you may explore yourself or with others.

As we will see, we are in the throes of the greatest reformation in history. This is a bold and unabashed claim. It is also very true. Whereas the sixteenth-century Reformation was largely European and foundationally religious, our current reformation is global and secular. However, one part of our incredible reformation encompasses organized religions of all stripes and types. Likewise, this reformation is reforming how we consider and utilize spirituality. Spirituality is becoming a much-studied, researched, and thoroughly discussed topic in postmodernism. Naturally, this great global reformation and age of countless genuine paradigm shifts surrounds and encompasses Western Society, Western Christianity, and Western spirituality. Throughout this book, we will explore elements of postmodernism and how it exists in these three areas.

This exploration of our postmodern reformation is not exhaustive. Nevertheless, it is comprehensive. It offers sufficient insights, information, and musings to articulate the reality of our "brave new world" by delving into postmodernism in Western Society, Western Christianity, and Western spirituality. This exploration weaves some academic insights and musings while attempting to maintain a light, "easy to read" approach. Thus, this effort attempts to be both profane and accessible. Given the nature of this endeavour, we will pose various questions. These are societal questions needing examination and attention.

To illustrate our postmodern global reformation, think about the following simile. Imagine a snowball. In the early days of the paradigm shift in the New Reformation, it was a small snowball. As it rolled downhill, as if traveling through time, it gathered momentum along with more and more snow. It became bigger and bigger and rolled faster and faster. The snow on the surface symbolized newly accumulated knowledge. However, it soon disappeared because another layer of snow, containing more knowledge, covered it. In a short time, there were layers and layers of newer snow and/ or newer knowledge. In other words, recent adaptations or new ideas soon give way to newer ideas or adaptations.

As the snowball grows, it rolls over everything in its path. It rolls over humility, and it absorbs, covers, and buries civility. It becomes an all-consuming "me-ism." Then suddenly one day, freezing rain, as a fine invisible mist, begins. It covers the large snowball and provides a thick crust. The New Reformation is a sudden change. For decades scientists said this "freezing rain" would take place. They said it wasn't a matter of "if" but "when." The "when" took place during the New Reformation. It forever transformed the snowball and altered the world. The fine freezing rain was COVID-19. The snowball became a tremendous crushing ice machine!

For almost all of human history, change or evolution moved slowly. Small adaptations or adoptions took place. In the Postmodern Reformation, change is both fast and often. If the change in the past moved at the speed of a horse and buggy, in our postmodern world it became an F1 racing car moving at 200 mph. Then, in a twinkle or flash of time, with the onset and encompassing reality of COVID-19, change occurred at the speed of rockets!

Suddenly in Western Society, we saw hand sanitizers everywhere. When allowed outside the home, people were to keep six feet from each other and wear a facemask. Shuttered places included retail stores, social services offices, religious institutions, government offices, and countless commercial and manufacturing shops. We learned that PPE meant "personal protective equipment," and we learned that it was in short supply. We learned that this was the "new normal." We witnessed a great global infection and high death rates. We witnessed concern and denial. Physically, emotionally, financially, mentally, and spiritually, people of all ages, all around the globe, suffered.

Before we can explore how Western Christianity and Western spirituality are experiencing a massive reformation, we must first give some attention to postmodernism. This is Chapter One. While we may easily acknowledge we are in the postmodern world, we need to establish some background for this declaration. Only then can we assess what change, or evolution, is emerging and how it affects Western Christianity and redefines postmodern Western spirituality.

Chapter Two focuses on postmodernism and Western Christianity, and Chapter Three addresses postmodern spirituality. Given what is taking place in postmodernism, it's appropriate that we dedicate Chapter Four to an examination of the "Spiritual but Not Religious" situation. The chapters that follow build upon these foundations, but they might also be described as stand-alone chapters or separate essays on postmodernism and Western spirituality. Chapter Five addresses concepts of spirituality and the brain. Chapter Six delves into spirituality and mindfulness. In Chapter Seven, we consider spirituality, loneliness versus solitude, stillness, surrender, and serenity.

One topic that's receiving much academic attention is spirituality and education. This is the focus of Chapter Eight. Much of this academic attention deals with students in higher education (colleges and universities). This is because they are the group closest to academics! However, high school and elementary school students and their teachers are beginning to receive attention from researchers as well. Likewise, nursing, medical services, workplaces, and other businesses are also embracing spirituality.

Chapter Nine explores some notions of our spiritual future and the future of spirituality.

At the end of each chapter, I have included some discussion questions, which you may explore by yourself or with others. Take time to pray (if so inclined), ponder, reflect, and ruminate on these questions. Let them filter through you and allow them to percolate. Don't try to answer any too quickly. In other words, be a little anti-postmodern by taking time and space before seeking a solution or answer. Use knowledge and especially wisdom to temper your opinions. Sadly, in postmodernism we are quick with opinions and slow on information with ourselves and when conversing with others. Listen deeply to yourself, and intentionally listen to others. If you try to make your opinions heard, others will hear you saying, "I am right; listen to me." In turn, the message is also, "I'm not interested in you, just me." It's alienating and polarizing. Share thoughtful images quietly and with care.

Appendix A, "A Practical Model of Spirituality and Learning Rooted in Adult Learning Principles," illustrates how people gathered in small groups, using adult education principles, can develop, enhance, or re-discover their "spirit-voice." I developed this model and it was "road-tested" and refined in some small groups at St. Andrew's Episcopal Church in York, Pennsylvania during my tenure. In this model, postmodern adult learning principles shift from historical top-down, teacher (or the church) knows all and others follow, to group sharing, learner-centered activities, and discovery.

As noted in the introductory account of Chapter Eight, there is a great deal of growing interest in spirituality beyond our historic religious institutions. Janet Groen and Jeffrey Jacob in 2006 wrote:

> During this past decade, the interest in spirituality has increased significantly and has been discussed and written about within various contexts such as business, (Fox, 1995) and health care (Do Rozario, 1997; Wright, 2004). Specifically, within the education setting, authors such as Jones (1995), Bohac-Clarke (2002) and Miller (1999) have begun to make connections between teaching practice and spirituality, particularly at the K-12 level. In addition there has been an increasing interest in the spiritual and transformative dimensions of adult learning (Dirkx, 1997; Hunt, 1998; Westrup, 1998; English & Gillen, 2000; Tisdell, 2000). These authors have made links between spirituality and transformative learning, spirituality and adult development, and spiritual learning processes in adult learning. Qualitative research studies that have linked adult education and spirituality have been conducted by Groen (2004) and English (2001).[5]

Other research supports this development.[6] While there is growth in these fields, one must wonder how much of this is an interest in spirituality or a product of consumerism. David Tacey, writer and analytical psychologist (among other professional skills), elegantly observes this:

Spiritualism has enormous commercial appeal and marketing potential, because the businesses and industries of consumer capitalism are always striving to produce, package and sell things that will give life that extra boost or that missing dimension. In an exhausted, flat and spiritually empty society, spiritualism appears as one of our favourite addictions, since it presents spirit as a fabulous product to be consumed, or a toy to be played with in our boredom and depression. It is eminently marketable, and supplies us with parodies of spirit in a society that can no longer tell the difference between genuine spirituality and spiritualistic diversions or entertainment. By fixing spirit in a fabulous space readily manipulated by commercial industries, we are prevented from discovering richness, depth and transformation in the spaces that we normally inhabit ...[7]

Whatever the motives, spirituality is being explored as never before. Paul Heelas summarizes this phenomenon well:

For obvious reasons, this kind of data provides only a rough guide. Nevertheless, a simple search using Google serves to indicate the relative popularity of ways in which spirituality has come to be considered. At the end of January 2006, a straightforward search for "spirituality and ..." on Google.com resulted in the following figures: spirituality and health, 20,400,000; spirituality and business, 16,100,000 (with Peter Senge heading the list); spirituality and education, 14,800,000, spirituality and enlightenment, 2,200,000. A search at the end of January 2007, now using Google.co.uk, provides the same sequencing: health, 1,270,000 business, 1,200,000; education, 918,000 and enlightenment, 132,000. With this pulse of public, quasi-academic and academic interest in mind, I adopt the same sequence....[8]

Finally, it seems appropriate throughout this endeavor to provide some long and short quotations from other writers. My words alone only cannot capture the depth or breadth of the data. Likewise, the words and thoughts of others serve to stimulate and validate elements of spirituality in the postmodern world. To appreciate the detailed thoughts of these gifted and insightful authors, take time to ponder their words and the picture they paint. Perhaps you may need to read a quotation several times to glean some insights. As stated, some of the quotes are long. This is intentional. Remember this! This is to encourage you to see a broader and likely more well-rounded perspective. It's unusual to insert long quotes because authors like readers to focus on their thoughts and words. Authors generally consider the words of others as simply supportive arguments. In this effort, however, the thoughts of others are not to draw the reader into this writing alone. They serve as a tool to encourage the reader to read and digest the books, articles, journals, papers, and writings of others.

In broad terms, this introduction outlined the Age of Entitlement. The focus is on how Western Society and Western Christianity are evolving and how they affect Western spirituality. Figuratively speaking, we live in Huxley's *Brave New World*, where technology has replaced God. At the same time, we're no longer in Dorothy's Kansas. We traveled somewhere over the rainbow and found ourselves in *Oz*! In our *Oz*, we find new and unknown social and personal challenges and problems in front of us.

In the 2020–2021 period, while experiencing our *Brave New World,* the radical transformation called postmodernism transformed! We learned the term "COVID-19." Likewise, the word "pandemic" became one of the most common words people heard, saw, and experienced. Perhaps it was a word that many learned to spell! In this period we learned social distancing and to wear masks. People had to encounter and partake in that very un-postmodern experience and forgotten virtue—patience.

Before the global pandemic, a person could be in serious legal trouble for wearing a mask into a bank. During the pandemic, one was in trouble if attending to the bank without one. In the past, one faced potential jail time for wearing a mask into a bank. With COVID around us, one faced potential death for not wearing one anywhere! In the first case, the State (or Queen, eh?) could invoke penalties for the violation. In the second case, one's thoughtlessness was judge, jury, and possible executioner. In early Western Society's postmodernism, men used to display women's garters from their automobile's rear-view mirror. Today, many use that mirror to carry facemasks. The world is topsy-turvy.

This amplified reality hit Western Christianity quite hard inasmuch that normative religious services and other celebrations, such as weddings, funerals, and baptisms, stopped for months. We morphed from valuing wedding invitations to appreciating being one of the few selected in funeral invitations. In the past, wedding size was sometimes only restricted by the size of the church or hall. Today, weddings and funerals have gathering restrictions. In many cases, weddings were postponed!

For centuries, religious institutions in Western Society kept church doors open as a way to suggest that they were open to receive people, and with hopes to fill all the seats. With COVID-19, this changed. Today, we have R.S.V.P. and reserved seating. Will people return or, because of the pandemic, find it a convenient way to opt out. Some may use this as a sincere call to deepen their faith experience, while others may use it as an opportunity to abandon their place of worship. In early postmodernism, religious institutions across Western Society were largely full. People attended regularly. As postmodernism progressed, some regulars became semi-regular members. A few years later, for a variety of reasons, other regulars became semi-regular, and the first semi-regulars became seasonal visitors. A few years later, more regulars slid into being semi-regular worshipers. The second shift of semi-regulars become seasonal visitors, meaning mostly Christmas and Easter. Likewise, the current crop of seasonal visitors, who were the first group to become semi-regular, just stop attending. I wonder what these changes will do to postmodern spirituality. What do you think? This paradigm shift within a paradigm shift radically transformed Western Society and Western Christianity. Sequentially, Western spirituality naturally began morphing amidst its already greatest transformation.

Unprecedented health issues have gripped every corner of the globe. We learned that even the richest and most prepared counties weren't as prepared for this pandemic disaster as they thought. It was natural and expected that massive unemployment and economic woes would expand in this world crisis. Both short-term and long-term effects continue to emerge. In light of these massive developments, we must ask, "How do these developments affect postmodern spirituality?" The answer to the question is unclear. It will be some time before we can truly discover the short-term and long-term effects. All we can declare is that our brave new world might transition into a braver newer world.

As the pandemic advanced, it brought much of the world to a crawl. As the world slowly stalled, online services experienced incredible expansion. People who never considered online shopping felt it necessary—out of fear, convenience, or necessity—to buy online, and this included meals and groceries! In Western Society, the growth was so vast and consistent it became the "new normal." Naturally, it made one wonder about the return and future of traditional bricks and mortar stores. One wondered about the employment of an immeasurable number of displaced retail workers.

When the pandemic exploded across the world, schools at all levels, in most places, shut down for the year. The following September, schools around the globe grappled with ideas on how to re-open. Much anxiety existed. Across Western Society, governments felt incredible financial pressure to have parents return to work and, in turn, spend money to keep the economy from potential collapse! Likewise, there were strong urges for students to recapture and engage in their learning structure. This meant reopening schools. School administrations at all levels considered realistic, viable options. Issues of health and safety were vital concerns. Many places looked at scenarios such as online learning, reducing class sizes, or even alternating school days. The success and failure of various programs depended on keeping the virus at bay. Some places were more cautious than others. It will be some time before accurate short-term and long-term effects measure the success of re-opening. Additionally, it will take time to see how the pandemic affected the emotional, physical, cognitive, and spiritual lives of students, teachers, instructors, administrators, and parents.

As social creatures, what is the future? How long are we to keep six feet apart? As many stories inform us, those who flaunt this proven health guideline and continue to party, worship, or meet in large groups are prone to catch and spread the virus. In many ways, we again must wonder how this will affect postmodern spirituality. This is a major question that can only be answered in due time. Likewise, in the natural anxiety the pandemic is creating, we must wonder if we are further polarizing ourselves. Will we only seek instant, supportive, and affirming preconceived answers, or will we become willing to take a chance and explore issues in depth once more? Again, only time will tell!

In 1945, Rogers and Hammerstein introduced the musical *Carousel*. From this production, the song "You'll Never Walk Alone" reached fabulous fame. Decades later, female and male sole singers, groups, and instrumentalists continue to make cover copies of this song. It is the anthem of the Liverpool Football Club. Their fans sing it lustfully. Today, some make it an ode to the front-line workers who work in hospitals and nursing homes. It's an ode to teachers and those bravely working in retail settings serving others. It's a spiritual call as we attempt to cope with the Coronavirus. It's a spiritual call to learn that despite much adversity, one can walk and be at peace with oneself. It's a spiritual call that offers hope. Since copyright laws are a quagmire filled with potential landmines, I suggest you search online for the lyrics of the first verse of this song. Read these words slowly and give yourself time to reflect on them.

Amidst the greatest societal paradigm shift in history, we found another shift taking place. The world changed. We need to understand how spirituality is changing. This is a daunting task. We don't know what direction this evolution will take. It's like that old advertising motto stating that half of the money spent on advertising is wasted, but nobody knows what half! Clearly, to garner some glimpses of postmodern spirituality, we must examine the big picture, from a variety of perspectives. We need to develop some comprehension of postmodernism, of postmodernism in Western Society. In turn, we need to enlighten ourselves on how this affects Western Christianity, and then how these realities impact and re-shape Western spirituality.

Questions to ponder and discuss
Introduction

❶ One of the facets of postmodernism is the erosion of rootedness. This applies to both individuals and society. Spend some time making lists and reflecting on how this affects you.

❷ If you consider that we live in an inverted bell curve, where the edges attract much attention and the middle seems void, where are you—in the middle, left edge, or right edge? How do you arrive at that spot? How can you move closer to the middle?

CHAPTER ONE

POSTMODERNISM AND WESTERN SOCIETY

Historically, we've identified pivotal ages of history by major themes of the period. These themes largely and accurately describe those specific periods. For example, we have the Iron Age, the Dark Ages, and the Age of Enlightenment. We might unmistakably label our postmodern time as the Age of Entitlement! Others may state that we live in the Cyber Age, the Digital Age, the Age of Entertainment, or the Age of the Global Village. Perhaps the Age of Self-Indulgence or Age of Consumption are accurate and other potential identifiers of our postmodern society. In 2018, historian Yuval Harari in *21 Lessons for the 21ˢᵗ Century* stated that we are in the Age of Bewilderment.[1] Whatever the title—entitlement, cyber, digital, global village, entertainment, or bewilderment—our time is marked as a period of accelerated, continuous change.

At the end of the nineteenth century, we began to witness the slow glide from modernism to postmodernism. The Great War, the Great Depression, and World War II were significant parts of the shift. The Great War, as with many wars, began a period of changes. Armies needed new ways to beat the enemy. Cavalry charges, in time and after much procrastination, gave way to tanks. Aircraft became more advanced, viable, and useful. The Great Depression in Western Society saw millions leave the farm or

1

rural lives for the hope of a better life in cities. New Deal work projects saw countless massive national and local projects, long overdue and stymied with years of discussion, begin with much earnest effort to get people working. World War II helped end the depression by forcing governments to finance resources towards manufacturing countless products needed for the war effort. It also became necessary, and in time acceptable, for women, like the allegorical Rosie the Riveter, to enter (and remain) in Western Society's workforce.

In the 1950s, with the onset and development of suburbs, an ever-expanding middle class, and incredible new technologies, the postmodern shift began. Modernism gave way to a model that prompted bigger, faster, stronger, and more adaptable. The new reality focused on "You." The rise of ever-increasing disposable income, which was a marked move from centuries of most people living in survival mode, was another significant contributing factor. The rise of more and better accessible communication products also evolved. Instead of going to the movie theatre for short newsreel stories, people stayed home and watched long newscasts on television. By the 1960s, this increasing wave of growth became constant big surfs with much growth, expansion, and evolution.

Furthermore, cheaper and faster global and national transportation infrastructure added to this shift. For example, look at the rapid increase of automobile ownership in North America following World War II. The Model T became the first affordable luxury for many in America before World War II; however, these autos weren't designed to drive across the county. The models introduced after World War II (some with fancy fins!), along with the installation and paving of the American Interstate system and thousands of miles of new, well-paved roads across North America, opened up travel for all. The motel industry arose and catered to the flood of holiday travelers. In time, because of increasing disposable wealth and dual incomes, began the rise of two automobile families. In 1900 in Western Society, there were almost no automobiles. A mere seventy years later, many families owned two automobiles, and people traveled across the county with ease. In early postmodernism, we shifted from tough "arm strong" steering to power-assisted steering. Later in postmodernism, we began seeing self-driving automobiles. We moved from driving with intense control and effort to having artificial intelligence do much of the work of navigating, driving, and even parking. Sadly, in the early stages of this development, we assumed so much that some people slept while behind the wheel, believing that the car didn't need them to drive! This is a great metaphor for spirituality. We shifted from intense participation to passive acceptance, yet we still expect the same result—to arrive safely at our destination.

Additionally, the increased development of public transportation helped reshape North American and Western Society. In relatively short order, historically speaking, Western Society moved from an agriculturally rooted world (note the pun!) to one in which most people live in cities. Cities grew horizontally and vertically. The next shift in postmodernism was the massive exodus to the suburban world.

In postmodernism, we witnessed immense, unrestricted national travel (pre-COVID), and incredible commercial production increases in terms of products, speed of production, and delivery, and infrastructures. Perhaps in our postmodern world, we should consider the Internet as the new interstate or superhighway. Unlike paved roads, the speed of Internet travel is incredible. This new superhighway is universal, with incredible speed limits, and while it still requires upgrades, it doesn't require paving. Sadly, like highways of old, crashes still take place.

Without debate, the development and rise of the general public education system, and later the greatly enhanced post-high school opportunities, changed Western Society and, very likely, Western Christianity! Likewise, the acceptance of significant numbers of female students changed the educational dynamics and expansion of colleges and universities following WW II. Later, the ever-increasing rise of minorities in post-secondary education emerged. Again, in a relatively short time period, we saw society transformed. In 1900, young men graduating high school were considered "well educated." Today, we have men and women undertaking postgraduate university programs and technological training to be "well educated." Our brave new world no longer reflects Dorothy's rural Kansas.

By the 1980s, the rate of growth in postmodernism accelerated exponentially! The universality of the personal computer (note the label— it's yours and belongs to no one else) altered us and how we work. We shifted from massive work computers to our desktop/personal empowering machine. Slow dial-up phone line Internet gave way to speedier delivery systems. Wal-Mart (as it was then spelled) and other early adapters (like Amazon) utilized computers and the Internet. These leaders streamlined product movement models. In many places, we became a "just in time" society. Manufacturing and inventory control became just in time. Nothing was put on a shelf. These workplace models also affected our emotions. We became reactive and responded to everything as it took place. We began to lose the ability to place emotions on the shelf and to ruminate and contemplate the best options or responses. Immediacy emotions replaced thoughtful, measured responses. For example, many looked for immediate sexual hook-ups to pacify a need, without any thought of a long-term emotional attachment to the other.

In postmodernism, human knowledge seemed to double at great rates, but it's impossible to continue at that rate. It's one thing to double one's knowledge from two to four, or four to eight. It's another to double from a trillion! Nevertheless, the "size" of our current bank of knowledge is extensive and overwhelming. It's reasonable to suggest that humanity accumulated more knowledge in the last decade than in all recorded history combined. Take a moment to ponder that piece of information. What does it say to you? How does it affect Western Society, Western Christianity, and Western spirituality? How does it affect you? In turn, we must ask if we have become any smarter or wiser. What do you think?

Furthermore, with the Internet, we can explore almost any question, at any place, at any time. The knowledge of the world is literally at our fingertips. Yet I wonder to what degree we take advantage of this gift. On the other hand, does it take advantage of us? Do we merely use the World Wide Web as an opportunity to be entertained with games such as Candy Crush? What do you think? Decades ago, famous architect Frank Lloyd Wright supposedly called television "chewing gum for the eyes."[2] I wonder if we can co-opt that image and say that our smartphones are chewing gum for our eyes. Again, what do you think?

Throughout this work, I will ask questions such as, "What do you think?" These are questions to cause you to pause and reflect. In postmodernism, we are quick to jump to conclusions and offer opinions. In a phrase, "We are long on opinions and short on information." Thus, having offered and provided some information, one should take time to "pause and ponder." Instead of jumping to instant answers, let the information and insights filter through you and, I hope, enlighten you. Be open-minded as you shift through this work. For example, consider the following:

> ... Plutarch tells the story of how Alexander the Great came upon the philosopher Diogenes examining a pile of human bones. "What are you looking for?" asked Alexander. Diogenes answered, "Something I cannot find." "And what is that?" "The difference between your father's bones and those of his slaves." Retelling this story, Anthony De Mello adds: "The following are just as indistinguishable: Catholic bones from Protestant bones. Hindu bones from Muslim bones. Arab bones from Israeli bones. Russian bones from American bones. The enlightened fail to see the difference even when the bones are clothed in flesh?"[3]

The development of the personal computer, then the Internet, and later smartphones, together with this accumulated bank of knowledge (or should we be more definitive and say "data"?) made the postmodern shift almost complete. How does this super information age of postmodernism affect and influence Western Society, Western Christianity, and Western spirituality? To say this another way, how do we look at the "bones" around us and determine what they are saying to us. All this needs further exploration.

To further illustrate the postmodern world, one need look no farther than the recent social reality of the love of "selfies." With the advent of the digital camera embedded in our smartphones, we are prone (can we say conditioned?) to take pictures of ourselves and then instantly post and share them with "followers" and the world. If it's not bad enough to be addicted to one's smartphone screen, it's worse when people remove themselves from interactions with others by the wearing of earbuds. In other words, we don't see or hear anything but what a four-inch screen provides us! The result is that we only satisfy the "me."

A mere sixty years ago, everyone sent exposed film from one's camera "away" to be developed. People waited a few weeks for a single or a double pack of black and white prints to return via the postal service. Today, we can take a color picture or video, "develop it," enhance it, and send or "mail it" around the globe moments after we clicked the picture. One can be 500 miles away and see grandchildren boarding the bus for their first day of school moments after it took place. We can even have images and videos of rogue police kneeling on the necks of people. All this is incredible. This is one of the new technological realities that fulfills and soothes our need for instant gratification. In turn, it creates the need within us to always seek soothing. It changed our minds, emotions, and spirit. For example, if your phone dings and says, "You have mail," you're now conditioned to instantly answer it or feel anxious until the task is accomplished!

Today, our pictures, captions, and stories are often one-way communications via various social media platforms. The typical message revolves around themes such as, "Look at me, look at my children, look at my dinner, look at my vacation spot, and, look at me, and look my friends around me." This fulfills a psychological need to feel self-worth, to brag, or to share one's excitement. When we send these photos, we expect them to be "liked" and perhaps shared on a network of "friends." In some cases, these are "friends" we only know through our digital environments. Sometimes after we post a picture or video we may feel slighted if we don't obtain the number of responses to which we feel entitled. We expect many "likes" to appease our sense of entitlement and instant gratification. Like alcohol or drugs, these photos and videos are the new postmodern fix! YouTube, Snapchat, and Tik-Tok are some of the platforms we utilize to feed and soothe this appetite.

Another significant benchmark of instant gratification in postmodernism can easily be defined by two words—credit cards. Brashly put, "Enjoy now, and pay later." Sadly, for many people, the constant need to accumulate items means making minimum payments on those numerous credit cards! Is this not a truly definitive definition of the postmodern person and the need to be gratified?

In the postmodern world, we expect (can we say demand?) that Amazon and others meet our "needs" by delivering our online orders quickly. This is because we need our gratification in near real-time. We delude ourselves when we believe these orders ship at no cost. Patience is a relic! Whereas a few decades ago we patiently waited a few weeks for the film to return, or catalog orders to show up, we now expect the package we ordered to be in our hands the next day. Amazon strives for same-day delivery in some major cities! One of the stalwarts of Western Christianity is rooted in a virtue called patience. It's a common image in the Bible: "Love is patient, love is kind, it isn't jealous, it doesn't brag, it isn't arrogant" (1 Corinthians 13:4, CEB). Also, "Conduct yourselves with all humility, gentleness, and patience. Accept each other with love" (Ephesians 4:2, CEB). At times, it seems that humility, gentleness, kindness, and patience are lost words, images, and values. Are these values defunct in postmodernism? What do you think? Furthermore, has boasting, bullying, and impatience replaced these attributes, and if so, to what degree? Again, what do you think?

To what degree have we morphed our expectation of instant gratification and a sense of entitlement into our postmodern religious and spiritual lives? Mull over the words of T. Byram Karasu, a noted psychiatrist and professor. He wrote:

> New Age psychotherapies promote search for the self— but never get beyond it. They are geared toward self-actualization, self-protection, and self-love (in the smallest sense of the word). They primarily offer quick-and-easy answers that derive from pleasure, not insight or enlightenment. In fact, they don't ask questions or look beneath the surface—of one's own myopic life. In this sense they are selfish—never selfless. In seeking instant gratification, they are indulgent, excessive, and exalt only the immediate moment—never eternity. They reject the simple life and instead urge their recipients to indulge hedonistic desires and pleasures, to seek narcissistic gains. In short, you can only get there by riding others.[4]

Do we have any of the reserve or patience like those who were lost and wandered for 40 years looking for the promised land? Do we appreciate those who spend 40 days in solitude working on self-understanding and seeking a direction in life? Do we understand that someone may not answer our last email of 40 minutes ago! Do we wait more than 40 seconds to check our phone after we hear some notification? Sadly, in postmodernism, we don't seem to welcome or value those who exude patience. Instead, we tend to pray: "God (or Higher Power), here is my prayer (which in postmodernism means my expectation). Answer it." Often we metaphorically add the phrase, "And I mean now! I give you five minutes, and if I receive no answer, I will know that you are neither God nor real." Perhaps we view the creator of the universe as a commodity that solely exists to appease our personalized needs. In turn, we expect to have our needs met before or excluding the needs of others! In other words, "God, your job is to make me happy." This is a significant postmodern reality!

To further define and explain postmodernism, we should ponder some more insights or illustrations to assist our understanding of the Age of Entitlement. Neuroscientist, cognitive psychologist, writer, and musician Daniel J. Levitin in *The Organized Mind: Thinking Straight in the Age of Information Overload* offers a wonderful and comprehensive insight:

> ... Our cell phones have become Swiss Army knife-like appliances that include a dictionary, calculator, Web browser, e-mail client, Game Boy, appointment calendar, voice recorder, guitar tuner, weather forecaster, GPS, texter, tweeter, Facebook updater, and flashlight. They're more powerful and do more things than the most advanced computer at IBM corporate headquarters thirty years ago. And we use them all the time, part of a twenty-first-century mania for cramming everything we do into every single spare moment of downtime. We text while we're walking across the street, catch up on e-mail while standing in line, and while having lunch with friends, we surreptitiously check to see what our *other* friends are doing. At the kitchen counter, cozy and secure in our domicile, we write our shopping lists on smartphones while we are listening to that wonderfully informative podcast on urban beekeeping.[5]

Without question, we are the most connected society in history. This is one foundational cornerstone of postmodernism. Likewise, much suggests that we are also the most disconnected society in history. Brené Brown in her classic *Daring Greatly: How the Courage to be Vulnerable Transforms the Way we Live, Love and Parent and Lead* describes our sense of connection and disconnectedness very well:

> With disconnection it's a similar story. We may have a couple of hundred friends on Facebook, plus a slew of colleagues, real-life friends, and neighbors, but we feel alone and unseen. Because we are hardwired for connection, disconnection always creates pain. Feeling disconnected can be a normal part of life and relationships, but when coupled with the shame of believing that we're disconnected because we're not worthy of connection, it creates a pain that we want to numb.

> One stop beyond disconnection is isolation, which presents real danger. Jean Baker Miller and Irene Stiver, relational-cultural theorists from the Stone Center at Wellesley College, have eloquently captured the extremity of isolation. They write, "We believe that the most terrifying and destructive feeling that a person can experience is psychological isolation. This is not the same as being alone. It is a feeling that one is locked out of the possibility of human connection and of being powerless to change the situation. In the extreme, psychological isolation can lead to a sense of hopelessness and desperation. People will do almost anything to escape this combination of condemned isolation and powerlessness."[6]

This is another foundational cornerstone of postmodernism. The greatest disease in our society is not cancer. It's personal isolationism or loneliness. We don't connect to ourselves or others. We don't connect to organized religions and community groups. It's ironic that in the age when any contact is but a click on our smartphone away that we are so disconnected. This is another postmodern reality.

A humorous but defining illustration of this is found in an early episode of the popular comedy television show *The Big Bang Theory*. To make a point, one of the lead male geek actors declares he has "212 friends on Myspace," to which his roommate responds, "Yes, and you've never met any of them."[7] To wit, how much are we ever truly connected with others? Sometimes we expend so much energy by expanding our "friends" list that we neglect those who are already our true friends. Sometimes we're so busy "friending" and collecting "likes" that we fail to feed current relationships. Likewise, how much attention and deep connection do we truly afford others? What do you think? How much inner attention do we give ourselves? Are we so busy friending and seeking instant gratification that we're failing (or failed) to even friend ourselves? What do you think?

When we're "friending" and posting stories, it's often a one-way communication: "I share, you like." It's a communication saying, "Respond to me." It's a monologue, not a dialogue. It's not a conversation; it's "talking" and seeking positive reactions. Feedback only takes a second when you can click and "like" the sent message. We're anxious to see how many "friends" will give us a mere second of attention! Instead of the historical image of God creating humanity, we now conceive ourselves as God-like since we have the power to have countless "likes" that feed our egos. Sometimes world leaders, corporation heads, church leaders, etc. act as if they can do whatever they like because of this false sense of power, control, and self-importance. This is not just a postmodern reality. It's a historic reality. However, in postmodernism, we see images of absolutism abounding. R. Scott Smith spells out the notion of absolutes very well in his 2005 book, *Truth and the New Kind of Christian: The Emerging Effects of Postmodernism in the Church*:

> ... McLaren says that modern Christians are controlling and not compassionate. They are Pharisaical, legalistic, arrogant, rigid, and uptight, and they want to keep things safe doctrinally and avoid heresy. Furthermore, they want salvation and the Christian life pinned down to nice,

neat categories and simple formulas. The transmission of information, rather than the transformation of people becomes the focus of discipleship. But these approaches lead to tremendous internal struggles when we face problems that resist such explanations and approaches, says McLaren, for there are no new insights beyond such formulas. In the cases of people with such problems, their problems are compounded because there are no people with whom they can open up. Their questions or doubts cannot be examined, if we must have absolute certainty in our beliefs. We put ourselves in a very restrictive box, and when life becomes messy and we hurt and struggle, we can end up in a crisis of faith, much like what McLaren himself experienced. Furthermore, Christians tend to treat dogmas as free-floating abstractions, and by trying to figure out all of life by means of neat, tidy categories, they by and large lose their sense of wonder over who God is ...[8]

In postmodernism, we expect friends and followers to appease our needs. We must wonder if altruism—the belief that acting for others is right and normal—has become archaic. Does not the need for constant affirmation add to our being self-absorbed? In other words, we are creating a loop of needs. First, we greatly desire "to be liked," and when affirmed, it makes us even more certain that we are important, and the cycle repeats. What do you think of this notion? Take time to ponder this idea. We need people to like what we post because we want to believe (howbeit wrongly) that it matches them really "liking" us. It feeds our entitlement and gratification. These affirmations are fleeting and feed our surface emotion without becoming entrenched in our deeper being. If surface gratification is soothed, we often feel no need to take the happiness deeper because we're busy reveling in that instant happy spot and are also seeking the next happy fix! How often do we post restaurant meals or cooked meals so we can have others say, "Wow," even if they're not interested?

If we're busy and consumed by reaching out and trying to expand and increase ourselves by having others affirm us, I wonder when we set aside time to reach into ourselves. As an adult education specialist who looks at connections between adults and spirituality, Janet Groen says, "In contrast, rather than looking outward and upward, our souls require us to look inward into ourselves. It is in our everyday experiences and our humanity that we find our soul. It is in our deepest feelings, dreams and longings that soul resides."[9] If we focus on reaching out to stroke our artificial ego, where is there time to reach in and truly grow? Some might suggest that in postmodernism we are superficial. Metaphorically, we might say we live lives that "are a mile wide but only an inch thick." I wonder if this epidemic of loneliness is leading us back to searching for spirituality in Western Society or taking us the other way into a spiritual abyss. In her dissertation on adult learning theories and spirituality, Laura Brown describes this skillfully:

> Forman (2004) suggests other factors that have contributed to the growing interest in spirituality. In his book about grassroots spirituality, he argues that the American fast-paced, technological focused life style in combination with demographic shifts away from rural life have contributed to our sense of worry about alienation and aloneness as well as our concern about superficial relationships and lives that lack significance. Communities no longer revolve around strong nuclear or extended families, and people no longer share life-histories with neighbors or people from work which contributes to these feelings of alienation and feeling alone. Forman also cites the disillusionment with science and rationality to provide meaning and fulfillment as another reason for this growth in spiritual interests.[10]

Instead of being overly involved in busyness and avoiding quiet, we need to embrace quiet, loneliness, and solitude. Mother Theresa also articulated this reality of loneliness when she wrote:

> The greatest disease in the West today is not TB or leprosy; it is being unwanted, unloved, and uncared for. We can

cure physical diseases with medicine, but the only cure for loneliness, despair, and hopelessness is love. There are many in the worlds that are dying for a piece of bread, and there are many more dying for a little love. The poverty in the West is a different kind of poverty—it is not only a poverty of loneliness but also of spirituality. There's a hunger for love, as there is a hunger for God.[11]

Similarly, the notion of postmodernism and our fractured, ungrounded shallow lives are well expressed by psychologist David Myers, who vividly notes that:

More than ever, we have big houses and broken homes, high incomes and low morale. We celebrate prosperity but yearn for purpose. We cherish freedom but long for connection. It is a time, I conclude, to dream a new American dream, one we positive psychologists hope to help make reality.[12]

Take a moment to consider his words!

I sometimes wonder since we seem so disconnected from others, organized religions, and ourselves, if there's any connection between these disconnections and violence. This is a deep question. What do you think? Has loneliness, a sense of despair, and feelings of hopelessness become factors that result in some people driving cars and vans into crowded streets of people? Does it trigger people to shoot up schools, nightclubs, churches, and workplaces? Perhaps when some feel unloved or unconnected they react with the total opposite emotions of anger and hate and project those feelings towards others. Is this a broad assumption? Perhaps. Yet this observance seems to need societal attention.

It seems that individuals and nations are withdrawing and becoming isolationists because we have forgotten how to reach out and embrace others. We fail to embrace others because we've forgotten how to embrace ourselves. We need to rediscover wholly holiness and holy wholeness! Mull over the following words of adult educator, the late Linda Vogel. She presented this timeless image over twenty years ago. However, as we move onward in postmodernism, it is becoming more poignant.

> As persons seek to become whole, their ways of being and relating have the potential to be transformed so that the persons are truer to who they are and to who they are becoming. This shift releases them so that they can be open to and accepting of others. When persons are able to embrace all that they are—claiming gifts, naming wounds, and owning questions—there is a greater freedom to be present for others as well. To reckon with our spiritual selves requires that we look both inward and outward— engaging the wounds and seeking the healing that can lead to wholeness.[13]

We must ask to what degree is the human need for purpose disappearing when we're seemingly handing this trait over to machines. Inventor and futurist Ray Kurzweil, in *The Age of Spiritual Machine: When Computers Exceed Human Intelligence*, beautifully describes the rise of the computer. Kurzweil explains how computers have surpassed the capabilities of the human mind and are taking on essential human traits. In turn, this naturally leads to the question, "Are computers evolving and can they become spiritual!"[14] This is another question for us to contemplate.

Likewise, computers are becoming more adept at everything humans can do, but in some things much better. The question becomes, "What can computers do to replace us?"[15] In pondering this question, I can't help but think of Irving Berlin's great song from *Annie Get Your Gun,* where Annie and a male gunman sing that they are better than the other. In postmodernism, it's the computer singing to humanity: "Anything you can do, I can do better!" Perhaps this may include being spiritual. What do you think? Don't brush off this question lightly.

Is our seeming loss of self-identification and declining ability to connect with others making us prone to embrace polarization? After all, it's becoming easier to hold an opinion than have a conversation! Is this dilemma making us vulnerable to extremism? If we seek appeasement through "likes" on social media and don't afford ourselves time for reflection or self-care, are we not becoming shallow? In turn, by shifting virtues and thinking over to computers, we add to this. I believe these questions need addressing.

Briefly, postmodernism in Western Society seems to manifest as people living fractured lives of quiet desperation and loneliness. We are surrounded by many but unknown to most. In turn, we expend much energy keeping busy and attempting to feed our entitlement. For example:

> ... Comedian Louis (Louis) C. K. jokes about our sense of entitlement regarding technology. He marvels that "everything is amazing right now and nobody is happy." Louis mocks those who get impatient when they have to wait a few seconds to get a cell phone signal ... FROM SPACE! The fruits of technology are often ingratitude and impatience. We don't want to be short-tempered and demanding, but we have come to expect technology to be at our beck and call. Could a deeper understanding of technology broaden our sense of appreciation? If we receive technology more as a God-given gift and privilege, could we grow in gratitude? How might stepping away from the conveniences of technology sharpen our perceptions and quicken our spirit?[16]

We must wonder if our sense of entitlement and the need for gratification are the result of our brains being rewired. Again, what do you think?

In *The Shallows: What the Internet Is doing to Our Brains,* which won the Pulitzer Prize, author Nicholas Carr explains how the Reformation and printing press developed "deep reading or close reading." Reading and writing shifted from a small, select group of educated people to many. Ordinary people began to read books. In most cases, it was the Bible. People made efforts to "master" their thoughts.[17] Do we "deep read" today, or do we glance at bullet points and believe that we are very informed? What do you think?

For centuries, there were few books in Western Society. This is because they were handwritten. The printing press, invented in 1444, and the Reformation, which began in 1517, changed this. Today, despite the Internet and "screen addiction," printed books are still produced in vast numbers. Despite this reality, academics often consider textbooks only twenty years old as dated. This is because newer, "current" texts in our knowledge-infused postmodern society, which are typically built on those previous efforts, are considered more accurate and thorough. In other words, in some fields of study, textbooks that were the "bible" of their field for decades are regarded as obsolete. Such is postmodernism! We have more books than at any other time in history, but do we have fewer readers? This is a question that ought to be explored. What do you think? Do you read, read deep, or glance at bullet points?

Today, vast amounts of printed or screen matter occupy our lives. Every day we experience a constant barrage of books, newspapers, computers, tablets, phone calls, texts, twitters, and ever-flowing data and information. Every day we touch our phones thousands of times, even if we're not answering a phone call. Consequently, we may find it hard to discern or read deeply. Today, we typically do not read deeply; instead, we skim. This means we look at bullet points, watch highlights, or listen to sound bytes. Despite selecting meager information, we feel informed. Sadly, many write political speeches with only the media in mind so they can hone in on a few pertinent sensationalist comments for radio or television. This means that the media (and perhaps society) ignores most of the text or information. Perhaps in postmodernism the sound byte is the full speech, and the bulk of the speech now serves as filler. How do we discern appropriately and fairly based on meager information? Sadly, we're naturally accustomed to continuously relying upon the same sources, so we neglect other sources. This suggests that instead of developing well-rounded opinions based on much information and thought, we are impatient and settle on narrow views that reinforce previous opinions. This leads to polarization. In other words, in the age of vast information, we often settle for listening to and accepting information from small, closed loops or echo chambers. What do think of this? Do you listen or read broadly or from a few "trusted" sources?

In the past, television news attempted to offer unvarnished, reasonably discerned, accurate news reports. Today, news reporting seems to offer opinionated, biased editorials. The unpleasant is either filtered out or used to make the case more substantial. With shortening attention spans, scanning without absorbing, and seeking and affirming polarized views, we seem to have drifted a great deal in postmodernism. Mainstream media have taken on the sensationalistic approach formerly the purview of the tabloids. Since people quickly tune in and then tune out, it became essential for mainstream media to adopt attention-grabbing pictures, titles, and stories to attract readers. The use of "yellow journalism," which is an exaggeration of trivial or distorted accounting to create a favorable spin, is not news—it's a ratings game to increase viewership, make money, and satisfy advertisers. In other words, real, unbiased news seems to have less exposure and may be of secondary importance! News outlets don't offer news—they offer ratings to draw in advertisers! This shift from news accounts to opinion pieces creates bias and affects Western Society, Western Christianity, and Western spirituality. What do you think? Whereas news sources and media used to be dedicated to educating the populace on the issues and news of the day, it now seems that they're dedicated to entertaining the populace on the issues and news of the day. Again, what do you think of that comment? To what degree is it true?

Over the years, television also conditioned us to develop shorter attention spans. Shows are interspersed with many commercials. Over the decades, due to increased costs and shorter attention spans, it was logical that the length of some commercials became shorter. Shows are now shorter and commercial time longer! Today, we have the two-second commercial! The Internet accelerated this decline. This is significant. Our shorter attention span influences all aspects of Western Society, Western Christianity, and Western spirituality. Here is an insightful comment:

> The average attention span is five minutes. Ten years ago, it used to be 12 minutes. How can our attention span be less than half of what it used to be? What's changed? The answer is … the internet. The internet is ever present in our society. Nowadays, you can be connected anywhere at

any time to speedy internet services ... We expect instant gratification from the internet. Pages on the web need to load at breakneck speed. A study found that a one-second delay in page load time can result in 11% fewer page views, 16% decreased customer satisfaction and 7% lost conversions ... Bullet pointing information is popular these days. When the information is already organized and chunked, our brain doesn't have to go the extra mile and do the work itself. Twitter has a character limit of 140. When Facebook statuses are less than 70 characters, they get more likes than those that are more.[18]

Since we skim and glide through data, it seems natural that we would even consider downsizing the Bible! We did. Yes, there's a *Reader's Digest* version. Why? So we can easily digest the Digest. Clearly, by gliding and skimming, we don't take information or scriptures deep into ourselves. We reduce scriptures to bullet points to affirm our preconceived opinions. It's hard to discern scripture, or any data, when we seem overloaded with facts and information. It's hard to discern when we live with compressed and compacted time.

Jean M. Twenge and W. Keith Campbell, who we hear much from, in 2010 wrote *The Narcissism Epidemic: Living in an Age of Uncertainty*. In it, they explain this societal shift quite well. Their explanation provides us with great insight into the effects of postmodernism on Western Christianity and Western spirituality:

A disease model of narcissism gives a picture of how narcissism might grow and spread. Diseases need specific conditions to become epidemic: a host (a person or group who has the disease), a means of transmission (a way for the disease to move from one person to another), and a new host (a person or group who catches the disease). We already know that both individual Americans and our shared culture are becoming more narcissistic over time. Thus a host is in place. And narcissism has a means of transmission through the media and the Internet. The narcissistic behavior that brings attention to one person can, through the magic of the Internet, be spread instantly around the globe. Other cultures are increasingly becoming infected with narcissism, becoming hosts for the fast-moving virus of egotism, materialism, celebrity worship, entitlement, and self-centeredness. As epidemiologists can tell you, a virus that spreads from many people and many points can quickly overtake an entire population.[19]

With postmodernism, we live in an ever-increasingly narcissistic world enveloped by "Me-ism." Perhaps you've heard famous sports figures refer to themselves in the third person! And others we might say perceive themselves as, "A legend in their own time." With "Me-ism," it seems that many can be identified as "A legend in their own mind!" Without discussion, we can easily note that the rise of "Me-ism" is directly affecting the decline of organized religions, community clubs, fraternal organizations, and volunteerism. Instead of a desire to help others, it seems that our first desire is for others to help us! Instead of freely giving, we seem to give the message, "I may help others only after I am satisfied." In turn, this "Me-ism" is helping to create an environment of greater polarization and confrontation across all spectrums of society. After all, if one is the "center of the universe," should not others conform and support your perceptions, your opinions, and your ideas? What do you think of this emerging reality? Consider how you deal with others, your life, and various situations. Be unusual and take time to reflect upon this! For an in-depth discussion on the decline of organized religions, community clubs, fraternal organizations, and volunteerism, again consider Putnam's book.

In large part, the rise of individualism and "Me-ism" is a result of readily accessible worldly knowledge, data, and information. It's important to state that by having the world readily available, we have gained a sense of power and self-proclaimed expertise. Since we tend to only search for data and information that is within our comfort zone, we feel affirmed when data confirms our truncated views. A final illustration of postmodernism states:

... Clearly, more information has improved our lot in life. The advances in science, especially health and medicine, are staggering. The rise in literacy has lifted many out of poverty. A Maasai warrior with an Android smartphone has access to more information that the president of the United States did just fifteen years ago. Farmers in Central and South America are helped by their newfound ability to know the fair market value of their goods via smartphones. Thanks to more accurate and accessible information, they negotiate from a position of greater knowledge, strength, and profitability. So where does information lead? "Can it lead to wisdom" Kelly suggests, "Theologians should team up with nerds to study information as the entity closest to God."[20]

How does living in the postmodern world change society and us? A significant change is that where modernism focused on institutions, our postmodern focus is on the individual. This shift is so complete that we no longer offer institutions much trust or obedience. We are increasingly suspicious of institutions, such as governments, banks, and the religious. In the past, we often expected institutions to guide and direct us. We were loyal to our institutions. This is no longer true. In recent decades, various financial scandals and many religious sex scandals reduced and eroded this trust. In part, some of these institutions brought shame, disgrace, and humiliation upon themselves. Postmodern thinking did the rest. Bob Dylan, the American musician, poet, and Nobel Prize winner, rightly mused in the 1960s that "the times they are a' changing."

The evidence seems to tell us that in postmodernism, we value style over substance. Kelly Besecke, a freelance writer, in 2014, wrote, *You Can't Put God in a Box: Thoughtful Spirituality in the Rational Age*:

What Eliot said in poetry, the people in my field sites said in prose. Parker Palmer, giving a public lecture, said, "our society has limited vision. It's hard to look around and not see the many ways our society encourages death, rather than encouraging life." And Common Ground's Ron described the disenchanted world as a world without soul, a world that's all surface and no substance.[21]

We value politicians who sound good (to us) over policy outlines. In our eager, quick-fix world of shallow thinking, packaging trumps content. Sadly, we have declined to the point where we accept stylist "tweets" and "bullet point" headlines and news that is critical of institutions as sufficient information on which to make "personal, well-informed decisions." Overall, we seem to appreciate shallow, quick-moving, and changing waters over mastering deep water or deep reading.

Historically, Western Society and Western Christianity were rooted in countless stories of people in the Old and New Testament and in Christian history. In many of these stories, as previously noted, people either had great patience or needed patience. Today we lack patience. Bluntly, God is now Google! If we have a question, we want it answered instantly. If a question pops into our head, out pops the phone. This is an endemic social reality that is conditioning us to salivate when we hear bells ringing. If you don't know what this is referring to, call Google and say "Pavlo's dogs." In postmodernism, we can walk across a room and, speaking in a normal voice, say "Hey, Google, or Alexis, or Siri." And unlike waiting for God, these machines instantly answer our pleas. We're no longer willing to spend time like Moses wandering and waiting for the right moment for God to speak. We no longer allow ourselves to sit patiently and let that "still, small voice" within us help us discern, weigh in, or mull over issues. Today, Google responds to our needs, and it very rarely says "No." Google et al instantly answers our question and offers us 1, 10, 10,000, 1 million, or 10 million potential answers. These "answers" are arranged and ranked. Algorithms select the answers that they "think" we want.

Naturally, these emerging evolutionary (revolutionary) factors bear much weight on human development, Western Society, and the corresponding religious institutions in Western Christianity. In *The Chrysalis Effect: The Metamorphosis of Global Culture* (2009), the late Philip Slater, sociologist and writer, accurately suggests and describes our postmodern reality:

> We're used to riding the rapids of technological change, but social change, historically, has proceeded at the pace of a stream meandering through a dense swamp. The recent speed of social change has put a strain on our adaptive capabilities. We've had to adjust not merely to computers and cell phones and the Internet, but to the changing status of women and minorities, the sexual revolution, the decline of the nuclear family, the global economy, the increasing meaninglessness of national boundaries, the ecological movement, the bewildering concepts of modern physics, and so on. All in a few decades ... Some people talk about a "culture war" between the West and Islam. But the real culture clash is taking place *within* Islam and *within* the West. This is not a conflict between nations, or between religions, or between left and right. The conflict is within every nation, every political party, every religious tradition, every institution, every individual. [22]

He is best known for his 1970 book, *In Pursuit of Loneliness*. Fifty years later, this commentary on society is still relevant as elitists seek control of much in society. What do you think of his comments concerning the real issues being within ourselves?

One of the earliest and still foundational efforts that describes the move from our religious world to spirituality is the 2005 book *The Spiritual Revolution: Why Religion Is Giving Way to Spirituality*. Written by Paul Heelas and Linda Woodhead, with assistance from Benjamin Seel, Bronislaw Szerszynski, and Karin Tusting, this is an excellent read. In my view, it offers a fair, balanced, and unvarnished examination of our postmodern reality. Likewise, it's obvious that our brave new world, even before COVID-19, was immersed in radical social change that created much distrust and confusion. In Western Society, since our historical roots seem to be uprooted and paved over with a stream of information, we don't have time to assimilate or absorb much before it evolves again.

Questions to ponder and discuss
Chapter One

Postmodernism and Western Society

1 In postmodern society, we are swimming in overwhelming data and information. How can you unabashedly shift through and seek wisdom?

2 In postmodernism, we can see incredible developments in travel, education, information, communication, and the rise of social media. How has this affected you? Which affects you the most and the least?

3 We are the most connected society in history and also the least connected. Are you disconnected from others? To what degree? Are you disconnected from yourself (be tough and be honest)?

4 Loneliness is a global disease. Does it apply to you?

CHAPTER TWO

POSTMODERNISM AND WESTERN CHRISTIANITY

The postmodern world is under unprecedented flux and great expansion. A massive collection of paradigm shifts is bombarding Western Society and, in turn, Western Christianity. With a sense of feeling overloaded, both Western Society and Western Christianity are forcing people to grapple with immense, often-overpowering issues.

For example, consider one of the foundational tenets of Western Christianity—the Bible. In postmodernism, a plethora of new Bible translations and paraphrases were developed. Most of these seek to provide a more accurate, word-to-word or thought-to-thought translation. Many desire to make ancient languages more readable in English. Sadly, some "translations" seem to champion specific political or religious views. Take a moment to think back on the conversations (dare we say, confrontations?) in which churches in Western Christianity used the Bible to "talk" about slavery, homosexuality, gay marriage, and gay ordination! Not only was there much anger from one denomination to another, but even within denominations and congregations. We will explore some of this more fully.

For centuries, Western Christianity was firmly rooted in and tied to the King James Version for religious and spiritual development. Yet even this foundational English translation adhered to political pressure, since King James refused to have the word "tyrant" translated as such! He didn't want people to think of him as a tyrant, although he often was! There is no perfect translation. Sadly, given the number of translations and paraphrases, there are now some bad versions available. In the past, academics and church scholars laboriously worked on translations. In postmodernism, anyone with a computer and agenda can churn out self-edited copies. In other words, esteemed and thoughtful filters to create a good end product seem to give way, in some cases, to "translators" deciding what the end will look like. Instead of a journey, they begin with the destination!

Following World War II, some updated versions and newer translations arose. Years later, the floodgates opened and countless new translations and paraphrases appeared. Naturally, some felt threatened and responded with knee-jerk reactions, proclaiming the KJV as the only and inerrant voice of God. As to be expected, this situation led to polarization. In postmodernism, with many threats abounding, many sought solace in one of their dearest personal and community values—the Bible. While some do believe the world is changing and unraveling around them, they seek to hold to their valuable, unchangeable, inerrant Bible to guide them. Popular and well-versed writer Dorothy Butler Bass describes this reaction of postmodernism well in her 2012 book, *Christianity after Religion: The End of Church and the Birth of a New Spiritual Awakening*:

> ... Fundamentalist preachers look at this situation and shake their heads, warning against the devil appearing as an angel of light, decrying how easy it is to fall into heresy, and how the evil one roams about tempting God's children. To them, the 1970s revival went on the skids— neither their converts' lives not their attempt to convert culture unfolded as planned. They are busily training new troops to correct the course and return America (and the rest of the Christian world) to old-time religion and God's righteous path. They envision a global sawdust trail to convert the heathen masses and restore biblical inerrancy, family values, social order, clerical authority, theological

orthodoxy, sexual purity, free-market capitalism, and Protestant piety.[1]

Today, some churches ordain women, whereas a mere short century year ago, that action was unfathomable. Some churches now marry same-sex couples. Again, a mere fifty years ago, it was radical for churches to marry divorced people. Much is changing in Western Christianity. In postmodernism, various Christian denominations, and many "stand-alone" or independent churches, face sailing into swirling and uncharted waters. While Jesus commanded waters to be still, it's clear that current church leaders don't have that ability. Postmodernism demands action instead of pondering reflections. Sadly, some unabashedly declared that Hurricane Katrina was God's punishment on gays.

Today's leaders wrestle with what to maintain, what to adopt, and what to discard in the ever-changing and shifting landscape. One vital challenging question is, "What do we keep, and what do we let go of?" For example, "If we keep certain doctrines, we lose members. However, if we discard those same doctrines, we lose members. Moreover, if we do nothing to avoid doctrinal or personality conflicts, we will also lose members." Sometimes in early postmodernism denial or stall was an acceptable answer. However, as our societal shift continues, it seems more drastic responses are needed to catch up to the radically changing environment. Likewise, it's difficult to consider changes when one is preoccupied with putting out fires!

The religious shift in postmodernism is so radical that in the few decades following World War II, Western Christianity, which had experienced massive and unprecedented growth, began to experience massive and unprecedented decline! We must acknowledge this situation. The growth was, in part, due to population expansion (the baby boom), post-war immigration from Europe, and the shift from rural to city to suburb living. Greater disposable income led to the building of countless new churches, or building expansions, and new programs. Yet within a half-century, this boom gave way to decline. Many new suburban churches and city churches amalgamated or closed. The decline was so intense that labels such as "post-denominationalism" and the "Age of Post-Christianity" are increasingly in use.[2]

Just before the Reformation, Europe was smoldering with many restrictive and oppressive ideas that questioned Western Christianity. At that time, Western Christianity meant the Roman Catholic Church. It had a monopoly. In turn, it was the most powerful institution in Europe. Naturally, the church, as with any monopoly, sought to suppress the cauldron of new thoughts. Then one day, a disgruntled Roman Catholic monk, frustrated with the lack of response or conversation, happened to be the right person acting at the right moment in time. This monk wrote out his ignored ideas and complaints. He nailed these 95 thoughts on a church door. Martin Luther was the monk, and he was the spark that ignited the Reformation. He opened the smoldering floodgates of emerging religious and social thoughts. In addition, the growing use of a recent invention of a converted wine press into a printing tool greatly helped. The corresponding use of ink that didn't run or smudge was also instrumental in this process. Together this created a perfect storm, and a religious and cultural explosion erupted and ushered in significant societal paradigm shifts.

The Reformation saw many books, pamphlets, and treatises that objectively and progressively articulated and debated various thoughts. Despite much conflict, violence, and polarization, this was also an age of deep thought—a practice that seems to be fading. Nicholas Carr wrote, "The practice of deep reading that became popular in the wake of Gutenberg's invention, in which "the quiet was part of the meaning, part of the mind," will continue to fade, in all likelihood becoming the province of a small and dwindling elite."[3]

Today, we are amidst much violence in our homes, communities, nations, and the global village. We have polarizing thoughts with an eroding middle ground (and middle class). Violence, racism, and sexism are rampant, and we as a society seem to lack deep thought, deep thinking, and conversations that can help us evolve! In other words, our first response in our impatience to issues is often to draw lines in the sand. Instead of a pleasant conversation, we jump to demanding confrontation. This is widespread in Western Society and Western Christianity, and it weighs heavily on postmodern spirituality. This needs exploration.

For much of recorded history, we depended on the exploration of information and questions to help us discover answers. Answers led people to ask more questions. Metaphorically, we might say we created spirals of expanding insights. In postmodernism, however, it seems that we begin with answers and then search for information and questions that support that answer. Thus, we moved from spiraling outward to spiraling inward! When we spiral outward, we move into the unknown. We face challenges, new wonders, and potential responses that give us a sense of awe. However, in postmodernism we tend to spiral inward, where we discover information, opinions, and thoughts that already support what we know. Likewise, when we spiral inward, our focus doesn't expand—it contracts. Either wittingly or unwittingly, this narrow focus leads to assuming the righteousness of our answer and the potential rejection of any contrary information or opinion. In postmodern Western Christianity, to what degree did the churches spiral outward or inward? How much effort was afforded to the status quo? In addition, how did these actions encourage or suppress spiritual growth? These are vital questions to ponder. How do you answer these questions?

In our postmodern religious world, we haven't abandoned objectivity, but it is reduced for the sake of more subjective opinions and personalized views. We post one-way communications expecting and anticipating others to approve. English sociologist and anthropologist Paul Heelas, and English sociologist and religious studies specialist Linda Woodhead, write that people moved from external, objective roles of "duties and obligations" to "a turn, and even towards a life lived by reference to one's own subjective experiences." They also suggest that this subjective focus is endemic:

> ... What we will see is that both self-understanding and socio-cultural arrangements have been developing in a "person-centred" or "subjectivity-centred" direction. In education culture, we see a turn towards the "child-centred" or "learner-centred"; in purchasing culture towards the "consumer-centred"; in health culture, towards the "patient-centred"; in work culture, towards the personal development of employees. Each of these shifts

involves a turn away from a more hierarchical, deferential, life-as order of things in which the teacher, the shopkeeper, the doctor, the manager was "god". Thus those institutions that cater for the unique subjective-lives of the "centred" are on the increase, whilst those that continue to operate in life-as mode find themselves out of step with the times ...[4]

This suggests that instead of looking at issues through broad perspectives, we now tend to keep reinforcing and affirming narrow and often very subjective views. In postmodern Western Christianity, we often hear the mantra that churches want to grow. What we don't hear in the subtle and sublime undercurrent is that one is to grow in the prescribed church- approved manner. This means that people reinforce narrow, subjective views. Because we are seemingly meeting the church's agenda, we are pleased, because it matches our personalized agenda. Instead of saying, "I am meeting the needs of the faith," the image is, "Isn't it great that the needs of the faith are what I already am working on." Likewise, we discount and reject agendas and items that don't fit in our prescribed fixed boxes or those of the church or other religious institutions.

It's important to remember that before the Reformation there was one church. We may say that from its earliest days the Roman Catholic Church was the first truly non-governmental multinational organization! It was the only common denominator found in the nations and principalities of Europe. It was so powerful that instead of taking on the languages of these many nations, it offered one language to all—Latin. The message was that "we provide one common language to everyone." The Church controlled or influenced much of the thinking and actions of the leaders. This isn't a criticism but merely an observation of what took place at that point in history.

Historically, the Roman Catholic Church relied upon a "one-size-fits-all" model. In other words, Rome set the standard and norms to which everyone was to conform. It still does. The Reformation saw cracks and then great divisions in this forced conformity. This model was built upon sincere agendas; however, it was also fraught with some leaders who were corrupt opportunists. The veneer that covered some of this corruption faded and became quite visible and, for some, normative, such as the selling of indulgences, which were religious pardons sold to lawbreakers. One could rob and steal and then pay off the church for a "get out of jail free card."

In time, Protestantism and nation-states became part of the new social fabric. In many ways, Rome continued to uphold itself as the official church and the others as pretenders. It still operates in the "one-size-fits-all" model. While this works in-house, it no longer commands the same dominance or influence elsewhere. While the Roman Catholic Church believed it made it through the Reformation largely intact, I wonder if it assumes that it will weather postmodernism with the same approach. This is not likely going to happen.

In the postmodern world, the "one-size-fits-all" model collapsed. We no longer seem comforted or fed by "off the rack" institutional, hierarchical, fixed, and rigid models of theology, doctrine, or liturgy. This is significant. We tend to like the complete opposite! We like creating our own "mix-and-match" theology, doctrines, liturgies, and spiritualities. We no longer adhere to or like fixed, stable, orderly, authority-centered models or hierarchies. We are abandoning orthodox boundaries, church buildings, and certainty for a very different reality.[3] Not only do we "mix and match," but we often do so on a whim. We don't seem to care if we coordinate in our mix and matches, as long as they feed our present and immediate needs. If we feel that our immediate needs are less than adequately met, we shift and search for other mixes and matches. This is central in postmodern Western Christianity. For example, instead of conforming to religious norms, we expect religious norms to conform to us. This is a significant reversal of the past. Moreover, if we don't feel appeased, we seek out other ways to meet our needs. Instead of the "one-size-fits-all," we've morphed to a model that is "all-sizes-fits-one." We don't conform to religious institutions in Western Christianity—we expect them to conform to us. If not, we take one body and wallet elsewhere! In the past, that wasn't considered an option. Today it seems to be standard practice.

Before the Reformation, it was natural for the Roman Catholic Church to operate with the mentality of "father-knows-best." The parish priest was the Father, or guiding parent, of the local community. Again, this model was mostly genuine and sincere. It remains largely genuine and sincere—and it still exists. The priest was (and is) the sage giving advice and instructions on how to live. Historically, the local community priest's role was to keep records, hence the term "cleric"! Yet this model was and is sometimes fraught with issues of abuse. The elevated place of priests in a community can lead to elitism. This model is prone to downplay the place and roles of people who are not ordained. In other words, elite classism. Sometimes this model morphs and becomes "father-knows-everything." In turn, this can develop into the sad situation of "father-can-do-anything." As Lord Acton mused, "Absolute power corrupts absolutely." Thus, abusive power and control seduces some into being sexual abusers.

Before the Reformation, and until the rise of general education, most in holy orders acted genuinely as pastoral shepherds to people who couldn't read or write. In our educated postmodern world, this archaic model needs to fade away. This and other elitist models in Western Christianity stymie spiritual growth and personal development. Sadly, sometimes elite leaders refuse to reform because the lust for power and control defines their leadership. It is intoxicating. What is the incentive to change when one is more worried about power and control than the future of their religious institution?

The "father-knows-best" model is counter to emergent postmodern values. The religious model of "father-knows-best" eventually shifted to individualized "I-know-best." Unfortunately, many leaders of elite models are blind to this shift and are struggling to maintain their exalted positions. The "father-knows-everything" model gave way to "I-know-everything" and in turn to the "I-can-do-anything" image. What does this mean for Western Christianity? It means we no longer believe we need the priest or pastor "telling" us how to live or die! What do you think? Likewise, to whom do we turn for assistance with postmodern spirituality since we're abandoning models of the past? What do you think?

It took about five centuries following the Reformation for Martin Luther's ideal of the "priesthood of all believers" and other budding religious and theological ideas, such as letting the scriptures speak to the individual, to emerge. Academic James Herrick, who often writes about technology and spirituality, explains this quite well:

Indeed, the Reformation in northern Europe under the leadership of Martin Luther is typically associated with a return to the Bible as the standard of religious truth. However, a number of scholars have pointed out that this powerful Christian movement contributed importantly to skepticism's rise in modern Europe ... Perhaps another of the Reformation's guiding principles, the priesthood of all believers, which placed biblical interpretation in the hands of the individual believer, contributed to this effect.

Of critical importance to later developments is the commitment of Reformation leaders to private interpretation of the Scriptures. "The Pandora's box that Luther opened at Leipzig," writes Richard Popkin, "was to have the most far-reaching consequences, not just in theology but throughout man's entire intellectual realm." Similarly, Roscoe Pound argues that "private interpretation of the Bible" had the effect of elevating individual reason.[5]

As just noted, the Reformation encouraged people to view and think about scripture without the specific need for clergy to provide interpretations; they were still communities of believers. In postmodernism, this shifted. It shifted significantly. Instead of people collectively acting "as the church," we seem to act and believe individually. At best, we reverted to religious tribalism. At worst, we are now often "a church of one." We may be with others, but only because they are very much like us. Much tribalism exists in Western Society and Western Christianity. For example:

Despite platitudes and rhetoric, many Christians, or churches do not want much to change. For example, we seek to hold to models that still give us that "Old Time Gospel Hour." Most tend to prefer keeping change at a slow process, under much control, and limited to the small tinkering. If we are genuinely open to the unfolding of self that is involved in transformation, we will generally encounter resistance in most of the places that we normally expect support. Families, community, and culture often conspire to keep us safely in a place of conformity. As noted by Richard Rohr, most religion—and this certainly includes Christianity—is more tribal than transformational.[6]

These postmodern realities continue to diminish the place of organized religions in Western Society. Given the history of Western Society, this typically means Western Christianity. Nevertheless, Western Christianity in the postmodernism world must learn to be nimble! Unfortunately, as with many institutions, the leaders would rather plod along making small, incremental changes than take any substantial risks. By not taking risks, what are we risking? Sadly, because of this "slow-go" mentality, many religious institutions in Western Christianity are suffering. If we use the retirement metaphor, we can say that from the early day of postmodernism, Western Christianity was in the "go-go" phase. It's now near the end of the "slow-go" phase. If not urgently addressed, it will become "no-go." Likewise, many churches and denominations may then move into the "no-no" state we usually call death.

Historically, the mainline churches were the first to feel this postmodern shift, and recently the Evangelical movement organizations are feeling the pinch. The Evangelical churches once saw much growth at the expense of mainline churches. They absorbed disenfranchised members and added people who felt disdain for the traditional religious institutions. However, they too are slowly waning. But given the lack of a long history and permanent locked-in thinking and practices, they tend to be more nimble than mainline churches.

Mainline churches in Western Christianity typically lived with fixed liturgies and fluid theology. Amid the growth of postmodernism and uncertainty, the Evangelical churches grew and flourished because they often offered fluid liturgy and safe, fixed theology. John Dornauer illustrates this well:

> Cameron Trimble, Executive Director of the Center for Progressive Christianity, puts it this way: "While

conservative churches are less flexible with their theology, they are incredibly adaptable when it comes to their ritual and liturgy. Progressive Christianity, on the other hand, is has a very flexible theology, but refuses to change its ritual and liturgy."[7]

Nevertheless, as the postmodern reality took hold, this changed. Much of Western Christianity, meaning mainline and Evangelical denominations, and individual churches are attempting to cope with declining membership, reduced attendance, smaller income, and a downward sliding influence. Likewise, we sometimes now stretch full-time ordained leadership beyond manageable levels. We increase the geographical areas they serve and/ or their workload. This is done to continue a full-time position. Part-time ordained and lay leadership often fulfill roles previously reserved for full-time clergy. As noted earlier, new suburban and city churches are following the lead of rural congregations and are shutting down or amalgamating. Instead of the Great Commission to preach the gospel to help people spiritually grow (and to grow the church), we find much energy and attention directed towards survival realities. Leaders who deny this reality are in denial themselves. Furthermore, replacing the waning interest in religious institutions across Western Christianity is a new postmodern phenomenon—the SBNR movement (those who are Spiritual But Not Religious).

For much of history, we were a rural society. People belonged to the church of their parents and grandparents. It was a social norm and expectation. One knew all their neighbors. In this fixed, staid society, one could raise eyebrows and voice displeasure if a Protestant and Roman Catholic intermarried. The churches and parents considered this anathema. Protestants married Protestants, and hopefully from the same stripes, while Roman Catholics were expected to marry other Roman Catholics. And if a non-Roman Catholic married a Roman Catholic, the expectation was that they would become Roman Catholic. "What did love have to do with it?" when fixed protocols were abounding!

In postmodernism, we don't worry too much if Protestants and Roman Catholics marry each other. However, some still raise their eyebrows and voice displeasure if inter-racial or same-sex couples discuss their desire to marry. This shift is significant. The former social and religious boundaries that kept Protestants and Roman Catholics from marrying no longer exist. It's now common for Protestants and Roman Catholics to marry a partner who belongs to no church, or even had no religious upbringing! Ironically, some couples with no church or marginalized church affiliation still seek an institutional church as the setting for their wedding. Is this because they want the traditional "churchy" look, or is it because they have some small spirituality calling them to seek the sacrament of marriage? What do you think?

After centuries of arranged marriages based on sustaining both families, we saw a shift to where women and men married for love. We shifted from the celebrated "man and wife" marriage of the same religious background to almost any variation! We saw the shift to husband and wife, wife and wife, and husband and husband across racial, cultural, and religious traditions. At the same time, marriage gave way to short-term, long-term, and serial relationships. These were "without the benefit of clergy." This secular reality is now our societal norm!

For many centuries, it was the standard practice in Western Christianity for couples to "marry-for-as-long as-we-both-shall-live." Divorce was possible for royalty, nobles, and others in the autocracy, but for others, it was rarely an option. It was expensive and brought a significant stigma for those not in the upper class. Women did not have rights or status. Mutuality didn't exist. Arranged marriages were the norm and for the survival and benefit of both families. In postmodernism, couples no longer feel any social pressure to marry. Today, relationships often seem rooted in the notion that "We-will-live-together-for-as-long-we-both-shall-love." In turn, divorce is so much a part of our postmodern culture that to meet the demand court cases move quickly and we have no-fault divorce. These changes are a great paradigm shift from the past. What do you think? Paul Taylor describes the postmodern view of marriage quite well:

> ... A 2013 research paper, "Knot Yet: The Benefits and Costs of Delayed Marriage," did a wonderful job showing how young adults view marriage as a "capstone" rather

than "cornerstone" arrangement—"something they do after they have all their other ducks in a row, rather than a foundation for launching into adulthood and parenthood." Given this new cultural framework for marriage, it's no surprise that it's the high-achieving young adults who are most likely to get hitched. "Marriage has become a status symbol," writes Cherlin, "a highly regarded marker of a successful personal life... Something young adults do after they and their live-in partners have good jobs and a nice apartment."[8]

For these and other reasons, today's people don't feel compelled to be married. The past stigma of divorce or pre-marital sex is over. Today, we even have "starter marriages!"[9] People don't feel stigmatized if they don't belong to a church. Instead of memberships, our foundation of entitlement entices us to be nothing more than samplers.[10] We sample relationships, we sample churches, we sample careers, we sample life, always looking for the short-term fulfillment of the "me needs."

Another shift in Western Christianity surrounds our approach to worship or liturgy. The historical practice and thinking of worship and liturgy was "the work of the people" to praise God. From the earliest Christian liturgies through the Reformation and beyond, people gathered with the focus to praise God. Yet in our time, one of the most common questions people ask themselves after worship is, "What did I receive in the church today?" or "What is the church doing for me?" Is this not a monumental shift? What do you think?

We moved away from people meeting the expectations and needs of the church. We moved from the notion of giving to God to the radical idea of, "What am I receiving from God." We now embrace the model in which individuals expect the church to meet their needs. It seems that if our needs aren't being met, people easily shift, without guilt or shame, to another church, to another denomination, or to secularism. Instead of seeing themselves at fault for failing to worship God, people may find it easy to cast blame on pastors, policies, and practices. Likewise, the days of brand loyalty are over. Again, what do you think? What can you add to this conversation?

In response to postmodernism, some rail and believe that they must fight "spiritual warfare." They see the world abandoning historical values. It's "us against the world." In large part, this approach is founded upon the notion that those who deem themselves as favored by God must confront all others, and others are styled as "sinners" as opposed "the elect." Those in spiritual warfare see themselves as God's chosen, and they must battle all others. It's reflective of postmodernism because it's rooted in polarization and confrontational thinking. If one is busy attacking others from an assumed superior position, little time, energy, or interest exists to explore "Is this right?" In other words, the "favored people" believe themselves as God's insiders and thus chosen to preserve God's world. By the way, many (can we say, most?) of these "chosen warriors" prefer the King James Bible. Throughout postmodernism, this approach smacks of polarizing and confrontational elitism. Because many gather in like-minded group settings, (can we say tribal?) people reinforce the idea that they are "the chosen" or "elect." As with postmodern realities, this tunnel vision is destructive. In my view, this Christian view is unchristian. However, despite internal issues challenging Western Christianity, one of the most significant issues in postmodernism is not found in the shifting of religious ideals but in how do we deal with apathy!

Sadly, in postmodernism, the Christian churches that grow are those who are revising the gospel. Instead of answering the call to look after the weak, the poor, the widow, and the orphan, they read ancient scriptures as though they intend twenty-first-century Western Society Christians to be successful. They seek personalized affirmation. The personified image that Jesus is for them seems counter to the message Jesus spent most of his time affirming while assisting the marginalized. This image is well explained by Jean Twenge and W. Keith Campbell:

> Many churches around the country now promote "prosperity Christianity," or the idea, as one book puts it, that God Wants You to Be Rich …Of the four largest megachurches in the United States, three teach some

version of "prosperity"—the idea that God doesn't want you to be poor. "The tragedy is that Christianity had become a yes-man for the culture," says Stephen Prothero, chairman of the religion department at Boston University.[11]

Instead of working to help the poor and others, many seek religious institutions that tell them the gospel says, "God wants us, and desires us, to have material wealth and success." The prosperity gospel churches are reflective of the postmodern mind. It seems that their version of the gospels was conceived specifically to address the postmodern American. This is ironic because in biblical times, people understood their place. In biblical times, the poor knew they would always be poor. There was no middle class. People were wealthy or poor. The poor paid high taxes to help the rich maintain their lifestyle. In other words, the poor often gravitated to Jesus because he made being poor somewhat bearable. He also offered hope and grace. He helped their survival mode mentality and made difficult situations bearable. He helped people move from darkness and shadows into light, meaning from sadness to joy. He made people feel spiritually alive. Unfortunately, making people spiritually alive didn't bode well with the religious and wealthy elites. They felt threatened by the massive potential of the poor to rise up! I wonder to what degree this is still a problem. To what degree does Western Christianity address people's religious needs ahead of spiritual needs? If Western Christianity tried to focus on spiritual needs, it would cause institutions to make paradigm shifts! What are your thoughts?

Linda A. Mercadente, in *Belief without Borders: Inside the Minds of the Spiritual but Not Religious*, provides a wonderful metaphorical illustration:

> ... Jewish theologian and sociologist Will Herberg warned of a "cut flower culture" where moral principles eventually die once they are cut off from their from their scriptural and intellectual roots. "cut flowers retain their original beauty and fragrance, but only so long as retain the vitality that they have drawn from their now-severed roots: after that is exhausted, they wither and die," he wrote in *Judaism and*

Modern Man. Other fields join the worried ranks because it seems that Americans are increasingly separated from each other, segmented, market-driven, virtualized, and specialized in work and leisure. In fact, there are many studies showing emotional and physical health benefits of religious faith and memebership. Social scientists contend that religion, even if not perfect, has always been a strong glue and beneficent presence in American society[12]

Dr. Mercadente is the opposite of most SBNR people. She grew up in a non-religious home, found her spiritual self, and is now a professor of theology!

The glue eroded more in the boomer generation, who as postmodern people began to see religion and worship quite differently than their parents. Craig Kennet Miller, an ordained United Methodist cleric who directs discipleship ministries for his denomination, explains in *Boomer Spirituality: Seven Values for the Second Half of Life* how battles over worship instruments took place. In a simple image, the parents who supported the sole use of the traditional church organ versus drums and guitars won many battles. However, they lost the war because the boomers left Western Christianity.[13]

At the beginning of postmodernism, the decline and changing situation of religion in Western Society can be partly attributed to the automobile! For centuries, most people couldn't travel any distance. One's life was one's village. How far could one reasonably walk or ride, and return, in a day? With the onset of families having one, and later two or more, family automobiles, we saw a true paradigm shift. In a phrase, we shifted from the "community church" to "church communities." This is monumental. This is significant. Now instead of a melting pot of people in one's village worshipping as one, we see people travel and gravitate to people who like the same theology and worship structure. In other words, people use to travel a very short distance to go to church, but in postmodernism, they may travel 20 miles (32.187 kilometers for Canadians, eh?) or more to worship in a church that they like and, in turn, likes them! These religious changes brought transformation to Western spirituality.

Today with the new superhighway called the Internet, we don't even have to leave home to attend church. COVID-19 magnified this reality. Think about this reality in these terms: In the 1960s, adults wore their "Sunday best" to attend church. Then as postmodernism progressed, and relaxed attitudes developed, men began to feel comfortable shedding ties, and women their fanciest dresses. Today, we don't even have to leave the bedroom to attend church. We can now Zoom church while wearing our favorite pajamas. While I have no problem with that, I sincerely hope that those who dress in that manner will, at least, wear the appropriate liturgical color—green for most of the year, white for Christmas and Easter, purple for Lent, etc. For those of a non-liturgical church, plaids and paisleys are suitable and reasonable weekend church attire. These factors show great religious and social paradigm shifts.

We shifted from being with people who lived life near us, to being with people who are like us. Instead of attending church because of its location, we now chose churches because they resemble people who think like us—in other words, a shift from people conforming to the community, to having a community that conforms to us! Once more, this indicates that in the postmodern world and in Western Christianity, we seek a church that meets our specific needs, whatever they may be, each week! It's only after meeting our needs that we feel empowered, if so inclined, to meet God's needs or those of others. Such is postmodernism and the unaware self-centered, self-absorbed lives we lead. After all, we want (expect) God to make us happy! These changes influence and modify our spirituality.

Some other shifts in postmodern Western Christianity show that theological thinking and approaches to dogma and liturgy are much different from any time in history. From the earliest days of Christendom through the Reformation and to postmodernism, one significant, central image was that one's faith served to help earn one's way into heaven. Throughout Western Society's history, most people lived life at the survival level. Thus, having often endured "hell-on-earth," one looked forward to receiving one's "reward in heaven." Much of Western Christianity supported this viewpoint. Some still do. While the church preached about the "heavenly home," many messages were rooted in another image—we are helping you "avoid hell." Negative reinforcement works well. Theology of earning one's way into heaven and receiving advice on how to avoid damnation were great tools to uphold power and control over people. Postmodernism is changing that image. Again, mull over some very thoughtful words offered by Jean Twenge and W. Keith Campbell:

> This is a very different view of God and religion than was common just a few decades ago. Back then, religion had expectations of you; it was not a vehicle for fulfilling your dreams. There were rules for behavior (no adultery, no idols before God, go to church, don't lie or steal, don't work on the Sabbath, don't covet your neighbor's stuff), and you'd better follow them or you would be doomed to hell (or, at the very least, you'd have to face up to your sins, confess them, and do penance). Many of today's preachers say that God still doesn't want you to sin, but he also wants you to have a big house ...[14]

Today, people place greater value on having a good earthly life than on thoughts of afterlife rewards. It seems that the medieval image has faded. Thanks be to God. In part, people now live beyond survival mode. Today, people are blessed with disposable incomes, better education, healthcare, and less controlling religiousness. These are some are reasons for this change. We might say that we are abandoning negative reinforcement for more positive approaches. Rutger Bregman, in his monumental book on positivism, *Humankind: A Hopeful History*, explains that we are prone to seek, reinforce, and adhere to the negative. Yet he affirms that we thrive on hope and kindness.[15]

Bunyan's classic medieval work, *Pilgrim's Progress*, brilliantly explored the negative images of avoiding hell. He wrote of life's journey and its challenge and rewards. In postmodernism, with all its medical marvels and longer lifespans, we don't want to hear of potential rewards in the afterlife. Instead, as noted, we desire guidance on how to live our earthly lives. Instead of the "afterlife," we want "the life we are here after." This is a tectonic shift.

Tied to this in a postmodernism image, Western Christianity added to its demise by telling people they were "saved." People responded by thinking, *If I'm saved, why do still need the church?* Instead of thinking of salvation as an ongoing reality, postmodernism took it as a benchmark, and people moved on and away from the church. We no longer see clergy and Western Christianity as the sole, or "soul," conduit to God. In 1967, A. H. Van den Heuvel, quoting Dietrich Bonhoeffer (one of the first to describe postmodernism), said, "I began by saying that God is being increasingly edged out of the world, now that it has come of age. Knowledge and life are thought to be perfectly possible without him ..."[16]

Likewise in postmodernism, without much conscious awareness, Western Christianity began to take on the characteristics and attributes of rising secularism within Western Society. This is a major shift. In the Reformation, the sacred influenced social changes, but now social churches are influencing the sacred. A good illustration of this shift centers on the clergy. Historically, people recognized clergy as God's representatives. They spoke for God and to God. Clergy were respected for their call to ministry and their sense of "being." In postmodernism and secularism, this changed dramatically. People and church structures, while still acknowledging the "being" role of the clergy, began to measure them on what they had accomplished. We began evaluating what they "did" as opposed to who they were. Hence, we shifted from acknowledging clergy for their sense of prayer and their leadership roles in worship and the community. We shifted, likely unconsciously, to secular success-business-centered models—in other words, from being to doing. We shifted from prayer, presence, and pause to production and proficiency. This shift is substantial, and it is still evolving.

Additionally, in the last fifty or sixty years, we shifted from the nuclear family of a male parent working outside the home and a female parent at home with children to various models. For example, it's normal for both parents to work outside the home, or to be a single-parent family, or to be a blended family. We see same-sex families. We see families with and without children. In our Western postmodern society, the largest "family" group today is the family of one person.[17] This is a significant social shift. In part, the decline of the centrality of the nuclear family mirrors the decline of organized religion. Despite massive societal shifts, churches have rarely adapted to regard new models of family. For some churches in Western Christianity, the nuclear family remains the only acceptable model. Some may embrace single-family units, but they still quietly yearn for families. Why do these realities exist? They sincerely believe in their need to have a new generation to continue the church. Yet can't single people, particularly older singles, also fulfill this desire?

Literature professor Gene Veith Jr., in *Postmodern Times: A Guide to Contemporary Thought and Culture*, notes many new realities. In a pivotal thought, he states:

> The old paradigm taught that if you have the right teaching, you will experience God. The new paradigm says that if you experience God, you will have the right teaching. Not only is objective doctrine minimized in favor of subjective experience; experience actually becomes the criterion for evaluating doctrine.[18]

We will come across the notion of "right-thinking" again in the last chapter.

He also wrote much saying that instead of the church focusing on various doctrinal changes, it should focus on how to change lives.[19] We might surmise that instead of offering people religion or new models in the postmodern world, we might do well to focus on spiritual development. Instead of hoping for people to come to church to meet its needs, the postmodern focus of Western Christianity might be, "How can we assist you in your spiritual journey?" For me, this is foundational for Western Christianity and indeed Western Society.

If we were to provide one overall encompassing and definitive phrase to explain religion in Western Society before postmodernism, we might say that it operated with a prescriptive foundation.[20] In prescriptive models, Western Christianity told people what to believe and how to act. In postmodernism, with some certainty, the focus should be on descriptive models. Instead of top-down fixed lists of "this is what you need to do," we need to shift to a bottom-up, fluid model. Prescriptive models that are top-down set the agenda and measure how people respond and perform. In descriptive models, leadership must be prepared to respond to a broad array of ideas, thoughts, and notions. In other words, a prescriptive approach can be very narrow (this is right, that is wrong), whereas a descriptive model is always wide (hmm, that's a good question to ponder). Prescriptive models naturally enhance and support rules that exist, whereas descriptive models are always evolving. In other words, we need to discern from within and seek views from others like and unlike us. We need to affirm, challenge, sustain, and confront our thinking and actions. These images of prescriptive/descriptive are not trite or simplistic.

In our descriptive postmodern Western Christianity, where we are the center of the universe, we tend to see the world through the lens of our own eyes. Descriptive models aren't perfect, as prescriptive models believed they were. It's easier to affirm fixed prescriptions than to explore challenging descriptions. In turn, we often seek those who have similar and, therefore, affirming views.

Perhaps one of the most profane ways to describe postmodern Western Christianity is in the simple yet complete image that we shifted from embracing the historical Christ for the personal Jesus. The personification of this "Me-ism" is the shift from the hymn "The Church's One Foundation" to the Christian rock in which we personalized faith and ask, "Who Am I" by Casting Crowns, and the constant theme is "I am yours." This is not to cast aspersions upon Casting Crowns but to illustrate how postmodern Western Christianity moved to "Me-ism." While the phrases "Who am I" and "I am yours" are spiritual, the thrust revolves around individualized support from the Creator. We've shifted from the historical collective approach to one that placates the postmodern individual. In postmodernism, instead of saying that Jesus died for humanity, we reduce this to, "Jesus died for me." If we undertake a "deep or close reading" of postmodern religion, we find that Jesus often personifies the American ideal of prosperity, success, and entitlement. For example, "If you're one of the elect, you are saved while others are not." It's elitism. Some churches in Western Christianity embrace this approach. In a phrase, they have co-opted postmodern culture to be their postmodern religion. This is a noteworthy point to ponder. What do you think? Take your time.

Jesus spent much time caring, healing, and supporting outcasts and non-Jews. He didn't wine and dine with his society's elect—the Temple officials or Roman overloads. Jesus, in many stories, supported women. At the time of Jesus, women had little status. In the New Testament, women are rarely named because they had no status except as an "add-on" to the husband! Jesus never talked about becoming wealthy, except for the wealth gained by serving others. Jesus was annoyed when his disciples pursued ego and self-service. Jesus was not a twenty-first-century American, yet sometimes he seems like the personification of that image. Instead of his efforts of inclusivity (he even talked with non-Jews!), he sometimes seems exclusive to one brand of Western Christianity. Does this adoption of Jesus reshape postmodern spirituality. What do you think? Muse on this.

In our postmodern society, we impose our culture and religion upon Jesus. Instead of us becoming Christ-like, we make Christ to be like us. This is a profound shift. Consider the image presented by a professor of psychology, William Indick, in his 2015 book, *Digital God: How Technology Will Reshape Spirituality*. He wrote in vivid, descriptive detail:

> ... The religious trend of the past few millennia will be flipped ... The new digital idols will allow us to fashion our own graven images of God in way we wish. The personalization, preceptualization, and sensualization of the experience of God may even lead a reversal back to pre-monotheistic spiritualities ...digital simulation will give us the power to create our own spiritual perception, as vivid as any dream ...[21]

Later in that book he wrote, "In the Digital Age, as in the Paleolithic Age, each man will be a prophet, each woman an oracle, and each individual will behold a perception of his own personal Digital God."[22] We've morphed from humanity being created in the representation of God to God be created into the image our personal, ever-shifting image of what we desire. At first glance, this is better than Nietzsche's image of "God is dead." But that was a philosophical idea, while the notion that the Creator is being defined by the Creations is not!

For many centuries, the sacred influenced the secular. Western Christianity provided great influence and direction to Western Society. In the last few decades, postmodernism reversed this reality. In other words, the secular now conditions the sacred! For eons, monarchs and political leaders were cautious on how they acted lest they experience the wrath of the institutional church. When the priest or other cleric spoke to you, shame, humiliation, and correction followed. King Henry VIII is a great example of one who ignored this maxim. Today the opposite seems dominant. Church leaders are wary about making controversial political statements, fearing the wrath and/or backlash of the government and a potential financial loss. Leaders are fearful of lost revenue from members, who today are more political than religious but think they're acting religiously! Ponder this! Sometimes this is so subtle we're unaware of the situation. Again, take time to mull this over.

Western Christianity continues to find the postmodern and secular swing perplexing. It seems to be "bewitched, bothered, and bewildered." History often shows that institutions are slow to perceive and respond to shifting cultural mores. To add to this dilemma, it's natural for the religious institutions in Western Society and Western Christianity to offer typical, traditional, religious responses to these postmodern issues. But people aren't seeking religious responses. People desire (and can we say demand?) spiritual responses. Unfortunately, the aforementioned institutions may believe they're offering spiritual responses when in fact the response is still largely religious. Sociologist David Lyon, in his 2000 publication, *Jesus in Disneyland: Religion in Postmodern Time*, quite thoroughly explores this reality.[23] Writing fifteen years later, sociologist Josh Packard, in *Church Refugees: Sociologists Reveal Why People Are DONE with Church but Not Their Faith*, explains this very well. He interviewed many people who explained why they left the church:

> ... While everyone's story is unique, there are some common tensions that emerge among the dechurched. They wanted community ... and got judgment. They wanted to affect the life of the church ... and got bureaucracy. They wanted conversation ... and got doctrine. They wanted

meaningful engagement with the world ... and got moral prescription.[24]

Wow, someone else offers an example of prescriptions versus descriptions!

Western Christianity in postmodernism is radically different from any other time in history. Secularism took over from the sacred. Self-authority took over from religious authority.[25] I like how Reg Bibby describes this shift when he explores four social shifts. He wrote that we moved from dominance to diversity, from obligation to gratification, from deference to discernment, and from homes to careers.[26] I suggest that one read that short but powerful and descriptive list again and consider the depth of Bibby's thoughts. In turn, I wonder if postmodern society turned religion into a talisman. A talisman is an object believed to have magical properties. What are your thoughts? Take some time to ponder these difficult but vital postmodern questions.

All this raises the question: "As postmodern Western Christianity is radically different than in the past, is it not logical that spirituality, which was often perceived as a 'subset' of Western Christianity, is also different?" What are your thoughts? What images have occurred to you thus far? In *A Church at Risk: The Challenge of Spiritually Hungry Adults*, former academic dean and researcher Marcel Dumestre describes how the postmodern shift is causing Western Society and Western Christianity to reconsider spirituality:

> We live in a fast-changing world. The anxiety of our era thrusts us toward questions of ultimacy at a time when world events and scientific discoveries occur at blinding speed. Our cultural "blindness" compels the need for direction, clarity, and vision—the stuff of spirituality. Adult Christian spirituality is an awakening to the search for meaning at the deepest levels of human experience. This awakening is not a singular event. It is a journey of discovery with periods of setback as well as advancement ... We have a crisis of opinion about the purpose of religion

and the meaning of spirituality. Some ministers view spirituality as the sole province of religion. They see other expressions of spirituality as "flaky" religious experimentalism. Likewise, many Americans have written off formal Christian religion as incapable of providing meaningful spirituality. This conflict is complex because it involves deeply personal and often passionately held beliefs, as well as a lot of misconceptions about religion and spirituality.[27]

We need to explore this dilemma more thoroughly. This is a challenge for mainline and sideline Western Christianity. Evidence suggests they have a deadline. They must do more than constantly address denominational or congregational speed bumps. If ignored, there may be no resurrection for these churches!

Questions to ponder and discuss
Chapter Two

Postmodernism and Western Christianity

1 The "father-knows-everything" model gave way to "I-know-everything" and then to an "I-can-do-anything" image. What does this mean for Western Christianity? What does it mean to you?

2 We no longer believe we need the priest or pastor "telling" us how to live or die! So to whom do we turn for assistance, since we are abandoning models of the past?

3 Why do couples with little or no real religious experience still desire a church wedding? Is it more than the traditional setting?

4 Instead of asking, "What did I receive in the church today?" or "What is the church doing for me?" think about, "What did I give to God or others in worship?"

5 In your discerned thoughts, consider, "To what degree does Western Christianity afford to religious needs, and afford to spiritual needs? Which dominates?"

6 If Western Christianity was to try to focus on spiritual needs, would the result cause institutions to make paradigm shifts?

CHAPTER THREE

POSTMODERN SPIRITUALITY

This book is not an all-encompassing presentation, yet it sufficiently shows that we live in the postmodern world. It's a period of radical and monumental change and societal shifts. Likewise, I hope that the presented information has shown, to so degree, how Western Christianity is also amid a period of radical and monumental change and shifts. These tectonic shifts are more extensive than the Reformation!

Since Western Society and Western Christianity are in the middle of colossal re-ordering, it's natural to ask, "How do we deal with spirituality in postmodern Western Society and Western Christianity?" In other words, "What is spirituality in the Age of Entitlement?" In addition, "How is it manifested?" We must also ask if spirituality is different than in ages past. The answer to this profound question is "Yes" and "No." People continue to ask and explore the same questions they historically asked, such as "Who am I?" and "What is my purpose?" However, in postmodernism, the context of these questions is different than in the past. What do you think? Is the context of our questions different from even a mere sixty years ago? Can you answer this dilemma?

For centuries, people typically looked to the institutional church for guidance and spiritual answers. However, this most exclusive of all monopolies no longer exists. People now look in many places beyond the institutional church for answers. Given the level of secularism in Western

Society, it's quite likely that some in our postmodern society have never approached or considered looking at religious institutions for any spiritual guidance! Given its decline and various sexual and financial scandals, it's logical that people look for guidance in alternative places. The embattled institutions do themselves no favors when after discovery of wrong they choose to be silent. They fail to see how this further erodes public trust. While they may think they will endure this like historical battles of the past, the reality is that the battle is already lost. It's lost when your troops, aka parishioners, leave! Unlike in the past, postmodern people have no qualms about metaphorically jumping ship!

Likewise, we are witnessing a shift from a religiosity that was doctrinal, fixed, rigid, hierarchical, and head-centered, to a postmodern model. In this emerging model, realities are ambiguous—doctrines of Monday can be different by Friday, and one can hold many divergent opinions (at the same time). This new model is fluid (to meet your ever-changing immediate needs), is rooted in the self, and is heart-dominant. This is central to postmodern spirituality.

While we may be using the same words as in the past, much suggests that people today are exploring spirituality with fresh, new eyes. As Antoine de Saint-Exupéry's *Little Prince* said, "It is only in the heart that one can see rightly, what is essential is invisible to the eye." Today, the heart leads to what we see. It directs what we accept and to what we chose to believe. Instead of coming to spirituality through "head" centered or focused programs, we tend to gravitate to "heart" centered programs in our spiritual journeys. Today, the head affirms the heart. In classical spirituality, the heart often affirmed the head! It's important to remember that for most of Western Christianity's history, the religious institutions were interested that the people learned through their instructions. They weren't interested in how they felt about issues.[1] This isn't a condemnation but an observation of church scholars sincerely desiring people to learn set, prescribed practices to be close to God, to be close to their faith, and, if honest, to be close to the rules of the institution!

Exploring spirituality is timeless. Many centuries ago, written on the forecourt of the Temple of Apollo in Delphi, were the words, "Know Thyself." This theme of knowing yourself is explicitly spoken and often implied in the gospel stories of Jesus, and indeed throughout the Bible. The spirituality of knowing oneself is a theme in the sacred books of other religions. Spirituality addresses the human condition and isn't restricted to religions or denominations, despite the claims of some to exclusivity. Throughout history, writers have explored this foundational human condition. One of the most well-known and iconic examples comes from Act I, scene 3, of *Hamlet*. In this passage, William Shakespeare heightens this essential human theme when he writes of Polonius preparing his compulsive and erring son, Laertes, for travel to France. The son is being sent away to avoid potential conflicts. In this famous father-to-son address, we find many classic phases. Of these, perhaps the most famous is, "This above all else, to thine own self be true." This notes the ageless call, indeed our deepest spiritual call, to look inward.

This call continues today. As previously noted, we are the most and least connected people in history. We are people with many issues confronting our spiritual journeys. Fundamentally, we are seemingly forgetting to connect deeply within ourselves. In our often shallow and superficial world, where everything is fleeting, this is significant. We must dig deeper into ourselves and avoid the postmodern reality of often being superficial and shallow. We are truly spiritually alive when we learn to connect with who we are, with others, and, for many, with a Creator image. In 2002, cleric, academic, and writer J. Philip Newell, in *Echo of the Soul: The Sacredness of the Human Body*, wrote that, "The Irish novelist James Joyce describes one of his characters as living at a distance from himself. That is a fine description of how most of us live much of the time, at a distance from our true selves."[2] Are we individually and collectively distant from ourselves? Are you distant from yourself? Take time and ponder this deep question. Strive to be honest. To your own self be true! Sadly, in postmodernism, despite the urge to find ourselves and to be true to ourselves, we seem to be at a loss over who we are. We are in a dilemma.

Alexander W. Astin illustrates this well. He spent 42 years as a UCLA professor and dedicated his career to researching the spirituality of college students. His studies, and those research studies he often shared with his wife, Helen S. Astin, and Jennifer A. Lindholm, explored how young adults view spirituality and spiritually connect. Their combined research culminated in the "must-read" 2010 publication, *Cultivating the Spirit: How College Can Enhance Students' Lives*. In a 2003 UCLA press release, Alexander Astin is quoted:

> The great traditions at the core of a liberal arts education were grounded in the maxim, 'know thyself,'" Astin said. "But today developing self-awareness receives little attention on campuses, and academic work has become divorced from students' most deeply felt values. At the same time, the spiritual growth of students, in the broadest sense, receives virtually no attention in discussions about educational reform."[3]

Astin and many others studying and researching spirituality often use university and college students for analysis. For many disciplines engaged in academic research, college students represent the most viable and accessible social group.[4] In other words, why look for a research group to study when you're already surrounded by easily reached, motivated, and inquisitive students! Astin, Astin, and Lindholm's extensive and detailed work followed rigorous academic research standards. Their combined effort was a substantial longitudinal (meaning long-term) study with well-structured questions. They follow this firm and unquestionable foundation in all their studies. Their 2010 tome notes:

> ... Another consideration that stimulated our interest in studying students' spiritual development is the manner in which students' concerns and values have been changing over recent decades. Annual surveys of entering college freshmen (Pryor et al., 2007) show that the personal goal of "being very well off financially" has grown dramatically in popularity, while the value of 'developing a meaningful philosophy of life"—which was the highest-ranked concern in the 1970s—has declined sharply among students. This is not completely surprising to us. Over time, students have become more anxious about their futures and more

overwhelmed by everything they have to do, balancing school with paid employment, worrying about being able to finance their college education and finding a job after college. At the same time, these personal concerns are exacerbated by national and global changes: of its natural resources, and religious and political conflicts that result in bloodshed and destruction around the globe.[5]

Their research showed that from the 1970s onward, students' interest in altruism, or unselfish efforts to benefit others, declined as growth in self-interest increased. The search for self-interest was materialistic. This matched societal shifts in postmodernism. Can we say "Me-ism?" We must wonder if the desire for personal, self-centered goals in students grew at the same rate as interest in their souls declined? The evidence seems to affirm this move. This is yet another significant insight. It's worthy to ponder and reflect upon. Astin, Astin, and Lindholm, however, projected hope. At the end of their work, they wrote:

> In short, we believe that the findings of this study constitute a powerful argument in support of the proposition that higher education should attend more to students' spiritual development. Assisting more students to grow spiritually will help to create a new generation of young adults who are more caring, more globally aware, and more committed to social justice than previous generations, and who are able to employ greater equanimity in responding to the many stresses and tensions of our rapidly changing technological society.[6]

We too must seek help to become inwardly aware and outwardly active to live deep, spirit-filled lives. Adult educator Al Lauzon, in 2001, explained this human need quite well when he wrote:

> Spirituality, as a construct, is an elusive concept and hard to describe to others, yet it is a major organizing principle in our lives, it is the source from where we often derive

meaning, and it informs many of our major life choices. Sinnott (2001) defines spirituality as "one's personal relation to the sacred or transcendent, a relation that then informs other relationships, and the meaning of one's life" (p.99). It is, I believe, only in encountering the spiritual that we can begin to understand it. Palmer (1993) captures the essence of spirituality when he writes that "authentic spirituality opens us to truth—whatever truth may be, whatever truth takes us. Such a spirituality does not dictate where we must go, but trusts that any path of knowledge.[7]

In looking at the deep question "Is spirituality different today than in ages past?", it's essential to also consider the relationship between religion and spirituality. This is because historically, religion and spirituality were accepted as one reality. If one was religious, one was spiritual. If one was spiritual, it was because of religious practices. This relationship is no longer true. We now see spirituality divorced from religion. For many in postmodernism, delving into one's spiritual life is void of religious parameters. Are religion and spirituality in postmodernism the same as religion and spirituality in the past? The answer is "No." We will continue to explore this changing and evolving relationship.

As noted, for much of Western Christianity's history, spirituality and religion were largely synonymous. This is well documented.[8] Today, we see religion and spirituality as separate. Spirituality is valued, but not always viewed through traditional sacred languages, rituals, or symbols. Graham Rossiter, a professor at a Roman Catholic university in Australia, explains this situation quite well:

> ... [he] proposed that "spirituality" was a pivotal personal development construct in discussions of both religious education and nonreligious spiritual education. The contrast "spirituality" has significant roots in both the religious sphere and the ordinary secular human sphere. The word originated within Christianity, and until relatively recent times, the words "religious" and "spiritual"

tended to be synonymous—spirituality was the equivalent of religiosity. Spirituality has also been used as a secular construct for interpreting aspects of personal, spiritual and moral development in a nonreligious way. It is thus strategically placed like a bridge connecting traditional religious ways of seeing people in God's universe with contemporary secular, psychological ways of interpreting personal development. Another valuable quality of spirituality is its growing connection with education (both religious and secular).[9]

Rossiter, in 2014, described how students in the Australian Roman Catholic school system, with which he is well-versed, learn most of their spiritual views from external, secular sources. This is a monumental insight. Can we extrapolate this notion in postmodernism to where sacred people use the secular world to define their spiritual health? What are your thoughts?

Perhaps we can say that postmodern spirituality is now perceived, studied, and accepted as the human condition instead of being considered a religious condition. Conversely, in postmodernism, many like to describe the human condition by borrowing an image from the French philosopher Pierre Teilhard de Chardin. In 1955, in *The Phenomenon of Man*, reportedly was the first to state that, "We are not human beings having a spiritual experience. We are spiritual beings having a human experience." Given the evidence presented thus far, it seems that we are indeed spiritual beings. But are we spiritual beings having a human experience, humans disconnected from our spiritual selves, or spiritual people who are forgetting (or forgotten) what it means to be spiritual? This is a complex matter that the future will decide. What are your thoughts on these three scenarios?

Nevertheless, it seems that we must consider that we are spiritual beings who need to learn, or relearn, what it means to be spiritual! This is often neglected, ignored, or forgotten in postmodernism. When we need to relearn what it means to be spiritual, the obvious question is, "When did we forget what it means to be spiritual?" Is this true or partially true? Take a minute to think about this question. Do we need to re-discover spirituality from scratch? Do we need to determine what spirituality means?

The word *spirit* comes from the Latin word *spiritus,* which means breath. The word in Greek, *pneuma,* means air or wind. The word in Hebrew is *ruach* or spirit. In the Bible, the word wind, spirit, Spirit, and breath often use the same Hebrew or Greek word that we re-interpret in English. The choice of each image is according to the context of the sentence or situation. These words each mean something different, but they have one essential commonality. In every language, the notion of spirit implicitly carries with it the idea that our spirit is something we need to live. Our spirit fills our being and is in all of us. The word *spiritus* is also interpreted as inspiration. It is our life, our sustenance.[10] Is your inspiration your spirit talking to you? What do you think?

Does it seem daunting to explore spirituality in our postmodern society? I think so. It's a topic that is constantly spiraling outward and becoming broader and deeper. Here's a fun illustration of this dilemma. In the movie *Shrek,* the quiet, solitude-loving hermit ogre (Shrek) is constantly annoyed by the ever chipper and yapping social donkey. The ogre, who does not like others and prefers solitude, at one point reluctantly sheds the walls around him and unwittingly describes himself to the donkey. He says he is complicated. He says that he's like an onion, as there are layers. Indeed, postmodern spirituality is complicated and can be explored and approached from "multiple levels and multiple perspectives."[11] However, such an exhaustive search is obviously beyond the scope of this endeavor.

In 2014, Margaret Benefiel, Lois W. Fry, and David Geigle, in a journal article on spirituality and religion, noted that there are at least 20 research efforts exploring spirituality in the workplace.[12] In 2017, a more extensive exploration titled, "Workplace Spirituality Annotated Bibliography" by Judi Neal, listed about 150 articles and books that explore this single topic of postmodern spirituality.[13] Given that she has an extensive background in exploring and researching workplace spirituality, this list is quite credible! Can you imagine 150 scholarly efforts dedicated to understanding contemporary workplace spirituality? Postmodern spirituality is receiving much necessary attention!

Likewise, research in various fields of education is increasing—read Chapter Eight! In recent years, many books, articles, and dissertations have dived into the spirituality of teachers and students, both at the grade school and high school level. As previously noted, college students and college professors already received much earlier attention.[14] In addition, nursing and medical programs are also looking at spirituality.[15]

Through my readings, I discovered over 100 different fields, beyond the traditional efforts of religious institutions, researching spirituality. This indicates a growing social interest in the topic (see Appendix B). Sadly, while many disciplines are now engaged in researching spirituality, Western Christianity seems to be standing pat. In other words, religious institutions are still trying to entice people by offering rebranded, centuries-old favorites and models. Bluntly, the packaging is new but the product is largely still the same. This isn't surprising, since religious institutions in Western Christianity are notoriously slow to adopt and reform. Medieval practices of prayer and contemplation are still highly valued (as they should be), but other approaches or thoughts are often viewed with contempt and skepticism. The Reformation took place because the institutional church lived in denial and didn't see or accept the world changing around it. Here is a question: Is this failure being repeated by postmodern religious institutions? What do you think?

Spirituality is being widely explored by a vast array of disciplines using varied approaches and from diverse backgrounds. This still begs the question, "What is postmodern spirituality?" This is a tough question to consider, since it has layers. It's an even tougher question to answer. For most of history, Western Christianity and spirituality were synonymous. In their 2016 publication, *Fragmented Lives: Finding Faith in the Age of Uncertainty,* William Sachs and Michael Bos wrote, "A recent study found ninety-two definitions for spirituality, and still growing."[16] Ponder this. Given this vast and varied list can we truly define and explore postmodern spirituality with certainty? In my view, we can at least try!

In part, one of the benchmarks of postmodernism is diversity. A second benchmark is the lack of foundational morals or rootedness. We're always in flux to meet our ever-changing needs. A third benchmark is the lack of a central core or focal point. In other words, we hold many vital central ideas at the same time. There's no common societal idea or direction. Could the lack of a central guiding principle lead us to grasp only a few notions of postmodern spirituality? Are only a few notions or concepts within our ability to grapple? Can we embrace 92 definitions? Or do we seek the ones that suit us? How often do we change our decision so that we end up always being appeased? Do you think we have broad, well-accepted definitions, or as with much in postmodernism, do we reduce what we consider spirituality according to our personal and selective experiences and small sphere of knowledge? These are profound questions needing further consideration.

One of the benchmarks of postmodernism, as well noted, is instant gratification. Today, if one suddenly desires the baseball statistics of the baseball player Marvelous Marv Thornberry, or the recipe for a particular dessert, or to find if kerfuffle is a real word, eh, all one has to do is ask the phone. Within a split-second, algorithms supply countless responses. This is our new norm. We don't have to attend a library or wait until we get home to find a reference book. We simply speak or salivate like Pavlov's dogs, and our need is gratified. If we assume this social and cultural reality of instant answers is the norm, how do we mesh this actuality with postmodern spirituality? To this notion, journalist Paul Taylor wrote:

> ... For each expert who said that Millennials' use of digital technologies would empower them to learn more than previous generations and become more adept at finding answers to deep questions, a different expert worried that this generation will exhibit a thirst for instant gratification and quick fixes, a loss of patience, and a lack of deep-thinking ability due to what one referred to as "fast-twitch wiring.[17]

According to this statement, it seems that we may need to rediscover and utilize historical religious and spiritual practices. We may need to weave our past into our present. We may need this to direct the future. We require patience, deep thinking, and thoughtful responses. In a phrase, we need to add depth to our shallow, narrow lives. Instead of focusing on overt talking (without listening to anyone but ourselves) and instant gratification, we need to rediscover the human need to journey inward. In other words, we need to recapture everything that is a postmodern contradiction.

It seems that postmodern spirituality, in all forms, is calling us to listen within to the "still, small voice." But do postmodern people truly listen? But as the 2,600-year-old image from 1 Kings 19:12, in the NRSV states we need to listen to the "still, small voice." We are still called to take part in "deep, inward listening." It's a call to avoid external and internal noise and distractions, to discern deeply and not to seek fast answers. In other words, we aren't to use our common, busy, and loud surface voice. Instead, we need to cultivate our often quiet and softer inner voice. Working on inward listening and silence may be quite a monumental mountain to climb, since much of these practices seem forgotten in postmodernism. To work on inward listening and silence is a life-long journey. Can we do this? Can we avoid the postmodern trap of being easily distracted? Can we concentrate on listening to our souls instead of reaching for the phone? This is difficult, because we're often busy listening to a terrifying news item on global climate change or COVID-19. We may be glued to the news of some celebrity or sports icon doing something bizarre. And yes, some are addicted to these types of stories. Can we call them inconsequential distractions? Can we avoid the addiction to our various electronic devices that condition and control us? Kelly Besecke, in 2014, wrote:

> Spirituality is about depth and vitality. People who want a rich spiritual life are looking for a deeper awareness, a heightened consciousness; they want to experience more of the meaning and intricacy of life. They want to feel truly alive—to feel engaged, to find life compelling. They want to feel centered and grounded in something eternal. They want a sense that there's more there than meets the eye. They want a little bit of magic. They want an antidote to what they experience as the flat, literalistic materialism of modern society—an antidote to its shallowness and apparent meaninglessness. They want a broader base, a deeper foundation, and a higher horizon ...[18]

In postmodernism, some people suggest we compartmentalize our faith just as we compartmentalize other parts of our lives.[19] Instead of the center of our lives focusing on the farm, our village, and our church, we have evolved into broader, diverse lives. In the medieval world, one's world was typically small because of daylight walking or riding requirements. Consequently, one was often limited to the number of people one met in their lifetime. The traveling merchant met more people, but compared to today, it was a small number. I wonder if a mall sees more merchants and shoppers in a day than merchants met in their lifetime a few centuries ago. What do you think?

In our postmodern world, we have our family obligations, our children's school, and sports commitments. We have our work environments, and we attend shopping malls and shops either in person or online. We have our sports clubs and perhaps even a church community. In the past, the same people belonged to almost everything the same! Our world is no longer the farm, village, or local church; it is much, much more. Today, we typically meet those who are interested in what we are interested in. We can call this the rise of tribalism. We do this instead of meeting our next-door neighbors. This is a reality in postmodernism.

Religion and spirituality moved from being foundational and central to just being one of life's many selective, possible commodities. We must relearn what it is to discern and examine our desires and intentions, as well as to distinguish "what is deep from what is shallow, what is free from what is compulsive."[20] Can we do this? Do you think we can? Can you do this? While we can't return to the simple, small-world life of the past, we can make conscious decisions on how to move spiritually forward in the global village.

To some degree, both Western Christianity and Western Society have slowly discovered that their historical models of giving answers to people have eroded. They gave way to models in which people prefer asking and exploring questions. The stock answers of the past no longer work. Besides, the answers being offered may not even apply to the questions being asked. The focus of the institution is to provide an answer without deep regard for the question. Western Christianity sometimes still utilizes the "father-knows-best" approach. Likewise, these institutions may say to read the Westminster Confession, or look at the Creeds, or pay attention to a specific Papal Encyclical. Others may say, "The Bible says that ..." Can we call these responses denial? Instead of deep listening, exhausted leadership finds it easier and less taxing to provide old answers than to assist people in totally exploring their questions. When one is used to giving answers, it's hard to shift and help explore questions. This needs a tad more attention.

Some religious institutions in Western Christianity remain largely conditioned and locked into giving answers, and they rebuff efforts to evolve. They have difficulty seeing beyond the practice of giving answers. They can't see that people aren't interested in the provided answers. By the time many of these institutions began to realize that the old models were no longer viable, they were severely hemorrhaging members and their viability. For some institutions or congregations, it was too late to adapt. Others endeavored to respond, metaphorically, with the image of "rearranging deck chairs on the *Titanic!*" Some religious institutions and congregations have sunk. Others are sinking, but they continue to bail while living in denial. Bailing may only keep them afloat for a short time. In postmodernism, spirituality is about exploring questions, not about receiving answers. Ivana Milojević, an educator and researcher with an interest in sociology and the future, describes this situation well:

> According to Palmer (1999b), however, spirituality is less about teaching truths than about helping with articulating and thinking about particular questions. He argues that people rarely raise spiritual issues, partly because of "the embarrassed silence that may greet us if we ask our real questions aloud." (Palmer 1999b) But also, another, perhaps even more significant reason why people don't ask these questions is because someone will try to given them "The Answer" (ibid.). Spirituality is not about answers but about questions such as: *"Does my life have meaning and purpose?" "Do I have gifts that the world wants and needs?" "Whom and what can I trust?" "How can I rise above my fears?" "How do I deal with suffering, my own and that of my family and friends?" "How does one maintain hope?" "What about death?". . . "How shall I live today knowing that someday I will die?"*[21]

This lesson of exploring questions ahead of offering answers was learned by some and ignored by others. In 2012, we can note the profound image of the shift from the historic millennial religious monopoly of spirituality to sudden secular domination when Amazon's book list on spirituality was listed at almost 158,000 choices.[22] I wonder what the count might be at the moment you are reading this! I'll wait while you Google!

As the evidence suggests, postmodern Western Society is quite fascinated by spirituality. In turn, we saw that over time, we moved from where Western Christianity and spirituality were synonymous to the point where people want to delve into spirituality without religion! Today, ever-decreasing numbers do not adhere to any religious institution, and even fewer attend worship. Could it be that those religious institutions in Western Society because of closed-minded elitism, scandals, and the propensity to give answers instead of explore questions, brought about their demise? And if so, to what degree did this hasten the decline? What are your thoughts?

Ironically, church attendance still swells at Christmas and Easter. But is this because of religious convictions, or does it socially seem appropriate? Do people attend because of religious needs, or is it a social action, like attending the Santa Claus parade? We must wonder if numbers swell because people still have remnants of their religious heritage somewhere inside them. Are there enough remnant thoughts of spirituality/religion that bring them to Easter Sunday yet not enough to have them attend other Holy Week or Sunday religious services? Perhaps, at some level, this is an attempt to be spiritual without realizing it. Re-read and ponder these questions.

Sadly, while numbers still swell at Easter and Christmas, they are but a shadow of attendance at those religious festivals just a few decades ago. Could it be that people, at some level, are looking at the old familiar church for affirmation? In 2006, Liesa Stamm, then Senior Associate at Rutgers University Center for Children and Childhood Studies, explained that in postmodernism, people are looking for spirituality beyond models of historical Western Christianity. She vividly describes this:

> The essence of this transformation centers on a basic shift
> in the experience of everyday religious life from established
> religious institutions and their associated theologies,
> doctrines, and prescribed practices to a focus on the self
> and the personal spirituality of seeking ... In previous

decades Americans sought *social belonging* through their association with churches and synagogues, and practiced religion in terms of socially defined expectations and beliefs, what Wuthnow calls a *spirituality of dwelling* ... Symbolic of the shift in the locus of American spirituality from dwelling to personal quest, a large percentage of Americans no longer belong to or attend churches or synagogues. The established Protestant and Catholic churches are losing their historical religious control of the American population, and the so-called alternative spiritualities are flourishing.[23]

Could part of the problem be that the church and people need to discover some common ground? Could part of the problem be that both church and people need to find what they are truly seeking before jumping to solutions? What do you think?

In the early days of postmodernism, during the 1950s to 1970s, people still held to some connections to religious institutions. However, do we today? In *Religion in Britain Since 1945*, written in 1994, sociologist Grace Davie said, "people believe but that they just don't belong."[24] This is a theme that runs throughout the book. By 2005, a mere decade later, quantitative social scientist David Voas, and Alasdair Crockett, who studied and lectured on the sociology of religion, and died shortly after penning an article, wrote in that piece declaring that BWB (believing without belonging) "was an interesting idea, but it is a time for the slogan to enter honorable retirement."[25] What can we conclude from these remarks? Let us break that down!

It likely means that the older people who belonged and believed gave way to those who marginally belonged but still believed. Those who believed and belonged are dying off. Those who marginally believed but were part-time worshipers are declining. Those who never believed or belonged are replacing those two groups. As it is sometimes expressed, the church is one generation from extinction.

Western Christianity moved from the center of society and world dominance to the margins. Today we often hear that the mainline churches of the past are thought of as the sideline churches. To phrase this another way, mainline Western Christianity shifted from being the principal lead actor on center stage to being, at best, a supporting cast member, or at worst, an unaccredited walk-on role. In current postmodernism, the fate that befell mainline churches has also infected the religious institutions that took their place. This suggests that all Western Christianity might end up with walk-on roles!

A sincere question, but alas beyond the scope of this effort, asks us to ponder the future of Western Christianity. Some may choose to blame other world religions for this decline. Yet how much of the decline is the postmodern shift to "Me-ism?" We shifted from the historical "life-as religious people" to the current model of "subjective-life" spirituality.[26] We might say that apathy is another noteworthy reason for this situation. Perhaps you could take some time to ponder questions about the apparent demise of Western Christianity. Please consider the discussion questions at the end of the chapter as a place to stop and ruminate (what an awesome word, *ruminate*, it even sound delicious and fruitful).

Traditionally, we derived much of our spiritual core from the spiritual language found in our religious foundations. It was our main and dominant source. Since we now live in the post-denominational, post-Christian world, are we losing, or have we lost, the source of our religious languages and spiritual language? If this is indeed taking place, and I think it is, what are the new sources for our spirituality? Likewise, how do we create and utilize a spiritual language that others can speak? How do we discern the new sources? Do we embrace answers that for a moment appease our needs and then move on? In our fluidity, we may accept one source on Monday but deny it by Friday. We might use one spiritual word Monday but deny it by Tuesday because it's suddenly either lacking or we evolved its meaning. Alas, many questions abound. The question of where are we getting our spiritual words and concepts in postmodernism is an "incredible onion-like (Shrek-like)" question because it has layers. In other words, when you peel a layer off postmodern spirituality you discover another deeper layer. In turn, it's a foundational question for all spiritual people and Western Society to wrestle with and find their spiritual word and idea source because it's the starting point of true spiritual identity.

It's easy to define religion. Given the historic connected relationship between the religions of Western Christianity, and the current separate realities of Western Christianity and Western spirituality, it's important to take a moment to look at how we define religion. We have already discovered that there are at least 92 definitions of spirituality. Adult educators with interests in spirituality, Leona English and Marie Gillen, clarified this for us when they wrote that "religion is based on an organized set of principles shared by a group, whereas spirituality is the expression of an individual's quest for meaning. Although religion and spirituality may be connected, they do not have to be."[27] Professor of religious studies, Eugene Gallagher, elaborated on this in 2009 when he quoted the ideas of Bruce Speck:

> Speck draws out an animating fear of compulsion and denial of individual agency when he asserts that "religion has traditionally been engaged in the work of converting people to a particular viewpoint." Further, "religion denotes a set of precepts that must be affirmed." Spirituality, on the other hand, is a matter of personal preference and "allows flexibility because nobody has to believe in a prescribed set of precepts."[28]

In another article published in 2009, four authors in the same journal (but different issue) as Gallagher wrote:

> There is often misunderstanding between the concepts of spirituality and religion and that terrifies many and they tend to shy away from both topics. "It is important to note that religion (an organized belief system) and spirituality (an inner longing for meaning and community) are not the same thing." "Religion is based on an organized set of principles shared by a group whereas spirituality is the expression of an individual's quest for meaning." Spirituality is "the human quest for personal meaning and mutual relationships among people, nonhuman environment and for some god." "Religion focuses more

upon the specific group and the organization, while spirituality is more generic, and may even encompass more than one religious approach."[29]

In an unflattering 1997 comment, Marcel Dumestre, whom we met earlier, provides what I think is a common but repressed and unpopular opinion:

> An unconscious and unfortunate tendency of many ministers is to put the institutional concerns of religion above spirituality. Raising funds for church buildings, paying salaries, dealing with internal church conflicts, and the many other dimensions of institutional life can overwhelm the primary purpose of church life—mature spirituality. Most Americans consider these institutional preoccupations as reasons for religion's lack of relevancy. The common complaint, "My religion is getting in the way of my spirituality," expresses it well.[30]

Please read that again. It bears much truth. I think it's correct to state that all too often we let religions in Western Christianity hinder our spiritual needs. It's not likely intentional. It's easier, more visible, and career-wise to build up the church compared to assisting the quiet, personal, and spiritual growth of individuals. We address the "seen and touchable" rather than the "unseen and unknown."

Much suggests we are still amid the birth pangs of trying to define spirituality. Some define spirituality as "a way of being and experiencing that comes about through awareness of a transcendent dimension and that is characterized by certain identifiable values in regard to self, others, nature, life, and whatever one considers the Ultimate."[31] Others say spirituality is "an awareness of something greater than ourselves ... [that] moves one *outward* to others as an expression of one's spiritual experiences."[32] Leona English and Marie Gillen's 2000 wonderfully edited work described the situation very well. It's an insightful observation. In their editor's notes, they wrote:

> Spirituality! Like dandelions in the spring, the term is cropping up everywhere. There are books, magazine

articles, newsletters, conferences, tapes, even Web sites dealing with the subject. The explosion of interest in spirituality gives rise to tantalizing questions: Why this interest now? Is it a response to the spiritual malaise at the end of a thousand-year epoch! Is it merely what is referred to as millennium hype, or disillusionment with materialistic gains?... What is spirituality? Can it be defined? In some respects, it has such a variety of meanings that defining it is like trying to pin jelly to a wall; it does not stick. Miller (1985) refers to it as a "weasel word" (p. 66) and in his view the word is almost meaningless. But there are others who have tried to come to grips with the term. Harris (1996) refers to it as "our way of being in the world in the light of the Mystery at the core of the universe; a mystery that some of us call God" (p. 15). She distinguishes two different and almost opposite meanings of the term spirituality—one marked by withdrawal from the world and the other marked by immersion in the world. The latter distinction, which is characterized by a social and political dimension, is what interests us as adult educators. Further clarification from Van Ness (1996) is also helpful. He distinguishes between religious spirituality and secular spirituality. The fact that people are religious does not mean that they are spiritual. As Van Ness points out, "A secular spirituality is neither validated nor invalidated by religious varieties of spirituality. Its status is related to them but separable" (p. 1). In other words, religion is based on an organized set of principles shared by a group, whereas spirituality is the expression of an individual's quest for meaning. Although religion and spirituality may be connected, they are not necessarily.[33]

Before postmodernism, spirituality was almost exclusively within the realm of Western Christianity. Institutional religious organizations defined spirituality. Today, spirituality is defined and explored by educators, sociologists, psychologists, branches of the medical community, and even those in the financial/business community.[34]

Evidently, in postmodernism, anyone can define, explain, and explore spirituality. We even try to measure spirituality (look at Appendix C). In postmodern spirituality, we are sailing into uncharted and explored waters. We need to learn to harness the winds and tides. However, we must first untie ourselves from the dock and let go! Can we take a risk and search for new definitions and ideas? In turn, can we look into the past as we cast into the future? One of the clearest and most profound images of defining spirituality in Western Christianity is well explained by Richard C. Halverson, Chaplain to the American Senate from 1981–1994. Countless Internet sources declare that he reportedly said:

> In the beginning, the church was a fellowship of men and women centering on the living Christ. Then the church moved to Greece, where it became a philosophy. Then it moved to Rome, where it became an institution. Next, it moved to Europe where it became a culture, and, finally, it moved to America where it became an enterprise.

In the seemingly natural progress of postmodernism of Western Society and Western Christianity, we saw religion treated as an enterprise. Is it natural that we will now treat spirituality as an enterprise? Sadly, I think this is taking place. For example, we have many monthly or quarterly magazines that focus on spirituality, including *Spiritual Healing, Spirit and Destiny, Spirituality and Health, Soul and Spirit, The Spiritist, Awkenings, Guideposts, Christianity Today*, and one called *Mind, Body, Spirit*. I wonder to what degree these magazines mesh with or appease our postmodernism concept of spirituality that we can define as DIY—do-it-yourself. What do you think? Has postmodern spirituality morphed into a consumer commodity that is well marketed to appeasing our immediate and instantaneous needs, or is it the "still, small voice" that lives within us?

Today, various academic journals give attention to spirituality, including the *Journal of the Study of Spirituality, Journal of Spirituality in Mental Health, The International Journal of Religion and Spirituality in Society, Psychology of Religion and Spirituality, Spiritus: A Journal of Christian Spirituality, Studies in Spirituality*, and *Spirituality and Health*

International. I wonder to what degree these academic journals mesh with or appease our postmodernism concept of spirituality. What do you think?

This brings me to a question implied throughout this book. If we live in an individualistic Western Society, how can we undertake corporate, common spirituality? We used to have this when we went to church, but since most no longer attend church, where can we find this today? This is a significant question well beyond the scope of this book! It's a vital question that needs urgent attention by many! Ponder this idea and consider the discussion questions at the end of the chapter. These questions, and those peppered throughout, serve to take you deeper in your exploration of spirituality. We must move beyond being shallow, reactionary, and instantly gratified.

One of the attributes of corporate spirituality is that it provides checks and balances. Again, if we are the center of the universe, and Google is one of our best guides, how can we shift to shared spirituality where we can and should cooperate and learn from others? Perhaps we appreciate corporate spirituality when it meets our individualized needs. Where and how can individualized needs address corporate spirituality and Western Society? This is a complex issue. Once more, we have layers!

When we are learning or rediscovering our spirituality, we must value patience. Likewise, we must add depth by honest self-examination. We must shed superficial, shallow, and perhaps self-patronizing answers for honest, well-formed responses that have depth and worth. A wonderful illustration of this come from the musical *Les Misérables.*

One main lead is ex-convict Jean Valjean. Another is Javert, the dogged police inspector who sees his mission as finding some way to discredit Valjean's yellow passport or restricted pardon. At one point in the chase, Valjean stops and ponders his criminal past. He stole bread to feed others and experience the gifts and joy he received in giving to others. As a "free" man, Valjean wonders what direction his life should take. Does he run, or does he fight for justice? As he mulls this matter over, he sings a pivotal song. Appropriately, this song is titled "Who Am I?" It revolves around the foundational spiritual question, "Who am I?" and causes Jean to assess his life, who he was, and who he became. He pulls these two thoughts together and assesses whether he has changed or evolved! His spiritual journey mirrors our foundational spiritual journeys and questions.

The song is full of Jean Valjean asking "Who am I." The words challenge him into a deep, complex yearning. By the end of the song, his tone is greatly changed. He found his answer. With great joy and conviction (note the pun!), he sings with gusto. Given incredible copyright issues, I again suggest you Google, Firefox, Chrome, or whatever and find the lyrics to verse one. Better yet, listen to the song. There are many fine renditions on YouTube. Listen deeply to the words, the tone, and the feelings.

The final cry of "Who am I?" evolved and became a cry of affirmation and acceptance. He knows who he is. He is no longer a broken convict but a happy, free, and peaceful man. He is transformed from *Who am I?* to *Who I am.* We too need to sing our song. In postmodern spirituality, a common tune we should sing is, "Who am I? I am a spiritual being!" and "I am a spiritual being always in the process of becoming who I am." As Jean Valjean is dying at the end of the musical, we hear the prophetic, and I think truly insightful, spiritual words, "To love another person is to see the face of God."

Jean found his spirit-voice and felt blessed that he was able to care for others. He was able to avoid the "Me-ism" inherent and epitomized in the single-minded thoughts of police inspector Javert. Javert's single-minded "Catch the thief" was rooted in "Me-ism." He was incapable of introspection or asking, "Who am I?" As a result, when he finally gained insight into the reformed and incredible loving and caring Jean Valjean, his only response was to commit suicide. The characters were both one-dimensional. One, rooted in love, journeyed in and found himself; the other, rooted in anger, did not.

Les Misérables is set during the French Revolution. At that time, France was a religious society, and Jean Valjean appropriately sang "To love another person is to see the face of God." But what about postmodernism, where God and/or the religious institutions in Western Society are often sidelined, neglected, ignored, or forgotten. How could we phrase this insightful spiritual phrase? Could we say, "To love another person is to see the spirit of God or another soul"? What do you think? This is a good question to ponder, since we're rarely religious but still spiritual. As we will see in Chapter Four, most people in Western Society think of themselves as spiritual but not religious!

Questions to ponder and discuss
Chapter Three

Postmodernism and Western Spirituality

❶ Today, many people seem to receive much of their spiritual input from secular sources. Can you identify these?

❷ The Reformation took place because the institutional church lived in denial and didn't see or accept the world changing. Is this failure being repeated by postmodern religious institutions?

❸ Do you practice inward listening? Are you patient?

❹ Do you find that our religious institutions are more apt at offering answers than exploring questions? Can you offer examples? Ponder this.

❺ Why is it that numbers swell at Christmas and Easter in Western Christianity? Is this a social expectation, a sliver of spiritual need, or deep longing for something unknown? Or is it another image or combination of any of these notions?

❻ What is the source of your spiritual language?

❼ If you aren't a "lone ranger," spiritually speaking, where is your source of common, corporate spirituality?

CHAPTER FOUR

SPIRITUAL BUT NOT RELIGIOUS

Histry evolves slowly. However, in the last six decades (give or take a few years), the opposite took place; it evolved very quickly. We are in the most profound and drastic social, cultural, and human transformation in history. This is a true paradigm shift. Without question, even before COVID-19, this was the most substantial makeover in human history. This revolution includes the dismantling of Western Christianity. In a short period of time, Western Christianity fell from a commanding social presence. It fell so far that many now ignore, or even despise, these various religious institutions. At best, Western Christianity moved from domination to marginalization. This happened for many reasons.

One of the principal reasons was the constant denial and lack of action by religious institutions to address child and other sexual abuses. Their silence and lack of remorse upon discovery showed arrogance. The message was, "Protect the institution at all costs." Second, the stand of some religious institutions on sexuality and birth control and/or abortion irked many. Third, in postmodernism, discussions on same-sex issues emerged from the shadows. It's not surprising that people began to boycott religious institutions. Some church members left because their religious institution supported same-sex unions, and others because the institution didn't support same-sex unions.

I wonder if this was a real significant issue or decline, perhaps it was a manifestation of something else! Yes, these hot topics caused many to leave their church; however, I can't help but wonder if other social factors were unconsciously in play. Perhaps in postmodernism people couldn't identify, or verbalize, other powerful factors, such as the rise of "Me-ism," in their decision. In other words, people said they left because of positions on sexuality, but I wonder if this was more the trigger on an already loaded gun! Were people already inclined to less church attendance, religiosity, and commitment? Perhaps they consciously or unconsciously merged these factors into their displeasure on sexuality positions. What do you think? Nevertheless, the decline of Western Christianity created a void. People desired spirituality but no longer felt they needed or wanted religious institutions involved. People continue to look for ways to fill this void. As we will discover, in many situations the spiritual void was filled by the spiritual but not religious folk.

Although only a few religious leaders and institutions failed to maintain the high moral standards championed by the gospels, societal blame fell upon many Christian institutions. Many members felt betrayed. People who no longer regularly attended worship also felt betrayed. People who never attended worship felt betrayed. In a phrase, Western Christianity forgot humility and care. Consequently, it failed. George Hunter, in *How to Reach Secular People*, describes this beautifully:

> If the first cause of Christianity's loss of influence upon western people and culture was such a series of events—Renaissance, Reformation, Nationalism, Science, Enlightenment, and Urbanization,[12] the second cause was the Church's pathological pattern of responses to these events—responses that undermined the Church's credibility and distanced the people from her witness. [1]

I can't but help but wonder if the decline of Western Christianity closely matched the corresponding rate of growth in individualism. There must be some correlation. What do you think? Likewise, what about the relationship between the decline of organized Western Christianity and its sense of community and the quick rise of privatized spirituality? This is a pivotal and central question for Western society and Western Christianity. We saw the great upsurge in individualism and secularism replacing

Western Christianity. In turn, the environment was ripe for people to be SBNR—spiritual but not religious.

As a corollary to these activities, we saw the development and the rise of an individualized God. We personalized Jesus. One of the catchphrases in postmodern Western Christianity is "Jesus is MY personal Savior." Instead of serving the call of Jesus to care for the world, we now call Jesus to serve our individualized, specific needs. The tradition of "Jesus died for the sins of the world" was replaced with "Jesus died for ME." This is, in my view, significant! Take a few moments and consider the differences.

As noted earlier, the largest churches in America proclaim the Prosperity Gospel—that is, "God wants you to be rich." But, that's a secular interpretation, because Jesus talked about caring for the poor, widowed, and marginalized. Another vital component of this postmodern personalized faith is reflected in the statement, "If your needs are not like my needs, I am right, and you are wrong because Jesus loves ME." We are selective about who we "know" Jesus loves. Instead of us reflecting images of being Christ-like, we flipped the image and see Christ as just like us!

About thirty years ago, a famous television preacher sat at a desk and spoke directly to the camera (meaning you). But instead of the cross or other traditional Christian symbols behind him, the American flag was on prominent display. Did this mean that God was American? Did it mean that God favors Americans over others? Again, secularism seems to be rewriting the gospel. All this feeds our postmodern egos because we delude ourselves by thinking we are great Christians when, in fact, we're making Christ into a human image. He is a savior to those like us.

From these evolutionary actions, we saw Western society quietly morph into creating and affirming the notion of personalized spirituality. Alone, each of these activities is significant, but together they represent a monumental and significant social paradigm shift. To borrow an image from Walt Kelly's classic *Pogo* cartoon, "We have seen the enemy, and he is us!" Western Christianity was and is responsible for its decline. Coupled with rising secularism, people desired spirituality apart from traditional venues.

In postmodernism, we became alienated from institutions. We became alienated from God. Sadly, we became alienated from ourselves. We began to live and believe in a false façade we created around ourselves. Since we live in self-created, ever-changing illusions, we never feel complete. Moreover, in vain efforts to feel whole or complete, we constantly seek quick fixes and instant gratification to soothe us. In doing so, we created our undoing. In postmodernism, we seek "Happy Meals," but these quick, instant-gratification spiritual endeavors don't satisfy us. We are forgetting to live on balanced spiritual diets because of spirituality on the go.

When people in Western Christianity created, denied, and covered up various scandals, it created an environment of fallibility and distrust. Western Christianity's apparent aloofness, real or imagined, enabled people to move towards individualism. While sexual scandals involving children is vile, the silence maintained after much documented and supported evidence is equally vile. As some articulated, the silent response by the institutions was deafening. What do you think of the failure of institutions to respond to scandals in terms of private and public trust? To paraphrase societal thinking, "If Western Christianity is seemingly aloof, it is clear that they aren't interested in me!" This made the rise of cultural individualism ripe for people to shed religiosity. Yet many yearn for fulfillment by seeking alternative forms of spirituality. Marcel Dumestre eloquently described this view in 1997 in *A Church at Risk: The Challenge of Spiritually Hungry Adults*:

> For far too many adults religion has either lost its relevancy or has presented a regressive, dangerously naïve view of life. The scandals of tele-evangelism, clergy pedophilia, and various other forms of abuse are all too obvious. These problems are the sensational ones that mass media love, maybe a little too much. And too many churches today treat their adult members as spiritual children. A childish spirituality is not appropriate for adults, and they know it. Yet, paradoxically, a childish spirituality keeps many adults tied to their churches. For most people, those ties retard adult growth through fear of death and an uncertain afterlife. It is true that the more complex life's problems are the more we seek simple answers. Religion can give simple,

direct answers, but sometimes the answers are instead simplistic—the mark of childish spirituality.[2]

Besides Western Christianity's failure to address scandals and its inability to read and adjust to changing social realities, we must not forget the vital role of science. For hundreds of years, religious institutions in Western society tried to squash scientific advances that threatened their prestige, authority, power, and control. Instead of dealing with science, these institutions took the position of confrontation. We might say their motto was, "It is us, the religious institutions, that guide and govern your life. We do so under the authority of God. Listen to us. Science is from men, not God; therefore, it naturally corrupts your thinking!" To illustrate this, ponder the decision of the Roman Catholic Church in 1992. After 350 years, and a 13-year investigation, it apologized to Galileo. He had declared that the earth revolved around the sun, and not the sun around the earth. Perhaps the length of the investigation was not so much to say Galileo was correct but served to seek ways of saying, "We weren't wrong because we adhered to the thinking of the day, while he did not."

As a result of the refusal of religious institutions to evolve, their steadfast conflict with science accelerated when people began accepting medical insights and healing instead of adhering to historical practices and phrases, such as "It is God's will." People might have been dubious about the rise of science, but when health issues arose and remedies were forthcoming, the scales were tipped in favor of science. Consequently, science gained much traction. As science gained traction, it never lost its momentum. Religious institutions failed to see this, and they failed to see that they were stuck in the mud, whereas science plowed ahead. In a phrase, Western society evolved and Western Christianity devolved. With the advent of Western society valuing science over the religious institutions that refused to see the worth of science, it was natural for spiritually seeking persons to jettison religion!

The classic Western Christianity versus science scenario was the battle of faith against Darwinism. In America, the famous Scopes Monkey trial pitted William Jennings Bryan (defending religious views and creationism) against Clarence Darrow (a secularist defending the accused). The battle was in a small Tennessee courtroom. Evolution won and became a standard school science program. Alas, in some religious realms, this battle still takes place nearly a century later!

It's ironic that in the quest for easy, simple, and affirming answers in our fractured, fragmented postmodern society that creationists are seeking, once more, to have their views restored to classrooms. In other words, in our uncomfortable state, we wish to turn back to a time when we had comfortable, safe answers. Did you know there's a museum in Kentucky devoted to humanity living in the age of dinosaurs? In other words, "Science is wrong since we have the infallible Genesis accounts of creation as illustrated in this display!" (The sarcasm is mine, and I own it.) As Yuval Harari, in *21 Lessons for the 21st Century*, writes:

> For thousands of years people believed that authority came from divine laws rather than from the human heart, and that we should therefore sanctify the word of God rather than human liberty. Only in the last few centuries did the source of authority shift from celestial deities to flesh-and-blood humans.
>
> Soon authority might shift again—from humans to algorithms. Just as divine authority was legitimized by religious mythologies, and human authority was justified by the liberal story, so the coming technological revolution might establish the authority of Big Data algorithms ...[3]

We shifted from total belief in religious leaders giving us "God's Word" to algorithms that suggest music, make book choices for us, and recommend what we need to consume! Whereas in the past God gave us the answer, we now have algorithms that provide answers. Algorithms also steer us to asking questions that fit the provided answers. Take more than a few moments to truly think about this. Algorithms take us to where we want to be, not to God. Ponder that sentence.

In a world of infinite choices, algorithms direct us to limited, pre-chosen selections that fit our previous history. Instead of expanding and opening our minds, our thinking, and our spirit, we have a narrowing of thoughts that are reinforced. Since we validate our narrowing view, it's no surprise that polarization is a benchmark in postmodernism. I wonder if we're now on the verge of having algorithms suggest our mental, physical, and, yes, spiritual decisions. What do you think of this? Be open-minded when you mull this over.

Indeed, with all the social, cultural, and religious upheaval in postmodernism, it's fascinating that many continue to crave a spiritual life. The result is that in Western society, the fastest-growing segment of the population are those who are Spiritual but Not Religious (SBNR).

Freelance writer Kelly Besecke describes the rise of the postmodern SBNR phenomena quite well. We must repeat a previous passage from her work. Perhaps your thoughts, now stimulated (I hope), might read this differently:

> Spirituality is about depth and vitality. People who want a rich spiritual life are looking for a deeper awareness, a heightened consciousness; they want to experience more of the meaning and intricacy of life. They want to feel truly alive—to feel engaged, to find life compelling. They want to feel centered and grounded in something eternal. They want a sense that there's more there than meets the eye. They want a little bit of magic. They want an antidote to what they experience as the flat, literalistic materialism of modern society—an antidote to its shallowness and apparent meaninglessness. They want a broader base, a deeper foundation, and a higher horizon ...[4]

As often noted, for much of history, religion and spirituality were synonymous. If one was religious, one was spiritual. If one was spiritual, it was because one was religious. In postmodernism, we view these as separate and perhaps unequal entities. Is this not a significant social shift? From this idea of people being spiritual but not necessarily religious, we have four distinct groups in Western society.

First, some continue to be religious and spiritual. Second, some religious people lack spirituality. (Yes, Virginia, like Santa, this is possible. Perhaps you know some.) Third, some profess spirituality but aren't religious. The fourth group consists of those who don't think of themselves as either religious or spiritual. Many call this fourth group the NONEs.

It's not necessary to discuss those who are religious and spiritual. Likewise, we won't address those who say they are religious but seemingly lack a sense of the spiritual. However, it might behoove religious institutions, if not too threatened, to research this group. The results might be enlightening! At some point, quality research on the NONEs seems very necessary. This is because they are on their way, via evolution, to being the largest and most dominant group in Western society. Whereas religious and spiritual people tend to be organized in groups, the NONEs are individuals who rarely talk or imagine spirituality or religion. Dorothy Butler Bass defines NONEs:

> And, to underscore the fact that Americans now have more choices in their spiritual and religious lives, young adults are far more likely to be "nones" than their more religiously obligated grandparents—somewhere between 25 and 30 percent of adults under thirty claim no religious affiliation. Although the United States still comprises many Christians and has a history of religious diversity, the percentage of Christians in the United States has clearly declined, and religious diversity is more obvious and widespread across the population than ever before. By 2010, in a stunning change, America's third largest religious group—and one of its youngest—is "unaffiliated," an independently minded group, with no single issue, theology, or view of God; the "nones" include atheists, agnostics, "nothing in particular," religiously oriented and secular unaffiliated people. If these trends continue at the current pace, "nones" and other religions combined will outnumber Christians in the United States by about 2042.[5]

Paul Taylor, in *The Next America: Boomers, Millennials, and the Looming Generational Showdown,* echoes this argument. He outlines four main reasons for NONEs. First, they are a political backlash to the rise and power of the conservative right. Second, with delays in marriage, the youth of today are breaking from the historic religious cycle of their ancestors. Third, young people, who make up the largest number of NONEs, are socially disengaged. In other words, they are embracing self-interests, or "Me-ism". "Me-ism" will be well explored throughout this book. Fourth, NONEs are a product of secularization.[6] In a short, vivid description of the NONEs, Taylor stated:

> Yet another theory loosely links the rise of the unaffiliated to what some observers contend has been a general decline in "social capital"—a tendency among Americans to live more separate lives and engage in fewer communal activities, famously summed up by sociologist Robert Putnam as "bowling alone."In this view, the growth of the religious "nones" is just one manifestation of much broader social disengagement.[7]

The NONEs are mostly the young people frustrated with the directions of the past and unhappy with the present; as a result, they tend to create and live in their own social reality.

Our attention, consequently, largely concerns the third group, or those who identify as spiritual but not religious (SBNR). As we begin to look at the development and growth of the SBNR phenomena, it's necessary to clarify how we believe this social element originated. In 1991, Barna wrote:

> The Church in America is in desperate need of a new model for the local church. We currently develop churches based on a model of ministry that was developed several hundred years ago, rejecting the fact that the society for which that model was designed no longer exists. The constant cry of the unchurched—"the church is irrelevant to the way I live"—cannot be addressed until the model itself is renewed to acknowledge that the times have changed. Our approach to meeting people's needs with the unchanging truths of the gospel must reflect our sensitivity to that change.[8]

As postmodernism evolved, it seems that people saw religious institutions as being so "heavenly" minded that they didn't meet the challenge of addressing people's "earthly" needs. In the past, people simply desired to "make it into heaven." In postmodernism, people in our individualized world aren't interested in the afterlife. In a popular phrase, instead of the afterlife, people are interested in the life they are after. In other words, how do I live my faith and life and meet my current needs? Rightly or wrongly, these perceptions caused people to drift away. This and other noted reasons made the time ripe for people to assume the role of "spiritual but not religious."

This growing societal phenomenon receives much attention because this segment of the population is rapidly becoming a dominant social reality! This is a dramatic shift. In a very short period of time, we transitioned from most people being spiritual and religious to the point where being religious is sometimes considered suspect! What do you think of this opinion? Take time to ponder and not rush to a quick answer.

Historically, people often organized themselves according to religious tradition. It was one's foundational community. The SBNR phenomenon, however, doesn't exist in organized social communities. For the most part, they lack cohesive, structured communities. If we were to classify or seek a common thread, we might say that the SBNRs and other postmodern people are consumers of the here and now. They tend to consume and live in a constant flux of ever-changing moods and fads. Sociology professor Yuk-Lin Renita Wong, and sociologist and therapist Jana Vinsky, explain this:

> Divorcing spirituality from its historical-religious roots
> makes it easier for the spiritual consumers to feel free to take
> up and appropriate at will cultural or Indigenous practices
> they define as "spiritual-but-not-religious." Practices from
> Asian traditions, such as yoga and mindfulness practice,
> are used as "techniques" or "methods" for the healing of
> the Western body, mind and spirit—the new "trinity" in
> the "spiritual-but-not-religious" discourse.[9]

Similarly, the next year, adult educator Riyad Ahmed Shahjahan wrote:

This is the point at which the first privatization—involving the creation of individual, consumer-oriented spiritualities—begins to overlap with an increasing emphasis upon a second privatization of religion—that is, the tailoring of spiritual teachings to the demands of economy and of individual self-expression to business success.[10]

In the past, people frequently defined themselves by their membership in a religious institution, congregation, or worship location. Today, people don't need a religious history to be credible! Instead of identifying features such as "As a child, I attended the oldest church in Eccles, Manchester," or "I grew up at St. Peter's Anglican Church, Scarborough," we have many small identifiers. This is because we are fragmented and as such carry numerous small and often short term "tags," such as, "I coached in the Philipsburg-Osceola Soccer League," or "I love the York Revolution of the Atlantic Baseball League." Instead of religious identifications, we identify ourselves by membership in our various sports affiliations or fan clubs, some consumer groups, our workplace, or where we live in our just-in-time society. For example, how long does it take when we meet a new person to ask where they work or live so we may connect with them more fully? I know when clergy sometimes meet other clerics, one of the first questions voiced while searching for commonality is, "And what is the size of your congregation?"

Since we live in a just-in-time society, we're free to shift in and out of organizations without issue. Instead of life-long memberships, we now have situational memberships. As our situations change and evolve, or devolve, our memberships change. After a few years, we may no longer feel inclined to coach or attend Little League baseball games.

Likewise, we move out of our religious heritage or background to whatever we desire, and when we desire it. Lifelong membership in a single church is giving way to "pray-as-you-go" models, and in turn to "play-as-we-go." To achieve our need, we may feel inclined to venture to a new religious organization, or into none! Hence the rise of the SBNRs and NONEs.

Today, many still wear crosses or emblems to denote their religious community. Sadly, however, in some settings, this practice has drifted so much that religious symbols are banned. In June 2019, Quebec passed Bill-21, effectively banning government employees such as police, court employees, prison guards, teachers, etc. from wearing any symbols. This wide-sweeping bill covers (or I guess, uncovers) Muslim hijabs, Jewish skullcaps, and Sikh turbans. This also includes Catholic crosses in a province that for decades was the most religious and Roman Catholic in Canada. Today it's one of the most secular. The banning of symbols shows how much secularism now dominates laws, customs, and practices. Ironically many governments across Western society begin meetings with prayer, and then quickly move into business forgetting the context of the prayer.

However, with the overall decline of religious symbols (Bill-21 notwithstanding), we witnessed an incredible increase in people wearing sports appeal symbols! I guess this means in Quebec you can't wear a hijab or turban, but a Montréal Canadiéns (in this case, this is the right spelling, eh!) lapel pin, baseball hat or sweater is perfectly fine! One can wear a red scarf to champion their pledge to Manchester United in English football, or wear a wedged shaped cheese-head hat supporting the Green Bay Packers. Even small-town teams, universities, and high schools market apparel. This is the new normal.

When monks and nuns wore distinctive habits, and people wore crosses, the statement was, "I belong to Christ." Today when we wear sports apparel, our statement is, "This is my team." The classic example is the Dallas Cowboys football team, which markets itself as "America's team." Postmodern marketing even encourages sports teams to "update" their icons and colors periodically so people will need to purchase new apparel. This is quite a leap from when football teams introduced helmet decals many decades ago! When the marketing for this began, the Pittsburgh Steelers were dubious. To save costs, they placed the decal on only one side of the helmet. This unusual practice continues. The evidence in Western society where SBNRs dominate is clear—the fan base of today's teams have much religious zeal.

In postmodernism, one's focus shifted. Society moved from considering the needs of others to looking after oneself. When one belonged to Christ, it was both a religious and spiritual commitment. Today, as noted, some sports fans "religiously" support their team, but is this a spiritual connection?

What do you think? Instead of being for Christ, one's postmodern message is "Look at me, I'm a fan of ..." In some cases, this is perhaps true. For example, some die-hard sports fans are buried in their team-inspire casket![11] Furthermore, some people give their chosen political party such devotion that it seems to match the fervor of a crusade. One's next-door neighbor and friend of decades may now be seen as an inhuman degenerate. They may need to face an inquisition! (I wish this was just sarcasm, but alas, there is some truth in this.) This religious zeal in the political realm, without the checks and balances of Western Christianity, will greatly damage Western society unless we rediscover our souls! I wonder how many of these zealots are religious and spiritual, just spiritual, or SBNRs. This is a good question for others to ponder and address.

Sadly, Western Christianity, unless championing loud, fundamentalist opinions, seems to be largely neutered. Both traditional Western Christianity and the new forms that are enjoying power and control, enhanced by secularism, need to dig deep and find themselves. To use a Christian metaphor, they need to come to terms with the pain and hurt of Good Friday, and experience "the dark night of the soul" in silence, and then wrestle with meaning until willing and able to let go of the past and, in turn, experience the resurrection of Easter.

In addition, the postmodern era shifted from fixed, solid foundations to fluid, revolving connections. This helped create NONEs and SBNR people! Instead of a lifelong connection to one church and community, we float to what we want, when we want it. In postmodernism, one can be socially acceptable by being spiritually free of religiosity! I ask, "Is this not a true paradigm shift?" What are your thoughts?

In an insightful 2005 publication titled, *The Spiritual Revolution: Why Religion Is Giving Way to Spirituality (Religion and Spirituality in the Modern World)*, Heelas and Woodhead wrote:

> ... we are witnessing a tectonic shift in the sacred landscape that will prove even more significant that the Protestant Reformation of the sixteenth century. What we are living through, they argue, is nothing less than radical change in which religion—namely Christianity—has been eclipsed

by spirituality (Luckmann, 1967, 1990; Campbell, 1999). Since this 'spiritual revolution claim' is the most striking and provocative claim being made about the contemporary sacred scene ...[12]

This tectonic shift to subjectivity and individualized self-importance brought down various religious institutions in Western society. Various scandals in Western Christianity added to this decline.[13] The results indicate that the sacred and secular largely reversed roles! The shame of being secular person in a religious society disappeared and many religious people felt shame for the actions of their churches. Likewise, religious people tended to become less religious, and those already less religious became lesser religious. Consequently, the largest segment in Western society became SBNRs.

While it's beyond our scope to explore the NONES in detail, I think they represent the natural progression in Western society. They will influence Western society and Western Christianity into becoming increasingly even less religious and, in a short time, less spiritual. The NONES are quite likely people whose parents were already distant, alienated, or removed from religious experiences.[14] I wonder if we can consider the idea that in the next few generations, the NONES will replace the SBNRs as the largest social group in Western society. This is a profound question Western society should consider exploring. What do you think? Thus, those who are religious and spiritual could, within a few years, reside on the fringe of society. Is this idea speculative? Yes. Yet this seemingly represents the direction Western society is heading! What do you think of this potential outcome? Moreover do you feel threatened or appeased by this societal shift?

In time, the SBNR group, because of roots in individualism and the lack of familiar foundational communities, may naturally begin to decline. Again, is this speculative? Absolutely. Is it possible? Absolutely. In 2009, cultural sociologist Penny Edgell spoke to this potential reality when she wrote:

The religious landscape of the United States is in a period of long-term, fundamental transformation, and all of the evidence suggests that today's emerging adults will provide a catalyst that accelerates this transformation. Since 1990, the percentage of Americans who claim no religious identity has more than doubled, from 7% to 15%. There is a focus on *spirituality*—as a way of talking about experiences of connection and transcendence, as a way to designate a wide-ranging set of practices used to connect with the sacred, and as an expression of a critical distance from organized religion. At least 20% of Americans identify as "spiritual and not religious," and over 40% identify as both spiritual and religious. There has been a reaction against the recent politicization of religion; the "culture wars" have caused some Christians to turn away from their religious identity altogether, and surveys show a new preference for more distance between religious leaders and politics.[15]

The shift from the domination of Western Christianity to the domination of the SBNRs and soon the NONEs represents a further step in the evolution of postmodernism. I wonder to what degree COVID-19 will affect this shift in the short-term and the long-term. We can only speculate. However, the shift to SBNRs, and perhaps NONEs, is real. As Drescher states: "perhaps, of middle-class entitlement … church is a discretionary activity, not an essential one."[16] This issue requires attention. This issue, in my opinion, as a spiritual and religious person, needs our attention.

It's clear that if we don't explore the growing SBNR situation, the Christian message of going forth to evangelize will fail. It will fail badly. For much of Western Christianity, the focus of evangelism was to get people to join the church and "be like us." Today, when church leaders ask their people, "What can we do to grow?", the answer from the stakeholders remains rooted in those insider perceptions. Despite changing formats and ideas, we still have the same foundational image of wanting people to join religious institutions on the terms of those already on the inside. We deny the reality that people have already given us their answer. It is no. Those in religious institutions are often blind to the needs of outsiders because they're consumed with panic and thoughts of survival. Many religious institutions failed because they could not, did not, or would not adjust to meet "Me-ism." Other religious institutions, often those formed in postmodernism, more easily adopted themselves to meet "Me-ism." Naturally those with less entrenched history and rituals were able to make changes and shifts more readily. Does not the shift to "Me-ism" suit SBNRs? After all, we search for satisfaction and comfort ahead of suffering and challenges. In other words, we desire Easter's joy and resurrected experience without traveling through the agony of Good Friday.

It would behoove those in religious institutions to ask those not in religious institutions what it would take to bring people back into the flock. In other words, how would religious institutions in Western Christianity strive to seriously address and respond to the SBNRs? This is often threatening because it may mean that religious institutions must embrace radical change! Yet it's imperative for religious institutions of all stripes and types to endeavor to address the identified needs of non-members. Sadly, if the institutions don't genuinely attempt to meet the needs after asking people what they need, they give the disillusioned further reason to be disillusioned! Sadly, much of Western Christianity is so entrenched in various models, lacking in imagination, and nervous of great risks, that they find it difficult to think about alternatives. After all, if these substantial risks were undertaken, religious institutions could jeopardize losing those already inside. Instead of seeing potential gains, leaders often focus on potential losses. The result is that few take great risks. Consequently, the SBNR segment continues to grow!

Having stated this situation, I must say that many religious institutions in Western society openly addressed issues surrounding sexuality. Conversations in an age of constant confrontation take courage. Talking about abortion and LGBQT+ issues required risks. Religious institutions were forced to address these formerly ignored, chastised issues or to attack those who held those values because postmodern secularism expected these matters needed attention. Religious institutions in postmodernism had to take their head out of the sand and deal with these public issues. Living in denial was so much easier.

But is Western Christianity too entrenched in old attitudes and baggage to explore many challenges? One of the most famous and telling statements regarding the decline of Western Christianity is: "We have never done it that way before!" Alas, how can Western Christianity move out of its comfort zone? How can we move Western Christianity from thinking, "We need people to meet our needs," to the old prophetic call, "How can we meet the needs of the people?" What are your thoughts? In turn, how do SBNR people respond to the pleas of Western Christianity?

In postmodernism, Western Christianity must do more than offer traditional safe, predictable programs. Solutions that served well for centuries do not effectively or efficiently always serve our society. Unfortunately, Western Christianity and other institutions failed to perceive that "The Moving Finger writes, and, having writ, moves on." Yet before we bemoan the potential reality of becoming a NONE society, we have the opportunity to look at how spirituality is currently part of people's lives. We need to build upon that foundation. We urgently need to try to understand the emerging social reality of SBNRs! We need to see how they perceive and use spirituality.

We must assume that it's extremely unlikely that Western society will ever return to being a predominantly Christian society. Consequently, Western Christianity should endeavor to address people's spiritual needs rather than promote its religious programs. In my opinion, this is critical. Unless we address people's spiritual needs, we could morph into a society that is increasingly polarized, constantly angry, very vindictive, and often confrontational. Some may say we crossed that bridge some time ago. Others may say we are at the tipping point. Yet we may sadly say that others are in denial and fail to see this taking place! Instead of entrenched programs that wittingly and unwittingly suggest to outsiders, "come and be like us," Western Christianity must retool and focus on postmodern spirituality. This is an immense task in the predominant D-I-Y (do-it-yourself) spiritual environment. Western Christianity must make efforts to address the rise and stature of the SBNRs.

You may wonder why I'm championing the role of the Western Christian churches. In addition, why do I seem to be acting as a vanguard of needed reform? The answer is simple. The religious institutions in Western society own the history, the tools, and the skills, unlike any other organization in society, to respond to people's postmodern spiritual needs. This is a fact. However, while Western Christianity owns these tools, we might ask, "Are these institutions interested?" Ay, there's the rub.

You might think this writing is nudging Western Christianity to undertake more initiatives to address spirituality in Western society while ignoring other faiths. It's not my intention to ignore other faiths, but as an ordained Christian cleric, I am speaking to and from my tradition. I can do no other. It would be bold and presumptive to contemplate Jewish, Hindu, or Islamic faith traditions of which I know little. However, with some clarity I can say that they face the same postmodern dilemma as Western Christianity—that of being relevant in an SBNR world. These religious groups all face decreasing membership, declining attendance, and growing disinterest. In other words, apathy.

In postmodernism, parts of Western Christianity made various moral and ethical missteps, and these greatly undermined their message and credibility. It shouldn't be surprising that people simply chose to spend their time and money in other ways. As an academic turned full-time prodigious writer, Phyllis Tickle tells us in unflattering terms that as Western Christianity began failing, the SBNRs filled the void.[17] Although describing the postmodern social reality in Canada, sociologist Reg Bibby' book, *Beyond the Gods & Back: Religion's Demise and Rise and Why it Matters,* generally speaks to all of Western society. It's a long quotation, but like other lengthy passages, it serves the purpose of exposing readers to the deep, insightful thoughts of others. The quotation urges readers to take time to ponder and reflect upon the writer's thoughts. It is a quotation of some substance:

> Put simply, secularization refers to the decline in the influence of organized religion. While the line is not perfectly straight, it nonetheless is linear: secularization proceeds in a fairly relentless and non-reversible fashion.
>
> Dobbelaere, the Belgian sociologist, offered an important clarification of the concept in pointing out that it has at

least three major dimensions—institutional, personal, and organizational. The spheres of life over which religion has authority decrease and its role becomes more and more specialized; religion has less and less of an impact on the daily lives of individuals—what Berger has referred to as "a secularization of consciousness"; and religious organizations themselves are increasingly influenced by society and culture in the way they operate—their goals, their means, their content, and the way they measure success, for example ... They argued back in the early 1960s that, despite high levels of religious participation in America, secularization was already rampant. Their explanation was that secularization was taking the form of "secularization from within" rather than "secularization from without." On the surface religion was flourishing; but if one looked more closely, they said, the structures and content of religion in the U.S. were being ravished by secularism. By way of one memorable illustration, Berger wrote that, when it came to values, "American Christians [held] the same values as anyone else—only with more emphatic solemnity."[18]

Undoubtedly, our society has a much less common corporate moral foundation than in previous generations. This was replaced with ever-increasing individualism, the addiction to instant gratification, and personalization. Instead of living with a firm, fixed foundation, we morphed to fluid, ever-flowing urges that we must appease. Ponder this metaphor: instead of living anchored lives, we are constantly drifting and pushed by prevailing blowing winds. In postmodern Western society, we must understand that people consistently abandoned former safe anchors of religion. Today, people prefer to sail on tides, currents, and winds of constant change and what-feels-right-at-this-moment. Instead of tacking and working to reach a destination, we allow winds to direct us. Postmodernism is constant change and constant chaos. It's no wonder people often feel overloaded and respond with anger, confrontation, and, sadly, rage. For centuries, Western society looked for direction from substantive sources, such as the Ten Commandments. These commandments were so foundational that you'd think they were carved in stone. Today, we seem to keep our ever-evolving laws date-stamped on phones.

In keeping with the sailing metaphor, the late Peter Vaill wrote much on organizational leadership, change, and spirituality. He weaved several essays into a compiled work called *Managing as a Performing Art: New Ideas of a World of Chaotic Change*. In this work, he described our postmodern reality as living in a "permanent white water world." He also said people need to work "spiritually smarter."[19] Despite the decline of structured Western Christianity, and while on chaotic white water currents, people still yearn for spiritual meaning. How can we address this complex, ever-shifting situation in our SBNR dominated society?

Having noted the context and some of the processes involved in the rise of the SBNR reality, we must now turn our attention to some of the content of this SBNR phenomenon. Sadly, in postmodernism, with our short attention span and reliance upon Wikipedia and Google (et al) as our standard source of information, we often look for the path of least resistance when pursuing answers. We follow it without taking into consideration any alternatives. In other words, we often limit our approach to looking at societal and personal issues. This means that if we sincerely desire to discover and understand the core reality of people who are spiritual but not religious, we must utilize a broader approach. It's vital to understand why and how we moved away from a society that gathered in comfortable long-term settings, such as in religious institutions. We must understand how we moved from family meals to the place where we utilize drive-through, fast food eateries for unsatisfying but quick "happy meals." I wonder if we realize that the happy meals we use to feed our sense of spirituality are fatty and lack nutrients! In other words, while fast food satisfies us for a short time, it leaves us wanting more. Instead of having full, family and/ or community sit-down meals, we slipped into the postmodern spiritual world described by Reg Bibby in 1987 when he described us as eating "à la carte."[20] We pick and chose from the buffet what we desire and ignore a proper diet! Ponder this illustration of moving from full communal and/ or nutritious family where interactions abound to individualized fast-fun meals we gobble down while on the run. What does this reality say to you?

To discuss properly the SBNR society, we must first observe how religiosity and spirituality are different. Arthur W. Chickering, Jon C. Dalton, and Liesa Stamm, academics with expertise in educational leadership, provide some terrific insights in *Encouraging Authenticity & Spirituality in Higher Education*. In this collection of essays, Jon Dalton provides an excellent example of how students see the differences between religion and spirituality:

> Ask most college students the difference between religion and spirituality and they are likely to tell you that religion is about a lot of external rules and rituals, whereas spirituality is a soul-searching inward journey. They are inclined to see religion as going to church, obeying commandments, following someone else's rules, and participating in a formal religious organization. They see spirituality as having to do with their personal journey toward greater purpose and meaning, a journey that helps them understand their place in the world and their relationship to transcendent values and purposes ... thus it is not surprising that students' participation in formal religious activities usually declines in college, whereas their interest in spirituality increases.[21]

Many of the thoughts of these students are reflective of images expressed in Western society. Six years after Chickering, Dalton, and Stamm's book, church historian Diana Butler-Bass, in one of her many books, provided us with another insightful and encompassing explanation. In observing religion and spirituality, she wrote this long but very authoritative piece. Take time to contemplate and allow it to percolate within you. She wrote:

> What do you think of when you hear the word "spiritual"? When you hear the word "religious"? In a very unscientific experiment over the course of a year and a half, I asked groups with whom I was working to play a word association game with me. On a whiteboard, I drew two columns, one

headed with "Spirituality," the other with "Religion," and had them list in each column words they associated with that term. I worked with Groups in Texas and Toronto, New Jersey and Newport Beach, Colorado and Columbus, Sydney and Seattle. Interestingly enough, they all came up with almost the same lists:

Spirituality	Religion
experience	institution
connection	organization
transcendence	rules
searching	order
intuition	dogma
prayer	authority
meditation	beliefs
nature	buildings
energy	structure
open	defined
wisdom	principles
inner life	hierarchy
12-steps	orthodoxy
Inclusive	boundaries
doubt	certainty

Depending upon the gathering, the words showed up in different order and with different emotional content. Groups in Seattle, Toronto, and Newport Beach quickly and energetically filled out the "spirituality" column, offering testimonies to the power of nature, prayer, and meditation in their lives, whereas New Jersey Presbyterians were skeptical of "spirituality" and warmly described "order," "structure," "orthodoxy," and "beliefs" in the "religion" column. Many groups included these words and went beyond them, filling flip charts and whiteboards with related terms. In addition to positive words, there were negative terms as well.

Some described "spirituality" as "individualistic," "selfish," "lacking an ethical compass," and "self-centered" and accused those who talk about spirituality of contributing to the decline of the church or of turning their backs on social justice. But "religion" got the worst of it: "cold," "outdated," "rigid," "hurtful," "narrow," "controlling," "embarrassing," and "mean." And those words came from people who were church members! No matter the region or denomination, all of the groups associated spirituality with experience and religion with institutions ...[22]

Medical doctor and writer George Vaillant, in *Spiritual Evolution: How We Are Wired for Faith, Hope, and Love,* also gave an astute observation of the difference between religion and spirituality. He is more eloquent than I could ever write:

> The first difference is that religion refers to the interpersonal and institutional aspects of religiosity/spirituality that are derived from engaging with a formal religious group's doctrines, values, traditions, and co-members. By contrast, spirituality refers to the psychological experiences of religiosity/spirituality that relate to an individual's sense of connection with something transcendent (be it a defined deity, truth, beauty, or anything else considered to be greater than self) and are manifested by the emotions of awe, gratitude, love, compassion, and forgiveness. Second, religion arises from culture; spirituality arises from biology. Religion and cults are as different from spirituality as environment is from genes. Like culture and language, religious faith traditions bind us to our own community and isolate us from the communities of others. Like breathing, our spirituality is common to us all. On the one hand, religion asks us to learn from the experience of or tribe; spirituality urges us to savor our own experience. On the other hand, religion helps us to mistrust the experience of other tribes; spirituality helps us to regard the experience of the foreigner as valuable too.[23]

The origin of the term SBNR is unlikely to be resolved. Among the first to explore this emerging social force was trailblazer Wade Clark Roof. This acknowledge author died in 2019. He was versed in sociology and the psychology of religion. In 1993, he wrote the pioneering work, *A Generation of Seekers: The Spiritual Journeys of the Baby Boom Generation,* and in 1999, *Spiritual Marketplace: Baby Boomers and the Remaking of American Religion.*

In 1997, Brian Zinnbauer, Kenneth Pargament, and others in a qualitative article in the *Journal for Scientific Study of Religion* made a valiant effort to describe the meaning of spirituality and religion by explaining the evolution into SBNR as "fuzzy" to "unfuzzy."[24] Four years later, professor of religious studies Robert C. Fuller wrote *Spiritual but Not Religious: Understanding Unchurched America.* It was another early exploration of the SBNR reality. Of Fuller's work, Diana Butler Bass plainly says:

> … [he]points out, however, the popular definitions of the words diverged throughout the twentieth century: "The word *spiritual* gradually came to be associated with the private realm of thought and experience, while the word *religious* came to be connected with the public realm of membership in that religious institutions, participation in formal ritual, and adherence to official denominational doctrines." Not only did the words come to signify different aspects of faith by the early twenty-first century, but the terms "spiritual" and "religious" have become laden with emotional connotations. In general, "spirituality" is taken as a positive term, whereas "religion" is often negative; spirituality is understood as somehow more authentic, religion as having "a somewhat cynical orientation." Indeed, one British researcher found that Americans, Canadians, and British who identified as spiritual were more "socially desirable" than those who defined themselves as religious—that is, they were more appealing life partners.[25]

As well noted, this SBNR reality represents a true paradigm shift. We moved from church weddings and funerals that were part of our total social fabric to an ever decreasing number. Here's a question to think about: In our SBNR culture, to what degree do church weddings take place because of their historical setting and architecture, or because people genuinely are religious and spiritual? What percentage would you give to each? In many European countries, weddings (if they take place) are civil ceremonies. If so inclined, a religious blessing and ceremony may follow. In postmodern Western society, some conversations in Christianity about secularizing weddings took place. Why did various religious institutions engage in this conversation? It was, I think, because the unorganized but massive SBNR reality pushed some clergy and religious institutions to the opinion: "Why should we give much time and attention to couples we'll never see in church again?" Western Christianity and other religious institutions began considering their options! A few decades ago, such conversations were unheard of and unfathomable.

In postmodernism, religious marriages declined as couples chose to live together in either long-term committed, or serial relationships. This took place because the historical repercussions of this social taboo disappeared. As the number of religious weddings declined, there was a corresponding natural decline in the sacrament of baptism. I wonder how many Gen Zs can even define the meaning of baptism? This is an interesting question. What do you think? In postmodernism, Western Christianity slid from being a mainline social staple to being a sideline discretionary option. I wonder to what degree SBNRs and others utilize religious institutions because they view them in some way as being a talisman. Perhaps couples are seeking a religious/spiritual experience without being aware of such. What do you think? What is next? What do you think will transpire?

In many ways, Dorothy Butler Bass is correct that part of the postmodern shift from Christianity into SBNR was the desire to seek new definitions of "God." She wrote:

> ... The plethora of new survey data does not indicate either apocalypse or secularization. Instead, it points toward a different possibility: a turn away from the old

gods in search of new ones. In such a situation, diversity is a given (since no new norm has arisen) and dogmatism is a problem (since there are so many options and no single option can claim to be the ultimate answer). Indeed, statistical research might prove that philosopher Robert Wright is more correct when he suggests that God is currently undergoing an "evolution" than Richard Dawkins is when he claims that God is a delusion. Not an end, but a beginning? Are there signs of longing in the midst of the discontent? Are new answers arising as people question the old gods?[26]

The postmodern SBNRs are seeking new beginnings and new ideas of God (perhaps better stated as a small "g" god or gods).[27] Historically speaking, SBNRs are a recent social entity, and they're an entity without religious or deep community connections. Yet in Western society, they're the most common social segment. In time, they may surrender this reality to the NONEs. This possibility of NONE domination, as previously noted, bears immediate investigation by social scientists, and perhaps by Western Christianity.

After exploring how and why (or the context and process) of SBNRs evolving to be our most common social segment in society, we can now turn our attention and truly discover, "Who are the SBNRs?" In 2012, prolific writer Dorothy Butler-Bass wrote that in the last few decades, many countries began asking who saw themselves as SBNR. She said that the results were "both surprising and steady." Those questioned in the United States hovered around 30%. In other countries, SBNRs were self stylized by 40% of Canadians, approximately 25% of Australians, and 51% of those in Great Britain.[28]

In 2015, the Pew Research Center followed up their 2012 survey and found that nearly 23.9% of Americans identified themselves as SBNR. Geographically, the Mountain census area, which reported 5% of the population as SBNR in 1990, saw this jump to 26% in the 2014 US Census! In a quarter-century, the SBNRs in that area doubled twice! The 2014 US

Census showed SNBR people were almost evenly distributed across the nation. Consider their results:

	% of Population SBNR	% Growth of SBNR 2007–2014
The Pacific States	29%	26%
The Mountain States	26%	44%
The West North Central States	30%	33%
The West South Central States	17%	55%
The East North Central States	24%	50%
The East South Central States	16%	30%
The New England States	30%	30%
The Middle Atlantic States	22%	57%
The South Atlantic States	21%	40%

These figures come from Elizabeth Drescher's detailed book, *Choosing Our Religion: The Spiritual Lives of America's Nones.*[29] Drescher, who is a professor of religions, calls the SBNRs the NONEs, meaning they have no religion but are spiritual. Most others typically define the NONEs as those who are neither religious nor spiritual. Drescher's book is one of the most comprehensive and astute works looking at the development of the SBNRs. The cover of her book shows religious symbols of the world's major religions. Beneath each symbol is a box. The boxes are not checked. However, there is a blank space next to these various religious symbols. This represents the SBNRs. This blank space is marked with a large red checkmark. This indicates the vitality of the SBNRs. Most research on SBNRs deals with America. Unfortunately, this precludes trends in Canada, Mexico, and Europe. Studying the SBNR growth is also largely an American undertaking. Unfortunately, of the little research on the SBNR situation of Canada, almost all of it is from sociologist Reg Bibby. We will look at the Canadian situation shortly.

We find the SBNR people uniformly spread across America, except in the "Bible Belt" in the eastern southern states. The growth rate of the

SBNRs from 2007 to 2014 in the various areas ranged from 26% to 57% of "adherents." This suggests, without question, that the SBNR is a national reality, not regional. According to gender, SBNRs are almost evenly split.[30] However, according to Elizabeth Garbhart, in terms of ethnic background, SBNRs are typically white (84.8%).[31] Garbhart's notes are from her 2015 Master of Science dissertation thesis from the University of North Texas.

A *Fact Tank* article by the Pew Research Center pegs the ethic rates as 65% white, 11% black, 14% Hispanic, and 10% as all others.[32] While the discrepancies might be explained by research structures or sample size, the fact remains: Caucasians dominate the SBNRs. To date, the SBNRs in America are geographically diverse but split almost equally between female or male. What are some other identifiers of SBNRs?

First, according to Garbhart, SBNRs tend to perceive themselves as "elite," or middle to the upper class.[33] *Fact Tank* states that 29% are high school graduates or less; 37% had some college experience; and 34% were college graduates.[34] Conversely, Drescher, quoting another Pew Research document, says that 38% were high school graduates, 32% had some college, 18% graduated college, and 11% were postgraduates. SBNRs tend to be well educated. However, as Drescher shows, those quoted education levels closely resemble the general population of the United States.[35]

Second, it's interesting to look at the age groups of the SBNR population. The first two columns are from a September 2017 *Fact Tank* survey by Pew Research Center. The third column is from Drescher, citing a 2015 Pew Research Center report. The fourth column is another survey cited in the aforementioned 2017 *Fact Tank* article.

	Age	2012	2017[36]	2015[37]	2017[38]
Gen Z	18–29	20%	20%	35%	22%
Gen Y (or Millennials)	30–49	20%	29%	37%	36%
Gen X	50–64	21%	29%	19%	30%
Baby Boomers	65+	14%	17%	9%	12%

While the 2015 survey seems to offer results different from the other three surveys, we can agree that most SBNRs tend to be younger people. This mirrors the period when distrust in religious institutions began taking place—in other words, the SBNRs likely are void of religious practices, experiences, and exposure.

As distrust of institutions, apathy, "Me-ism," secularism, consumerism, and commercialism evolve, we need to add the more recent phenomena of screen addiction. These realities continue to assimilate into our personal lives and social fabric. This trend is expanding. As Gabhart stated in her qualitative-based, well-researched thesis:

> By far, the strongest predictor of being "spiritual but not religious' among the variables I examined was having "no" religion at age 16 ... The majority of SBNR adults in the United States seem to have identified with a religious organization in their teens. The rejection of religion at an early age a relatively rare, but very powerful predictor of becoming SBNR's.[39]

Again I find it fascinating that almost all the SBNR research takes place in the United States. Some comes from the United Kingdom, but there's little taking place in the rest of Europe. Given the vast American research, it's interesting to see similarities and differences between them and their Canadian neighbor (neighbour in Canada, eh). According to Bibby, the age groups of SBNRs in Canada closely resembles the American experience.[40] Whereas in 2015, 20–30% of Americans identified as SBNR, 39% of Canadians stated that they were SBNR.[41] This isn't surprising, as unlike Europe and Canada, America remains a country of active church membership and participation for many Gen Ys and Zs. However, the United States is beginning to experience the same slide. Conceivably, the far right and near far right religious institutions are reacting to this slide by seeking to entrench themselves in the past. This, however, didn't work for mainline churches that previously experienced the same slide in membership, prestige, and income! What do you think?

We can state that the United States is becoming a dominant SBNR nation. In terms of age groups, the religious slide in Canada is evenly spread across all age groups.

	Canada[42]	United States[43]
	2015	2015
Millennials	37%	22%
Gen Xers	42%	36%
Boomers	41%	30%
Pre-Boomers	29%	12%

The surprise is that Millennials in America have yet to seemingly fall prey to the same level of distrust of institutions, apathy, "Me-ism", secularism, consumerism, and commercialism as previous generations. Perhaps this is, in part, due to their higher attendance in religious institutions, unlike Canada and Europe. They have yet to ride the stride of the declining slide because they often chose to hide! When mainline churches chose to ignore changes, they suffered. In time, the powerful Evangelical right will follow suit.

Despite their great on-screen addictions, Millennials seem to be less cynical. Perhaps their concerns about the environment, climate change, and related issues have established or reconnected a spiritual awareness within them. Perhaps they value nature and balanced relationships, or harmony between oneself, society, and the world, more than previous postmoderns. Perhaps they're freely seeing and seeking spirituality beyond religious institutions. Bibby writes, "The research suggests that large numbers are not only finding alternatives to conventional expressions of spirituality but are also finding these alternatives to be highly functional."[44] This is emerging as a significant postmodern feature.

Having looked at where, how, and who are the SBNRs, it's essential to observe some of those "highly functional alternatives to conventional expressions of spirituality" that SBNRs utilize. Furthermore, it would be useful to add to the conversation the reasons why SBNRs exist in postmodern Western society.

Postmodern Western society saw the rise of commercialization and consumerism. In many places before postmodernism, stores were often closed Wednesday afternoons and Sunday. Consumerism pushed against these "Blue laws." Consumerism won. Even though people had the same amount of money to spend the other six days a week, "Me-ism" prevailed. Then Sunday shopping gave way to some stores that boast of 24/7 hours. People in postmodernism have disposable income that other generations did not. To meet this "need," Western society created more places to spend it.

The rise of malls was an early postmodern innovation. Likewise, colleges and universities learned the marketing appeal of malls and advertising. "Students become consumers experiencing 'the same kind of freedom they enjoyed in shopping malls,' and adult educators, 'become increasingly de-skilled as they surrendered their agency as a teacher for the less pro-active role of broker of commodified educational services.'"[45] In other words, there was some shifting from "this is what we need to teach" to "what society wants you to learn." Instead of students fitting the parameters of institutions of higher education, higher education institutions modified themselves to appeal to students. Marketing appealed to "Me-ism." Yes, courses, programs, and academics were indicated, but sports and social life were also highly noted. These institutions in the postmodern world greatly expanded their offerings. In turn, students can even "stream" their courses and lectures while in their jammies and/or even in distant cities. With the onset of COVID-19, this streaming action greatly increased.

Just as bricks and mortar malls began to fall out of favor, bricks and mortar campuses, in part because of COVID-19, are facing the same dilemma. We must also note that it's much cheaper to stream courses than pay staff and maintain buildings. Will post-secondary education bodies ever be like the past, or will they too evolve? Time will tell. What do you think? In the past, universities and colleges often chose their student. Today, students chose their school. This means that institutions of higher education compete for students. In a phrase, it's an educational marketplace. Perhaps that term is misleading, since many people don't attend institutions of higher education for an education but instead to train for a job! I wonder if SBNR students and religiously minded students approach this emerging model differently than in the recent past. Oh, how I wish someone would research this!

Malls in early postmodernism became the new commercial marketplace. They became Sunday's church! With malls and educational institutions, and recently online shopping, becoming Western society's marketplaces and norms, we must ask the following profound question: "Did religious institutions morph into religious marketplaces?" What do you think? Take time and consider that question. This will help us understand the SBNRs more fully.

Gene Veith describes this matter well:

> ... The ultimate postmodernist structure may be Minnesota's Mall of America, a mall and a theme park rolled into one. As someone who occasionally goes to both malls and theme parks, I do not want to put them down. That would be both snobbish and modernist. They are wonders of free enterprise and American culture. Trips to a mall or to Disneyland are essentially innocent activities. Malls and theme parks do, however, exalt consumerism and entertainment as the prime values, an attitude that, if allowed to run out of control, could be deeply problematic from a Christian perspective.
>
> Sometimes today churches resemble malls or theme parks, not only in their architecture but in the way people think about them. Megachurches sometimes resemble malls— with the parking lots, atriums, information booths, and shops featuring Christian merchandise. Employing marketing research and addressing people accustomed to the variety of choices offered at the local mall, these megachurches offer a range of activities and interest groups catering to every taste. Robert Schuller's Crystal Cathedral is something like a religious theme park, featuring babbling brooks and luxuriant plant life (inside the building) and multimedia sensory overload.
>
> Just as the gospel can be proclaimed in a modernist auditorium as well as in a traditional sanctuary, Christ can certainly be preached in a postmodernist architectural setting. The problem comes when the mind-set of the

malls and the theme parks becomes confused with Christianity.[46]

In Western society, postmodern shifts saw colleges and universities take on the values of educational marketplaces. They now compete for students (and dollars). Malls replaced the centuries-old model of main street shopping. The ten jewelry stores that once existed on Front Street either closed or moved to malls. Main Street shopping couldn't compete with the lure of malls. Malls became the preferred consumer marketplace. Yet in the accelerated pace of postmodernism, we are witnessing the death of the mall. Online shopping is now the consumer marketplace. Today, many online websites are hopelessly chasing Amazon in the competition for consumers. COVID-19 unintentionally increased this shift. What does the future hold? What do you think the next model will look like?

Some evidence shows that newer religious institutions, like the big box churches, tried to match the development of the big box store. Since we shop at the big box store, is it not natural that we should be drawn to investigate the big box churches? Big box stores became Main Street with less walking, no poor weather, and other conveniences. To meet the consumer of the big box store, some of the large big box churches even have their own Starbucks coffee shops on the campus! It seems that these new religious institutions captivated a postmodern tool unheard of or unattractive to mainline churches—marketing! Western Christianity, like Western society, became religious marketplaces. Furthermore, while attracting some to the big box church, the majority in society, the SBNRs, still preferred the big box store and other social activities over attending big box churches.

In postmodernism, much to the chagrin of the historical mainline institutions, consumer competition for souls took place. Instead of people fitting the prescribed parameters of religious institutions, various savvy religious institutions learned that they needed to appeal to consumer expectations of people. The churches in Western Christianity that grew were the ones that made Jesus look like their members! Consider this: some in America seemingly describe Jesus not as a first-century inclusive Jew but as the epitome of a white, twenty-first-century Evangelical American! In other words, instead of calling people to be Christ-like, Jesus was marketed to mirror the postmodern person. Diarmuid Ó Murchú, an Irish Roman Catholic priest, social psychologist, and author of many books on spirituality, describes this phenomena this way:

> To what extent is our anthropocentric compulsiveness—"man is the measure of all things"—the dominant underlying motivation of the focus on the personal relationship with Jesus? Are we not in danger of reducing God-in-Jesus to our image and likeness? And, insofar as the relationship tends to be described in patriarchal terms (even in the case of the loving father) is there not a subtle spiritualism at work, seeking to elicit subservience and compliance that may be quite alien to the freedom of the children of God? [47]

Jean Twenge and W. Keith Campbell, whom we met earlier, provide another insightful perspective:

> ... Thus the classic solution to permanent cultural change is not to directly challenge core cultural ideas, but instead co-opt them to fit a new vision. A classic example is the migration of religions across cultures. When Christianity entered Europe, it co-opted the ethnic traits of its inhabitants and the features of existing pagan religions. Jesus became a white guy with blue eyes and blond hair, Christmas involved a tree with lights during the winter solstice, and Easter was celebrated with an egg-carrying bunny in the spring ... In a more negative example, Hitler rose to power by wielding Teutonic myths, stories of Aryan history, ancient symbols like the swastika, and the long-standing prejudice against Jews in Europe. Hitler turned German culture into something very ugly and twisted, but he did it using core ideas from the existing culture ... This is exactly what happened to build the narcissism epidemic. We went from an independent but community-oriented

culture to one that can accept, without irony, the idea that admiring oneself is all-important, and believes that self-centeredness is necessary for success in life. These changes were not imposed by a dictator, imperial fiat, or religious decree. Instead, the changes built of themselves slowly, so that they seem a natural part of who we are.[48]

In postmodernism, new religious groups sprouted up. Likewise, many televangelists boomed and largely faded in the 1980s, because of their messages that informed the masses they were the specific pathway to heaven (for only $99.99 to them per month), and also they served as the conduit to meet personal needs. One even said to touch the television and feel his power coming through to you—if anything, it was static electricity. They were the "perfect storm" for a commercial and consumer-driven society. In short order, many older religious institutions began crashing because their religious fronts seemingly fell to a few postmodern snake oil sellers interested in greed and self-glorification. In time, financial scandals, lies, and other issues fittingly brought many of these charlatans to the edge, and they were cancelled on television. No masses, no mass income! While child abuse and financial scandals wore heavily upon mainline churches, the greed of the televangelists also sank public trust in Western Christianity.

Without question, in postmodernism, religious marketplaces became "spiritual marketplaces." In 1999, in *Spiritual Marketplace: Baby Boomers and the Remaking of American Religion,* sociologist Wade Clark Roof coined this now-iconic phrase. This term speaks to the SBNRs of postmodernism. In a tip of the hat to this forerunner of much postmodern research on spirituality, Reg Bibby wrote:

> ... Highly-respected sociologist Wade Clark Roof, for example, has written extensively on how the American Baby Boomer era has seen a major shift from involvement in organized religion to highly individualistic spiritual quests. Moreover, he has described how a burgeoning spirituality industry has emerged in response to such interests, resulting in lively "spiritual marketplaces."
> For Roof, three features in the U.S. have stood out.

The first is the sheer numbers of people involved in pursuing spiritual needs. Many who have lost traditional religious groundings are looking for new and fresh moorings. Others who are still religiously grounded are looking for further enrichment.

Second, a dominant theme is self-understanding. Consequently Roof speaks of quest, seeking, and searching.

Third, somewhat paradoxically, the spiritual yearnings are leading many beyond the self-focused, self-fulfillment themes of the 1960s and 70s. Now, he says, that quest has moved beyond consumption and materialism. "Popular spirituality may appear shallow, indeed flaky," Roof writes. But it also "reflects a deep hunger for a self-transformation that is both genuine and personally satisfying." His reading is that the current religious situation among American Boomers "is characterized not so much by a loss of faith as a qualitative shift from unquestioned belief to a more open, questing mood."[49]

From Roof and others, Bibby concluded:

> ... Consequently, there is every reason to expect that any movement away from organized religion will typically not result in the demise of spiritual interest.
>
> On the contrary, "religious defection" will see many individuals move toward highly personalized forms of spirituality, and cultures will respond with increasingly lively "spiritual marketplaces."[50]

Take time to re-read that insightful passage. In turn, read and reflect upon the following deep, thoughtful quotes. First, Robert Fuller, a religious studies professor, and another early voice explaining the rise and place of the SBNR development also explains the spiritual marketplace quite well:

> ... Unchurched sources of spiritual thought have competed quite successfully in America's "spiritual marketplace." Like all marketplaces, the spiritual marketplace is ultimately driven by consumer demand. Churched and unchurched alike look to this marketplace for ideas that

meet their practical religious concerns; and, increasingly, these concerns seem to lead them to supplement the teachings of our established churches by drawing on one or more alternative spiritual philosophies. Recent surveys have convinced Wade Clark Roof that the nation's spiritual marketplace is changing. He believes that over the past two decades there has been "a qualitative shift from unquestioned belief to a more open, questioning mood." The sheer variety of spiritual philosophies available in today's marketplace makes it difficult for thoughtful people to believe that anyone religious system has a monopoly on truth. And, with a growing shift in emphasis from the producers of religious ideas (e.g., the churches or the Bible) to the consumer of religious ideas, there is a corresponding emphasis on spiritualities that are tailored to everyday concerns. The concerns that characterize the "spiritual, but not religious" sector of the population would thus appear to be causing the marketplace to operate differently. The traditions that emerged to address these concerns now affect how a large number of educated Americans understand personal spirituality. These changes in American religious life raise fascinating questions. Where are we headed? What will personal spirituality be like in the future? Has religion become captive to the marketplace, at the mercy of passing whims or fads? How might we evaluate the pros and cons of the trends set in motion by America's unchurched spiritual traditions?[51]

In a phrase, in the spiritual marketplace, everything is open for business! This leads us to a second image to ponder. British authors Paul Heelas and Linda Woodhead, et al, in 2005, wrote:

Terms like spirituality, holism, New Age, mind-body-spirit, yoga, feng shui, chi and chakra have become more common in the general culture than traditional Christian vocabulary. Even a cursory glance around the local bookshop or a stroll around the shopping centre leaves little doubt that Christianity has a new competitor in "the spiritual marketplace". "The times", it seems, "they are a-changing." Indeed the times are a-changin ...[52]

Amidst the changing times, consumerism consumed and consumes us. Adding <u>c</u>ommercialism, <u>c</u>onstantly <u>c</u>hanging <u>c</u>hoices, and <u>c</u>olossal <u>c</u>onveniences to this mix and we are beleaguered. It's no wonder we allow AI (artificial intelligence) and algorithms to condition and guide our lives. It seems as though we avoid complex thinking in favor of undemanding decisions. With all these "<u>c</u>" attributes on top of us, it's natural that we're becoming more and more SBNRs! Given this postmodern reality, we must ask, "Where do SBNRs shop in the spiritual marketplace?"

Elizabeth Drescher, in her well-rounded and researched book, *Choosing our Religion: The Spiritual Lives of America's Nones*, provides much insight into where the SBNRs feed their spiritual needs. For Drescher the four most foundational places where postmoderns find spirituality she styles as the 4Fs—family, friends, food, and fido.[53] She uses the word fido to keep with the letter "f," and it's a catchphrase for pets. Drescher devotes a chapter to this foundational spiritual focus of SBNRs. Throughout her extensive interviews, she noted that "at least two of these '4Fs' came up for every person who talked with me when I asked them to describe the practices or activities that were particularly important to them spiritually."[54] I can't help but wonder if these 4Fs are largely rooted in the personal desires, needs, and wants of people. In other words, "Me-ism" developed, modulated, controlled, and now manages one's spiritual world. I ask, in these self-serving feedings, "Where is their external authority?" and "How can one be accountable if one is only accountable to oneself?" This means if people don't like the feedback from family and/or friends, food, or even fido, they disconnect or distance themselves and seek another family member, other friends, other foods, and new pets to slack their urgent spiritual need. Do they quickly re-order to what makes them happy. What are your thoughts? Is it happiness just for the moment, or happiness that is deeply embodied in oneself? How does an assessment take place? Furthermore, can these

SBNRs ignore anyone and anything that don't immediately spiritually feed them? What do think?

The 4Fs are the top-rated sources of SBNR spirituality, but they're not the only items on Drescher's list. Other spiritual resources, in ranked order, are prayer, music, nature, art, and physical activity. Other people affirm these spiritual resources.[55]

According to Barna in 2016, one of the most popular resources for SBNR spirituality is sitting or communicating with nature.[56] "And why not, considering the real sense of personal autonomy one gains from time outside."[57] Historically speaking, in a short period of time we shifted from a religious-spiritual society that mostly saw spirituality existing in places of worship or prayer to seeing spiritual resources everywhere. We moved from corporate, shared experiences to highly personalized individual experiences. In a phrase coined by Robert Wuthnow and affirmed by others, we shifted from the "spirituality of dwelling" to a "spirituality of seeking."[58] Clark Wade Roof also used that image.[59] In 2009, Lambert, commenting on Robert Wuthrow's 1998 research, wrote:

> In 1998, the sociologist Robert Wuthnow claimed that the search for salvation and religious meaning in the United States had twice been reoriented since Weber's analysis in the early twentieth century. In order to make his point, Wuthnow fashioned a narrative of American religious history that made the 1950s the high point for a "spirituality of dwelling" in *After Heaven: Spirituality in America Since the 1950s*. The nineteenth-century religious landscape of the United States was quite diverse with an odd collection of religious communities, spiritualists, and mind power adherents, but in 1956 church membership totaled 80 percent of all Americans—the highest level in history. From this, Wuthnow concluded that religious leaders of the mid-twentieth century convinced the American public that congregational membership and congregational participation, "dwelling" Wuthnow called it, was the highest form of spiritual expression.

Congregations thus held something close to a monopoly
on spirituality and religious life.[60]

Without question, in Western society, postmodernism made a
significant shift from religious institutions owning spirituality to
spirituality being seen almost everywhere else. This shift from "spirituality
of dwelling" to "spirituality of seeking," tied with the significant decline
of membership, attendance, and adherence to religious institutions in
Western Christianity, marks a significant paradigm change. Instead of
people flocking to religious institutions for spiritual feeding, they began
seeking spiritual food everywhere but those institutions.

Those who remain religious and spiritual may dream of recruiting
and growing, but as long as religious institutions in Western society act as
gatekeepers of the past, and desire people to come to church "to be like us,"
they'll only find failure and disillusionment, and the slide will continue. The
slide will continue for mainline churches and for the religious right-leaning
religious institutions. Instead, the need of the religious and spiritual is to
follow a radical act of returning to one's roots. The origin of the word "root"
is the same as "radishes." Hence, to be radical truly means to return to one's
foundation before clouded by history and dogma! From being gatekeepers
of what was, the challenge for places of worship is to evolve and be door-
openers of the future. In other words, Western Christianity should be open
to the SBNRs and attempt to address their needs instead of the needs of
the institution. Western Christianity should return to the original model
in ministry—listening and responding, not telling and directing. Stephen
Brookfield, one of the world's foremost esteemed thinkers and author of
many books on adult education and critical thinking, beautifully describes
the problem of people being gatekeepers rather than door-openers. In his
1987 classic, *Developing Critical Thinkers: Challenging Adults to Explore
Alternative Ways of Thinking and Acting*, he poetically wrote:

> ... who encourage people to ask... awkward questions
> about imbalances in power structures and wealth
> distribution are likely to be criticized by gatekeepers of the
> dominant culture. Helpers who try to promote political
> learning may risk (at best) public criticism or (at worst)

loss of their livelihoods or, in some regimes, even their lives.[61]

Nearly forty years ago, Mark Kinzer called Western Christianity to return to its roots. He brilliantly described this when he wrote:

> ... Christianity is challenged to adapt itself and apply itself to a drastically new environment. This is not the first time Christianity has been so challenged ... In every great missionary endeavor and in the transition to every new challenge to new adaptation and application. And in every successful response has been guided by the same principle: adapt whenever possible to the thought and habits of the new environment in order to apply and preach the gospel, but never compromise essential Christian truths ... The church must now adapt itself and apply itself to a society that is in many ways unlike any that has ever existed before, a society in which change is the norm, and which therefore poses a slightly different challenge today than it did yesterday, and which will pose a new and unprecedented challenge.[62]

Western Christianity must do much to remain viable in our postmodern Western society. It will never return to being a dominant mainstream entity. This is especially true in Europe and North America. Valiant efforts are required to even remain as sideline players. If Western Christianity doesn't adapt and adopt new ways to meet spiritual needs, it could continue to slide. Evidence indicates the shift from mainline to the sideline is real. The shift to borderline is emerging. The next stage, of being on a lifeline, is quite realistic unless drastic actions are undertaken.

One part of postmodernism sometimes overlooked is that the pipeline of Protestants, Catholics, and Orthodox Christians from Europe to North America after World War II dried up a few years ago, thus contributing to the decline of Western Christianity. Many of these immigrants brought strong religious/spiritual practices with them to North America, and perhaps slowed the decline of Christianity there. Another factor in this postmodern decline was the shift from large to small families, reducing the number of people belonging to and attending Western religious institutions. Ponder these images. In recent decades, the pipeline of immigrants has typically been from non-Christian countries. Sadly and unfortunately, some entrenched white Christians in North America find this new trend threatening. In turn, instead of working to build up their religious communities, efforts are put into tearing these newer newcomer "others" down. It would benefit Western Christianity in North America if it would contemplate the mainline/sideline/borderline/birth-line/lifeline/pipeline images with open-minded thinking and care.

However, as the Barna Group published in March 2020, there are some glimpses of hope:

> Kinnaman summarized the implications of the research this way: "More than two and half decades' worth of tracking research shows that Americans are softening in their practice of Christianity. These stunning changes raise questions and suggest urgent implications.

> "First, *why* are things changing and *how* can so much change be occurring? Social research is very limited in answering how or why questions, yet it's very effective in demonstrating that change is, in fact, happening—and at a relatively rapid pace. Other research (for example, this summary) shows that the U.S. population is undergoing major religious, social, demographic and digital change. The rise of digital life, including social media, the economic crisis, changing attitudes about social issues and the emergence of younger generations on the scene are some of the factors that are likely to form undercurrents recalibrating Americans' connection to faith and to Christianity.

> "Second, the research raises urgent questions for church leaders about the nature of the relationship Americans

have to Christian practice. What redefines and what anchors the churchgoing, Bible reading and prayer of adults? Among the interesting stories in the data is that private practices of faith—such as prayer and Scripture intake—aren't sliding as much as church attendance.

"Finally, the study shows reasons for continued hope and for additional reflection. For example, generational change is certainly taking place, but older generations (Boomers and Elders) are drifting away from conventional church attendance at roughly the same pace as younger generations (Gen X and Millennials). Why is that? What can church leaders do to engage the one-quarter of Millennials who remain active in Christian practice? How can the Bible-loyal readers continue to form the bedrock of a resilient Church? In what ways can prayer—the most universal of spiritual activities—be sparked to create spiritual renewal in this society?"[63]

It's fair to declare that the SBNRs are the dominant segment in the United States and Western society. Their numbers will continue to grow. Unlike organized groups, one of the rare common facets of SBNBs is distrust of organized religions. They fill this void by seeking fulfillment in individualized personal spiritual venues. Instead of a common communal foundation, we morphed into a society of individuals always in the fluid flux of becoming what we think we might want to be. I wonder if we are ever truly satisfied, since we lack checks and balances that existed in historical spiritual and religious practices. What do you think of this observation?

I can't help but wonder if the largely white, middle to upper-class, conservative, Evangelical movement is exerting social and political muscle pressure in response to the growth of SBNR. I am positive there is some correlation. However, is it 10% or 75%? How much of this correlation is a conscious activity and how much is an unconscious relationship? How would you rate the percentages?

It's interesting to think about the relationship between the conservative, Evangelical movement and SBNRs, and to mull over the decline of Western

Christianity in Western society and the shift to the highly personalized and individualized SBNR reality. While many may decry the loss of the dominance of Western Christianity, we must applaud the news that people are spiritually hungry and often actively seeking varied approaches for nourishment. In 2004, David Tacey, whom we met much earlier in this work, wrote optimistically of the new spiritual age surrounding and enveloping Western society:

> ... This is a people's revolution. It is taking place because society's loss of meaning is becoming painfully obvious, especially to the young, the disenfranchised and to all who suffer. It is a counter-cultural revolution, a romantic rebellion against the rise of materialism, inhumanity, and economic rationalism. Because this interest is rising from below, it may take some time before the mainstream institutions in health, education, politics, journalism, and religion are able to catch up with it. To date, there has been much suspicion and resistance, and a tendency to lump everything spiritual into the category "New Age", where it is damned and forgotten. There has not been enough discrimination, because we do not know how to see this blurred and repressed area of our own experience.

> ... This revolution involves a democratization of the spirit. It is about individuals taking authority into their own hands, and refusing to be told what to think or believe. It is about personal autonomy and experimentation with the use of direct experience of the world as a kind of laboratory of the spirit. There is a new desire to observe, create theories, and test these against the facts of our experience. We seem to be applying the scientific method of our spiritual lives. Not all this investigation is happy or profitable, and this is all the more reason why public institutions must eventually take up a dialogue with popular spirituality.[64]

While the SBNRs are the personification of postmodern Western Spirituality, I can't help but wonder if they abandoned the "spirituality of dwelling" altogether. Instead of dwelling in venues of Western Christianity, they now dwell in secular institutions of education and consumerism (and, to a degree, the religious marketplace). To what degree did these new places truly become spiritual marketplaces? This is a fascinating question. Likewise, in our consumer-oriented secular society, to what degree have we assumed consumer-oriented secular spirituality? Did these institutions or marketplaces help define the SBNRs, or did the SBNRs define these places? It is likely mixed, but to what percentage would be an interesting study.

Some of the hallmarks of postmodernism are algorithms, bar codes, point of sale inventory tracking, and SKUs. With these tools, we have nearly perfected the "just-in-time" society! For example, to maximize profits and reduce expenses, we only deliver products to retail locations or manufacturers as they need them. Thus, almost nothing, or very few items, ever go on a shelf. Instead of six of product "A" on a shelf, we have one, and the other five are in the back room or on the delivery truck. With the space saved from six product As on a shelf, we now have space for products B, C, and D. Hence, a broader consumer choice is available. Besides, it means reduced storage and retrieval costs. We've come a long way from Henry Ford's statement that people could have the Model T car in any color they wanted, as long as it was black. Speaking of automobiles, today's engines, built-n Japan, arrive at the American assembly plant just in time to be placed directly into a vehicle! In *Door to Door: The Magnificent, Maddening, Mysterious World of Transportation,* Pulitzer prize-winning journalist Edward Hume's insightful 2016 book, we read:

> … In the end, the iPhone has a transportation footprint at least as great as a 240,000-mile trip to the moon, and most or all of the way back. The wonder of this is compounded by the fact that this transportation intensity is a strategy to *increase* efficiency and lower cost.[65]

Fellow journalist Thomas L. Friedman, in *The World Is Flat: A Brief History of the Twenty-First Century,* wrote:

... In 1983, Wal-Mart invested in point-of-sale terminals, which simultaneously rang up sales and tracked inventory deductions for rapid resupply. Four years later, it installed a large-scale satellite system linking all of the stores to company headquarters, giving Wal-Mart's central computer system real-time inventory data and paving the way for a supply chain greased by information and humming down to the last atom of efficiency. A major supplier can now tap into Wal-Mart's Retail Link private extranet system to see exactly how its products are selling and when it might need to up its production ...[66]

We've created even more dependence upon instant gratification, but instead of just appeasing people's needs, it also placates the marketplace. Given the prevalent postmodern societal phenomenon that swept across Western society, I can't help but wonder if we're evolving into a "just-in-time" spirituality. Do we truly have a spirituality of consumerism?[67] How does this mesh with SBNRs who are looking for a spirituality that meets today's specific urgent need. Are they influenced more by "just-in-time" secular spiritual phenomenon than those who are religious? I do not know. This is a question that would be interesting to examine. What are your thoughts?

The concept of spirituality hasn't changed; however, how we look at, use, and approach spirituality is involved in great reform unlike at any other period of history. In this the greatest, broadest, and most wide-sweeping reformation in history, people continue to seek venues to nurture their spirituality. People remain hungry. Instead of feasting in religious institutions, as in the past, people now consume spiritual food everywhere else! They often seek "just-in-time" nourishment. We can't turn back the clock, but we can challenge religious institutions to weave secular ideas with their foundation tools to help feed postmodern people. Perhaps if Western Christianity was more adaptable about adaptation, without surrounding core values and beliefs, there might be a shift from NONEs and SBNRs who are dissatisfied with self projections and/or in need of a community! What are your thoughts on this bold statement?

Questions to ponder and discuss
Chapter Four

Spiritual but Not Religious

1. Do you think there is a correlation between the decline of Western Christianity and the rise of "Me-ism"? Furthermore, can this be attributed to the decline of communities?

2. Are algorithms "taking over" much of our mental, physical, and even spiritual decision- making?

3. Will the NONEs replace the SBNRs as the largest group in Western society, and if so, when do you think the tipping point date will be?

4. How can one be accountable if one is only accountable to oneself?

5. Are you more of a gatekeeper of the past or door-opener to the future? If you belong to a religious institution, what is their dominant position?

6. Are SBNR's influenced more by "just-in-time" secular spiritual phenomenon than those who are religious?

7. Make a list of your sources of spirituality and then see how many fit within Drescher's list of 4 Fs

CHAPTER FIVE

SPIRITUALITY AND THE BRAIN

The Age of Entitlement saw the beginning of incredible advances and innovations across Western society. Many of these incredible gains were in the field of medicine. We continue to see the fantastic development of life-saving drugs, medical procedures, and various other practices. In the past, people wanted the mature family doctor because that doctor had much experience. Today, we seem to prefer recently graduated doctors because they know the latest medicines and practices! Indeed, much is changing in the medical world.

In postmodernism, we live longer lives. I'd like to say this advantage also provided healthier lives. Alas, I cannot. In part, television (and now small screen) addictions, tied to manufacturing automation of fast foods and snacks, such as potato chips, resulted in people being active couch potatoes. Our poor diets and physically inactive lives counter any advances gained! In other words, we live longer and we live sicker!

In the past, when we were an agrarian society, work and home life gave us the required essential physical activity. Today, in our fragmented specialized society, we seek physical activity in specialty stores. We call these gyms! Some prefer the cheaper practice of jogging or walking on their own. Many partake in these practices, but most prefer watching physical activities (which we call sports) while eating chips as couch coaching potatoes! This satirical comment is sadly too true.

One branch of medicine now receiving tremendous attention is brain research. There is much study on how the brain works or does not work. One eminent researcher, neuroanatomist Jill Bolte Taylor, has looked at the effect strokes have on the brain. She suffered a stroke and consequently turned her theories into practice! Jill recovered from her stroke and wrote about her experience and insights in her award-winning account, *My Stroke of Insight: A Brain Scientist's Personal Journey.* My impression is that after her recovery, Taylor seemed to have reinvented herself as gentler, and gentler on herself.

Besides much work on how the brain deals with strokes and other functions, there is much research on how drugs interact with the brain. You may recall how Dr. Oliver Sacks discovered the beneficial effects of a drug that awakened (sadly, only for a short time) catatonic patients. Taylor and Sack's stories are just two well-known examples of brain research in postmodernism.

Besides these neurological studies,[1] we see psychiatrists, psychologists, and other clinicians finding new ways to assist those with mental health issues.[2] We no longer spin people in chairs to throw the mental illness out, or cover their head with a box to quiet them (you can Google these and other past "useful" mental health practices). Today, medications stimulate or dampen various brain chemicals. We can say that there's a postmodern surge in theories, practices, and beneficial results! There are also investigations ongoing into how the Internet is affecting and rewiring our brains![3] We have studies that examine near-death experiences (aka NDE), spirituality, and the brain.[4] Some even wonder if we are "Wired for God."[5] Similarly, some genuinely ask, "Are we hardwired for God?"[6] Evidently, postmodern Western society is asking, "What is the relationship between spirituality and the brain?"

We must begin by stating that this evolutionary field offers potential great insights into the human condition. As with any new field of research, some efforts are spectacular, while others are speculative. Some efforts achieve merit, while others are more controversial. Alas, it isn't always easy to discern the difference! Despite limitations, this effort will try to filter some sustained facts from those considered farfetched. Nevertheless, we must recall that sometimes farfetched facts or opinions, in time, are justified. Remember the story about Galileo, the universe, and the church!

We shouldn't be surprised that a variety of books on spirituality and the brain sell very well in both academic and popular outlets, such as Matthew Alper's *The "God" Part of the Brain: A Scientific Interpretation of Human Spirituality and God*, Nicholas Carr's *The Shallows: What the Internet Is doing to Our Brains*, and Lionel Tiger and Michael McGuire's *God's Brain*.[7] Some of these authors, such as Newberg, continue to garner attention, gain a following, and, in turn, stimulate more studies of the relationship between the brain and spirituality.

In exploring the relationship between our brain and spirituality, it seems vital that we begin by asking the significant foundational question: "Are our brains different in postmodernism than before postmodernism?" It's a question never explored or considered previously in history. In other words, no other generation considered whether their brains were different than their forbearers'. In fairness, it's highly unlikely that this question even arose, since the brain and its functions were largely unknown. However, for us, it's a good question to help answer our basic life question, "Who am I?" I highly recommend Nicholas Carr's work as a useful place to begin exploring this question. It provides much insight in a readable manner on how the Internet is truly rewiring and changing our postmodern Western brain. As you read the quote below, consider that Carr's book was printed in 2010. In our accelerated postmodern society, some may call this effort "dated." Carr wrote:

> As the uses of the Internet have proliferated, the time we devote to the medium has grown apace, even as speedier connections have allowed us to do more during every minute we're logged on. By 2009, adults in North America were spending an average of twelve hours online a week, double the average in 2005. If you consider only those adults with Internet access, online hours jump considerably, to more than seventeen a week. For younger adults, the figure is higher still, with people in their twenties spending more than nineteen hours a week online. American children between the ages of two and eleven were using the Net about eleven hours a week in 2009, an increase of more

than sixty percent since 2004. The typical European adult was online nearly eight hours a week in 2009, up about thirty percent since 2005. Europeans in their twenties were online about twelve hours a week on average. A 2008 international survey of 27,500 adults between the ages of eighteen and fifty-five found that people are spending thirty percent of their leisure time online, with the Chinese being the most intensive surfers, devoting forty-four percent of their off-work hours to the Net. ... These figures don't include the time people spend using their mobile phones and other handheld computers to exchange text messages, which also continues to increase rapidly. Text messaging now represents one of the most common uses of computers, particularly for the young. By the beginning of 2009, the average American cell phone user was sending or receiving nearly 400 texts a month, more than a fourfold increase from 2006. The average American teen was sending or receiving a mind-boggling 2,272 texts a month. Worldwide, well over two trillion text messages zip between mobile phones every year, far outstripping the number of voice calls.[13] Thanks to our ever-present messaging systems and devices, we "never really have to disconnect," says Danah Boyd, a social scientist ...[8]

This 2010 book contains mathematical figures that, in postmodern terms, are light years behind us! I wonder what the numbers may be a decade after the publication of this book. What do you think?

In our age of instant gratification and immediate responses, we no longer read or think deeply. In postmodernism, our spiritual selves and brains have changed because we are prone to gloss and rush rather than ponder and pause. Books allow thoughts to settle and ripen, whereas web browsing does not.[9] I ask you, does not the popular and commonly used term "browsing" clearly define what we do on the Internet? Instead of deep probing with conscious and unconscious reflection, we now settle for superficial, trivial, and seemingly ready-made answers. We are easily appeased.

In a wonderful analogy of this dilemma of rewired brains, Nicholas Carr quotes playwright Richard Foreman, who offers a succinct, vivid, and wonderful image of our society as spread thin by describing us a pancake people.[10] In another analogy, we might say we used to approached life as a school essay question. It required research and constructed arguments that were organized and compiled. Finally, one offered a viable coherent conclusion. Today, instead of molding a complex essay, we often settle for simple true and false tests. Likewise, we prefer multiple choice, where the answer beckons a good guess. Our chosen goal is to complete the task as quickly as possible. To give deep thought or consideration is not an objective. Yet even at the end of the simple test, we have an emotional rush that reinforces the notion that we accomplished something. Sadly, we value emotional appeasement more than the test, never mind constructing a valuable life essay.

Historically, we used to read and think to gain detailed information. We would distill and filter this information to make good and wise decisions. Then after some useful, ponderous reflection, we made what we hoped was an excellent choice. Likewise, we were open to hearing information contrary to our views to help us create a more well-rounded and viable position. Today, we skim data on the web (which is often tailored to our personalized algorithms) and we jump to conclusions and results so that we can move on to the next pressing and more immediate issue! Instead of reading news items on the web, we scan the bullet points. Instead of using several news sources, we often use the ones suited to our predisposed ideas. Since we utilize the Internet in this manner, it seems that brain rewiring is alive. To what degree the Internet is changing us, however, is a significant question. Is this rewiring affecting spiritually? What do you think?

Another way our brain and spirituality are morphing is that we no longer date the next-door girl or boy. In the past, restricted by geography, income, and our agricultural roots, we likely dated a person we'd known for most of our lives. Today, we don't afford ourselves the same time to learn about the other. With a larger field to draw upon, we tend to marry someone we met just a few years ago. At the extremes in the postmodern reality, we succumb to speed dating, where we talk to a variety of potential partners for just a few timed minutes. Instead of looking for a lifelong partner, we may shop for a mate with no goal in mind except a short-term sexual experience. Nowadays, online dating is a massive billion-dollar industry that uses algorithms to pre-select compatible mates:

> ...The biggest change in dating between 2004 and 2014 was that one-third of all marriages in America began with online relationships, compared to a fraction of that in the decade before. Half of these marriages began on dating sites, the rest via social media, chat rooms, instant messages, and the like. In 1995, it was still so rare for a marriage to have begun online that newspapers would report it, breathlessly, as something weirdly futuristic and kind of freakish ... This behavioral change isn't so much because the Internet itself or the dating options have changed; it's because the population of Internet users has changed. Online dating used to be stigmatized as a creepier extension of the somewhat seedy world of 1960s and 1970s personal ads—the last online dating became irrelevant as a new generation of users emerged for whom online contact was already well know, respectable, and established. And, like fax machines and e-mail, the system works only when a large number of people use it. This started to occur around 1999–2000. By 2014, twenty years after the introduction of online dating, younger users have a higher probability of embracing it because they have been active users of the Internet since they were little children, for education, shopping, entertainment, games, socializing, looking for a job, getting news and gossip, watching videos, and listening to music ... Asynchrony allows both parties to gather their thoughts in their own time before responding, and thus to present their best selves without all of the pressure and anxiety that occurs in synchronous real-time interactions. Have you ever left a conversation only to realize hours later the thing you wish you had said? Online dating solves that ...[11]

While a whimsical exaggeration or a flippant image, we might say that in the past we rejoiced with those who celebrated 50 years of marriage. Now the focus seems to be on those who successfully enjoyed a 50-second speed date! We've moved from 50 years of dedicated marriage to one-night "hook-ups." Does this shift from commitment to momentary gratification not affect one's spiritual self and one's brain? What do you think?

We also read and digest information differently than in the past. Mull over the following comment:

> Today the real question is not what technology *does for us* but what technology *does to us* i.e. to our ways of thinking and to our sense of being human ... It has also been seen that a growing number of contemporary media theorists and cultural critics are concerned about what they perceive to be the *rewiring of the human brain*.[12]

Without question, the Internet made changes to how we read, write, date, etc. For example, what has happened to common punctuation such as semi-colons, capital letters, and sentence structure because rewired brains speak before they think? We text short messages and dread making long comments with good sentence structure. How have our "evolving" brains affected relationships that are vastly different from previous generations? Yours, mine, and ours is a postmodern reality. The Internet fundamentally changed how we date, form, and uphold relationships. As the above quote tells us, we often seem to focus on what postmodern technology is *doing for us* with little reflection or attention to what it *is doing to us*. We have radical new approaches to making "informed decisions."[13]

Throughout our postmodern lives, we spend our days making more informed decisions than any previous generation. This is for several reasons. Simply put, we face more information, complex issues, and questions requiring resolution than in the past. From our origins, the act of making informed decisions has been an integral part of the human condition. However, in postmodernism, this became more complicated and multifaceted. The following example truly illustrates this plight (or benefit?) befalling Western society:

... In 1976, the average supermarket stocked 9,000 unique products; today that number has ballooned to 40,000 of them, yet the average person gets 80%-85% of their needs in only 150 different supermarket items. That means that we need to ignore 39,850 items in the store. And that's just supermarkets—it's been estimated that there are over one million products in the United States today (based on SKUs, or stock-keeping units, those little bar codes on things we buy).

All this ignoring and deciding comes with a cost. Neuroscientists have discovered that unproductivity and loss of drive can result from decision overload. Although most of us have no trouble ranking the importance of decisions if asked to do so, our brains don't automatically do this.[14]

Unlike in the past, in postmodernism, we have more multiple choices on more questions than at any other time in history. We are often overwhelmed. As a result, our brain filters and reduces our choices to previously known patterns. Given our conditioning, we also make many quick, spontaneous decisions. I wonder how many of our daily decisions receive thoughtful reflection. In the past, we maybe faced four choices, and we took time to evaluate the merits of each choice. Now we can be faced with four hundred choices. It's impossible to process and consider this volume. Consequently, our brain uses algorithms to reduce the choices to a few recognized or similar options. Since we're confronted with many decisions, we typically allot little time to our decision, and we don't fully evaluate the merits of the decision we just made. In turn, when significant decisions are before us, we may lack the skills to deeply reflect and make a decision because the process of spiritual reflection has mummified! What do you think? Try to take more than a few moments to ponder this before you make a decision (he asked with a satirical grin!).

The evidence is clear: in our postmodern environment, the Internet reshaped and rewired how we make informed decisions, how we shop, how we date, and how we begin or end relationships. It changed how we read and how we think. If our brains and habits are transformed, we must assume that our spiritual lives also experienced a transformation. In our *Brave New World*, can we, like Dorothy Gale in *The Wizard of Oz*, metaphorically wonder if we are in Kansas anymore? Like Dorothy, how do we meet and interact with our own Tin Man? How can we in the postmodern reformation acknowledge, energize, and begin to re-utilize our spirituality and brains?

With the knowledge explosion, it's not surprising to find Western society looking for connections between spirituality and brain chemicals.[15] Some research suggests that there are true connections. Likewise, others believe this field is mostly speculative. Some even call the rising field of study between the brain (and/or brain chemicals) and religion and spirituality "neurotheology." In 2014, philosopher Alireza Sayadmansour wrote that:

> ... scholars in this field, strive up front to explain the neurological ground for spiritual experiences such as "perception that time, fear or self-consciousness have dissolved spiritual awe; oneness with the universe ... Ultimately, neurotheology must be considered as multidisciplinary study that requires substantial integration of divergent field."[16]

If this is true, we no longer live in Dorothy's Kansas. Four years after Sayadmansour's definition, Jimmy Kyriacou wrote that he rejects extreme views supporting or denying a relationship between spirituality and the brain. In seeking a realistic perspective and balance, he wrote:

> Firstly, the term "neurotheology" is often used interchangeably with the term "spiritual neuroscience". Secondly, neurotheology studies *correlations* between neural phenomena. i.e. brain processes, with subjective experiences of spirituality. Thirdly, we have the claim that there is a neurological and evolutionary basis for these experiences. It is in this third area that most of the controversy arises.[17]

Kyriacou, a South African lawyer who was once an Advocate of the Supreme Court of South Africa, also holds a graduate degree in spirituality. In writing about neurotheology, he said that a few years ago only a few people considered it a topic of interest, but that is now changing. He noted that this field of study owes its foundation to Andrew Newberg. Kyriacou wrote:

> Researcher Andrew Newberg represents perhaps the most balanced treatment of the topic we will encounter. Without seeking to prove or "explain away" the content of religious and spiritual experiences, his work represents an attempt to describe what is going on in the brain when such experiences are taking place.[18]

Newberg is a medical doctor in Philadelphia with an extensive background in radiology, emergency medicine, and psychology. He's the director of the Marcus Institute of Integrative Health. He founded this institute so medical doctors could treat patients' wholeness—body, mind, and spirit. Much of Newberg's success and ongoing research originated with the warm reception of his 2010 book, *How God Changes Your Brain: Breakthrough Findings from a Leading Neuroscientist*. It garnered much respect and attention for how it dealt with the context, process, and content of spirituality and the brain. Without question, it stimulated extensive further investigation by Newberg and others. In this early fundamental benchmark book, Newberg stated:

> ... Our research has led us to the following conclusions:
>
> 1. Each part of the brain constructs a different perception of God.
> Every human brain assembles its perceptions of God in uniquely different ways, thus giving God different qualities of meaning and value.
> Spiritual practices, even when stripped of religious beliefs, enhance the neural functioning of the brain in ways that improve physical and emotional health. Intense, long-term contemplation of God and other spiritual values appears to permanently change the structure of those parts of the brain

that control our moods, give rise to our conscious notions
of self, and shape our sensory perceptions of the world.

Contemplative practices strengthen a specific neurological circuit that
generates peacefulness, social awareness, and compassion for others.[19]

Throughout this judicious and well-presented book, Newberg makes
numerous references to the benefits of meditation on spirituality and brain
health.[20] He also states that "The serotonin released during meditation
may also be responsible for the enhanced visual imagery and sensory
experiences often reported during intense spiritual practice ..."[21] His
research also interestingly declares that yawning is a healthy activity!
Seriously. He wrote:

> So what is the underlying mechanism that makes yawning
> such an essential tool? Besides activating the precuneus, it
> regulates the temperature and metabolism of your brain.
> It takes a lot of neural energy to stay consciously alert, and
> as you work your way up the evolutionary ladder, brains
> become less energy efficient. Yawning probably evolved as
> a way to cool down the overly active mammalian brain,
> especially in the areas of the frontal lobe. Some have
> even argued that it is a primitive form of empathy. Most
> vertebrates yawn, but it is only contagious among humans,
> great apes, macaque monkeys, and chimpanzees.[22]

(You may yawn at this point, but not too long). To feed, enhance,
and stimulate our brain and spirituality, reflect upon the eight activities
Newberg suggests we need for spiritual aliveness. He says we should smile,
stay intellectually active, consciously relax, yawn, meditate, undertake
aerobic exercise, engage in dialogue with others, and have faith.[23]

The same year that Newberg published his book, Kevin Nelson, a
professor of neurology, published *The Spiritual Doorway in the Brain: A
Neurologist's Search for the God Experience*. This book is mostly devoted to
analyzing NDEs (near-death experiences). He attempts to decipher bonds
between spiritual awareness and the brain. This work didn't receive the

same reception as Newberg's. Apart from focusing upon an emerging area of study, much of the information seems rooted in anecdotal illustrations. Research seems based on these stories. Perhaps Nelson felt that the newness of the research needed stories to show how many people have experienced NDEs and can explain more NDE experiences than society realizes. Given the infancy of this branch of science and theology, we must declare that Nelson's thoughts, like Newberg's, may spark future investigations. In recent years, research into NDEs continues to acquire ever-increasing interest and attention, both from scientists and theologians.

In 2009, George Vaillant, an American psychiatrist and professor at Harvard Medical School, wrote *Spiritual Evolution: How We Are Wired for Faith, Hope, and Love*. In this work, he speaks of humanity's inherent spirituality. Instead of being a society focused on negative emotions, he champions the call to address positive human emotions—emotions that embrace our spiritual lives. He notes that not everyone shares that care:

> ... By 1990 modern science fully accepted the reality of emotion, but to many, positive emotions remained unmentionable. Consider that in 2004 the leading American text the *Comprehensive Textbook of Psychiatry*, half a million lines in length, devotes 100 to 600 lines each to shame, guilt, terrorism, anger, hate, and sin, thousands of lines to depression and anxiety, but only five lines to hope, one line to joy, and not a single line to faith, compassion, forgiveness, or love.[24]

In 1944, lyricist Johnny Mercer penned words saying that we need to "Ac-cent-tchu-ate the Positive." In postmodernism, Vaillant suggests it is vital to look for the positive. As the old song states, "You've got to accentuate the positive, eliminate the negative, and latch on to the affirmative." Vaillant supports this and notes how spirituality and one's brain make connections:

> Modern neuroscience, exemplified by brain imaging and neurochemistry, has shown us that our brain's most recently evolved centers, especially in our left neocortex,

mediate language, ideas, theology, scientific analysis—
and idiosyncratic religious belief. In contrast, our right
neocortex mediates music, emotion, symbols, and sense
of spiritual wholes. The same small area of the brain that
on the left interprets words, on the right interprets music.
Just as the musical score is linked to the verbal lyrics, just
so is emotion linked to science.[25]

Instead of looking at negative emotions and various controlling
doctrines and dogmas, Valliant contends that we need to look at positive
emotions and their connections. In recent decades, counseling approaches
began using models that support positive therapy! At the end of his
thought-provoking book, Valliant writes the following. It requires slow,
careful reading and absorption. In other words, read it and let it percolate
and filter within you. Then after a period of silence, re-assess its meaning.
In other words, "What do you deeply think of this invigorating opinion?"
Valliant wrote:

> ... religion arises from culture; spirituality arises
> from biology. Religion and cults are as different from
> spirituality as environment is from genes. Like culture
> and language, religious faith traditions bind us to our
> own community and isolate us from the communities of
> others. Like breathing, our spirituality is common to us
> all. On the one hand, religion asks us to learn from the
> experience of our tribe; spirituality urges us to savor our
> own experience. On the other hand, religion helps us to
> mistrust the experience of other tribes; spirituality helps
> us to regard the experience of the foreigner as valuable too.
> Over the short term, fear of strangers and xenophobia are
> social virtues. Over the long term, avoiding inbreeding by
> embracing strangers is genetic necessity.[26]

In 2016, Mike McHargue penned, *Finding God in the Waves: How
I Lost My Faith and Found It Again through Science*. While filled with

many anecdotal stories and accounts, this reflective work describes how by reading the Bible, he lost his faith. Then as an atheist and scientist, he found God and a spiritual life! In this fun to read, fluid book, he brings scientific insights to his story—and, perhaps, to our story. For example, he describes the importance of the brain because it uses 20% of our nutrients, and 25% of the oxygen as it cares for us.[27] He notes that there is no scientific consensus locating a "God-spot" in our brains.[28] However, there is something:

> In the brains of atheists, *God* is a noun, a noun no more real than *tooth fairy* or *unicorn*. But believers have a rich neurological network that encapsulates God through feelings and experiences that are difficult to articulate with mere language.[29]

Throughout the book, he describes his quest to find God and spiritual fulfillment. He notes that he discovered that despite much prayer and care, he was analyzing life instead of experiencing life. Do you do that? Take some time and honestly assess this for yourself! He said that while he was looking in the wrong places, and in the wrong way, God found him. McHargue describes how conversations with others paved the way, and God found him. He describes hearing and accepting that doubt is not the opposite of faith. He thanks one for sharing Brené Brown's (a sociologist and well-known author) images. He found that doubt and faith need each other for spiritual growth and life to take place.

This image of doubt is reminiscent of comments made by John Hull. In 1985, in *What Prevents Christian Adults from Learning?*, Hull wrote that doubt is part of the spiritual journey:

> When adults have doubts about their faith, they accuse themselves of being disloyal to it. Similarly, when adults have doubts about themselves, they can sometimes be nervous about learning more about religion in case this should lead to further loss of self. To learn would be to admit doubt, and thus to fail in loyalty. To learn something new about these valued objects of faith might mean that

one's own self-evaluation would undergo a change, and if the result of learning was to discredit the object of faith, the self-would similarly be devalued.[30]

When McHargue embraced doubt, he found joy and faith. Additionally, he says that hugs helped. His path back was "paved with grace by those who received my doubt in love."[31] For much of Western Christianity's history, doubt was denied. If one doubted, one lacked faith. It was a tool of power wielded and used by the church to keep people under control. Yet we now know that true faith, and true spirituality, embrace doubt. We need to tell our hearts and our brains that doubt is an essential part of our spiritual lives.

In his 2003 Penn State doctoral dissertation, Frank Milacci, quoting adult educator Tara Fenwick (2001), said, "Questioning, doubting, and dark introspection are not seen as a loss of faith, but accepted as part of the spiritual journey.[32] Eight years later, Brian McLaren, an author of many books on postmodern Christianity, wrote *Naked Spirituality: A Life with God in 12 Simple Words*. He quotes the well-known and influential hermit and writer Thomas Merton:

> The best way to pray is: stop. Let prayer pray within you, whether you know it or not. This means a deep awareness of our true inner identity. It implies a life of faith, but also of doubt. You can't have faith without doubt. Give up the business of suppressing doubt. Doubt and faith are two sides of the same thing. Faith will grow out of doubt, the real doubt. We don't pray right because we evade doubt. Thomas Merton[33]

While some churches in Western Christianity sadly like to portray doubt as a failure of faith, the truth is that by condemning people who have doubts, they're endeavoring to keep people into narrow, locked, predetermined concepts. Instead of assisting people to explore questions, these churches are only geared to give answers. Thinking and growth are restricted to programmed venues. In my view, Jesus helped his disciples and others explore doubts. Instead of the historical label of Doubting Thomas, we should see Thomas as one having questions, and when he sees the risen Jesus, he has his answer. Jesus didn't rebuke Thomas but added to the story by saying that others are going to experience joy because of His resurrection. Take the opportunity to consider this passage. Here is the story of Thomas from John 20:24–31 (CEB):

> Thomas, the one called *Didymus*, one of the Twelve, wasn't with the disciples when Jesus came. The other disciples told him, "We've seen the Lord!" But he replied, "Unless I see the nail marks in his hands, put my finger in the wounds left by the nails, and put my hand into his side, I won't believe." After eight days his disciples were again in a house and Thomas was with them. Even though the doors were locked, Jesus entered and stood among them. He said, "Peace be with you." Then he said to Thomas, "Put your finger here. Look at my hands. Put your hand into my side. No more disbelief. Believe!" Thomas responded to Jesus, "My Lord and my God!"[29] Jesus replied, "Do you believe because you see me? Happy are those who don't see and yet believe." Then Jesus did many other miraculous signs in his disciples' presence, signs that aren't recorded in this scroll. But these things are written so that you will believe that Jesus is the Christ, God's Son, and that believing, you will have life in his name.

In this story, Thomas is called *Didymus*, meaning "the twin." The other twin is never named, and the reason for this isn't explained. But in keeping with the biblical practice of sometimes using wordplay, we might say that Doubting Thomas was the twin to Faithful Thomas. While this image is a big stretch, and likely to provoke powerful non-positive emotion among many scholars and pseudo-scholars, it remains an image to ponder. What do you think of the idea of faith and doubt being two sides of the same coin? Jesus challenged people to think outside the box all the time. He challenged people to explore doubts, to take chances, to learn, and to grow.

We may or may not have a God-spot in our brain. In time, further research may shed light on this up-and-coming research topic. Mike McHargue's illustrative faith journey is similar to thousands of others. While the search continues to discover if we indeed have a God-spot, our brains already indicate we own God-pathways, and indeed spiritual pathways.

Historically throughout Western society and Western Christianity, people "were told" how to discover God in their hearts. In the prescribed manner given by church authorities, people followed the provided directions. The church said what the heart desired, and the brain (sometimes reluctantly) followed. Perhaps instead of the historical image of taking spirituality from our heart to our brain, we need to add the new image of taking spirituality from our brain to our hearts! As Parker Palmer wrote, "That is why the eleventh-century theologian St. Simeon described the deepest form of human knowing as the result of thinking with 'the mind descended into the heart.'"[34]

A well-accepted phrase says that "neurons that fire together are wired together." In other words, those who consistently pray, meditate, or follow a religious practice naturally create regular pathways, or streams, within their brain. Just as muscle memory in hands and feet work for pianists and organists, perhaps our brain works the same way in finding the spiritual that is within us. What do you think? It's interesting that a few years ago, Matthew Alper, a non-religious scientist, wrote:

> ... In the same way that planarians are "hardwired" to turn towards the light, humankind is "hardwired" to turn to a god or gods. Being that this impulse is cognitive in nature, it must originate from a part or parts of the brain. Consequently, there must exist specific neural connections from which our spiritual/religious cognitions, perceptions, sensations, and behaviors are generated. This would further suggest that should we sever or alter these neural connections, these "spiritual" parts of our brain, it would have a direct effect on one's spiritual consciousness.[35]

It seems that in being holy whole, we must weave our hearts, brains, and spirituality together. Professor of higher education Elizabeth Tisdell writes:

> It is interesting that wholeness, holiness, and health all have the same root: *hal,* "to be whole" (Sanford, 1977). The drive of spirituality is the drive to wholeness, to holiness, to health, and to making meaning of that wholeness. Fundamentally, this is what spirituality is about.[36]

It's critical to accept that "Spirituality is about wholeness. This point cannot be overemphasized. It is important to recognize the principle of an entirely seamless and interconnected reality that this entails."[37] Although referring to the world religions, the late Lionel Tiger, psychiatrist and neurophysiologist, and professor of anthropology Michael McGuire, could change the word "religion" to "spirituality," and thus to "spirituality and the brain." In 2010, their insightful book stated:

> Our proposal is that all religions differ but all share two destinies: they are the product of the human brain. They endure because of the strong influence of the product—religion—on brain function. The brain is a sturdy organ with common characteristics everywhere. A neurosurgeon can work confidently on a Vatican patient and another in Mecca. Same tissue, same mechanisms. And one such mechanism is a readiness to generate religions. Another is to respond positively and with conviction to what it has generated.[38]

Poetically, they style this as "Religion is to the brain what jogging is to the legs. It is a form of socioemotional and institutional exercise for the organ in our head."[39] If religion and spirituality are connected to our brains, and as we seek for a God-spot, let us acknowledge that God-pathways seem quite evident. They call this "brainsoothing!"

Let us conclude by considering a recent paper by the eminent Andrew Newberg. In 2017, he and six others publish a paper titled *Effect of a*

One-Week Spiritual Retreat on Dopamine and Serotonin Transporter Binding: A Preliminary Study. To the knowledge of the authors, no longitudinal studies of neurophysiological effects predate this study.[40] They note that many previous similar studies looked at the effects of meditation and brain imaging, yet the biological effects are thus far not truly examined.[41] While adopting a 30-day Ignatian retreat model to a short model, they used:

> single photon emission computed tomography (SPECT) imaging ... to measure changes in both dopamine transporter (DAT) and serotonin transporter (SERT) before and after subjects participated in the seven-day spiritual retreat. Given the psychological and spiritual changes anticipated, it was hypothesized that there would be significant changes in the dopamine and/or serotonin system.[42]

At the end of this well-documented journal article, the authors stated:

> This is the first study we are aware of that has attempted to measure changes in the dopamine and serotonin systems as the result of participating in an intensive seven-day retreat ... The findings, although preliminary, suggest that participating in a spiritual retreat can have a short-term impact on the brain's dopamine and serotonin function.[43]

In other words, they believe that spiritual practices truly affect brain chemicals. As valued scientists in a foundational research area, they believe that the evidence suggests a correlation between spiritual lives and the brain! They also yearn for future research. Nevertheless, it seems clear that the brain and its chemicals have connections to spirituality.[44] Furthermore, the human brain has spirituality flowing throughout it. What do you think of that budding image? Please imagine that spirituality is in your heart, not just your mind, and in your brain swimming around to feed you!

Questions to ponder and discuss
Chapter Five

Spirituality and the Brain

1 Does your heart tell your brain that doubt is needed in one's spiritual life?

2 Are our brains different in postmodernism than before postmodernism?

3 Are we hardwired to God, and are we hardwired to be spiritual?

4 How do you make well informed decisions?

5 Do you use "brainsoothing?" Perhaps you unconsciously do so. Think about it.

CHAPTER SIX

SPIRITUALITY AND MINDFULNESS

The emergence of spirituality from the overarching umbrella and shadow of religion in Western Christianity represents a transformative societal shift. Because of this, Western society was enabled to acknowledge and accepted the Eastern practice of mindfulness. In other words, mindfulness invaded some of the space that formerly belonged to Western Christianity. The materialization of mindfulness in postmodernism raised various questions for Western society: Is mindfulness the same as spirituality? Is mindfulness perhaps an element of spirituality? What are the differences between mindfulness and spirituality? These questions are important in trying to embrace postmodern spirituality in the Age of Entitlement.

The first question, "Is mindfulness the same as spirituality?", seems the logical and natural starting point. With the arrival of postmodernism, the subsequent decline of Western Christianity, and the reality of living in a global village, space opened up for conversations about mindfulness. We need to understand that what Christianity was to Western society, the Buddhist practice of mindfulness was to Eastern society. With the growth of secularism, along with the rise of "Me-ism," Western society felt free, or at least unencumbered, to consider Eastern spiritual practices such as mindfulness.

Given the centrality of individualism and personalized spirituality in Western society, the solitary practice of mindfulness seemed a natural fit.

With the many scandals that rocked Western Christianity, the quietness and tranquility of mindfulness became appealing. However, the question remains: Are spirituality and mindfulness the same? In 2016, the clinical psychologist Asimina Lazaridou, and Panagiotis Pentaris, a social work professor, offered a wonderful perspective:

> Spirituality and mindfulness have both been researched independently. Dearth of information let us void the strong links between the two, however. Spirituality is an experience of mindfulness, while mindfulness is practice to the spiritual ... Spiritual growth is the pattern for believing, whether that is religious belief or not, and mindfulness is a spiritual practice for becoming self-aware of that belief.[1]

Their definition seems to answer the first two questions. Mindfulness is not the same as spirituality. However, can we suggest it is a form of spiritual experience? Mindfulness is typically a private, personalized spiritual practice, whereas spirituality, despite its personalized forms, still tends to hold a broader social view.

With rampant "Me-ism," the time was ripe for mindfulness to take root and bloom in Western society. People were able to practice mindfulness while still considering other self-styled spiritual matters. As clinical psychologist Melissa Falb and her mentor, clinical psychologist and professor Kenneth Pargament, wrote, "Most mindfulness practices are solitary ones, carried out in silence. These practices clearly contribute to a range of positive effects ..."[2] Consequently, in the age of increasing "Me-ism" and personalized spirituality, the private, solitary act of mindfulness took off in Western society. In 2015, a British professor of education, and frequent author on Buddhist mindfulness and spirituality, Terry Hyland, wrote:

> An internet search on the concept of mindfulness retrieves around 18 million items and, in term of publications, numbers have grown from one or two in 1980 to around 400 per year in 2011 ...The growth of mindfulness publications has been exponential over the last few years.[3]

Naturally, given the historical tie Western society held to religion and spirituality, it's not surprising that in the early years of mindfulness, adjustments took place. Asimina Lazaridou and Panagiotis Pentaris describe this change:

> that often notions of spirituality overlap with religion and mindfulness. The latter appears to carry characteristics not so different from spirituality ... Mindfulness ... definitely employs a spiritual attitude towards the well-being of the individual.[4]

In other words, over time, mindfulness took on blended models in Western society. We might say that the Buddhist-centered concept of mindfulness became Westernized. We will explore this. First, we must explore the differences between mindfulness and spirituality.

In Chapter Three, we noted that Michael Sachs and William Bos found 92 definitions of spirituality. Without question, there are likely another 92 definitions! The broad and varied number of definitions is a clear indicator of postmodernism in Western society, as postmodernism is defined as having many centers. Mindfulness, however, tends to have few definitions. Perhaps this is because mindfulness is a specific spirituality. What are your thoughts? Leigh Burrows, who lectures on mindfulness, offers us comments on the thoughts of the early Western society adopter of mindfulness, Dr. Jon Kabat-Zinn: "In it most common form mindfulness has come to be associated with awareness and acceptance of present moment experience, with the aim of reducing an individual's stress and suffering."[5] Mindfulness is very much a spirituality rooted in the present and focused on positive thinking and reflection. Jean Twenge and W. Keith Campbell, in *The Narcissism Epidemic: Living in an Age of Uncertainty*, wrote that:

> Mindfulness, an outgrowth of traditional Buddhist practice, may also reduce narcissism and quiet the ego. Mindfulness is the awareness of the present moment—the thought, the feeling, and the physical experience—without negative judgment. This sounds simple but isn't.[6]

It's not a stretch to consider mindfulness as an excellent spiritual tool in addressing that greatest human question: "Who am I?"

We can trace the rise of mindfulness in Western society to the work of the aforementioned Jon Kabat-Zinn. He introduced mindfulness to the Massachusetts Medical School in 1979.[7] Armed with his doctorate in molecular biology, he began research on how body/mind interactions affect healing. Originally, this research dealt with those suffering from chronic pain or stress-related disorders, but it soon expanded into creating the tool Mindfulness-Based Stress Reduction (MSBR). Using this tool of mindfulness, he assisted the aforementioned people, along with those suffering from breast or prostate cancer. Later research papers note how these efforts were expanded and explored with those in prison, the corrections staff, and a variety of other settings. This tool led the way for the development of other mindfulness-directed resources. Look at Appendix D for further examples!

In recent decades, given the natural inquisitive nature of Western society, research into the application of mindfulness increased. But before looking at how Western society co-opted mindfulness, we must acknowledge its meaning in its pure, original Eastern Buddhist-centered origins:

> Mindfulness simply means "paying attention in any particular way: on purpose, in the present moment and non-judgmentally" in a way which "nurtures greater awareness, clarity and acceptance of present-moment reality."[8]

This is a good, full, and well-rounded definition of mindfulness. Yet, as noted, Western society enhanced and expanded this reality. A 2013 academic journal article by Leigh Burrows notes this progression:

> Mindfulness can however also be understood as "a spiritual awareness that is embodied and feelinful" (Stanley 2012 page 631). This relates to the North American medicine wheel teachings (Bopp et al, 1984) where spirituality is

seen to include being passionately involved in the world, compassion, anger at injustice, the refinement of feelings, empathy and the ability to set strong emotions aside to serve others.[9]

When Buddhism-mindfulness entered Western society, some of the initial leaders were nervous and leery. They wondered if it would gain acceptance. This was because of the lack of God-focused images. They were concerned that the inherent secularism of Buddhism would rub traditional Western Christianity the wrong way.[10] Whereas Western society (and Western Christianity) was external and God-focused, the Buddhist practice of mindfulness focused on inner-consciousness and reflection. In a phrase, until some postmodern thinking entered the scene, Western Christianity typically portrayed God as looking down on humanity. In turn, humanity looked up and reached out to God, striving to appease "him". Mindfulness, however, is quite different. Mindfulness is internal thinking, calling for reflection to enhance what exists and refine it. We might say that mindfulness is an internal audit! Additionally, Western Christianity with the predominant fall-redemption theology of good and evil, sin, punishment, and then reward, runs counter to the context of mindfulness, which "is defined as paying attention on purpose, in the present moment and, non-judgmentally ..."[11]

The subtle but ever continuous shift in postmodern Western society's secular-centered spirituality blunted the anticipated backlash of confrontation between pious Western Christianity and the emerging reception of mindfulness. Beginning with academic venues, mindfulness slowly gained acceptance. Naturally, among the first to embrace mindfulness were non-religious or semi-religious groups.[12] Western society historically used religion and spirituality to assist people in their lives and to earn their way into heaven! Mindfulness asks people to undertake positive inner self-discovery and to assist in self-healing.[13] Today, given the Western mind to develop analytic tools, many mindfulness tools or measurement programs exist. Again, consider looking for some examples in Appendix D.

Throughout history, societies constantly adopt and adapt to what is taking place around them. For example, Christianity took the Jewish

Passover and adopted this feast to be their principal and central act of worship, the Holy Eucharist, or Holy Communion, or the "love feast." Early Christianity took a pagan winter Roman celebration and turned it into Christmas. The practice of adopting and adapting religious rituals and spiritual practices continues. For example, we are adopting workplace mindfulness practices, and indeed much mindfulness in our post-Christian secular society. Perhaps the most extensively researched and used area of mindfulness is in the field of education.[14] What is your opinion of this new postmodern reality? In your view, how are these innovations addressing spirituality? You can Google and read the academic and various articles on mindfulness and associated topics yourself!

Before leaving the topic of mindfulness and spirituality, let us briefly explore mindfulness and education. This may heighten your overall inquisitiveness of the postmodern development of mindfulness in Western society. I first became aware of mindfulness in education when I read a news article some years ago. It was about elementary students asking if they could practice mindfulness instead of serving detentions. I recall that the students desired this practice to be part of their routine. It's essential and critical for child development for children to experience positive reinforcement and support. Mindfulness is healthier and more effective than the historical practice of giving punitive consequences.

In 2015, a wonderful and insightful article, published in the journal *Psychology*, began by saying:

> Mindfulness is also a burgeoning area of academic interest. Research investigating the phenomenon commenced in the early 1980s and by the close of 2012 there were approximately 2500 journal articles on the topic (Black, 2014). Due, in part, to positive findings in adult populations, mindfulness programs have been implemented in schools around the world (Albrecht, 2014) and there are now a substantial number of studies reporting on how mindfulness programs impact school communities (Albrecht, 2014; Burke, 2010; Harnett & Dawe, 2012; Shapiro et al., 2014).

Studies to date have predominately been outcome-based, with less focus on in-depth explorations using qualitative methodologies. In particular, there has been minimal research examining how young children (five to 12 years old) perceive the practice. It has been suggested that there is a critical need to explore this growing field of educational practice by using qualitative research methods (Roeser, Skinner, Beers, & Jennings, 2012). This gap in the field inspired the current research study, which focuses on understanding elementary school students' perspectives of learning mindfulness for the first time in an independent school located in New Zealand. The following research question was posed: What are students' perspectives of learning mindfulness practices at school?[15]

This well-researched and extensive examination of elementary school children and mindfulness, with its broad approach, is an excellent read. At the end of their thoughtful paper, the authors conclude with a long but very insightful analysis worth reflection:

> Findings indicate that there is value in the integration of mindfulness practice across student populations within the elementary school, and early learning settings. It may be important to start the program with teachers who already have an established mind body wellness, or mindfulness practice, or who are interested in participating in the program. Mindfulness practice also needs to include classroom teachers-not just counselors.
>
> Effective implementation of mindfulness practice should have flexibility and enable teachers and students to trust their intuition and to go with the flow. Further research is recommended to assess the affects on students of an ongoing application of mindful awareness, intention and presence techniques, and how mindfulness practices help to nourish and sustain student wellbeing.
>
> It is suggested that elementary student wellbeing be gauged on a regular and timely basis. Simple smiley face self-appraisal rubrics could help to capture the

student's voice, and measure student thoughts and feelings immediately after mindfulness activities; and student wellness throughout the academic year. Such self-evaluations may also serve as a personal wellbeing index for the children and are recommended for further research. Additional studies on how to measure the long-term benefits of mindfulness on student wellness are also recommended.

Conclusion

Mindfulness benefits the whole child—the mind, body and emotions and research suggests that mindfulness can affect academic performance, executive functioning, and feelings of connectedness with self, others and the environment. Mindfulness programs such as "Meditation Capsules" can positively impact the wellbeing of student populations in schools. The Meditation Capsules program has been shown to reduce stress, support the development of core character traits such as empathy and awareness of self, others, and the environment, and improve the happiness and wellbeing of students. It may also help to move individuals towards higher levels of wellness, to focus the attention of both the mind and body, and to assist with conflict resolution.[16]

I hope you take a few slow moments to re-read those words! Evidently, by practicing mindfulness, students experienced a sense of wholeness that was lacking before in their lives. Look at Appendix E to see a list of some of the extensive research into mindfulness as it pertains to students, teachers, and administrators.

In postmodern Western society, much mindfulness research originated with schoolchildren and youth. This research likely evolved from many schools embracing mindfulness because of the vast societal (and bodily) changes influencing adolescents – in other words, changes that needed caring attention. School students in postmodernism (even before COVID) face untold stress that didn't exist before. Students are expected to succeed ahead of all other tasks. To rephrase this, it means that getting straight "As" is much more valuable than students answering the pivotal "Who am I?" question. With the decline of much of our historic social fabric, schools seem to be expected to do more than teach academics. They now make effort to help students with emotional issues.[17] Because of dysfunctional families, societal and peer influences, overextended parent(s), and various other pressures, we can boldly state that students consciously or unconsciously see their school as a surrogate family.

Schools at all levels in postmodern Western society deal with a myriad of emotional and family issues. While private and systematic valiant efforts to care for students surround us, many realize that besides offering reactive assistance, such as counseling, it would be useful to provide students with proactive tools and guides. Schools now use mindfulness programs such as "Learning to BREATHE."[18] In 2015, Karen Ager, Nicole Albrecht, and Marc Cohen wrote that besides typical academic, outcome-based research, there was a lack of truly "listening to children's voices."[19] Schools use mindfulness to address many student needs such as stress.[20] Clearly, deep listening is also needed – especially if it doesn't take place at home. In 2016, the aforementioned Nicole Albrecht completed her Doctor of Philosophy degree with an extensive thesis based on school children and mindfulness. In her conclusion, she offers a fitting example of mindfulness and children:

> The findings from this study suggest that mainstream education is experiencing a paradigm shift. Practices that inspire a deep level of awareness, introspection and insight are inspiring and guiding the way teachers think, act and feel all over the world. I believe the motivation to teach children mindfulness originates from a need to create harmony—harmony within the individual, within the classroom, within the school, within society and the planet as a whole. Harmony is particularly critical at this moment in time as we live in a world in which the capacity to prevent conflicts and to resolve them in a timely fashion is practically nonexistent (UN Commissioner Guterres,

2015, as cited in Kitney, 2015, p. 46). Nourishing the seeds of wisdom and compassion and encouraging a mindful way of being to grow and thrive from an early age is one way peaceful individuals are trying to stem the tide of conflict.[21]

It's abundantly clear that the field of mindfulness and students is expanding to address broader and varied issues facing the postmodern student. In 2008, a published paper cited how mindfulness meditation "contributed to decrease anxiety an enhanced social skill and academic performance" among adolescents with learning disabilities."[22] It seems that though schools face immense pressure for students to be successful, mindfulness counters school and societal stress by allowing and encouraging students to explore, "Who am I?" Despite much deep resistance, evidence is mounting about the value for students of all ages to take part in mindfulness exercises.[23]

As with any new innovative endeavor, some research gives glowing reports of accomplishments, while others have mixed reviews or are inconclusive. Over time, the refinement of research practices, analysis, and experiences mold more complete and well-rounded mindfulness programs. In other words, over time, mindfulness within schools and elsewhere in Western society will continue to gain acceptance. There are even magazines devoted to mindfulness, such as *Mindful* and *Breathe*, and many other magazines have contained articles on mindfulness. If so inclined, Google this for yourself. With increased positive results and public acceptance, mindfulness has largely lost its stigma as an Eastern religion and is now considered a Western spiritual tool.

Since mindfulness is devoted to self-healing and mental rest, it seems a natural fit in the "Me-ism" world and society we reside in. One question, however, remains: How will postmodern Western "Me-ism" redefine mindfulness as it did Western Christianity and Western Spirituality? What are your thoughts?

Here is a few of my thoughts on that question. Mindfulness is truly a much-sought spiritual practice for various levels of schooling. This is great. It has established firm roots in Western society. This too is beneficial. However, this eastern Buddhist practice of inwardness has undergone Westernization. Like countless societies before some retooling took place in the new society. Just as Christianity adopted and reformed Jewish rituals and Roman holidays, our postmodern Western society has remolded mindfulness. This has displeased some who call these nuanced reforms McMindfulness.[24] Dr. Terry Hyland, an adult education professor in the United Kingdom and Buddhist has published much on mindfulness and Buddhist practices. Among his writings, he noted how Western society took mindfulness and subjected to McDonaldization. The result he called McMindfulness. In 2017, in the *Journal of Transformative Education,* he wrote:

> The reductionist, commodified forms of mindfulness practice – popularly known as McMindfulness – have been brought about by a number of processes operating within academia and the public socio-economic sphere. In the academic sphere, mindfulness has been taken up most energetically by psychologists, psychotherapists and educators, and … acknowledging the 'challenging circumstances relating to the major cultural and epistemological shifts' as Buddhist meditation was introduced into clinical and psychological settings, Kabat-Zinn (2015) has latterly acknowledged that there are 'opportunistic elements' for whom 'mindfulness has become a business.[25]

Hyland is not convinced that the reworked models are well construed and of much use in schools.[26] He isn't the only one worried about Westernized mindfulness. Among others, Ronald Purser a Professor of Management at San Francisco State University, and an ordained Buddhist teacher wrote, *McMindfulness: How Mindfulness Became the New Capitalist Spirituality* where he eloquently notes how consumerism and capitalism took over mindfulness. This matches the situation where consumerism and capitalism took over Western Christianity. Consequently, while it is important that we look at mindfulness in postmodernism we need to be conscious of the sources we use!

Questions to ponder and discuss
Chapter Six

Spirituality and Mindfulness

❶ How are mindfulness and spirituality the same? How are they different?

❷ The original purpose of mindfulness in Western society was geared to reduce stress and suffering. How did it evolve?

❸ There is a growing trend to use mindfulness in schools as a replacement for punitive detentions. What are your thoughts? Should this be expanded and encouraged?

❹ Some see mindfulness as an Eastern spiritual tool overtaking Western Spirituality. Take time and contemplate that notion.

CHAPTER SEVEN

SPIRITUALITY AND ISSUES OF LONELINESS ...

E ach year the Great Ormand Street Hospital in London, England receives undisclosed income from the royalties of J.M. Barrie's 1904 play, *The Boy Who Wouldn't Grow Up.* Most of us know the play and its later adaptations as *Peter Pan.* It's the well-known story of a boy in Neverland who loses his shadow, and he can't grow up until he finds it. Historically in literature, shadows often represent the past, or darkness. However, in this case, I think it means something very different. The shadow is neither pointing to his past nor is it dark. In one scene the shadow and Peter Pan are playful. Early in the play, before the shadow is lost, Peter and his shadow dance. Moreover, instead of pointing to the past, it guides Peter towards his future. Peter Pan's shadow is his soul, and until he understands and embraces his soul, he is stuck!

Peter and his shadow complement each other. They need each other to be complete. Throughout the story, Peter's friendship with Wendy, the eldest of the Darling children, enlivens him to try more fully to understand who he is. Consequently, when Peter is still and quiet, Wendy "sews" the shadow back on. She helps Peter heal and find his soul. In turn, Peter is finally able to engage in life. He can now grow up, and in time, face adult issues. Peter Pan's shadow represents Peter taking stock of his life. We might say he faced part of himself that he didn't want to face. Nevertheless, in doing so, he restored himself to wholeness. Peter became "holy whole." What about you? Are you whole? Do you face uncomfortable parts of your life? Like many postmodern people, are you so focused on moving forward that the thought of being still or taking stock of life seems unfathomable? Do you think and feel that you are wholly whole? Do you deny or dislodge this reality of your life? Do you fall into the trap of denying the denial? Likewise, do you consider yourself holy? What is your shadow? Hmm, think about that idea!

Postmodern people often seem incapable of silence or solitude. Truly, how can we be silent, reflective, or embrace solitude if we never turn ourselves off from noise? Today, our smartphones never leave our hands. Perhaps you've heard that texting while driving is now considered the cause of more traffic accidents than impaired driving.[1] If we're not connected in some way, we assume that something is wrong.

In the postmodern Western society, we may be addicted to playing one of the millions of online games. We may play a game alone or with others in a multiplayer game. We might even be playing with a "friend" in a foreign land, whose only contact with us is through a specific game. We could be on the phone talking. On the other hand, we may be exploring various social media postings or adding to our story with pictures of last night's dinner for the fifth time this week. Today, it seems that everyone crossing the street gives more attention to the phone than safely walking!

If we're constantly involved with our phones, computers, online social media, or older media such as television or radio, when do we have time for silence, stillness, and solitude? If noise surrounds us, can we appreciate silence? When are we ever still? Can we truly value or grasp solitude or serenity? Do you ever take time, and I mean more than a few seconds or minutes, to engage fully in silence, stillness, solitude, and serenity?

If loneliness isn't the greatest, it's at least one of the most prolific diseases of our time. This disease is so rampant that the British government created a cabinet-level department to address and combat loneliness! Without question, the Coronavirus increased isolation and loneliness, and it calls us to connect remotely with others. The isolation imposed (encouraged) for all societies during the crisis resulted in a great increases in mental illnesses. Those with issues became worse, and those bordering on mental illness often crossed over. Consider how isolation in some way led to more domestic violence, family and mass community shootings. But I wonder how many used this opportunity to embrace or try silence, stillness, solitude, and serenity.

Perhaps we spend so much time on our phones to avoid facing ourselves and pretending we aren't lonely. Do you think we avoid being still with ourselves? Do you use the addictive phone to avoid inner silence? If this is so, to what degree? Likewise, are we even aware that we are lonely? Or have we drifted so far from these spiritual attributes that we have difficulty identifying, never mind using, them as part of wholeness? Perhaps we live in a time when we're so immersed in looking at our phones that we've stopped looking around, seeing, and engaging our shadows. Heck, have you noticed that at family meals at restaurants, many people, if not all of them, are too busy on the phone to even notice those around them? Where can we be alive and proclaim, "Me and My Shadow" as we stroll down the avenue?

While we may call postmodernism the Age of Entitlement, or Bewilderment, or the Digital Age, some astutely call it the Age of Entertainment! We reduce news to short, palatable sound bytes that invade us 24/7. It seems that sports are never-ending, and we now can stream almost any show we want, when we want, and do this almost anywhere. Maybe given the lack of inner understanding, and the longing to be entertained, we might also call postmodernism the Age of Distraction. After all, much suggests that our attention spans are getting shorter! Overall, it seems that we have many obstacles or barriers inhibiting us from stillness and being fully alive.

To become fully alive, like Peter Pan, and to avoid loneliness, means becoming engaged with ourselves. To be fully alive on the outside, to one's family and friends, one's community and the world, requires us to be fully alive on the inside. Truly, if we're not fully alive on the inside, we can never be fully alive on the outside. In other words, if not living with inner peace, all we show the world is a façade. We become like those iconic Greek masks actors held over their faces to show tragedy and comedy, but we don't show the human range of real emotions—like loneliness.

To be fully alive means embracing our shadow, our soul, and our spirituality. This effort requires us to explore a sense of stillness, serenity, and solitude. Much also suggests that we must learn to surrender. When we can take these explorations and understand "Who am I," we break free of the postmodern dilemma of shallowness and discover a full, robust life and a deep sense of true spiritual well-being. To delve into the need for solitude, stillness, serenity, and surrender for good spiritual health, we need to observe the postmodern barriers of noise and loneliness. We begin by considering one of the great distractions of our times—noise.

One important postmodern obstacle to silence and solitude is talking. You are probably aware of this quotation often attributed to Stephen Covey: "Most people do not listen with the intent to understand; they listen with the intent to reply." In other words, we're so intent on our opinions and listening to the sound of our voice that we've forgotten how to listen to others. Not only do we not listen deeply, but the listening, at best, is superficial. Perhaps it's sadder to realize that in postmodernism, we have forgotten to listen to ourselves! Renown adult educator Parker Palmer reportedly stated that we sorely need to learn silence. This is difficult in our noisy world and noisy lives. Have we forgotten what silence is? We need to learn to be quiet, "So silence can speak." Other famous writers and deep thinkers echo this image:

Silence is the language God speaks, and everything else is a bad translation.

Thomas Keating

Silence is the language of God; it is also the language of the heart.

Dag Hammarskjöld

Real action is done in moments of silence.

Emerson

All of humanity's problems stem from man's inability to sit quietly in a room alone.

Blaise Pascal, in his work *Pensées*

These short, insightful, yet powerful quotations speak volumes. Others provided more detailed thoughts about silence, noise, and spirituality. In *The Rule of Benedict: Spirituality for the 21st Century,* Joan Chittister states:

> We live with noise pollution now and find silence a great burden, a frightening possibility. Muzak fills our elevators and earbuds wire us to MP3 files and TVs blare from every room in the house from morning till night. We say we do not have the time to think, but what we actually lack is the quiet to think. Yet, until we are able to have at least a little silence every day, both outside and in, both inside and out, we have no hope of coming to know either God or ourselves very well.[2]

To more fully embrace these thoughts on stillness, serenity, solitude, loneliness, and silence, it's of value to read these long and short quotes several times. Take time and slowly ponder their meaning. By undertaking this effort, one more deeply considers thoughts on these topics and moves further into oneself. In other words, by taking ownership of these quotations and thoughts, one enhances self-understanding—an understanding of your spirituality.

In a 1994 book on the role and place of spiritual leadership in the workplace, we find a striking image suggesting how we might move from noise to the gift of silence and spirituality.

> Silence is more than refraining from noise; it is the inner silence that allows us to reflect on the higher purpose, to question our decisions in the light of that purpose, and to seek strength not to betray it. It allows us to listen to the inner stirrings of the spirit. It is critical for making distinctions—between right and wrong, to discern what we ought to do. In a parable from Kenneth Blanchard and Norman Vincent Peale's *The Power of Ethical Management,* the mentor of a manager facing an ethical dilemma comments: "I am continually amazed at how

clear my thinking becomes afterward, particularly if I'm faced with a big problem. It's as if the answer I am seeking exists somewhere already, just waiting for me to tune in to it. The solitude, quiet, and reflection are the tuning-in process."[3]

A 2005 research project about adolescent students found that in terms of spiritual development, the next highest question after the great "Who Am I" question concerns longing for solitude and silence.[4] Silence breeds silence, and it circulates in a circle of constant development. A contemporary religious reflector of the church in the age of postmodernism, Brian McLaren, describes this beautifully:

> ... I don't know if this story about Mother Teresa is true or not, but it tells the truth whether or not it happened. Mother Teresa was asked by a reporter what she said to God when she prayed. She replied, "Mostly I just listen." The reporter then asked what God said to her. "Mostly he just listens," she replied. Could it be that the loving, attentive, mutual listening of the soul and the Spirit constitute the greatest expression of spirituality?[5]

Silence means listening. Earlier we quoted the ancient writing of 1 Kings 19:12, and it bears repeating: "And after the earthquake a fire, but the Lord was not in the fire; and after the fire a sound of sheer silence." Earlier we noted that this 2,600-year-old image captures much that is missing in postmodernism. It refers to God as being in the "still, small voice." Other translations are perhaps more accurate when they state *"God was in the sound of sheer silence."* Like the prophet Elijah in that story, we too can find answers to perplexing issues when we move into silence and stillness. Silence and stillness mean more than avoiding noise or bombarding distractions. It's an intentional movement inward. It's a spiritual movement to seek clarity.

Silence, solitude, and stillness are noble ideals. However, the reality of our noisy, easily distracted culture of shallow lives represents a difficulty we must overcome as we try to experience entering into silence, embracing solitude, and discovering quietness. If it's hard to enter into these spiritual practices, it's even harder to be disciplined and make them part of one's being. In other words, it's a monumental task to journey inward to know oneself. As the poet Pablo Neruda said, "Perhaps a huge silence might interrupt this sadness of never understanding ourselves, and with threatening ourselves with death."[6] This image is reiterated by Parker Palmer, who wrote:

> Contemporary images of what it means to be spiritual tend to value the inward search over the outward act, silence over sound, solitude over interaction, centeredness and quietude and balance over engagement and animation and struggle. If one is called monastic life, those images can be empowering. But if one is called to the world of action, the same images can disenfranchise the soul, for they tend to devalue the energies of active life rather than encourage us to move with those energies toward wholeness.[7]

Likewise, R. Scott Smith, a professor of ethics and moral knowledge in California, in 2005 wrote another insightful image to ponder:

> Silence is a catalyst of solitude; it prepares the way for inner seclusion and enables us to listen to the quiet voice of the Spirit. Few of us have experienced silence, and most people find it to be uncomfortable at first. Silence is at odds with the din of our culture and the popular addiction to noise and hubbub. This discipline relates not only to finding places of silence in our surroundings but also to times of restricted speech in the presence of others.[8]

These authors skillfully state that to make the effort to enter into solitude means facing one's loneliness. Noted theologian Henri Nouwen, who left tenured academic life to live in a L'Arche community of differently-abled adults, once wrote:

> ... the spiritual life is that constant movement between the
> poles of loneliness and solitude, hostility and hospitality,
> illusion and prayer. The more we come to the painful
> confession of our loneliness, hostilities and illusions, the
> more we are able to see solitude, hospitality and prayer as
> part of the vision of our life.[9]

One of the greatest social diseases in Western society is loneliness. To move fully into stillness, solitude, and inner serenity suggests that we must come to terms with loneliness. Laura Beres, a social worker with many publications to her name on mindfulness, spirituality, and critical reflection, attended an Anglican convent while completing her doctorate. While there, she read a reader on Henri Nouwen:

> Instead of running away from our loneliness and trying
> to forget or deny it, we have to protect it and turn it into a
> fruitful solitude. To live a spiritual life we must first find
> the courage to enter into the desert of our loneliness and
> to change it by gentle and persistent efforts into a garden
> of solitude.[10]

Truly, we need to enter into our loneliness, our desert, and address "the dark night of the soul." John of the Cross, a sixteenth-century Spanish mystic and poet coined this iconic phrase. We now use this term throughout literature to describe the journey from darkness and fractured life into a new dawn and healthy new spiritual beginnings. To enter into loneliness and discover solitude, serenity, stillness, and silence requires us to turn off the radio and smartphone. Better yet, we need to place them away from us so they are not a distraction.

In *Selling Spirituality: The Silent Takeover of Religion*, Jeremy Carrette and Richard King, both professors of religion in English universities, attest that in postmodernism with the rise of psychology and the demise of religion, the social dimension of spirituality and the self were separated and "contributed to a new cultural malaise—the loneliness and isolation of contemporary individualism."[11] What do you think of that? How did the rise of science and secularism separate our internal spirituality from known practices that were typically religious?

We must learn to recapture the joy of solitude. This takes place when we heal from loneliness. As noted, we tend to be distracted from considering loneliness. While it's a great social and private disease, I wonder if it's broader and deeper than we acknowledge in Western society. Given the reality that people spend so much time being busy, could it be that they don't know they are lonely? This is a question worthy of research! If we were to be collectively willing to face this issue, would we discover the root of many social ills? Or conversely, if we were collectively willing to face this issue, would we discover the root of many social ills? We must address loneliness to enter into spiritual wholeness. As Cardinal Basil Hulme said, "We shall never be safe in the market place unless we are at home in the desert."[12] In entering the desert, the dark night of the soul, or the spaces in our lives we have ignored or neglected, we begin our journey to heal ourselves and move towards wholeness. With wholeness, we are truly able to fully embrace being involved with others.

Part of the journey into solitude needs silence. Part of the journey requires stillness. Another part of the journey requests serenity. Part of the journey calls us to surrender. Stillness, serenity, and surrender are values that are opposite to those prevalent in the postmodern person. Stillness is being still! It means emptying before filling. Stillness means emptying by changing the water. This could mean removing stagnant, still water for fresh, clean, spring water. Stillness requires patience. Silence means not making noise. Mastering stillness and silence leads to solitude and serenity. In turn, it's a process of surrendering who one thinks they are to who they are, and who one is becoming. All told, it is a journey to discover, "Who am I?"

Patience is not a postmodern quality. Stillness takes patience and practice. Stillness takes hard work! Stillness and silence are essential for the postmodern spiritual person. Stillness, solitude, and silence seem counter-cultural to the postmodern world, yet these are paramount for spiritual maturity. Another postmodern value we need to recapture is surrender. David Benner, a noted psychologist, in *Spirituality and the Awakening Self: The Sacred Journey of Transformation*, wrote:

Contemplative stillness is essential because it allows us to step back from the ordinary background noise of consciousness at our respective level of self-development and organization. It allows us to notice our preoccupations and identifications and set them aside in an act of surrender. The goal is not to eliminate anything but to release everything. For only then do we discover that we are not defined by what we hold, but by whom we are held.[13]

Before we explore images of surrender, it's fitting to end thoughts on stillness by considering an image by Sir William Osler. Osler, a Canadian physician, trained in medicine at Montreal's McGill University. He was one of the four founders and the first Chief of Staff at Johns Hopkins Hospital in Baltimore. Some call him the Father of Modern Medicine. This image is one that we should all share with our various doctors. And some of us have more doctors than others! Medical doctor and clinical professor of medicine Rachel Naomi Remen, in a 1999 edited book on spirituality, wrote:

Sir William Osler is often misquoted as having said that objectivity is the single most important trait of the true physician. He spoke in Latin and the word which is usually translated as "objectivity" is *aequinimitas. Aequinimitas* does not mean 'objectivity," it means 'mental stillness" or inner peace." Inner peace is an important quality for anyone whose daily work puts them in contact with human suffering. But this is not the outcome of distancing oneself from life, rather it is about knowing life so intimately that one has become able to trust and accept life so intimately that one has become able to trust and accept life whole, embracing its darkness in order to know its grace.[14]

Should we expect our doctors to value and seek inner stillness as they endeavor to heal us? In turn, we should ask ourselves objectively to practice our mental stillness or inner peace.

Surrender like silence, solitude, serenity, and stillness is a word that's abhorred in postmodernism. Sadly, we often think we need to be winners, to be in control, to have others submit to us—after all, we are the center of everything! Surrender, however, is required to achieve spiritual maturity. Surrender is a giving away to find God and/or community.[15] Surrender can be described as letting go of control, letting go of agendas, opinions, and thoughts. Throughout historical Western Christianity, there existed the strong image of surrender, and in turn, letting God take control.[16] Alas, we are fearful of letting go. We lack the trust to let go. We have no trust in our shadows. We have no trust in ourselves. Noted psychiatrist, theologian, and author Gerald May, in *The Awakened Heart: Opening Yourself to the Love You Need*, wrote these words about surrendering:

> Dag Hammarskjöld, United Nations Secretary General and Nobel Peace laureate, wrote these words in 1961: "I don't know Who—or what—put the question. I don't know when it was put. I don't even remember answering. But at some moment I did answer Yes to Someone— or Something—and from that hour I was certain that existence is meaningful and that, therefore, my life, in self-surrender, had a goal."[17]

The image of surrender, or surrendering, is well entrenched in Western Christianity's history. Popular reformist theologian and author Matthew Fox wrote, "The dark night of the soul descends on us all and the proper response is not addiction, such as shopping, alcohol, drugs, TV, sex or religion, but rather to be with the darkness and learn from it."[18] I wonder if we can add addiction to wealth to his list? Fox, however, is correct in stating that people attempt to fill their inner void with addictions and distractions. The idea of surrendering is rare in postmodernism. Yet we have a secular organization that leads many to spiritual fulfillment through surrendering. While its foundation was religious, it is truly a secular gem. This secular organization is very gifted in helping souls find their spiritual selves. This organization is known by its acronym–A.A. It helps those who hit the bottom and live in darkness to find light and steps to wholeness.

In 1935, the creators of Alcoholic Anonymous, Bill W. and Bob S., used spiritual images from Dr. Samuel Shoemaker, an American Episcopal priest. They created the "Big Book." It calls people to reform by looking inward and belonging to a community! To help the newly admitting alcoholic to become involved, each is asked to attend 90 meetings in 90 days. Just as a Christian cannot be solitary, neither can members of A.A. It's in this community, or fellowship, where members face their common dark night of the soul and their brokenness, and they share their plight and hopes. Through twelve progressive steps, spiritual healing takes place. In *Thirsty for God: A Brief History of Christian Spirituality*, Bradley Holt wonderfully describes this phenomenon:

> The twelve steps are a program that includes several features of earlier spirituality, such as a soul friend, daily examen, restitution, surrender to God, and sharing your belief with others. It focuses on the discovery and overcoming of irrational, harmful habits that have at their root the insistence that "I am God." The root of addiction is seen to be spiritual, and healing begins by surrender to grace, the gift of God.[19]

A.A. prides itself on avoiding religious dogma and ritual. Instead, it focuses on offering spiritual healing.[20] Alcoholism, loneliness, and lack of self-esteem are connected. The A.A. program helps members to spend their lives examining the essential, "Who am I" question and trains people to surrender to "the higher power" and be healed. Is this not a truly marvelous spiritual program? It catches people who are finally willing to be open and vulnerable. It helps those in much pain—physical, emotional, and spiritual—to address their dark night of the soul. When the night is faced, light may enter. Through community and sequential spiritual practices, a new life of sobriety and hope emerges. It catches people when they are ready. In a similar way, a Buddhist monk talking to the famous hermit Thomas Merton once said, "We don't teach meditation to the young monks. They are not ready for it until they stop slamming doors."[21] If young monks must stop slamming doors and drunks admit their failures and seek renewal, what does it take for others (meaning you and me) to enter into oneself and seek becoming a mature spiritual person? Can you answer this question, or are you like the postmodern person who is distracted, shallow, and unable to respond? Be true to yourself!

Here are some further thoughts on stillness. First, we collectively need stillness in Western society and Western Christianity. Second, we need stillness in our own lives. To personalize this situation, I ask: "Can you intentionally avoid the noise around you and find stillness and solitude?" Did you answer no? Did you say "No" because it's scary, or you're uninterested? Or did you answer yes? Did you declare, "I need to discover this lost part of my life"?

To be spiritually mature and alive, it's essential to make silence and, if possible, solitude an essential part of rediscovering who we are. We must use silence in our quest to discover, "Who am I?" Sadly, the obstacle of noise prevents us from finding stillness and solitude. From birth to death, noise surrounds us. Today we have noise-canceling headphones that cut out external noise so that we can hear only the noise the program wants us to hear! Elevators, malls, our homes, and everywhere we turn is noisy. British born essayist Pico Iyer, in *The Art of Stillness* (2014), wrote:

> Anyone reading this book will take in as much information today as Shakespeare took in over a lifetime. Researchers in the new field of interruption science have found that it takes an average of twenty-five minutes to recover from a phone call. Yet such interruptions come every eleven minutes— which means we're never caught up with our lives.[22]

Solitude is the end result of being patient with oneself, of delving into one's soul and holding on to stillness. Solitude may take a lifetime to master, and it might be a difficult task for most. If most of us can't achieve deep solitude in our lives, it would behoove us to learn, at the least, to somewhat master and appreciate stillness.

Being fully spiritually alive in postmodernism means embracing stillness and, if possible, solitude. This brings about serenity as you attach yourself to your shadow. One should approach this with anticipation and joy, not fear. Fear, unfortunately, is one of the greatest motivators in postmodernism, but fear doesn't help us find serenity; it's merely another distraction from discovering, "Who am I?" We need to give ourselves time and practice to achieve spiritual maturity.

We need to consider if we are lonely, and if so, we must truly embrace our darkness. We can't be alive to others unless we are first alive to ourselves. We must also embrace silence. We need to also avoid noise and the noise pollution that is invasive in the world. Of equal if not greater significance, we must avoid the noise within that distracts our inner selves. These are daunting tasks, but as noted, we need to talk less and listen more and deeply. In our age of short attention spans and distractibility, we must not be discouraged and quit. We must be patient with ourselves. All these tasks run counter to postmodernism. This doesn't mean they're not attainable if we practice, practice, and practice. The inward journey takes practice. As Brené Brown poetically wrote: "Stillness is not about focusing on nothingness: it's about creating a clearing. It's opening up an emotionally clutter-free space and allowing ourselves to feel and think and dream and question."[23] In another of her books, Brown stated:

> There's a quote that I share every time I talk about vulnerability and perfectionism. My fixation with these words from Leonard Cohen's song "Anthem" comes from how much comfort and hope they give me as I put "enough" into practice: "There's a crack in everything. That's how the light gets in."[24]

May you look and find your cracks and vulnerabilities. Embrace them. Instead of fearful elements to avoid, seeing them as opportunities to grow. Use silence and stillness and seek serenity as you journey to find, "Who am I?" Look for your shadow, use it, and let the light shine in. And then in harmony with yourself, you will have spiritual peace and fulfillment.

Questions to ponder and discuss
Chapter Seven

Spirituality: Loneliness Versus Solitude, Stillness, Surrender, and Serenity

1 Postmodernism is constant noise. If silence occurs, our first reaction may be, "Something is wrong!" Do you truly appreciate silence, and if so, how much and for how long?

2 Can we be quiet so silence can speak? Your thoughts?

3 As Joan Chittister wrote, "We live with noise pollution now and find silence a great burden, a frightening possibility ... We say we do not have the time to think, but what we actually lack is the quiet to think." What is your first reaction to this comment? After some reflection, what is your second reaction to this comment? Third, are your reactions the same or different?

4 Try to define silence, stillness, serenity, surrender, and solitude. What do the results mean to you?

5 Consider this tough and probing question. It requires one to go deep and be honest: Are you lonely?

CHAPTER EIGHT

SPIRITUALITY AND EDUCATION

This writing has included numerous observations on spirituality and education, and spirituality and mindfulness. This chapter, however, looks at the theme of education and spirituality in detail. As noted in the introduction, much of the research in spirituality and education is rooted in papers, books, and journal articles describing spirituality and higher education. This is defined as college and university students and other scenarios. This area of great research was and is well explored because of the ready accessibility researchers have to those nearby—eager students! Today, those students in higher education still receive much attention. However, it's increasingly clear that researchers investigate spirituality at all levels of education: primary school students and their teachers, high school students or adolescents and their teachers, and the aforementioned college-age students and instructors. Likewise, some adult programs of education are also studied. Researchers explore these and related fields in a variety of ways. There's clearly a link between spirituality and education. A delightful definition of education upholds this notion:

> *Educare,* the root of the word *education,* means "to lead forth the hidden wholeness," the innate integrity that is every person. And as such, there is a place where "to educate" and "to heal" mean the same thing. Educators are

healers. Educators and healers both trust in the wholeness of life and in the wholeness of people. Both have come to serve this wholeness.[1]

Education means to "lead one out," but for many, the journey out must begin by first journeying inward. Unless one walks into oneself and finds one's spiritual path, how can one truly find the right path in the world? The journey inward and outward must address one's pivotal question: "Who am I?" What do you think? Have you consciously journeyed inward? If so, how was the journey? Did you rush (as a typical postmodern) or did you take time to let images settle within you? Can you define how it helped you on your inward and outward journeys? What do you think of these questions? What questions would you ask?

Interestingly, those researching the topic of spirituality and education often write about journeys. Naturally, those writing are still largely focused on students in higher education settings[2] and adults.[3] There are also stories of the journeys of teachers. In describing this, adult educator Jerold Apps wrote:

> For the teacher, teaching means moving from telling to sharing, from adding to a learner's store of information to integrating new information with old, from serving as an expert source of knowledge to becoming a questioning, sharing journey leader. Teachers must deplore learner passivity and encourage active involvement. Teachers increasingly become students of context, for all learning occurs in an often complicated, ambiguous context.[4]

While the following passage refers to college students, I think we can apply the message to all students and teachers involved in their spiritual journey:

> To respect each student's solitary journey. To treat students as if they and their questions—all their questions!—are real. To help students bring words to the questions lying deep within them. To help them to see the world as a

whole, including the sacredness that lies within, around and among them. What wonderful possibility, and how much more of an education than simply 120 credits over four years. To my mind, that's a higher education worth the effort.[5]

We shouldn't be surprised at the importance the various levels of education place on the idea of a journey. Even after thousands of years, the notion of undertaking a journey remains part of our society's Judeo-Christian heritage. It's foundational in Western society. A journey is also an element in other religious and cultural traditions. When we shifted from a sacred-centered and religious-dominated Western society to postmodern secularism, it was natural that journeying became assimilated. We live in a world where the experiences of individuals, collective communities, and indeed all of society are built upon previous experiences. As expected, the postmodern secular society included public education when it adopted and adapted the notion of the journey. Consequently, it's important to explore a few of the roles journeying plays in the realm of spirituality and education.

It seems appropriate that we begin by observing young students. In turn, it's essential to then explore the spiritual lives of their teachers. Subsequently, we will explore young adults or adolescents and their teachers. Then we'll look at college and university students. As oft noted, this last group is among the most studied or researched groups in education and spirituality. As with the other groups, it is crucial to also discover insights into the spiritual lives of their educators. Finally, we will explore the spiritual lives of adults involved in education.

One of the first to appreciate and study the spirituality of children was psychiatrist Robert Coles. In one account, Coles notes that when he as a student was with his clinical analyst supervisor, they saw a particular child. Afterward, his supervisor said, "She's an *un*conventionally religious child. There's a spirituality at work in her, and we might explore her spiritual psychology."[6] The comment dazzled Coles. Little did he realize that he would soon develop and devote himself to a lifetime practice of studying the spiritual lives of children! He studied and assisted those who required psychiatric care and those who did not. He desired well-rounded views from children. In his medical practice, Coles routinely encouraged children to draw the face of God, or some religious picture, to help them describe their situation.[7] At times, Coles described the children's efforts as "soul searching."[8] His 1990 book, *The Spiritual Lives of Children,* is a work rich in insightful thoughts spoken by children. It contains illustrations by numerous children. For example, a girl of thirteen shared and cautioned Coles: "It's not important, where you think the soul is: it's what you're looking for with it, that's important."[9] Isn't this a profound image? Read her statement again. Andrew Wright, in a book exploring the development of spirituality in education, said of Coles:

> ... The obvious next step in the research process was to focus on children themselves. The last thirty years has seen a remarkable growth of such studies. An outstanding example is Robert Cole's *The Spiritual Life of Children* (1992), which presents a series of conversations with children gathered over an extended period of time and crossing cultural and religious boundaries. His research does not attempt to impose any closed interpretative framework on the conversations, but instead seeks to allow children to present their ultimate concerns for themselves, in their own terms. The richness of Coles' work is impossible to encapsulate in a brief summary, and the reader is urged to read this book.[10]

Wright's assessment is accurate! Throughout Cole's book, there are indeed many profound insights shared by children. Their thoughtful words are often overwhelming to adults, yet they show that even young children are soul seekers. They often sound like old souls! Indeed, as the Psalmist wrote about 3,000 years ago: "Out of the mouths of babes!" (Psalm 8:2). Children share deep, profound thoughts on life and spirituality. Adults need to stop talking and learn to condition themselves to listen deeply to children!

Since Cole's insightful, ground-breaking efforts, many have ventured into researching the spirituality of children. As recently as 2015, authors still note a need to appreciate the spiritual voices of children. Religious studies professor Annemie Dillen wrote:

> In line with much research about children's spirituality, one can state that children are often much more competent than we believe (Dillen, 2007a). The success of programs involving philosophizing with children, even with preschool toddlers, shows that we do not have to underestimate their capacities. Of course, the way in which the 'reflection' is organized and conceptualized varies, and one does not expect the same level of abstract reflection from young children and adolescents. Children are often very sensitive to symbols and stories, and are often able to see links with their own life experiences.[11]

Research suggests that children have a great deal to share. Why do adults have such difficulty in listening to and accepting insights from children? Is it ego or prejudice? Did you know that there's a journal on spirituality specifically dedicated to children, called the *International Journal of Children's Spirituality*?

We must acknowledge the spirituality of children. We must accept their spirituality without bias and without adult-based condescending attitudes. In turn, we should endeavor to enhance and expand the spirituality of children in schools. It shouldn't be an optional class or an add-on but a foundation from which all courses and classes flow. Is this revolutionary, or is it a needed evolutionary new reality? Is it pie-in-the-sky utopian dreaming or a sorely needed social adjustment? Your thoughts on this are___?

We sorely need to address the needs of the whole child. Sadly, there are obstacles. First, it's distressing that in our postmodern society, some still erroneously view this sincere goal as nothing more than a veiled effort to provide religious indoctrination.[12] In some circumstances, this is likely true, since some religious groups say they provide religious/spiritual education, while the curricula is really religious indoctrination. Consequently, this makes it difficult for legitimate spiritual efforts to gain any acceptance or credibility. We must educate all on the differences between religious education (and indoctrination) and spiritual formation. The need for children to be spiritually educated in schools is well explained throughout the 2014 textbook, *Global Perspectives and Context for Spirituality in Education*. Here the authors wrote:

> A concern for spirituality in education emerges from, but is not yet sufficiently valued by, today's post-secular, pluralistic, globalized societies, where a spiritual rebalancing can contribute to the social cohesion and wellbeing essential in promoting both prosperous and healthy communities. If children and young people are able to find a sense of self and identity, belonging and connectedness, and are able to make meaning from their life experiences through their school programs, they are more likely to develop into proactive, caring and compassionate citizens of the future.[13]

Besides the tension among close-minded, definitive, and highly selective practices of religious education, and the open-ended, explorative efforts of spiritual learning, another substantial obstacle revolves around the question, "How do we provide spirituality given the vast and often unwieldy definitions of spirituality?" As Ron Best, in *Global Perspectives and Context for Spirituality in Education*, beautifully wrote:

> In a liberal pluralist society, where respect for differences in values, beliefs and practices and the principles of multiculturalism, democratic rights and individual liberty are enshrined, finding answers to these questions that are acceptable to all, and offensive to none, is pretty well impossible ...[14]

A few pages later, he again most delightfully and accurately wrote:

> Such approaches seem not to get us any nearer the 'Holy Grail' of a clear definition acceptable to all, but they do indicate the key issues in the field, including whether the

spiritual is intrinsically linked with religion and belief in
God ...[15]

Published in 2014, this postmodern textbook is reflective of the place
spirituality needs in education.

The 2016 and 2020 American elections, for a variety of reasons, ushered
in a new era of greater polarization, confrontation, manipulation, distrust,
racism, sexism, and violence. Without casting blame, many changes in
governmental and social behavior tore the fabric of America and indeed
Western society. Issues that we considered to be declining were unmasked.
Sadly, the true dysfunctional reality of American emerged. In America,
the divisions between rich and poor, those with incredible medical care
and those with little or none, billionaires negotiating more wealth while
the basic minimum wage remained largely stagnant, became unbearable.
Some might say explosive. The rise of COVID-19 expanded rising issues
of violence and marginalization. This further polarized the nation. Many
saw systemic overreaction of white police on the minor (if any) crimes of
people of color. Today, we continue to see veiled forms of segregation and
oppression that originated in slavery.

In our incredible "Reformation," with the greatest paradigm shifts
in history all around us, we suddenly became subject to an even greater
shift. An invisible virus visibly brought global destructive social ills. In
turn, gains in spirituality and education seemed to evaporate or recede
in light of this new postmodern situation. Between COVID-19 and the
aforementioned expanding divisions, it's quite likely that gains made in
offering spiritual practices to students, including mindfulness, suffered
substantial setbacks.

To be blunt, with misperceptions of the separation between
religiousness and spirituality, and with the illustrated obstacles, I wonder
if we can even openly discuss offering spirituality to young school students.
Current conventional wisdom says that emotions and volatility in Western
society are too raw to begin any communication. Ann Trousdale, children's
education specialist in spirituality, also describes how barriers constrict the
development and use of spirituality in the classroom:

Children in the U.S. are growing up in an increasingly diverse society, bringing a variety of different spiritual backgrounds to their classrooms. These classrooms could be sites for nurturing the spirits of children while they learn about spiritual diversity in the United States and around the world; yet except in isolated cases, there is little acknowledgment of children's spirituality in U.S. public classrooms. There are a host of reasons that these opportunities are not taken advantage of: in addition to polarization along the political and religious spectrum, there is a conflating of spirituality with religion, a lack of education about children's spirituality, over interpretation of the First Amendment and case law surrounding it, fear of litigation, as well as simple public relations concerns for parental and local community response ... A perception of spiritual education as an area separate from religious education or indoctrination has not gained widespread understanding in the United States, yet there are efforts in that direction ...[16]

I wonder if conversations about spirituality, beginning with our youngest schoolchildren, could be a path of discovery and hope. Sadly, in our postmodern society of confrontation and alienation, where the gulf between people is widening, it's uncertain if the exploration of questions such as, "Who am I?" and "How can I be in harmony with others?" can take place. If allowed or encouraged, spiritual conversations with young children could make the vast empty void shrink the present gulf. It could be a great place to begin individual and societal healing and renewal. What do you think? I say yes. I believe we need to help children so that they can lead us in healing. Perhaps in the Age of Entitlement, one of the few areas to which one is righteously entitled is spiritual development in children so they may become holy whole.

In 2017, fully aware of issues of marginalization, alienation, radicalization, and polarization in Western society, and along with the domination of white researchers, Professor Marian de Souza, with graduate degrees in literature and in education, noted the thoughts of educator Audrey Lingley. To these, she added some additional ideas when she wrote how to think about the idea of spirituality in education:

> ... urgently require a spirituality responsive pedagogy that we espouse the qualities ... (that) should complement traditional models of human development. She described spiritual development as multidimensional process incorporating: (a) a disposition of genuine or authentic inquiry, (b) an engagement in a search for purpose and meaning, (c) an orientation of faith in regards to something largely than or beyond oneself, (d) a capacity for self-aware consciousness, (e) an interest in ethical relations and behaviors, and (f) the experience of awe, love, wonder, and transcendence.[17]

Yes, we need inclusive and expanded approaches stretching beyond historic WASP research. The age of white male dominated research must decline for diversity to climb. Diversity offers both a broad and more inclusive view, extending societal solutions since all souls are considered and addressed. In other words, Western society can no longer afford to fit into the parameters provided by elite white males. This sounds like a good, firm foundation on which to build new spiritual experiences. Quoting the late Warren Nord's 1995 insightful book, *Religion and American Education: Rethinking a National Dilemma*, John Miller, who wrote much on holistic learning, stated:

> We modern-day Americans have a spiritual problem. There is something fundamentally wrong with our culture. We who have succeeded so brilliantly in matters of economics, science and technology have been less successful in matters of the heart and soul. This is evident in our manners and our morale: in our entertainment and our politics; in our preoccupation with sex and violence; in the ways we do our jobs and in the failure of our

relationships; in our boredom and unhappiness in this, the richest of all societies.[18]

Miller wrote this astute insight in 2000. He also said, "Integrating spirituality into the life of the school means simply acknowledging that students have a life that needs nourishment."[19] In my opinion, this sentence says much about the state of spirituality and education in the preceding two decades. Read it again and think about it! Today, I believe the situation is more urgent. The gulf between learning and our souls is widening. When did lying, coercion, and insulting become an acceptable response in human behavior? Tied to this are many societal issues that need resolving. Can we say that we abandoned our roots and need to find them again? In addition to helping children, youth, and ourselves re-embrace moral values of respect for others—and ourselves—we begin to truly answer, "Who am I?" with spiritual integrity. Can children lead us back to wholeness? Will we let them? Will we learn humility as we attempt to feed our spirits?

In recent decades, in many places across Western society, limited finances saw schools cut teachers, teacher support, art, physical education, music, and other programs. These are all components that often offered undeclared yet great spiritual depth to the lives of children. A direct consequence of these actions was the reduction of spiritual enhancing programs and staff, and recent massive societal dissatisfaction, as students seemingly lack spiritual nourishment. They are at risk. In a time of their greatest need, we seem to be offering fewer and fewer resources in addressing the whole child. We live in a time when we should be enhancing spiritual growth but sadly seem to be drifting farther and farther from our roots. As a society and individuals, we are dying on the vine! What do you think? Can we recover and find our souls? Furthermore, are we interested in helping children explore their spirituality?

In postmodernism, we have sorely neglected to nurture the whole child, the young adolescent, the young adult, and adults. I sometimes wonder if we have truly succumbed to the pressures of Western society, which focuses on education models that promote success, material wealth, and consuming. Did we sell our souls? What do you think? To restate this, do we now glorify life in shallow selfhood or "Me-ism." Education seems motivated on making students of all ages aim for success and feel entitled to success. But what is deemed successful if we produce children and adults that are fractured, dysfunctional, and alienated from others or themselves? If one is fractured and broken, one can never be successful! We have created an environment in which one limps along, often in denial, and seeks a constant flow of new achievements. We consume much and are always thirsty because we're so prone to neglecting our need to journey inward. We need the journey inward to live our journey outward. Do we truly desire to create successful students or students who are whole? What are your thoughts? Can we fix this? Do we desire to fix this model of success versus wholeness?

We desire much on the horizontal plane. We are shallow and move through everything quickly. We are parched and must consume, but can we truly say that we savor what is around us? What do you think? The cost of the horizontal is that we neglected the vertical part of our lives, or the part no one sees—including ourselves.[20] As noted elsewhere, we want to gain the world but fail to see that the cost is our souls. Sadly, unwittingly and unaware, we never gained the world, as it remains forever elusive. Meanwhile, we still pay the cost to our souls and our wholeness. Perhaps we can redeem or reboot Western society and ourselves if we learn to adopt spiritual values! Perhaps students, school staff, and society could and should learn how to pause, reflect, and act. David Robson (not me, but an incredible British science writer), in *The Intelligence Trap: Why Smart People Make Dumb Mistakes*, notes that in Western schools when teachers ask students questions, they tend to pick a raised hand after only a few seconds. In other words, students don't respond to the question but to the opportunity to be picked. In Japan, Robson notes, teachers allow students more time to ponder and think.[21] We need to let stuff settle and move within us before we respond. Perhaps we can emulate the model of pausing.

Today, the "me2" (the women's movement of speaking out about sexual exploitation), BLM (Black Lives Matter), and other causes clearly show the inequalities and dissatisfactions that Western society has long covered up, denied, or, sadly, ignored. Without question, these mounting issues urgently need our attention. Perhaps by encouraging young children to experience spiritual growth we can turn the tide and stem another generational failure.

In writing about the need for us to be part of the spiritual growth of young children, Irish professors of education James O'Higgins Norman and Caroline Renehan (who holds doctorates in divinity and education) wrote:

> Too often, schools have focused largely on scholastic development to the extent that the interpersonal skills required for a full spiritual development are often neglected. Almost one hundred years ago John Dewey (1916/1966) argued that there is an intimate connection between education and the quality of societies. He claimed that democratic societies could only continue to exist if schools promoted exploration and growth rather than repressing expression and creativity. Progressive educationalists have identified the qualities that are needed to manage life intelligently and to participate in society, namely, critical thinking, problem solving, communicating and collaboration (Dewey, 1916/1966; Lindeman, 1926; Coyle, 1947; Williams, 2007), all of which can be promoted through spiritual development.[22]

These esteem authors are not alone in this assessment.[23]

To begin educating (note the typical historic word, as "teaching" is avoided) young school-aged children, it's essential to address their true need for wholeness. It is indeed proper to educate the whole child. All too often we are fragmented in our approach to education: gym at 9 a.m., math at 10, and band practice (if not cut by the budget) at 11. While they separately address the child's physical, emotional, and cognitive needs, they're not connected so that they feed each other. When they are linked, they begin to address the child's spirit. We need to weave all disciplines into common themes that speak to the whole child. Likewise, as education becomes vulnerable to financial pressures, traditional programs that address the children's spirit, such as gym, band, and art, are often the first courses dropped. In other words, courses that feed the soul disappear so that core academic courses that drive us to value success and entitlement are maintained. Do we want young students to see school as earning grades, or do we desire to help them value and explore life? What is more vital—"teaching to the test," which is noticeable and measurable, or helping young people discover who they are? The benefits of helping students discover the great "who am I" question are immense but perhaps rarely recognized or valued. Think about this: "What teachers do you remember? Are they the ones who made you work on the curricula, or the ones who met you as a person and helped you feel alive?" Take some time to ponder this question.

Young children are open to awe and wonder. They're open to learning about love, care and, compassion. They're open to learning about prejudice and hate. To counter hate, prejudice, and other negative values imposed on children, we need to help them learn to journey inward and then outward. The inward journey is to discover "I-ism," or "Who am I?" This is the opposite of "Me-ism." Our rampant postmodern image of entitlement revolves around "Me-ism." This is a sad social curse building up the ego and seeing oneself as the center of the universe. "I-ism," however, is not the glorification of the self but a genuine, deep effort of confronting "dark nights of the soul" and other issues to discover inner values of worth, joy, and empathy. By identifying and learning what works, along with other appreciating positive values, we can help children be healthy and whole. In turn, these children can move towards the vigorous view "of how to treat others as oneself." That is to say, to treat oneself and others with dignity and grace. We must encourage the young to find their spirit-voice because too often they feel reluctant to share.[24]

Educating children is more than teaching. Teaching historically means a teacher imparting information and providing tools to children. Education, viewed as learning, is a shared mutuality. In other words, the teacher helps children learn to give voice to their emotions and thoughts. Equally, the students help their teachers. The teacher is a fellow pilgrim. A teacher is not offering top-down knowledge. A teacher and children meet "in the middle," where both learn from the other. In other words, spiritual learning for young children is illustrated or modeled by teachers, who in turn are fed by the students. They learn the "language" of the other. When children sense that their teacher is a fellow pilgrim, they feel affirmed, and their level of trust increases. They also see examples of good practices on how to delve inward. Professor in art education and spirituality Laurel Campbell states this well:

However, Kessler (1998-99) finds that many educators feel the urgency to discuss spiritual wellness in light of serious social problems and self-destructive behavior, which is indicative of a "search for connection and meaning and an escape from the pain of not having a genuine source of spiritual fulfillment" in the generation currently in school. This discussion will need to include a serious study of not only how we teach, but also who we are as teachers. According to Palmer (1998), "Teaching, like any truly human activity, emerges from one's inwardness". He also believes that "connections made by good teachers are not in their methods, but in their hearts—meaning heart in the ancient sense, as the place where intellect and emotion and spirit will converge in the human self"[25]

Affirming this image of teachers and students, renowned educator and author Parker Palmer said, "good teachers join self and subject and students in the fabric of life"[26] Similarly, "the teacher sets the tone and the atmosphere of the classroom. When a student's soul is nurtured and developed, it follows then that the process must begin with the teacher's soul ... To ignore soul is to overlook an essential element in learning and development.[27] The basic need is for teachers to be beacons, fellow pilgrims, and refiners of images for students, which is well noted and superbly described by Clifford Mayes. Mayes, who holds a doctorate in cultural foundations of education and a doctorate in psychology, wrote the following. May I suggest you read it twice, slowly:

Unfortunately, there have been very few studies that look at the spiritual dimension of teacher reflectivity and practice. We need such research to give us a clearer understanding of how certain teachers ground their practice in axiological and spiritual concerns and convictions. I am presently engaged in a study of how veteran teachers in the graduate program in educational administration at my university have been shaped by their spiritual beliefs. We also need studies of how intending teachers' spiritual commitments manifest themselves in the teacher's daily classroom practice. For instance, in a recent article, I examined how my Mormon/Buddhist commitments have helped shape my teaching. The examination of how one's spirituality affects one's teaching a fascinating topic which needs to be much more visible in the literature on teacher reflectivity (Palmer, 1997).

By shying away from frank discussion and development of spirituality in our intending teachers (discussions that in some students will inevitably center around quite specific commitments to particular religious figures and doctrines), we do not fully serve those students and seriously compromise the depth and effectiveness of their reflectivity. In fact, I would argue that we actually do moral violence to such students by requiring that they "bracket off" the spiritual dimension of their existence as intellectually irrelevant or even institutionally unacceptable when, in fact, it does not have to be (Carter, 1993; Nord, 1995).[28]

The role of the teacher is to help young students make connections and to provide affirmation, help exploration, and share in those experiences. The open-minded, open-ended, non-judgmental spiritual education of young students should continue in high school. Here adolescents, with the guidance of teachers, can further deepen and expand their spiritual lives. Episcopal priest and educator specializing in the well-being of young children, Cheryl Minor, building upon the ground-breaking 2006 work of David Hay and Rebecca Nye, supports this. Both Hay and Nye are specialists in children's spirituality. Minor stated, "adults can foster relational consciousness by helping children keep an open mind, encouraging children to explore multiple ways of making sense of particular experiences or situations, and encouraging personal awareness ...[29] Building upon the 2009 work of Rebecca Nye, Minor wrote that young children need six spiritual conditions to thrive. They are space (the physical, emotional, and auditory), process (as opposed to product), imagination, relationships, intimacy, and trust.[30] Do we provide these spiritual needs in our elementary school systems? If not, where do we fall short? What about the school near you … where does it rate? What are your thoughts on the words of Cheryl Minor, David Hay, and Rebecca Nye?

In postmodern Western society, change is frequent and quick. Perhaps one of the most evident places is in our high schools. In the 1940s, teachers thought the top discipline concerns were:

1. talking out of turn
2. chewing gum
3. making noise
4. running in the hall
5. getting out of line
6. wearing improper clothing
7. not putting paper in a wastepaper basket.

Four decades later, the list was radically different. This time the responses were:

1. drug use
2. alcohol abuse
3. pregnancy
4. suicide
5. rape
6. robbery
7. assault[31]

Four decades later, mass school shootings are a regular (can we say monthly?) occurrence. In turn, countless schools have metal scanners on doors to check for weapons. They also use drug-sniffing dogs, CCTV cameras, and school police patrolling the facilities. This is a reality in many schools. It's quite a change from simply talking out of turn in the classroom! How do these incredible differences affect the spirituality of teenagers, younger students, teachers, and, sadly, many grieving parents?

In early postmodernism, parents were pleased to send children to school so they could learn to reach for and embrace the stars. Today, it is sad and often incomprehensible that all too many students in school suddenly experience the embrace of death! How will the short-term and long-term effects of COVID-19 hit students, classrooms, teachers, and staff? What do you think? How can we reduce violence and negative values and champion the need for spiritual wholeness? What thoughts do you have? Can we do this, or is it too late?

Despite these monumental shifts, high school students continue to ask the same timeless questions we all ask. As the late Rachael Kessler, champion of "emotional literacy," phrased it in 2005:

This concerns the exploration of existential questions that burst forth in adolescence. "Why am I am here?" "Does my life have a purpose? How do I find out what it is?" "Is there a meaning to life?" "Why should I live?" "What is life for?" "What does my future hold?" "What is my destiny?" "Is there life after death?" "Is there a God?" I've read these questions time and again when students write anonymously about their personal mysteries — their wonder, worries, curiosity, fear, and excitement.[32]

She identified seven areas where adolescents may explore spiritual development. These are:

(1) searching for meaning and purpose, (2) longing for solitude and silence, (3) urging for transcendence, (4) hungering for joy and delight, (5) developing creative drive, (6) calling for initiation, and (7) forming a deep connection. In the last case, Kessler meant "connecting deeply to nature, to their lineage, or to a higher power" (p. 105). For me, the deep connection is a Christian foundation, but it doesn't necessarily have to be Christian. Whether your spiritual beliefs are grounded in religion or your standpoint is more secular, I suggest that you combine the "life of the mind" with life in the spirit …[33]

Kessler isn't alone in identifying these universal questions of adolescents.[34] In my view, this list represents an ideal foundation on which high school students might mold and build their spiritual lives. In other words, by addressing the listed items, students begin the journey to deeper spiritual awareness and, in turn, wholeness. Kessler, who died in 2010 at age 63, wrote passionately about moulding the whole child, spiritually and educationally. Her classic 2000 book, *The Soul of Education: Helping Students Find Connection, Compassion, and Character at School,* should be valued by educators seeking to help children of all ages to be wholly holy and holy whole.

When looking at high school students, we determined the "who and when," and with Kessler's list before us, we have a viable image of "how" to approach matters spiritual. When we regard the shift from chewing gum in the class to thoughts about staying alive, we have identified a very definitive reason "why" we need to address matters spiritual. We might say we need to assist students to rediscover their roots. However, to be comprehensive and complete, we must hold these various images together. We must also address a pivotal question: "Where are the sources of adolescent spirituality?" In 2010, Graham Rossiter, a professor of religious and moral education in Australia, partly answers this question.

Rossiter both passionately and extensively wrote about spirituality and religious dynamics concerning the Australian Roman Catholic school system. This was often a challenging quest when one thinks about the rigid history of the Roman Catholic Church and emerging often opposite ideas posed by postmodern spirituality. This is a future question that others need to address!

Historically, for most Roman Catholics, the church and the church school system were often one's world. In turn, we might say that one's world was in three identical places: society, the church, and the school system. In postmodernism, this changed. Now for many Roman Catholics, one's world might include the church and/or the church school system. In the past, the church defined, directed, and governed one's spiritual (and we can say entire) life. That greatly faded with postmodernism. Unfortunately, it seems that senior church management often chose to ignore the shifting tides of society. Rossiter wrote that models that worked in the past do not, and cannot, work in postmodernism. He deftly wrote:

> If Catholic schools are to offer an education in spirituality
> that is relevant to the lives of pupils, then there is a need
> to understand and acknowledge their changed spiritual
> situation: for many, but not all, it is relatively secular,

> eclectic, subjective, individualistic and self-reliant; there
> is a strong interest in achieving a desirable lifestyle but
> little interest in connection with the church ...[35]

In my view, he brilliantly encourages the church to engage proactively in the future. Conversely, he also appeals for it to continue to uphold its roots.[36] He marvelously informed senior management what they needed to hear, but in such a brilliant way that he avoided a defensive backlash! He clearly explained that students in church schools no longer receive the bulk of their spiritual direction from the church or school. Instead, they glean insights from a "complex tapestry of influences of cultural meaning."[37] This includes many secular sources. For example, he noted that the cultural shift included the move from traditional religious spirituality. He said that factors such as the movement of people to cities; the separation between church and state; and the rise of science education, technology, and individualism are parts of the shifting tide away from traditional Catholic spirituality.[38] Although specifically addressing adolescents attending parochial schools in Australia, I think we can easily acknowledge and apply his arguments to high school students throughout Western society.

In Western society, high school students' evolution is very much a transition from childhood to adulthood. Students adjust to seek their emerging responsibilities and place in the world. They search for their place in classroom with peers, teachers, the general school environment. They search for new and expanding roles within their families and the local community. Students may wonder if they are the cool kids, or the cool kids' "sidekicks." In their search, they wonder if they're esteemed jocks or unnoticed geeks. They wonder if they're popular, or ghosts lurking under the radar. High school students often wonder if they are popular and, if so, with whom. This is a central and foundational reality for many. High school students fret over grades, sex, gossip, and social media. In postmodernism, students love and live on the many platforms of social media. It seems as if their hands are glued to their smartphones. Given that they grew up with smartphones, they truly believe that social media helps define who they are. While parents still provide some foundational spiritual guidance, social media and peers are increasingly vital for today's postmodern teens. It's the first place they turn with their friends. We must explore how social media can spiritually feed adolescents. To what degree does it satisfy or meet deep longings, or only offer constant but fleeting instant gratification? These are questions we should explore. What are you thinking at this time?

Recently, Pamela King, a professor of human development with a keen interest in the spirituality of adolescents, and Chris Boyatzis, a professor of psychology, wrote an extensive article on the religious and spiritual development of adolescents.[39] In part, they synthesize countless other research articles, meta-analysis reports, various historical research, and emerging trends. They note that postmodern adolescents are complex[40] and require much more research into their religiosity and spirituality.[41] They affirm the ongoing roles of parents,[42] but they note the strong role peers, especially peers of similar experiences, often provide.[43] Peers, they state, offer each other much "horizontal" support.[44] We must wonder, as with all postmodern people, where the vertical exists in their lives. How deep is the vertical compared to the wide swath of horizontal support? This a great question to be explored. What do you think about the horizontal/vertical split in terms of spirituality? I wonder if it should be a 50 – 50, 30 – 70, or even a 70 – 30 split. What percentages do think it should be, and in turn, should it change according to situations or be constant? Perhaps we can repeat Shrek's statement and say it is complicated and, like onions, has layers.

Carolyn Barry, Larry Nelson, Sahar Davarya, and Sirene Urry, in a 2010 article in the *International Journal of Behavioral Development*, also suggest that the place and role of media impacts adolescents and needs attention: "The Internet and video games also may be important forms of media that serve as socializing agents for emerging adults, and therefore justify the importance of further scientific inquiry."[45] Their notes on the relationship of parents, emerging adults, religion, and spirituality are quite comprehensive. Like King and Boyatzis, they also note the role peers play in the transformation adolescents experience.[46] In their conclusion, they state that these are few examples that show the necessity of "further theoretical work and empirical investigation."[47] Clearly, as we look at the spirituality of high school students, it seems vital that we develop programs that build upon their natural support systems. How can we utilize media and peers as positive tools in helping teens, or emerging adulthoods, discern the great "Who am I" questions of life?

There is evidence that children in public schools appreciate the use of silence and meditation. Many find that it helps them center and regroup amidst issues. Likewise, it's much better than serving detention. It is healing. Perhaps emerging adults, such as those in high school, could emulate the young and use silence to help them find their spirit-voice. Likewise, those who learn this tool in public school could further develop and utilize silence when journeying through high school and beyond. Clearly, "in-tune" educators are needed to aid students in expanding their spiritual selves. As Rachael Kessler noted:

> With everyone sitting in a circle where all can see and be seen, the council where all can see and be seen, the council process allows each person to speak without interruption or immediate response. Students learnt to listen deeply and discover what it feels like to be truly heard. Silence becomes a comfortable ally as we pause to digest one story and wait for the other to form, when teachers call for moments of reflection or when the room fills with feeling at the end of the class ... Since "we teach who we are," teachers who invite heart and soul into the classroom also find it essential to nurture their own spiritual development.[48]

Kessler, in her long career, wrote much about adolescent development. She developed a list she called the "Seven Gateways to the Soul of Education." She contended that if teachers and administrations were to follow and enhance these topics, both students and teachers would find greater contentment and harmony within themselves and the world around them. Kessler's list is:

1. Search for Meaning and Purpose
2. Longing for Silence and Solitude

3. Urge for Transcendence
4. Hunger for Joy and Delight
5. Creative Drive
6. Call for Initiation
7. Deep Connection[49]

Once more, the image of silence is prominent. Silence for adolescents seems contradictory to their lives, since they revel in noisy connections via peers, media, and phones 24/7! Yet silence can be a powerful tool to help them as emerging adults. Susan Schiller, a professor interested in holistic education and spirituality, beautifully and poetically writes:

> Silent meditation is a natural choice to enhance or deepen the quality of reverie. In the silent space of meditation soul and mind can mingle; imagination can freely move in a state of reverie and without the restraints of order or structure.[50]

Sharon Daloz Parks, in her well-loved, oft-quoted 2000 classic, *Big Questions, Worthy Dreams: Mentoring Young Adults in Their Search for Meaning, Purpose, and Faith,* adds to the notion of silence, which she calls "pause."

> Pause is powerful for young adults because it encourages cultivation of the inner life, honors the emerging inner authority of the young adult, and activates the awareness that he or she participates in the motion of life that transcends one's own efforts to manage and control, a reality larger than the scope of one's ego. The place of pause in the process of imagination is the place where each of us must go with the apparently irreconcilable tensions that constitute life's biggest questions. Initiation into the power of pause at once strengthens and chastens the imagination of the young adult and can be one of the greatest gifts of a mentoring environment.[51]

Like adolescents in high school, college students also ask themselves the timeless question, "Who am I?"[52] Indeed, people of all ages explore this age-old question. Throughout the world and in every generation, people have asked this central life question! Perhaps in our postmodern Western society, as people become more secular and insular, this question is more elusive. This may be true for recent and the current group of college students. They are part of the first generation lacking much, if any, religious background and, hence, experiences and language often tied to spirituality.[53] In other words, they've likely lost the instruments that showed how to spiritually play, talk, and exist!

In 2007, Larry Braskamp, a professor of education, beautifully described today's three groups of college students. He calls them the 3M mix: Millennials, Postmodern NeXter, and Missionary. In describing the Postmodern NeXter, he wrote:

> Students are consumer oriented, entertainment oriented, like instant gratification, have short event horizon, seek excellence-without effort, skeptical about life, intellectually disengaged, adaptable and pragmatic, entitlement focused, and are often stress about their life. Finally, they are close to parents.... (and) refers to the current group of young persons as "Generation Me.")[54]

Postmodern college students seem to be so present to the present that they look for quick answers to deep questions. They don't seem to afford the time (or silence) to looking backward to their spiritual heritage, or deep within themselves to satisfy the things they long for but also don't know how to approach. Fast food answers meet their immediate hunger, but at the same time, they unwittingly yearn for a full course, satisfying family meal.

Postmodern NeXter is the largest of the three groups identified by Braskamp. Although we may say that Generation Me are often self-serving, we must realize that they were born during the most revolutionary-evolution period of history. They were born in the greatest social, cultural paradigm shift ever experienced. This doesn't include the radical curvature in their lives and societies forced by COVID-19.

You've likely heard the comment that those born today will have a career(s) that didn't exist when they were born. Not that long ago, each generation followed the path of their parents. Many young women became mothers and home keepers, and young men either worked the family farm or learned the father's trade. Unlike previous generations that spent their whole career with one employer, today's youth will likely have several employers, and given COVID-19, they might spend many years working from home. They may be on contract to several firms instead of full-time employees. They may even work for themselves.

College students of the recent past and today are confronting life with unparallel situations in their personal, professional, and societal lives. Furthermore, this unprecedented reality has no substantial historical resources to call upon. While we might consider the ill-named Spanish Flu of 1917-18 as a resource to help us through the current global pandemic, reality informs us that we live in a radically different world than 1917. Travel, jobs, employed women professionals, computers, enormous population growth, and diversity are but a few examples of the differences between that pandemic and ours. Likewise, the average college and university student of 1917 is much different from the postmodern student. Those students were often elite, male, and white. Today, diversity reigns.

Without question, those styled Generation Me are living in the most unsettling period of history. For the most part, they have little religious experience and language, which historically helped students with spiritual awareness and embodiment. Postmodern students seem skeptical about their lives and society, yet they still yearn to find themselves. Perhaps more than any generation, they need to discover, discern, deepen, and develop their spiritual lives. In 1981, Howard Thurman, the great Quaker mystic, shared with a class of Spelman College a message that still rings true: "There is something in every one of you that waits and listens for the sound of the genuine in yourself."[55] We can also return to William Shakespeare's great and profound image, "This above all else, to thine own self be true." Being true to oneself means asking and answering the great question to which we always return: "Who am I?"

In 2007, adult educator Jennifer Lindholm wrote about this search:

To ignore the role of spirituality in personal development and professional behavior, higher education professor Elizabeth Tisdell asserts, is to overlook a potentially very powerful avenue through which many of us construct meaning and knowledge. Based on the findings from an ongoing national study called "Spirituality in Higher Education" ... agree with Tisdell. One of the most notable findings from the survey we administered in fall 2004 to 112,232 entering first-year college students at 236 campuses nationwide is that today's incoming students place significant personal emphasis on matters related to the interior dimensions of their lives. Moreover, they generally have a high expectations for the role that their college or university should play in their emotional and spiritual development ... In essence, they are searching for deeper meaning in their life, looking for ways to cultivate their inner self, seeking to be compassionate and charitable, and striving to determine what they think and feel about many issues confronting them and their communities.[56]

This position is not singular. Other adult educators with an interest in spirituality, such as Bruce Speck and Sherry Hoppe, also writing that year said:

Spiritual conversations allow students to engage in the process of self-discovery. In developing their own identity, students ask themselves questions about their identity, values, skills and vocation. While engaging in self-exploration, students ask: Who am I" What do I believe" How do I accept the things I cannot control? What has shaped me to be who I am today? And where am I going? These questions encourage self-reflection, value clarification, and discernment. The peer conversation, centered on these questions, not only leads to the self-discovery process but also prompts further engagement to understand one another in community.[57]

Those who attend college or university are as diverse a group as the general population. They are a very cosmopolitan group. Likewise, they have varied interests. There are students involved with technical trades, those who value the liberal arts, and many in highly specialized postgraduate research programs. Some students attend religious-affiliated schools, such as Liberty University or Brigham Young University, because they match and upholds the student's (and/or family's) religious and spiritual heritage. Other religious schools, such as Notre Dame and Boston College, while upholding strong ties and connections to their Roman Catholic foundation, tend to be much more varied in student membership. They also tend to value religious and spiritual mixture. Likewise, there are private and state schools that avoid religious matters, because religious views may taint academic objectivity. As adult educator Jon Dalton wrote in 2006:

> Things have gotten worse as higher education has moved increasingly toward a market-oriented enterprise model. Individual self-interest is the chief value communicated by the popular culture. Most colleges and universities reinforce this value in the curriculum and extracurriculum. Colleges market good jobs, good times, and the good life as their primary benefits. They promote their institutions as essential gateways to these high prizes of private self-interest and materialism.[58]

Yet amidst this move to post-high-school shifting to market-oriented models, many students realize through their ever-expanding and blossoming awareness that they are on a journey of discovery. Some only see academic discovery or a path to a career, while others see a broader image, which includes spiritual awareness. Dalton noted:

> When college students write or are asked about spirituality, they consistently describe it as a journey or quest that takes them inward into the unknown, unexamined

regions of their inner lives. It is a journey of introspection and reflection that students sometimes take alone and at other times in the company of others. When asked about the object or purpose of their spiritual journeys, college students often describe it as an inward search for purpose, meaning fulfillment, depth, wholeness, and authenticity. They describe a journey of discovery that is, in the end, not only about understanding themselves in a deeper and more authentic way but also about discovering their purpose and destiny in life and how these connect to what they believe is sacred and transcendent ...

College students take many paths on their inward journeys. Some make their spiritual searches within the context of a religious faith orientation ... Other students choose to explore paths outside the boundaries of a particular faith tradition and engage in spiritual searches that have little if any connection to any specific religious orientation. What is striking about the contemporary spirituality movement among college students is the wide variety of spiritual practices that students engage in and how receptive they are to exploring new forms of spiritual searching. For reasons that are not fully understood at this time, college students today seem to be very open and motivated to tackling the big questions that young people typically face during the college years.[59]

Ironically, as undergraduate students have their life horizons expanded, it's common for them to decline in their religious lives at the same time. "Some researchers have found that commitment to spiritual growth among traditional-age students may increase during college."[60] In other words, to address and enhance the full life of students, where each facet adds to the other, it would behoove institutions of higher learning to abandon their fears and embrace spiritual development.[61] In 2003, UCLA undertook an incredible national examination of students and spirituality. A press release of some findings bears much attention. Take the time to read this twice:

Today's college students show a very high level of interest and involvement in spirituality and religion, are actively engaged in a spiritual quest, and have high expectations for the role their universities will play in their spiritual and emotional development, according to a major new study released today. Four in five students have an interest in spirituality, three-fourths say they are "searching for meaning or purpose in life," and more than three-quarters believe in God.

These are some of the key findings of a survey conducted last fall of 112,232 freshmen attending 236 colleges and universities. The study, carried out by UCLA's Higher Education Research Institute (HERI), also analyzes how varying degrees of spirituality and religiousness translate into differences in students' political and social attitudes, psychological and physical well-being, and religious preference.

Some of the findings include:

- 80% are interested in spirituality
- 76% are searching for meaning/purpose in life
- 74% have discussions about the meaning of life with friends
- 81% attend religious services
- 80% discuss religion or spirituality with friends
- 79% believe in God
- 69% pray[62]

Two years later, Dr. Margaret Jablonski, who specialized in higher education issues such as women's leadership, also wrote that institutions of higher education need to address the whole student:

In short, by incorporating spirituality into the life of the college, all aspects of campus life become connected to the whole, and are thereby changed. I feel that I try to lead through example in the exploration of these critical questions on my own campus and through my work with NASPA in the larger academic community.

A new focus on spiritual development would have profound implications for higher education and for society as a whole. Students would be better prepared to meet the challenges of the global environment in which we live. Complex questions that cross culture, national, and economic boundaries, for example, could be approached from a holistic approach. Making meaning at the global level could be advanced if higher education provided the opportunities to explore knowledge in complex, connected, and holistic ways.[63]

Educational institutions must assist students in developing wholeness. Is it not better to build up a whole person than the sum of their parts? If we address parts, those parts may or may not develop. In turn, full development is stymied. However, if we address the whole student, and seek to address their sense of spirituality, it's natural that each part is touched, enhanced, and able to assist the rest of the student's sense of being. What are your thoughts on this?

Apart from an institutional fear of addressing spiritual matters, least perceived as being religious, it seems clear that leadership cannot embrace and offer spirituality unless they first embrace spirituality. As Garfield Kevin Hood notes in a 2006 journal article, "students often find the academy devoid of any 'morals' in its struggle to be sectarian and politically correct."[64] Again, "Beyond cultural norms, the Western paradigm of empirical, positivistic, objective, 'value-free' knowledge so cherished in traditional academia had no room for issues of faith, hope, and love (Palmer, 1993)."[65] Jon Dalton described the current scenario very vividly when he wrote:

Colleges and universities have become proficient at teaching students how to deconstruct, dissect, question, analyze, critique, and break down knowledge (Brooks, 2001). They do far less however, to help students construct, connect, and synthesize knowledge, experiences, end beliefs into an integrated whole life that makes possible what Palmer (2000) described as an "undivided life."[66]

It's clear that instructors need to connect with students, not the curriculum.[67] Dr. Laura Jones beautifully describes this:

> To reach deep inside students, where true learning takes place, we teachers must teach from our most authentic selves. Students can always tell when we're not. When classroom interactions are less than authentic, both teachers and students are to some extent merely going through the motions of formal education. This can create, as Parker Palmer, itinerant teacher of teachers and prolific author in spirituality and education, reminds us, a "great sadness" among all involved. Spirituality in education refers to no more—and no less—than a deep connection between student, teacher, and subject—a connection so honest, vital, and vibrant that it cannot help but be intensely relevant. Nourishment of this spark in the classroom allows it to flourish in the world, in the arenas of politics, medicine, engineering—wherever our students go after graduation.[68]

Later, she added:

> Palmer (2004) has expressed an illuminating analogy for the connections that comprise our spirituality. In previous times, during blizzards, farmers on the Great Plains would tie a rope from the back door to the barn to keep from getting lost in the driving snow. Spirituality is our rope, showing us the way home. When at home with ourselves and the world, we can be, as Palmer says, "healers in a wounded world." Palmer (1999) has also offered insight

into teacher-student connections: When students are asked to describe their good teachers, he recounted, the methods of teaching depicted varied—but all students described their good teachers as having "some sort of connective capacity, who connect themselves to their students, their students to each other, and everyone to the subject being studied"[69]

Students of all ages need to learn to embrace their deep spiritual lives. Teachers and instructors also need to deepen their lives. Together, students and teachers are harmoniously linked to discover the other and to share the journey. The curricular is part of the journey; it is not, however, the focus of the journey. By understanding the other, the curricular is enriched. Spiritual growth is not about earning grades, passing exams, or mandated proficiency goals. Spiritual growth is the journey, not the destination. It is the journey inward, towards the "*Educare*" that leads both the student and leaders to fully journey outward. Finally, one additional value needs to be stated. It is a value that is essential in all educational settings and speaks well of spiritual connectedness. Dr. Jude Westrup describes this:

> There's a story that goes something like this: There was a class that consistently achieved fantastic results in an area where students were "disadvantaged". They all graduated and went on to do creative and "contributive" things with their lives. An educational researcher following them all up, and they were, without exception "successful". He returned to the college they had been to, traced the teacher they shared and asked what she had done. "I loved them", was her answer.[70]

In many ways, this comment says everything about reaching out, being spiritually self aware, and openly being present to students of all ages.

Questions to ponder and discuss
Chapter Eight

Spirituality and Education

❶ Should spirituality be provided in public schools, and if so, beginning at what grade?

❷ If we offered spirituality in a non-religious manner or format, what would it look like for the young student (Grades 1–5), the middle-school aged student (Grades 6–8), the high school student (Grades 9–12), and the college student? If you desire, make a chart!

❸ What is the difference between teaching and helping people learn? Does this make a difference in providing spiritual learning?

❹ What teachers do you remember? Are they the ones who made you work on the curricula or the ones who seem to meet you as a person? Take your time with this!

❺ Would spiritual development in schools help reduce the violence, racism, bigotry, and classism that often overwhelm postmodern society?

❻ How does the spirituality of college students change the longer they're in college?

CHAPTER NINE

THE FUTURE

We need to acknowledge that we live in the greatest reformation in history. The growth of knowledge, data, and information continues to expand at unparalleled rates. For example, the U.S. Patent and Trademark Office took 130 years to register the first million patents. But it only took another 35 years to reach the second million. Then it was a mere 22 years to reach the third million. Seventeen years later, it reached four million. A decade after this, it reached the five million. Moreover, it took only eight more years to reach six million patents![1] I wonder how long it will take to reach seven million and eight million. Consider the postmodern world of YouTube. This Internet creation uploaded its first small short piece in April 2005. Fifteen years later, it grew to where the world watches a billion hours per day.[2] Knowledge, data, and information abound. So what will the future look like? How will this affect our spirits? What are your thoughts?

A mere sixty years ago, news footage from around the world entered our home on televisions during the nightly newscasts. The networks and/ or professional film contractors made these videos. Edited footage filled a determined space and time slot on the news. In postmodernism, everyone can shoot raw, unfiltered "videos" and instantly share them. Others may re-share these stories. This re-sharing is like building an upside-down pyramid! It doesn't take long for millions to view stupid, evil, dumb, sad, criminal, or incredible clips. Unlike edited, filtered, and planned news clips, these clips instantaneously bounce around the globe.

We emotionally respond to these clips. We respond to a cat "playing" the piano, or the inspired fellow who, like Spiderman, scaled a balcony to rescue a child. Sadly, we, like many millions, saw the 8-minute-46-seconds video of a police officer kneeling on the neck of George Floyd, a man screaming that he could not breathe. Later, updated tape showed that the act was actually 9 minutes and 29 seconds! It's sadder that this isn't an isolated case of violence in postmodern society – it is a regular situation. In turn, this and other footage feed our need for instantaneous news and postmodern thirst for instant gratification

In the past, newscasters provided a voice-over of the television video footage. They set the context for the viewers. The news was typically at 5 or 6 p.m. Today we stream it when we want. Today, we set the context. This is because we may too busy at those times and determine when we want the news to meet our need. Or because we may be shallow, utilize quick thinking, and respond or react immediately to matters, we're prone to predetermine the context or bias before we view the content. We are our own editors! Past generations realized, processed, and accepted filtered international, national, and local stories. Today, many are suspicious of the media, unless it supports their polarized opinions. As a result, we often respond without filters, or at best, with greatly reduced filters. We consider ourselves experts! We are our own (can we say, prejudiced?) filters. Heck, we don't even have to wait to watch the evening news anymore. In our "Me-ism" world, we can "stream" the news, or select segments of the news, when we want.

Bluntly, we chose to see the world through echo chambers of esteemed private perceptions. Thomas Friedman in *The World Is Flat: A Brief History of the Twenty-First Century,* articulated this dilemma very well in 2007:

> Too much connectivity may be bad not only for your peace
> of mind—it may not be healthy for society as a whole.
> When so many people can upload and globalize their voice,
> their video, their blog, their instant message—when it is
> so easy to do—it's also much more addictive for them and

for us. I am not sure it is good to have millions of people addicted to a form of communication that, by its nature, is unedited, spontaneous, unfiltered, and uncensored. There are some great bloggers and podcasters, who could be working anywhere, and the flat world has opened up wonderfully new opportunities for them to emerge—and even take down a TXU. I enjoy and respect their work. But there are plenty of others who either could really use an editor or should be keeping their thoughts to themselves— or reading a book or taking a class, rather than blogging and podcasting in their spare time.[3]

It seems awkward for postmoderns to impartially discern and appropriately filter and edit input. Thus, how do we constructively address future spiritual needs? How do we accomplish this, both as individuals and as a society? How do we approach spirituality that doesn't necessarily reinforce opinions we already own? Do we begin with conclusions and then search for the evidence to support them? As postmoderns, we are long on opinion and short on information. It's ironic that in the age of incredible information, we rely on reduced input to match preconceived and limited ideas. This is our tough but normal reality. How can we shift and become open to new and challenging spiritual insights? These are good questions to ponder regarding the future of our spiritual lives.

We tend to evaluate instantly those instantaneous stories captured on smartphones traveling around the globe. There's no time delay to digest or evaluate. Rightly or wrongly, we set the context ourselves. Naturally, knowing our history and mindset, algorithms always direct us to see similar stories that we may "like." We are channeled to stories we're likely to affirm. We don't see stories that offer a counter point of view. Algorithms direct us towards our comfort zones by guiding us to limited opinions. It's no wonder we're polarized. We are a society so polarized that armed violence exploded in the U.S. Capital building in January 2021. The world saw Americans weaponized and attacking Americans in the nation's most hallowed halls. The place that spoke of and championed democracy was stormed because people failed to believe that democracy was working.

Additionally, in our "Me-ism" world, we make ourselves the context and content. A 2017 report stated that a large number of Millennials are requesting plastic surgery. This increase can be attributed to the fact the average millennial takes 28,000 selfies annually.[4] Even if this statistic is exaggerated or inaccurate, it remains that with our smartphones and instant pictures, we do take incredibly more pictures than any previous generation. We take pictures of everything, and especially ourselves. This is postmodernism. This is "Me-ism." We evaluate everything around us on the basis that we are the center of the universe!

With our overload of information and difficulty in discerning this material fairly, we have a plague to address. It's a plague beyond the global pandemic wrought by COVID-19. To explain this plague in another way, mull over the following illustration. Imagine the wonderful challenge of choosing one of Baskin-Robbins' 31 flavors (31 was devised to match the days of a month). Now imagine a list of 31,000 choices. This big list is in constant flux, as B-R regularly adds and drops flavors. What ice cream flavor does one choose? Sometimes people may make an outlandish and spontaneous choice. However, for the most part, people tend to pick those flavors typically chosen in the past. We filter our decision to accept known and safe choices. In turn, we do the same with innovations, information, and videos that now swarm, and as some may say, choke, us! Gene Veith, in 1994, wrote:

> There is a difference, by the way, between "knowledge" and "information." Knowledge is substantial and tangible. Information is fleeting and ever-changing. The premodern and the modern value knowledge; the postmodern is obsessed with data.[5]

We have information from which we extract knowledge. Our plague is that the postmodern person needs to sift through much information to find viable, useful, and applicable knowledge. Alas, we often fall prey to known, predictable, and limited choices. Instead of increased knowledge expanding our selections, it serves to make our spheres more restrictive.

To extract knowledge from data and information, we require a special tool. We call this tool "wisdom!" I wonder how much we use wisdom compared to knee-jerk responses. Also, I wonder if we can discern the distinction between these responses. What are your thoughts? Ponder the next complex question deeply: "Is wisdom hard work and instant responses easy? If so, what do I tend to use most?" Be honest.

Another tool we need in this process is the gift of giving oneself time and attention to make use of wisdom. When one undertakes such an endeavor, it bodes well for one's spiritual wellness both today and in the future. Do we avoid giving ourselves time to think, ponder, and let knowledge percolate within us, or do we have a response to soothe ourselves? Sometimes the best answer to a question is, "Let me think about that." Then allow one's spirit time to work!

Take a moment to ponder the depth of your personal "footprint" (or should we say, brain print?) of information and knowledge. We each bring more than we likely realize to this postmodern dilemma of overwhelming data! Neuroscientist, cognitive psychologist, writer, and musician Daniel Levitin wrote in *The Organized Mind: Thinking Straight in the Age of Information Overload*:

> Just trying to keep our own media and electronic files organized can be overwhelming. Each of us has the equivalent of over half a million books stored on our computers, not to mention all the information stored in our cell phones or in the magnetic stripe on the back of our credit cards. We have created a world with 300 exabytes (300,000,000,000,000,000,000 pieces) of human-made information. If each of those pieces of information were written on a 3 x 5 index card and then spread out side by side, just one person's share—*your* share of this information—would cover every square inch of Massachusetts and Connecticut combined ...[6]

In terms of our knowledge and information explosion, 2014 was a lifetime ago! I wonder what would the current statistics look like. What are your thoughts? Let us explain this knowledge explosion and reductionist responses in one sentence: we are massive walking encyclopedia who often think and act from our *Reader's Digest* edition!

In the past, one of the major sources of seeking peace and comfort amidst tumultuous times such as plagues, wars, or social discord was spirituality and religion. Then the world changed. First, our tumultuous times seem to be unending because we're always in flux. For example, for most of Western history, people lived in a secure, stable society. While most lived in poverty or horrid conditions, people were accustomed to the way of life around them. Sons, as noted, characteristically followed fathers generation after generation on the family farm or the family trade. Ours is a very fluid society. In our lifetime, we may dramatically change our employers or careers several times. We may move great distances from our families. Likewise, we rarely live on the farm next to our parents' farm! The nuclear family is often no longer within the same city! For a vivid example, read your local obituaries and discover where children of the deceased live!

Second, Western society and Western Christianity were historically rooted in moral and cultural rules that were "carved in stone." In postmodernism, it seems that we keep today's rules regularly updated on our smartphones. Tied to this, the rise of "Me-ism," scandals throughout Western Christianity, tribalism, polarization, consumerism, and changing social mores are an integral part of our fluid society. Western Christianity was once entrenched, solid, and offered much security. Those days are gone. Between scandals and numerous social changes, it lost its predominant, sacred, hallowed, and favored position. Secularism and SBNRs assumed this place and space.

Postmodern Western society considers religion and spirituality as separate and distinct entities. In the last few decades, research into spirituality by educational, social, and medical scientists dramatically increased. At the same time, religious institutions in Western Christianity gave the impression that they remain comfortable with their fixed traditional, historic models, and practices. A sad but true saying within Western Christianity states, "That as it was in the beginning, is now, and evermore shall be." It's even sadder to see the lack of awareness of this position while one's ship is sinking. Ironically, while in freefall with decreasing social prestige, respect, falling memberships, declining attendance, and income, many are oblivious to the reformation all around them. Is this denial? Or is it avoidance? It's like the *Emperor's New Clothes*. Who's going to take a risk, be honest, and blow the whistle? What do you think? Western Christianity has many resources that could truly assist people in these tumultuous times. But is it so locked into the past that it fails to address reform and the fluid needs of people?[7] It seems that Western Christianity continuously fails to appropriately adapt to the changing world.

For much of Western Christianity's history, most people lived in poverty and distressing conditions. Consequently, for those who suffered on earth, the church promoted the notion that they would receive their reward in heaven. In postmodernism, people aren't interested in the heavenly reward. Instead, they desire a good earthly life. In her unpublished 2013 doctorate dissertation, Marlene Martin contends that this shift by humanity embraced a spiritual decline.[8] This means, in part, that instead of the "hereafter," people now "yearn after the here!"

Postmodernism challenges Western society, Western Christianity, and Western Spirituality to address the complex and ever-evolving human dilemma at the personal level and societal level. This intense global reality existed before COVID-19 took the world hostage and further enhanced the need for all to attend to spiritual matters. Clearly, in postmodernism, we must wonder, "What is the future of spirituality?" This is a significant personal and societal question. It is, in my opinion, a serious matter for Western society, Western Christianity, and Western Spirituality to engage. We shouldn't ignore this deeply foundational human crisis. After all, to do so will affect our souls! We sorely need to rediscover or enhance our spiritual selves. Like Dorothy, we are no longer in Kansas or acclimatizing to the dysfunctional *Brave New World*. We need to be like Peter Pan and discover our shadow (our spiritual selves) and sew it back on to be holy whole and/or wholly holy.

While Wendy enlightened Peter and sewed on his shadow, we too must be bold and willing to take risks. We need others to assist us in our spiritual journey of discovery. In turn, we need to assist others on their journeys. When we rediscover our spiritual selves, we can fly like Peter to "the second star to the right, and straight on to morning." In other words, we can move our lives forward rather than endure endless repeating cycles that affirm "Me-ism."

Richard Rohr, a Franciscan priest who spent a career in contemplation and writing, explained in his many books that we must move from our "False Self to our True Self." In the 2013 book, *Immortal Diamond: Searching for Our True Self,* he described this well. Ironically, like Barrie's *Peter Pan,* he alludes to shadows! Rohr in this insightful postmodern observation said:

There are *four major splits* from reality that we have all made in varying degrees to create our False Self:

1. We split from our shadow self and pretend to be idealized self.
2. We split our mind from our body and soul and live in our minds.
3. We split life from death and try to live our life without any "death."
4. We split ourselves from other selves and try to live apart, superior, and separate.[9]

Take a few moments, or perhaps longer, to look at these "splits" and assess them for yourself. How true are these comments for you?

Some call postmodernism the Age of Entitlement, others the Age of Bewilderment or the Digital Age. We might also style this as the Age of Entertainment, or the Age of Distraction. We might also call it the Age of Addictions because with reduced and declining attention spans, we can't remove our faces from staring at a two-inch handheld screen! We can boldly declare with some certainty that we are tethered to our phones—they are not tethered to us! We also face unprecedented addictions to drugs, alcohol, sexual abuses, domestic fights, and societal violence because we live on the edge of our emotions and avoid the inward journey. Early in postmodernism, many suggested that Buckminster Fuller called television "chewing gum for the eyes." Perhaps we can borrow this image and suggest that smartphones are now the chewing gum for our eyes. Have addictions and technology replaced our sense of wonder?[10]

In our "Me-ism" society, we are addicted to many things. Why? It is, in part, because we're seeking to avoid looking beyond the surface of our lives. A vivid example of the addiction to our smartphone screens is Gary

Turk's well-known YouTube video, "Look up." Some sources suggest it has 600 million views! Nevertheless, I can't help but wonder how many people it influenced to "look up." His social commentary on our shallowness and addiction describes our endemic social and private sadness, loneliness, and disconnection with the world. Watch this insightful video and take time to examine it and ask yourself, "What do I think of the message?" and "How much of this is me?"

In postmodernism, we are prone to desire and expect people to listen to us. We love it and feel affirmed when our words flow out of the mouths of others. Likewise, we are often so intent on what we want to say next that we afford little space to listen. Besides listening to us, we hope people look at us and "like" us on Facebook and other platforms. In other words, we yearn for external affirmation. Yet how much attention do we give to internal affirmation? How much attention do we ever afford to our spiritual lives or those of others? Are we so busy seeking others to like or love us in transitory, fleeting moments that we fail to see deep affections from others, and our self-awareness? How can we redeem this for ourselves and society? What do you think? Are we so concerned that we're "liked" that we may never think that we should "like" others. What are your thoughts?

For most of Western society's history, spirituality was prefabricated.[11] The religious institutions told people what they needed to do to be spiritual beings. This worked, since religiousness and spirituality were one and the same. However, with the separation of religion from spirituality, and with much suspicion of institutions and rampant "Me-ism," where do we now seek and hold spirituality? How do we advance spirituality beyond a cultural Prozac?[12]

With the daily (can we say, hourly?) overload of nonstop information and knowledge bombarding us through many sources, such as television news channels, the radio, our smartphones, the internet, and the social media, it's easy to become desensitized to the world around us. We become fatigued. I can recall my upset as a teenager when watching the famine in Biafra in the late 1960s when an interviewed aid worker stated that too much television coverage was bad for raising funds to feed the people. He said it would make people numb, and funds would slow down. That had a great impact on me because, like many, I thought that the more coverage the better!

Today with no walls or barriers, we may become fatigued with the information or knowledge around us. We may move away from thinking of others to solely addressing the self. In other words, to protect oneself from overload, "Me-ism" acts as a protective coating. Without question, the great pandemic of COVID-19 in postmodern Western society amplifies this evolving reality. Take a few moments and ponder the seemingly non-stop news, knowledge, information, and misinformation we have before us. We have esteemed scientists competing with a variety of "snake-oil" salespersons on the Internet and some news channels creating alternative truths. Sadly and unfortunately, many elect to downplay serious facets of this global crisis. For example, we hear that this is really a conspiracy to plant devices within us, or that it's a plot, like Nazism, or that sunshine or bleach will make the virus go away. We hear people championing the right to personal freedom. It's interesting that when queried on the news about how this may affect others, the answer is often sidestepped as they repeat or vocally strengthen their view of personal freedom. I wonder if placing freedom over caring for others isn't the current ultimate expression of "Me-ism." What do you think?

Where is the future of spirituality if we create roadblocks, and if we live with forever circling and reinforcing "Me-ism?" Richard Rohr, in *What the Mystics Know: Seven Pathways to Your Deeper Self*, describes this dilemma well:

> Living in the material world, with a physical body and in a culture of affluence that rewards the outer self, it is a both more difficult to know our spiritual self and all the more necessary. Our skin-encapsulated egos are the only self that we know and therefore our only beginning place. But they are not the only or even best place. That is our contemporary dilemma: (1) Our culture no longer values the inner journey. (2) We actively avoid and fear it. (3) In most cases we no longer even have the tools to go inward because (4) we are enamored of and entrapped in the private ego and its private edges. In such a culture, "The center cannot hold," at least for long.[13]

As explained elsewhere, it seems that we are shallow. Sadly, we expend so much energy looking for affirmation, we spread ourselves thin. As Gene Veith said:

> Jameson's comment that postmodern culture is "without depth" points to another stylistic feature of the arts. In contrast to modernism, postmodernism has, according to Harvey, a "fixation with appearances, surfaces, and instant impacts that have no sustaining power over time." A society devoted to instant gratification, conditioned by the immediacy of its information media and by its lack of moral restraints on immediate pleasure, will demand instant gratification in its arts and entertainment. While books encourage inner reflection, video images present only surface appearances. People who have no beliefs lack a sense of personal identity and an inner life. They are thus, in every sense of the term, superficial ...[14]

To repeat an image mentioned earlier in this work, are we a mile wide but only an inch thick?

It may be true that we're mostly unaware of the need "to look inward and also to act outward." What do you think? Do we likewise need to add depth to our lives? We will explore this critical image of the inward journey in this chapter. Have you ever wondered if you undertake enough inward reflection? Do you think you might begin to do more?

We can safely assume that the vast tidal wave and influx of information and knowledge isn't going to slow down. So how do we discern what is appropriate and avoid reinforcing tribal ideas that forever rotate within our narrow realms? Richard Hamm, a long-time parish cleric and later denominational administrator, describes this well:

> Postmodern society, with its capacity for creating "cultural niches," makes it possible for these generations to each live in its own little world without much real encounter with the others. Each generation has TV shows, music, movies,

and radio stations targeted to it. Each has magazines, cruise lines, automobiles, whole neighborhoods, and churches targeted to it.[15]

In other words, to expand our perspectives and break out of "cultural niches" and shallow self-serving limited perspectives, we must develop our spiritual selves! This includes learning to discover (dare we suggest, re-discover?) and utilize wisdom.

Wisdom means sorting through data, information, and knowledge. In 2010, professors of education, Elizabeth E. Bennett and Alexandra A. Bell, quoting the 1998 work of M.C. Harris, described the passage to finding wisdom:

> ... information is dynamic and evolutionary as value is added to transform observations into wisdom. He proposed a model that begins with data flowing from observation, which, when analyzed for classifications, produces information. Information explained leads to understanding, and the ability to predict produces knowledge. Wisdom is achieved when knowledge is used to create general laws. Very little data make it all the way through the process to the plane of wisdom, which is continually redefined in each era; what is wise in one historical moment is commonplace in another. This progression of refinement is greater than the sum of individual learning and affects the collective imagination of society.[16]

Wisdom, therefore, means including the input of others. To obtain wisdom means active listening to others and deeply listening to oneself! Renowned and popular populist author of postmodern spiritual thinking, Eckhart Tolle, echoed this notion in *Stillness Speaks* (2003) when he wrote:

> Do you need more knowledge? Is more information going to save the world, or faster computers, more scientific or

intellectual analysis? Is it not wisdom that humanity needs most at this time?

But what is wisdom and where is it to be found? Wisdom comes with the ability to be still. Just look and just listen. No more is needed. Being still, looking, and listening activates the non-conceptual intelligence within you. Let stillness direct your words and actions.[17]

Deep listening to oneself and others, along with life experiences, leads to spiritual growth.[18] However, these attributes aren't dominant in postmodernism. Instead of deep listening, we often seek quick responses or solutions that provide us with the "truth." Once we have "truth," we move on to other pressing matters. Deep, active listening is an art we need to re-cultivate in our quest to deepen our personal and corporate spirituality.

The late Dr. Eyatta Ficher, who dedicated herself to creating diversity in the classroom, describes this notion of listening beautifully:

The last process, communication through the heart, is the destination. The process, of listening provides a space for validation of the speaker and also allows the speaker to experience self-validity. I often wonder if something as simple, natural, and free as listening can change the course of the violent acts that are imposed on self and others. Listening is a transformative act. As Nelson (2000) so aptly states: "To listen. Not to grade. Not to psychoanalyze. Not to solve. Just to listen."[19]

Read this a second time. What does it say to you? Can you actively listen, and listen deeply? If so, both you and those with whom you talk need to learn to spiritually feed the other. In this way, the talker and listener enrich each other. The work of active listening and listening deeply requires practice and patience. Practice and patience are essential life attributes but sadly are not normative in postmodernism. This suggests that we have our work cut out for us as we search for our spiritual futures.

Since we seem to lead a life with narrow perspectives, our life experiences may lack variety. Instead of testing and sampling Baskin-Robbins' 31 flavors, or even the expanded menu, we tend to limit our selections to those that historically please us. If we love double chocolate fudge, why would we risk and taste raspberry-blueberry-orange-bubble gum! We are not prone to risks. Unwittingly, we prefer affirmation. This is normal human behavior. We channel our choices to predictable selections. However, it's becoming apparent that in our shallowness, we seem to be taking fewer risks. We choose not to risk any possible discomfort. What do you think? How often do accept an answer rather than struggle with a question? Give yourself some time to consider this matter. In turn, do you struggle or give up when solutions aren't readily available? Or do you preserve? Think about this.

It's in risks and in enduring discomfort that we grow as individuals both in character and in spirituality. In 1976, Henri Nouwen, a well known and much-published author on spiritual growth, elegantly wrote of inward-looking and risk-taking:

> The real spiritual guide is the one who, instead of advising us what to do or to whom to go, offers us a chance to stay alone and take the risk of entering into our own experience. He makes us see that pouring little bits of water on our dry land does not help, but that we will find a living well if we reach deep enough under the surface of our complaints …[20]

This need for inwardness, active listening, and risk-taking is essential to the future of spirituality! Others support this image. Here are some insightful quotes to ponder and contemplate. In other words, take some moments to practice some inward stillness and quietness to see how these thoughts mingle with your spirituality. Be prepared to take a risk to be enlightened! Read them each slowly, and then, if so inclined, read them again!

First, in 1998, an edited book of meditations of John Main, a Benedictine monk who gained an international following with his writings and meditation workshops, stated:

In entering into our own silence, we risk everything, for we risk our very being: 'So I said to my soul. "Be still."' The stillness of mind and body to which the mantra guides us is a preparation for entering this silence. It prepares us for our progression through the spheres of silence to see with wonder the light of our own spirit, and to know that light as something beyond our spirit and yet the source of it. This is a pilgrimage through our spheres of silence that we undertake in faith, putting our entire trust in what is only a dim apprehension of the authentic, the real, yet confident in doing so because it is authentic ...[21]

Also ponder the words of adult educator and nun Jane Vella, in 2000, wrote:

Whenever adults risk going to the core of their beliefs, they are apt to come face to face with the resources and wounds that are embedded in their spiritual selves. Growth and transformation become possible whenever adults connect their daily lives to their spiritual homes, that place where they grow toward wholeness.[22]

Dorothy MacKeracher, who taught adult learning practices for many years, writing in 2004, said:

The learning related to soul work takes time. It does not occur according to a plan or as a result of intentional intervention. If one attends to the soul with educated and steadfast imagination, change will take place without the individual being consciously aware of its happening. Moore concludes: "A genuine odyssey is not about piling up experiences. It is a deeply felt, risky, unpredictable tour of the soul."[23]

To journey inward means asking tough questions, but asking inward questions in postmodernism is not a common virtue. It's a practice needing revival for future spiritual growth. Israeli academic and author Yuval Harari's *21 Lessons for the 21st Century* provides us a succinct image of what the postmodern person needs to appreciate when seeking spiritual growth. He wrote: "Questions you cannot answer are usually far better for you than answers you cannot question."[24] We live in a period when it's easier to believe and accept answers and "truth" than to take time and explore questions. However, the answers we often accept are typically the answers of others. We must take ownership of our spiritual development. This means wrestling with our tough questions and being willing to accept that answers aren't always easily forthcoming!

In life, it's healthier to pose questions that are difficult to explore and answer than to have answers one cannot question. Jeanette Justice Fleming, for her 2005 doctoral dissertation, interviewed many people. One male shared:

> On this board he has written wisdom sayings over a period of several years that have meaning for him, inspire him, and reflect his world view. He pointed toward these as he shared his views about spirituality and said, "It may not be who I am, but who I aspiring to be."[25]

Thus, in exploring wisdom and insights from himself, he discovered that the foundational life question he was aiming to answer was, "Who am I?" He resolved that this task was vital to direct and uphold him as he grew into himself. He journeyed inward, explored questions, and moved forward on his journey of becoming a content spiritual person. This is the great spiritual quest that all should undertake.

As Dr. J. Philip Newell, who now is dedicated to full-time writing on spirituality, suggests, we need to reflect on the relationship between wisdom and humility:

> One of the true marks of wisdom therefore is humility, for although the wise may give voice to insights that have never been expressed, they know that the wellspring of wisdom is deeper than them and is pure gift. It is an everlasting stream flowing through them in new ways. And so, as

Ecclesiasticus says, 'honour yourself with humility. Again it needs to be said that humility is not a demeaning of the self, and certainly not a self-hatred. Humility is a returning to oneself, to the root of earth (humus) of one's being. Humility is about being reconnected to the ground of our soul. It is what Rabbi Kook calls a 'noble humility'... Knowledge without humility is an attempt to try to possess the power of truth for our own exclusive blessing with a disregard to the rest of life ...[26]

Is there a relationship between knowledge, wisdom, and humility? What do you think?

In my opinion, humility is a value not appreciated in postmodernism. Instead, we tend to perceive humility as a weakness in a society that prefers loudness, over-the-top self-proclamations, and examples of extreme self-confidence (can we say, arrogance?) and self-promotion. In other words, humility seems to be the opposite of the values championed and appreciated in postmodernism. This devaluing of humility is not new. Joan Chittister provides a grand illustration of this:

Later centuries distorted the notion and confused the concept of humility with lack of self-esteem and substituted the warped and useless practice of humiliations for the idea of humility. Eventually the thought of humility was rejected out of hand, and we have been left as a civilization to stew in the consequences of our arrogance ...[27]

Later in the same book, she added, "Humility, the lost virtue of our era, is crying to heaven for rediscovery. The development of nations, the preservation of the globe, the achievement of human community may well depend on it."[28] If we're to recapture humility, we must rediscover what it is. The late Madeleine L'Engle, well-known for her many writings, explained:

The root word of *humility* is *humus*, earth; to be *human*, too, comes from the same word; and the parables of Jesus which show the kind of humility he is seeking in us are often earthy, such as the parable of the workers in the vineyard, the parable of the seed and the sower and the parable of the prodigal son. We all have within us that same lack of humility as the workers who worked in the heat of the day and resented those who got equal pay for shorter hours of work; and we all understand the lack of humility in the elder son who was offended by his father's humble forgiveness.[29]

Mark Steffen, a missionary and later hospice and hospital chaplain, writing three decades later, offered this astute definition for us to ponder:

Humility, then can best be understood as having an honest and realistic awareness of who we are and who we are not. It is an understanding that we have both the potential and limitations, strengths and needs, and knowing what those are. Or in the negative, humility is not holding a false and unrealistically high view of ourselves. To be humble is to not be egotistical or self-absorbed. So, humility is the honest sense of being significant, yet interdependent, and others-concerned.[30]

Judy Rogers, professor and adult educator with a focus on spiritual development, built upon the thoughts of others when she wrote:

Emmons (1999) writes, "Humility is the realistic appraisal of one's strengths and weaknesses – neither overestimating nor underestimating them. To be humble is not to have a low opinion of oneself. It is to have an accurate opinion of oneself". (p. 171) Humility is the ability to keep your achievements and gifts in perspective, to be comfortable with who you are, to understand your faults, and to be free from arrogance and low self-esteem (Clark, 1992).[31]

Take a few moments to re-read these thoughts. Take time to let them settle, and with your spirit, reflect upon them! Take time to listen to your stillness. Like many, I like the poetic description presented in the New Revised Standard Version translation of 1 Kings 19:12: "And after the earthquake a fire, but the Lord was not in the fire; and after the fire a sound of sheer silence." In sheer silence and stillness, mull over the attributes of humility. Mull over how you can expand humility in your life and your community. It's a great response to combat postmodern "Me-ism."

While it" vital for spiritual growth to mull over humility in silence, it" equally important to accept the notion that silence is part of humility. Activist and author (with a focus on spirituality) Mae Cannon, in 2013, shared this idea when writing about Mother Teresa:

> Mother Teresa taught that humility, through the acknowledgment of weakness and mistakes and by keeping silence, is a manifestation of Christ- likeness. She believed that humility is not possible without silence: "Both humility and prayer grow from an ear, mind, and tongue that have lived in silence with God." In the silence of body, mind and spirit, God speaks and reveals himself. "If you face God in prayer and silence, God will speak to you," she said. "Then you will know that you are nothing. It is only when you realize your nothingness, your emptiness, that God can fill you with Himself."[32]

College president and adult educator Sherry Hoppe rightly declared that:

> Spiritual leaders must be humble enough to acknowledge mistakes, and more importantly, we must forgive each other when mistakes are made ... For a leader, beginning over again is usually just a reaching down into the core being for renewal and strength. So the inner journey continues and is the never-ending source undergirding the sacred responsibility of relationships. Central to that responsibility is compassion ... So we return to where we began: looking for the soul and spirit in the heart instead of the head.[33]

Perhaps one of the foremost authors on spirituality in postmodern Western society is the Benedictine nun, Sister Joan Chittister. She is the author of 60 books, often written from both a contemplative and activist perspective. In 1992, she published *The Rule of Benedict: Spirituality for the 21st Century.* St. Benedict (c. 480) was largely responsible for the growth and sustainability of the monastic way of life in Western society. We should accept this work of his as a major influence in the history of Western society. In his *Rule,* he described how a monastery was to be organized and how monks were to act. He gave structure to prayer, work, and sleep.

To a chaotic world, he gave order and a way to live in faith. Much of the *Rule* notes humility. In her book, Chittister eloquently makes note of this call. Please read and contemplate the following ideas. Again, let these long thoughts sift through you in silence. Do not rush through these gems.

> This is the degree of humility that calls for emotional stability, for holding on when things do not go our way, for withstanding the storms of life rather than having to flail and flail against the wind and, as a result, lose the opportunity to control ourselves when there is nothing else in life that we can control …

> To bear bad things, evil things, well is for Benedict a mark of humility, a mark of Christian maturity. It is a dour and difficult notion for the modern Christian to accept. The goal of the twenty-first century is to cure all diseases, order all inefficiency, topple all obstacles, end all stress, and prescribe immediate panaceas. We wait for nothing and put up with little and abide less and react with fury at irritations. We are a people without patience. We do not tolerate process. We cannot stomach delay. Persist. Persevere. Endure, Benedict says. It is good for the soul to temper it. God does not come on hoofbeats of mercury through streets of gold. God is in the dregs of our lives. That's why it takes humility to find God where God is not expected to be … Benedict is telling us that true humility

is simply a measure of the self that is taken without exaggerated approval or exaggerated guilt. Humility is the ability to know ourselves as God knows us and to know that it is the little we are that is precisely our claim on God. Humility is, then, the foundation for our relationship with God, our connectedness to others, our acceptance of ourselves, our way of using the goods of the earth and even our way of walking through the world, without arrogance, without domination, without scorn, without put-downs, without disdain, without self-centeredness. The more we know ourselves, the gentler we will be with others.[34]

The *Rule of St. Benedict* has a few very dedicated adherents in postmodernism. Do you know that postmodern people still benefit from a discipline developed by the Benedictine Order to follow the rules? In their deep and sincere desire to regulate prayer, worship, and an orderly practice and routine, we can thank them, and later the Cistercians, for the development and creation of the mechanical clock![35]

With our endemic quest and contiguous thirst to appease self-absorption, we must wonder how we can move back to finding humility and living simply. In our "Me-ism" society, we must ask if we are narcissistic, or do we border on narcissism. Here is a long quote from Jean Twenge and W. Keith Campbell to ponder that question:

In many ways, humility is the opposite of narcissism. Some people misconstrue humility as bad, equating it with shame or self-hatred. Humility is not the same as humiliation. True humility is a strength: the ability to see or evaluate yourself accurately and without defensiveness (notice we said "accurately," not "negatively"). Our friend and colleague Julie Exline, who researches humility, found that humble people are often surrounded by friends and family who support them and allow them to see themselves accurately. Sometimes this support comes through religion, as many religions emphasize humility. Overall, humble people are more connected to others. When you don't concentrate on pumping up the self, it is easier to relate to other people and the wider world. Many people think that humility is a virtue that only great leaders possess, like Gandhi or Mother Teresa, but everyone can practice humility by honestly appraising themselves, remembering the people who have helped and supported them, and truly valuing the lives of others ... Another treatment for narcissism comes from a surprising source: compassion for yourself. Kristin Neff, who did some of the first research on the concept, writes that compassion for yourself works because "people cannot always be, or get exactly, what they want. When this reality is denied or fought against, then suffering increases in the form of stress, frustration and self-criticism. When this reality is accepted with sympathy and kindness, then greater emotional equanimity is experienced." Compassion for yourself isn't about admiring or esteeming the self or making excuses for shoddy behavior—it means being kind to yourself while also accurately facing reality. "With self-compassion, you don't have to feel better than others to feel good about yourself."[36]

Perhaps you should re-read this last quote. What thoughts occurred as you read? Perhaps instead of labeling ourselves as narcissistic in our "me" centered society, we might fairly identify ourselves as "narcissistic-light, or narcissistic- very light." What is your reaction to this image?

Finding beneficial self-compassion and humility is essential for postmodern persons to rediscover themselves. Humility and self-compassion lead us back to who we used to be. When we are re-centered and spiritually alive, we can reach out and share that gift with others. There's an expression in Western Christianity, which says that we are "To let the Christ in me find the Christ in you." For those who call themselves Christian, this is, in my opinion, a fundamental image we need to build upon. For the many who have left Christianity in body and/or spirit, or those from other religious or cultural experiences, we might re-phrase this as, "I must use my spirit to find your spirit." In all scenarios, it is clear that all prosper, and all are served. To share in this growth, we must learn to listen to others. Likewise, we need to relearn the need to serve others.

The role of the early church was to follow the directions of Jesus to serve God and serve others. In keeping with this ideal, the early churches created and maintained a new social institution—the hospital. As well noted in postmodernism, Western society and Western Christianity morphed from serving others into "Me-ism." One elegantly expressed this when he wrote, "I was addicted to myself."[37] Clearly, we live in a society where we are prone to ask, "How can people and God best serve me?"

Using an image from Western Christianity, an all too often comment clergy may hear after worship is, "I didn't get anything from that sermon (and/or church service)." The best response we can offer to those who complain should be, "But what did you give to God or others?" A sad but indicative response in postmodernism and speaking from experience, the first response of many to the question of giving to God or others is to bestow money. This reeks of consumerism. In other words, people may not think that they need to give of themselves! Humility and all spiritual values are rooted in the image of, "It is not what we receive, but what we give!" This is true in non-Christian organizations as well. How can we in Western Christianity and Western society recapture the sacrificial nature of serving others? When we serve others, we also serve ourselves. To accomplish this bold act means reversing "Me-ism" to "we-ism." This is humility. To be a humble, content self, and feeling called and satisfied in cheerfully helping others with no expectations, is indeed a spiritual gift. The following quote is a stylish and accurate view of postmodern Western Christianity, yet Western society can adopt this illustration. Although written in 1994, it's even more poignant today. Gene Veith wrote:

> Christians, like everyone else in today's economy, are consumers, but they dare not apply consumer values to God. Notice the implications of the phrase "church shopping." Surely, shopping for a church in the same way we shop for a major appliance is dangerous. Instead of

looking for a church that teaches the Word of God, we sometimes look for a church that "fills our needs." The church does not exist to provide its members "services"; rather, it should challenge its members to engage in "service" to God and to their fellow human beings. When we think like consumers, we put ourselves first, picking and choosing what best corresponds to our desires. Christianity is a matter of truth, of submission to a Holy, righteous God whose authority over us is absolute and who in no way is subject to our consumer preferences. Christianity must not be tainted with consumerism.

Nor is the church a theme park. Our tendency in the postmodern age is to evaluate everything in terms of its entertainment value. Judging a worship service according to how entertaining it is misses the point. Choosing a church because we like the music or because the preacher tells funny jokes is dangerous. Worship is not entertainment, but coming into the presence of a holy God. A relationship with Christ is not contingent upon how good we feel. Rather, as those who worshiped in traditional churches were always reminded, it is a matter of being gathered into His cross.[38]

In serving others, we also discover and fulfill the basic human need for community. In a phrase, "human spirituality, like human welfare, is deeply rooted in relationship. Spirituality is rarely just about solitary gurus on mountaintops—not in the West, not in the East. Not anywhere."[39] Historically, people gathered, and still gather, to share religious and spiritual experiences. Today, with our global multi-cultural, diverse setting, it seems that Western Christianity and other religions need to embrace people within their community and assist all to find their spirit.

For eons, Western Christianity, and likely many Western religious groups, operated with the mentality of "Come to us; we have the answers you need." Today the mantra for all should be, "What can we do to help you find your spirit?" While appealing to individualism and "Me-ism" may seem to smack of postmodernism, the reality is this is the place where people are. All must bend and learn to meet people in their space. Then, and only then, are people able to enjoy religious organizations. We can't turn back the clock or avoid information and knowledge explosions, or consumerism, etc. We must learn to connect with others beyond "fitting in."[40]

As a community, people serve to assist, complement, challenge, and sustain each other on the collective and individual journey. As the old saying goes, "A bundle of sticks is stronger than a single stick." Thus, it makes logical sense to begin addressing people in their comfort zone to help them shift from "Me-ism" to "we-ism."[41] For the future of spirituality, it's essential that we address the idea of community. This doesn't mean supporting tribalism.

Tribalism, as noted, is part of postmodernism and is where like-minded people support each other and, unfortunately, may develop herd thinking. We are tribal in religious groups, ethnic groups, and skin color. At times, tribalism morphs and becomes fanatical, such as the John Birch Society, QAnon, Proud Boys, or Oath Keepers, etc. We need to rethink our identity from tribalism to community building. However, it's also necessary to note that this is a difficult leap!

> Consumerism starts with an assumption that is almost too obvious to state. Human beings must consume certain things in order to live. Postmodern tribalism offers a good reminder that cultural backgrounds influence how we view the world and play a key role in our sense of belonging and identity. None of these ideas is antithetical to Christianity, and the fact that we can find good in each of these should not surprise us. After all, God creates us as multidimensional beings—economic, aesthetic, psychological, political, spiritual, moral, biological, social beings who exist in specific times and cultures.[42]

We need to reverse tribalism from being ghettoized[43] and re-establish healthy, diverse communities. Community is people who have something in common but are open to disagree. We need to evolve from the "caterpillar 'me' to community butterfly."[44] The opposite of tribalism is community. As Parker Palmer once wrote:

> Paradoxically, as we enter more deeply into the true community of our lives, we are relieved of those fears that keep us from becoming the authentic selves we were born to be. Community and individuality are not an either/or choice, any more than life and death are. Instead, they are the poles of another great paradox. A culture of isolated individualism produces mass conformity because people who think they must bear life all alone are too fearful to take the risks of selfhood. But people who know that they are embedded in an eternal community are both freed and empowered to become who they were born to be.[45]

How do we recapture communities from our postmodern, tribal, and individualistic mindset? Although writing about virtual education, an image from Ros Stuart-Battle, quoting Sister Angela Ann Zukowski, Director of the University of Dayton's Institute for Pastoral Initiatives and Virtual Learning Community of Faith Formation, can easily be applied to any notion of community. She wrote that community is the 7 Cs. When these are present, we have vigorous communities. The list is, "conversation, collaboration, creativity, critical reflection, conversion, community and contemplation."[46] These seven actions can take place in a variety of community settings. They're also reflective of active listening, inward journeying, stillness, and humility. Dr. Deborah Cady notes that Sharon Parks, well-known for her work on adolescents and growth, also explains this need for community. She writes that Parks' five forms include:

> ... conventional community, diffuse community, mentoring community, self-selected group, and a community open to others. The mutual shaping relationship between one's identity and his or her community results in a developmental progressions not unlike the cognitive

theories where students progress from a closed, like-minded community to a more open, inclusive, and diverse community.[47]

Community is unlike exclusive, close-minded, and lockstep tribalism in which individuals have much in common. In a community, individuals may have a few things in common, but they also value and respect the differences others uphold or represent. Community is a willingness to disagree without judging others or feeling a need to be right. Community is needing each other. In a community, we listen to each other. To listen to those who truly differ from us, we must be bold enough to care about their opinions and thoughts:

> Our Western culture and its modern conveniences want us to push toward individualism and self-reliance. But our perceived self-sufficiency is a self-defeating illusion, because healthy life is life lived in community. We are members of the same team, and we are intended to travel through life in the company of others, for we are designed for interdependence ... Relationships are spiritual. They cannot be seen or touched, but they define us, and they hold us together meaningfully. Out spiritual health is best realized in community. For spiritual healing in the companionship of others is real ...[48]

Community is an open willingness to be in relationships without the need of being the center of attention. Community is accepting others for who they are with a desire that they accept you in the same way. Furthermore, in a healthy community, marginalization does not exist, and we wonder, "What can others teach me?"[49]

To move from postmodernism's mono-centered tribal groupings to healthy, diverse, engaging communities we must accept tolerance. We need to learn to be tolerant of those different from us. Intolerance, unfortunately, is rampant and reflective of postmodernism, where we often expect everybody to be like us and give little thought to their differences—after all, they "should be like me." Racism, gender conflicts, and violence (both domestic and societal) are indicative of intolerance and tribalism. To become tolerant, we should learn from great examples.

One interesting illustration to consider comes from A. A. Milne's *Winnie the Pooh*. Winnie, named after the Canadian city of Winnipeg, had a bunch of friends, including the human Christopher Robin (the real name of Milne's son). Among Pooh's animal friends was Tigger. Tigger was hyperactive about everything, all the time. He could be aggravating and exhausting with his non-stop excitability. At the other end of the spectrum was Eeyore. Eeyore's negativity was constant and deep, and it was as if he could truly suck all the brightness out of the sun! Everything was always wrong, sad, and negative. Yet no matter what took place, Pooh was loyal, accepting, and understanding of these two friends. If any of the friends in the stories were lost, they were all lost! All searched for the one supposed to be missing.

In a few words, Pooh was tolerant, accepting, and loving with his friends. We need to embrace, to grow spiritually by being tolerant, accepting, and loving. It's essential because it broadens our views, opinions, and acceptance of others. Pooh lived on friendship (and honey). Friendship must replace the postmodern reality of having countless situational shallow acquaintances. Friendship is sometimes defined as someone knowing everything about you and still liking you. Friends offer each other deep support and genuine care. Friends share joys and burdens, and consciously and unconsciously feed the spirit of the other.

All this poses a great challenge in postmodernism! It's as great a challenge as it is to instill silence and stillness. Read the next few quotes and then read re-read them. What do they say to you? First, consider the image of South African professor of Christian spirituality Marlene Martin, who wrote, "MacQuarrie (2000:64) argues that *spiritus* has a secondary meaning, *inspiration*, which literally means *breathing in* ... Jesus breathed not 'on' them but that he breathed 'into' them."[50] Reflect on that image for a few moments. Joan Chittister wrote:

> The difference between Benedict and other spiritual
> masters of his time lay in the fact that Benedict believed

that the spiritual life was not an exercise in spiritual gymnastics. It was to be nothing "harsh or burdensome." And it was not a private process. It was to be done in community with others. It was to be a "school" dedicated to "the good of all concerned." It was to be lived with "patience."[51]

Ponder the image painted by evangelist Dr. Ken Boa, who wrote:

> Dietrich Bonhoeffer in *Life Together* warned: "Let him who cannot be alone beware of community ... Let him who is not in community beware of being alone." Times deliberately spent away from interaction with other people nurture depth, perspective, purpose, and resolve. They deliver us from the tyranny and distractions of daily routine and prepare us for the next stage of the journey through an inner call rather than an external compulsion. By periodically distancing ourselves from schedules, noises, and crowds, we become less captivated by the demands and expectations of others and more captivated by the purposes of God. In this way, we measure and define ourselves in terms of what God thinks rather than what people think. This in turn empowers us to serve and show compassion to others, since we are less manipulated by human expectations and more alive to divine intentions.[52]

The final image to ponder comes from noted adult educator on spirituality Libby Tisdell, quoting an earlier work:

> Sharon Welch (1999) noted in her discussion of spirituality that the famous jazz pianist Mary Lou Williams would occasionally pause in midperformace to make the audience more attentive: "Listen! This will heal you!" (p. 19) she would say. This admonition, no doubt, got people's attention and it helped them listen in a new way. Significant spiritual experiences are like that.[53]

We understand the power and gift of music to heal. Mary Lou Williams (1910–1981) knew this when she said that people were stimulated to listen deeper. Her pause was a moment of silence amidst her music. Her pause asked others to pause and look inward.

Music is the combination of notes and silence. Without the brief silences between notes, music would be one continuous sound. Notes and silences work in harmony. We hear the notes, but it's the silence in between that gives music life.[54] We don't hear the silence, but it's essential to make the music sing. Moments of silence assist in making our hearts sing. It's in silence where we make sense of the notes and truly learn to look inward and then act outward. When should one begin this inward journey of weaving sound and silence to march spiritually into the future? The answer, of course, is right now.

For a wonderful example, think about the words spoken in the musical/movie, *The Music Man*. Scam-artist and extraordinary con man, "Professor" Harold Hill, is "working" on the good folks of River City. He wants them to buy his false presentations of creating a boys' band to overcome the problems he says they have. His agenda is to swindle the money to "buy instruments, etc." but then leave town to repeat the scam elsewhere. His roadblock is the staid town librarian, Marian Paroo. She doesn't buy into his cause. Consequently, he challenges her to live life. Instead of her whistle-blowing his swindle, he attempts to get her to change how she sees life. He says:

> Oh, my dear little librarian. You pile up enough tomorrows, and you'll find you are left with nothing but a lot of empty yesterdays. I don't know about you, but I'd like to make today worth remembering.[55]

In other words, she must break out of her staid, traditional, never-changing role and risk. As a result of their bantering, they fall in love! Together, Harold Hill and Marian Paroo, in their silences between notes, the notes being their conversations, discover the music they share! They fall in love. He was transformed from a non-musical swindler to successfully leading 76 trombones of the boys' marching band down Main Street to the joy of all. And she learned to smile.

Another common facet of postmodernism is that people prefer "style over substance." Easily and wantonly we blame marketing, consumerism, and shallowness for this reality. We must acknowledge that accepting how things present themselves, rather than how they should be, sways our actions. We're also appeased with how items look rather than how they perform. We spend billions on cosmetics and the latest "look at me" fashions. As previously noted, we spend much money on plastic surgery to upgrade our physical appearance. When will we realize that outward upgrades, of any form, do not appease the inner soul? When will we come to terms with the postmodern dilemma of style ahead of substance? Laura Brown, in her doctoral dissertation, quoting Robert Forman's *Grassroots Spirituality: What It Is, Why It Is Here, Where It Is Going*, provides a thoughtful illustration of this value:

> In addition, Forman (2004) suggests other factors that have contributed to the growing interest in spirituality. In his book about grassroots spirituality, he argues that the American fast-paced, technological focused life style in combination with demographic shifts away from rural life have contributed to our sense of worry about alienation and aloneness as well as our concern about superficial relationships and lives that lack significance. Communities no longer revolve around strong nuclear or extended families, and people no longer share life-histories with neighbors or people from work which contributes to these feelings of alienation and feeling alone. Forman also cites the disillusionment with science and rationality to provide meaning and fulfillment as another reason for this growth in spiritual interests. Forman recognizes that there are probably many reasons for the rise of spirituality in the past three decades, but he argues that there is considerable force behind this movement.[56]

Gene Veith also commented on this social problem and added much when he penned:

Postmodernists stress *style* over substance. Since there are no absolutes, any kind of objective meaning is problematic, including the notion of an absolute identity. The *surface* is more significant than the interior. This is true not only in the arts, as we shall see, but in social life. Life in the city, says Jonathan Raban, consists solely of role-playing. Everyone is *acting*. Everyone is affecting *style*. The office worker dons his power suit and plays the part of the corporate bureaucrat. After work, he plays another part with his friends. Whether he goes to a fern bar or a leather bar, whether he tries to impress women by being sensitive or macho, whether he projects himself as a free spirit or a world-weary cynic, it is all an act. And in the course of a day, he plays many parts.[57]

Does this suggest that we role-play throughout life rather than truly be ourselves? I sometimes think so. What do you think? If we spend much of our lives playing shallow roles to provide outward appearances of success, control, beauty, and value, when do we have time to address the deep part of ourselves? While loneliness is truly a vast and deep international disease, I wonder if people are lonely but don't realize it. I wonder how many suffer from matters of self-esteem because they're caught in the social game of style over substance. Having a healthy spiritual life feeds self-esteem, and self-esteem feeds one's spirit.[58] It's a healthy cycle. For the future of healthy individuals and societal spirituality, we need to value substance over style! This gives us meaning in life.[59] It helps us explore, "Who am I?"

For me, a basic and foundational notion embodied in the future of spirituality revolves around the adage "Are we more concerned about doing things right, or are we concerned about doing the right thing?" To re-phrase this, we should be bold and prepared to take risks. Or do we align with, "The comfortable pew"? The comfortable pew image defines much of postmodern Western Christianity. I wonder how much it also defines the SBNR or other tribal groups. We need to learn to let go to grow. This asks much of us as individuals and Western society. Again, it is an intense challenge for future spiritual development if we ask, "Are we more concerned about doing things right, or concerned about doing the right thing?"

For example, the Reformation took place because the Roman Catholic Church, which was the dominant societal and political power of that era, resisted all attempts, both large and small, to push their thinking and practices. For a long time, they constrained Western society into doing the right things (i.e., how to pray, how to follow rules, who to respect, and what to believe). Likewise, they assumed they were specifically ordained by God to monitor and uphold knowledge, to distill information, and when necessary, to impart wisdom. (Hmm, this also sounds like the ultra-right-wing Christians of today!)

The Roman Catholic Church of that era believed God called them to enforce these activities (remember the Galileo story). For many, the managed roles imposed upon people represented a sincere, humble, and kind effort, which they believed helped people live useful, religious, and spiritual lives. For others, however, it fulfilled a thirst for power and control over others and fulfilled self-glorification. Sadly, it remains an intoxicating human trait, never absent from any generation, culture, or corner of the earth. Lord Acton was right that absolute power absolutely corrupts.

However, one fateful day, one of the constrained, alienated, and restricted responded. A monk named Martin Luther, frustrated with the graft and the practice of indulgences, elitism, and approaches to scripture, hammered 95 opinions on a church door. He desired to bring change so people would be able to "Do the right things in life." Unknowingly and unwittingly, he hammered Western society into a paradigm shift we call the Reformation.[60] Naturally, and as expected, those stuck on holding on to "Doing things right" failed to comprehend the need to evolve. In turn, they couldn't see the need to "Do the right thing." This is true in the current reformation.

Martin Luther was the unwitting spark that ignited the powder keg for massive reform in Western Christianity and Western society. Today's reformation (as well explained earlier) is global and secular. However, the question remains: Who is still stuck on "Doing things right?" Can you name names or situations? Likewise, to what degree do you want to hold on to "doing everything right," and, to what degree are you prepared to undertake "doing the right things?" In other words, can you discern the difference between doing things right, and doing the right thing? Where do you see these two issues in society? For your spiritual future, can you risk? Finally, can you discern where Western society (and if so inclined, Western Christianity) needs to take a risk to spiritually mature into the future? Take some time to mull over these significant questions. Also mull over the words of Gene Veith:

The postmodernist rejection of objectivity pervades the evangelical church. "We have a generation that is less interested in cerebral arguments, linear thinking, theological systems," observes Leith Anderson, "and more interested in encountering the supernatural." Consequently, churchgoers operate with a different paradigm of spirituality. "The old paradigm taught that if you have the right teaching, you will experience God. The new paradigm says that if you experience God, you will have the right teaching."[6] Not only is objective doctrine minimized in favor of subjective experience; experience actually becomes the criterion for evaluating doctrine.[61]

In fairness, at the time of the Reformation, almost everyone in Western society was illiterate and, to a degree, needed assistance. Likewise, almost everyone belonged to the Roman Catholic Church. To make sure that people continued to "Do the right thing," the church didn't change traditional, time-tested, and valued liturgies, rules, autocratic bureaucracy, or policies. If nothing appeared to be broken, there was no need to fix it! In turn, it scoffed at innovations and budding thoughts. The implied message was, "The changing world is wrong; resist it, believe in us, and follow us in the right way!" The stubbornly entrenched leadership failed to see the gravity of evolution, like the printing press, emerging around them.

Historically, the Roman Catholic Church and mainline Western Christianity continue to cherish very slow change. The attitude is, "Let's stay with what we know works rather than risk and lose!" One writer expressed this very well:

The challenge is that bureaucracies, like all human systems, have a natural tendency to become self-serving, mired in obsolete methods (ruts), and preoccupied with control instead of with serving the mission for which they were created.[62]

Delightfully summarizing this stubbornness, George Hunter, author of several books on church development, or lack thereof, wrote:

> Bertrand Russell wrote in his *History of Western Philosophy* (with some exaggeration) that "the churches, everywhere, opposed for as long as they could, practically every innovation that made for an increase of happiness and knowledge here on earth."[63]

I'll leave it to historians, sociologists, and theologians to argue the sincerity and motivations of the church at the time. However, in fairness, I suspect that much of the local managers, such as the village priest, sincerely endeavored to do the work of the church and the gospel. Ironically, while much eventually "evolved," it was only because of postmodernism that the Roman Catholic Church moved beyond the sole use of the Latin liturgy. At last, people were able to worship in their native tongue.

Much of the future of spirituality depends on rediscovering or updating virtues such as humility, stillness, and active listening to oneself and others. It means serving others and shifting from tribalism to community. For Western Christianity, it means that instead of thinking of the traditional image of Christ breathing "on his disciples," to see him breathing into them. This is "God breathes in us." For non-Christians, I suggest being open to the notion of transcendence breathing in and through you. We need to pay attention to undertaking the right actions.

In our great reformation, we face new social realities. It will take time to accept these changes if we're inclined to move from "Me-ism" to "we-ism." However, to move where we are to where we must, we need to briefly consider the road we need to travel.

For most of the history of Western society, people existed in a hierarchical, vertical model. At the top was the King or monarch, then their appointed officials. Then we had the local chieftains. The average person was the peasant at the bottom. Naturally, they appeased all those above them.

The concurrent model existed in Western Christianity. At the top was God, then Jesus and the Holy Spirit. However, over the centuries, much time and attention centered on the question of Jesus and/or the Spirit being equal with God. The Pope, as expected, held the final word on all conversations and issues of faith and politics. Just below the Pope were the cardinals, then the local bishops, and then village priests. Again, the average people were the peasants at the bottom. They appeased all those above them. The church model was solely linear. With the Reformation, while the authority of the Pope remained unchanged in the Roman Catholic Church, the Protestants transferred this role to scripture. While the Protestants railed against the structure of the Roman model of top-down leadership, they often copied it.

Sadly, the competition for souls was, at times, bloody and violent. With the rise of postmodernism, these models changed. For example, the total control of the church by Anglican bishops in Western society gave way to "Being Episcopally led, but democratically governed." Thus, a sort of shared leadership developed. Throughout Protestantism, and to some degree in Catholicism, laypeople began assuming greater voices and roles! In part, we might say that for the first time if people weren't happy, they felt they could leave the church without intensive repercussions. Their wallets followed. The leadership noticed this and made some adaptations.

This mirrored much of what was transpiring in Western society—a shift from a narrow, vertical model of leadership (holding power and control) to a more universal horizontal model slowly grew. Instead of power and decision-making being in the hands of a few, it morphed into a broader base. Sadly, this broader base throughout Western society is still older, white men. Diversity of color, gender, sexual orientation remains a societal struggle. This is true in society and Western Christianity. Speaking of change in Western Christianity, college professor, church administrator, and parish cleric Thomas Hawkins identified this admirably when he wrote:

... the church needs to learn at the "speed of change." He notes that traditional hierarchal institutions must give way to increasing participatory models, and that <u>vertical</u> ways of thinking must give way to <u>horizontal</u> activities.[64]

Ironically, in this horizontal model, newcomers sometimes try to mimic the vertical models of the past and use confrontation to climb the ladders of success, power, and control. Perhaps one of the best descriptions of this shift is found in Thomas Friedman's *The World Is Flat: A Brief History of the Twenty-First Century*. Read and think about his astute words. Perhaps you might even read them twice:

> As the world starts to move from a primarily vertical—
> *command and control*—system for creating value to
> a more horizontal—*connect and collaborate*—value-
> creation model, and as we blow away more walls, ceilings,
> and floors at the same time, societies are going to find
> themselves facing a lot of very profound changes all at
> once. But these changes won't just affect how business gets
> done. They will affect how individuals, communities, and
> companies organize themselves, where companies and
> communities stop and start, how individuals balance their
> different identities as consumers, employees, shareholders,
> and citizens, how people define themselves politically, and
> what role government plays in managing all of this flux.
> This won't all happen overnight, but over time many roles,
> habits, political identities, and management practices that
> we had grown used to in the round world are going to
> have to be profoundly adjusted for the age of flatness...
> In the old world, where value was largely being created
> vertically, usually within a single company and from the
> top down, it was very easy to see who was on the top and
> who was on the bottom, who was exploiting and who was
> being exploited. But when the world starts to flatten out
> and value increasingly gets created horizontally (through

multiple forms of collaboration, in which individuals and little guys have much more power), who is on the top and who is on the bottom, who is exploiter and who is exploited, gets very complicated. Some of our old political reflexes no longer apply... This is what happens when you move from a vertical (command and control) world to a much more horizontal (connect and collaborate) flat world. Your boss can do his job *and your job*. He can be secretary of state and his own secretary. He can give you instructions day or night. So you are never out. You are always in. Therefore, you are always on. Bosses, if they are inclined, can collaborate more directly with more of their staff than ever before—no matter who they are or where they are in the hierarchy. But staffers will also have to work much harder to be better informed than their bosses. There are a lot more conversations between bosses and staffers today that start like this: "I know that already! I Googled it myself. Now what do I do about it?"[65]

Thomas Friedman then asks, "Now what do I do about it?" This a good question. What do you do to ensure the future of your spirituality? In turn, what do you do to further the future of society's spirituality? The quick answer is—you act! The right answer is—you act. You act and ask yourself, "Who am I?" Don't settle for spontaneous, glib answers. Take time to ponder yourself. This is not navel-gazing. It's a sincere opportunity to look at oneself beyond the façade we use in postmodernism. It's the opportunity to look beyond and beneath the forcefield or shield we create and cling to.

When Professor Howard Hill abandoned his outward distracting noise and looked inward, he began to make real music! Alice, in *Alice in Wonderland*, Lewis Carroll's iconic novel, stated, "Who in the world am I? Ah, that's the great puzzle." The journey down the rabbit hole, while filled with fantastical creatures, was Alice trying to figure life out. When Dorothy Gale in *The Wizard of Oz* accepted deep thinking, listened to her heart, and used the courage within herself (as shown to her by three traveling companions), she was able to travel inward. As a result, she found her soul, and she found herself back in Kansas. She journeyed to where she belonged.

When she was startled, Dorothy cried out, "Jiminy Crickets" to express her shock. Jiminy, however, truly came to life as a major character in *Pinocchio,* a Walt Disney movie. His name was a euphemism on Jesus Christ, and his role was to act as the puppet's conscience. As the spirit guide, he helped the wooden boy find himself and become a real boy. Peter Pan became spiritually complete when Wendy sewed his shadow on. Peter Pan was able to grow up! Jean Valjean, like Howard Hill, Alice, Dorothy Gale, Pinocchio, and Peter Pan, wrestled with the foundational question, "Who Am I?" Through the inward and soulful journey, he and each of these characters found themselves and their spirit. Can we do any less? Can you do anything less?

As noted much earlier in this work, thousands of years ago, thousands of people annually flocked to the Temple of Apollo in Delphi. As they entered the building, they were greeted with the inscription: GNOTHI SEAUTON—Know Thyself.[66] "Know thyself," as repeated by Jesus and Shakespeare, is a great way of stating, "Who am I?"

It's the most basic question of every generation, of Western society, and likely the whole globe. It's the question that from the dawn of conscious thought stimulated people to journey and explore within themselves! Additionally, it never changes. Yet it is a vastly different question in postmodernism than in any other generation. Yuval Harari explains this:

> By the middle of the twenty-first century, accelerating change plus longer life spans will make this traditional model obsolete. Life will come apart at the seams, and there will be less and less continuity between different periods of life. "Who am I?" will be more urgent and complicated question than ever before.[67]

It seems that in the middle of the expanding, speeding world there is an urgent need to find what we lost. Did we truly lose or misplaced our souls? Or did we put them in our back pocket and over time forgot where they were? Were we so busy working on our game face that we neglected the sorely needed inside work that is required?

To engage in spiritual growth means having an open mind and an open heart. The divergent branches of Western Christianity would do well to learn from each other. Mainline, or now more appropriately called sideline, churches need to add more heart or emotion as demonstrated and held valuable by Evangelicals and by postmoderns in general. The current success of the Evangelical movement is in part because they developed with the emergence of postmodernism. In other words, they didn't have theological, liturgical, political, or social baggage to overcome! When one thinks of Evangelicals, think of their emphasis on emotion and experience. Despite monumental obstacles, the Evangelical churches would do well to shift some attention from emotional foundations to investigating with a more cerebral approach. They need to weave horizontal emotions with vertical thinking to reach spiritual maturity. And in doing so, to use their term, they will be more Christ-like.

While it is utopian, if Catholicism, the reforming churches, and Evangelicals could discuss what they have in common rather than what pushes them apart, there's a chance that these institutions might recapture some of their vaulted positions in society. Even if that recaptured central place doesn't take place, they will still accomplish much for the poor, disenfranchised, and neglected in the world! However, all must take a risk to be open-minded.

To be open-minded means one must be prepared to let go of the past. While writing about Evangelicals and postmodernism, Carl Raschke, who writes on religions and spirituality in postmodernism, offered a most delightful illustration indicative of Western Christianity's failure. He noted how in the 1970s the Swiss watch industry, which had for decades dominated the world market, collapsed. They refused to adapt to the invention and innovation of the quartz watch. Ironically, it was the Swiss who invented the quartz watch.[68] R. Scott Smith, who wrote about postmodern religious trends, also wrote about the need for Western Christianity to be open-minded and reform. In 2005, commenting on Brian McLaren, a popular writer on emerging Western Christianity, Smith said:

Perhaps one of McLaren's most provocative comments about the influence of modernity on the church is his concern that though the church is here to serve, all too often it has become a purveyor of religious goods and services. In modernity's consumeristic orientation, too often the church has competed for "market share" and "clientele," or customers, with all other businesses and organizations that vie for our attention and loyalties. But the church does not exist to satisfy the demands of believers. Instead, the church needs to be a community that is faithful to the Lord Jesus, believing and living out our faith as He would have us live. That is, the church is a community of people who are engaged in a mission, to help reconcile the entire world under Jesus as Lord.[69]

Since Western Christianity and Western society need to acquire open-minded approaches in a close-minded, "me" centered world, the bottom line is that individuals must undertake that mission upon themselves. Perhaps the actions of the one (multiplied by many) can lead to the reformation of the institution! As Brené Brown writes:

We have to be able to talk about how we feel, what we need and desire, and we have to be able to listen with an open heart and an open mind. There is no intimacy without vulnerability. Yet another powerful example of vulnerability as courage.[70]

Throughout the centuries, governments, institutions, businesses of all sorts, and individuals realized that being open-minded often meant taking risks. Taking risks meant success or failure. While we enjoy success, we tend to be afraid of ridicule and shame if we fail. Yet taking risks is essential for the future of spirituality, both corporately and individually. Psychiatrist Curt Thompson skillfully, and with great poetic imagery, describes the need for risks:

However, I will argue that it is only through this process of being known that you come to know yourself and learn how to know others. There is no other way. To be known is to be pursued, examined, and shaken. To be known is to be loved and to have hopes and even demands placed on you. It is to risk, not only the furniture in your home being rearranged, but your floor plans being rewritten, your walls being demolished and reconstructed. To be known means that you allow your shame and guilt to be exposed—in order for them to be healed.[71]

Perhaps the greatest risk we ever undertake is entering oneself. It's a risk that requires patience, time, and courage. It requires stillness for insights to emerge. Instead of always chasing or looking for spirituality, sometimes the task is letting one's spirituality find you. When Jean Valjean stopped running (literally and figuratively) and was still and introspective, his spirit found him by the end of his searching song, "Who am I?" It found him when the silences and notes worked as one. Ponder the following:

In entering into our own silence, we risk everything, for we risk our very being: "So I said to my soul. 'Be still.'" The stillness of mind and body to which the mantra guides us is a preparation for entering this silence. It prepares us for our progression through the spheres of silence to see with wonder the light of our own spirit, and to know that light as something beyond our spirit and yet the source of it. This is a pilgrimage through our spheres of silence that we undertake in faith, putting our entire trust in what is only a dim apprehension of the authentic, the real, yet confident in doing so because it is authentic.[72]

I ask you to also consider a similar comment:

The learning related to soul work takes time. It does not occur according to a plan or as a result of intentional intervention. If one attends to the soul with educated and steadfast imagination, change will take place without the individual being consciously aware of its happening. Moore concludes: "A genuine odyssey is not about piling up experiences. It is a deeply felt, risky, unpredictable tour of the soul" (p. 230).[73]

Giving time, patience, and stillness to spiritual work is, historically speaking, holy work! It doesn't matter if one is religious or SBNR! These attributes also restore one to wholeness.[74] Perhaps we can clearly say that these attributes are spiritually nutritious. Likewise, to escape "Me-ism" and being self-absorbed, we need to step back and step into absorbing ourselves.

The future of spirituality for the postmodern individual is to take risks like Jean Valjean, Peter Pan, Dorothy Gale, et al., and to find who you truly are. Andrew Wright, "critical realist," in his astute book describes this as returning to an ancient mode: "As St. Augustine (354–430 CE) urged his readers: 'do not go outward, return within yourself ... in the inner man dwells truth' (Wright, 1996, p. 139)".[75] In turn, for individuals to collectively, in communities (not in tribes), to reform, society once more must look inward. In a time when Western society is fraught with polarization, consumerism, confrontation, and "Me-ism," people should accept their spiritual call to step back from these destructive values and re-discover themselves. I wonder as was we swirl with these negative values how many are willing to step back, step down, and step into themselves. What are your thoughts?

We must reform society from rampant "Look at me" to "Looking out for others." Australian psychotherapist and author David Tacey elegantly describes this journey. While he wrote addressing the need for Western Christianity to reform, we can adopt his image for all spiritual souls:

> When our internal wounds and divisions are healed, we gain the capacity and the courage to seek healing and wholeness in the world, and to act with mindfulness and sensitivity towards our internal and external environments. To recover one's 'vertical' connection with the sacred other is at the same time to restore and renew our 'horizontal'

> connections with self, others and the world. This, from
> a theological point of view, is the Cross of completion.[76]

It is to take the risk of discovering and living simply. It is being comfortable in your skin as you journey inward in humility and stillness and then, when able, to journey outward. When one journeys outward to serve others and build community, one also serves oneself. In postmodernism, where we love to hear others voice our words, we must shift to active listening. Discovering the voice of others adds to our depth. In the past, we discovered the voice of others in religious institutions. In postmodernism, we abandoned searching in those places and began to search ourselves. Sadly, we search to feed "Me-ism." But when we abandoned that search of self-absorption and embraced the "dark night of the soul," we found the search fruitful and filling.

In our privatized search of "Me-ism," it was natural to explore using our materialistic, secular foundation, because the deep, sacred roots of our past were severed. Diego Rinallo, Linda Scott, and Pauline Maclaran described this quest vividly in 2013. In their book on spirituality and consumption (yes, consumption), they wrote, "Spirituality is sublime. It smells of incense and everything that is good in humans. Consumption is instead mundane, materialistic, and ultimately soulless."[77]

In abandoning "Me-ism," which is shallow, for a true inner self and affirming "we-ism," we can begin to find community once more. Perhaps we might even rebuild Western Christianity from religious institutions with top-down rules and practices that suggest "Listen to us" to the role of being spiritual havens. Places that embrace and genuinely care about everyone's journey. We can build from the bottom-up, using deep listening and supporting the spiritual journeys of people ahead of political control or power.

It behooves Western Christianity, other religious practices, and SBNRs (Spiritual but not Religious), to belong to communities, to care for each other, and to humbly and deeply listen. We are called have to substance over style, depth over shallowness, and to explore questions rather than accept or look for quick answers. We require patience over instant gratification. If we can move in these directions, we might shift the great postmodern reformation towards another reformation—one in which all can spiritually proper. If we cannot embrace this challenge, the postmodern rush of destructive, all-consuming, self-centered affirmation will continue. Consider these words:

> As stated by Einstein in an impassioned plea to the nations of the world after our last world war, "Only a few short years remain in which to discover some spiritual basis for world brotherhood, or civilization as we now know it will certainly destroy itself."[78]

A final image comes from Erich Fromm an incredible postmodern seminal thinker, writer, and psychoanalyst. In 1976, he penned *To Have and To Be?* as a reflection on society. It is a fascinating read, and his projections are unfolding! He noted how the rise of mechanical tools changed society. It was becoming increasingly possible for everyone to have much. In other words, how people moved beyond survival and limited processions to embracing materialism, consumerism, and consumption. This was before computers and smartphones further amplified the progression of "having." At the same time, these new societal advantages made it possible for people to develop a greater sense of themselves in "being." Through much discussion, he showed that it was easier to succumb to seeking processions than to devote time to be introspective. Sadly, he suggested that we live in a society rooted in property, profit, and power.[79] He wrote how we must lose the need for greed and liberate ourselves for the needs truly needed for individuals and society. We need to discover, "Who am I."

Seriously, if we embrace and discover the depth of our spiritual lives, we might transform Western society from its Age of Entitlement to an Age of Empowerment where we embrace ourselves and one another. This book is only one of many passionately noting the deep, complex need to find spirituality in our dysfunctional postmodern society. The human need to be spiritual continues in our tremendous reformation. And while we may urgently seek and search for spirituality, one truth from the past remains—sometimes we just need to be still and silent to listen and let our spirit find us!

Questions to ponder and discuss
Chapter Nine

The Future of Spirituality!

❶ Are you more concerned about doing things right, or about doing the right thing? What is your dominant reality? Do not rush but take time to ponder this!

❷ "To be open-minded means one must be prepared to let go of the past." Is this you?

❸ How would you propose helping children, youth, and yourself to master silence?

❹ Is it possible for you to disconnect from all your connections and spend time connecting with yourself? Can you do this for an hour?

APPENDIX A

A PRACTICAL MODEL OF "SPIRITUALITY AND LEARNING:" ROOTED IN ADULT LEARNING PRINCIPLES

Overview

We know that for most of Christian history, religion and spirituality were synonymous. Being religious meant being spiritual, and being spiritual meant being religious. In our new reformation, this tradition is over. Significant shifts in social mores, such as the move of populations from the farms, to the city, and then to the suburbs, along with increased education levels and technology, were significant factors. Likewise, we moved from a sacred, religious society to a highly secular society in a very short time. Consequently, many in Western Society say they can be "spiritual without being religious."

While we are a society dominated by individualized SBNRs, much indicates that one cannot be a full, well-rounded, and spiritual person without community. If one is spiritual in isolation, all one truly accomplishes is affirming oneself without growth. One can't be truly spiritual alone! Furthermore, research suggests that people are spiritually hungry, and a few still seek fulfillment in religious institutions. Others seek spiritual guides through countless self-help books or a variety of other social activities, such as yoga. David Tacey identifies the religious world as "empty church but crowded pathways."[1]

One of the typical responses of Western Christianity in postmodernism is to offer traditional programs. In other words, they keep providing proven models rather than seek new pathways! For example, they offer programs in historical Augustinian, Benedictine, Carmelite, Cistercian, Dominican, Franciscan, and Ignatian spirituality. Some find these approaches useful, but in my opinion, part of this is denial, and part is a sincere belief that seems to say, "This has worked before and will work today. This will bring people back if we keep at it enough." In light of the great cultural shift overwhelming us, it's time to embrace new efforts to help people explore postmodern spirituality. We must move from the mindset of teaching "who and what we are in this denomination" to courses and programs that focus on adults learning about their spirituality.

We must move beyond historical and current conversations that typically hinge on conservative versus liberal, and confessional versus sacramental mindsets. We must move past contemporary conversations of orthodoxy (right beliefs and right thinking) and emergent/ emerging church scenarios. We must move into deep conversations on how to facilitate and support spiritual growth.

Churches have the natural infrastructure, experience, ability, and desire to meet people's spiritual needs. In today's environment, religious institutions should ask themselves, "Are we meeting our needs, or are we meeting the needs of those seeking spiritual assistance?"

Spirituality and Learning is a short program that tries to respond to the needs of those seeking spiritual assistance. It endeavors to meet the needs of adults using principles of adult education. In part, this means:

1. addressing the immediacy of applying new knowledge
2. utilizing praxis education, which is learning by doing
3. listening to others
4. listening to self
5. reflecting on and applying life experiences of adults.

In addition, adults are motivated to seek learning opportunities that relate directly to their needs. *Spirituality and Learning* attempts to respond to this need. Adults consciously or unconsciously are often rooted in self-directed learning. While *Spirituality and Learning* provides some formal structure, the format guides adults towards their goals in self-directed learning. Adults like to be invited to interpret what they are learning and discovering rather than be told what to believe. *Spirituality and Learning* supports emerging images of adult learning rather than the historical, traditional teaching. *Spirituality and Learning* hopes that adults desire, or yearn, to explore questions, especially questions that surround, "Who am I?" This is hard work compared to the historical stock of provided answers!

Spirituality and Learning embraces the whole person. It uses auditory, visual, environmental, and kinesthetic learning formats. It also addresses various adult thinking styles, such as a reflective practice, a creative practice, a practical practice, and a conceptual practice.[2] While there are many adult education models to facilitate learning, *Spirituality and Learning* appreciates and considers David Kolb's *Learning Style Inventory* as useful because it encourages adults to see their learning through concrete experiences, reflective observations, abstract conceptualization, and active experimentation.

Instead of the traditional vertical model, which offered one narrow approach to learning and was prescriptive (i.e., "this is what you need to know"), *Spirituality and Learning* is descriptive because it encourages a broad horizontal approach that endeavors to speaks to various learning and thinking styles. In historical prescriptive models, we may say the answer drives the questions, which will find the prescribed answer that is collectively identical for everyone. In descriptive models that are discovery-based, the questions asked lead to answers that are unique for everyone. Instead of being closed, it is a very open model.

Spirituality and Learning is a short, eight-week (two hours per week) program designed to respond to those who live with chaotic, busy, and perhaps fragmented lives. *Spirituality and Learning* intends to bring adults together for a period of intensely focused formation. In time, various small groups could elect to evolve and create long-term mutual sharing, support, and learning groups.

Spirituality and Learning encourages adults to use their spirituality as their source of learning. As liberation theologian and adult educator Gustov Gutiérrez often suggested, adults need *"to learn to drink from their own well."* This means that instead of the traditional models that *explain* spirituality, adults need to *explore* spirituality from within. This represents a shift from dominant outside voices to finding one's voice, or spirit-voice, with others. In turn, adults need to add perspectives and insights by listening to the spirit-voices of others. Instead of being isolated and creating one's own spirit-voice, which only affirms known positions and opinions, everyone offers and receives feedback from others. The methodology is explained later in this model. Whereas traditional top-down programs allow leaders to set the tone and direction, this short course, apart from some timing parameters, sees its tone and directions set by those involved.

Spirituality and Learning seeks to assist adults in discovering, enhancing, and deepening their spirit-voice. It doesn't provide packaged knowledge or give information. Instead, it asks adults to use their internal wisdom to seek insights. This seems counter-cultural to our polarized society that feels entitled to receive instant gratification. Spiritual growth takes time. Again, the approach of *Spirituality and Learning* seems to run contrary to trends in postmodernism, where we often settle for the superficial. It's not group therapy, an intervention, or a self-help support group. Instead, *Spirituality and Learning* is a group-driven enterprise in which individuals challenged each other and themselves to seek and expand their spirit-voice. *Spirituality and Learning* asks adults to listen, explore, write about, and ponder their spirituality.

In our fast-paced, busy society, it's essential that people learn to slow down, be still, and give time to listening to their spirit-voice. Your spirit-voice is the voice of God (or higher power) speaking within you. Thus, one must struggle to separate one's voice from God's voice. This challenge takes time, patience, and care and requires great discernment. It takes practice to step back and away from one's voice to encourage and allow the spirit-voice to speak! One tool some may find useful on this journey is to keep asking, "Am I using my spirit-voice?" Through constant and consistent practice, one can become accustomed to differentiating between one's voice and one's spirit-voice.

As individuals and a society, we need to step back from busyness and noise. We need to find stillness and silence, and as we mature, perhaps we can truly engage in solitude. Solitude is not a retreat from the world but a journey inward to help one live in the world.

Historically, education was rooted and entrenched in the notion of mastering skills. The focus was on achieving goals and acquiring proficiency knowledge. *Spirituality and Learning* doesn't look for adults to meet those types of goals or to develop proficiency. There are no clear answers because learning and discerning can be messy! It's not a linear climb but a journey through valleys and up to the mountaintops; it's feeling lost in a dark forest and hot deserts. The focus is on the journey, not the destination. Adult learning is "mystery learning" as much as "mastery learning." Sadly, society often downplays mystery learning, since we prefer to follow paths to safe, predictable, yet challenging resolutions. Mystery learning, even beyond Bloom's Taxonomy and other venues, is about stepping into the unknown. In the medieval world, when the world was thought to be flat, maps depicted oceans, and at the edge of the map, or in unexplored parts of the earth, the words, "Here be Dragons" often appeared. Mystery learning in spiritual growth means a willingness to walk off the map, though there may be dragons, into the unpredictable.

To meet diverse learning and thinking styles, and to avoid the traditional "one-size-fits all" educational programs, *Spirituality and Learning* provides a broader approach to learning, rooted in the student and not the curriculum or the instructor. In turn, *Spirituality and Learning* weaves and blends individual experiences with group experiences. While evidence indicates that much spiritual growth typically occurs privately, group settings provide essential balance and reflective opportunities. They offer support, stimulation, different viewpoints, and a safe place to share. Group settings also offer broader perspectives and a sense of community. Perhaps the greatest gift of group settings is that everyone is positively challenged and supports others. This includes those who may have very different views and perspectives. The group setting of this short course provides a place where people, in and with confidence, may share their deepest hurts and pains. In 2011, Jorge Ferrer, who wrote much on participatory spirituality, described the group experience well:

> Participatory enaction entails a model of spiritual engagement that does not simply reproduce certain tropes according to a given historical a priori, but rather

embarks upon the adventure of openness to the novelty and creativity of cognitive sciences ...[3]

The Individual Experience

In *Spirituality and Learning*, adults use three individual practices:

1. silence and solitude
2. journaling
3. contemplating and writing on the group's chosen weekly theme.

The **first practice** asks individuals to use silence and solitude. Silence means not talking. This is difficult given that the post-modern world is rooted in constant noise. Much in our consumer-driven society presses us to talk. Sometimes we talk even if we don't have anything to say! When we're talking, we aren't listening. Some suggest that we sometimes reduce prayer to talking to God (or Higher Power) without ever listening for God. Likewise, in our hectic world, when we take time to listen, we tend to be impatient! Silence means stepping back from actively seeking or undertaking a task. It's being still and doing nothing. In time, thoughts emerge. As one develops silence, one's spirit-voice can mature and deepen. In time, and with much practice, silence leads to solitude.

Solitude is the rare space of being comfortable with oneself. In 1993, noted educator Parker Palmer, in *To Know as We Are Known: Education as Spiritual Journey,* offered a wonderful definition of silence and solitude: "If knowledge allows us to receive the world as it is, solitude allows us to receive ourselves as we are. If silence gives us knowledge of the world, solitude gives us knowledge of ourselves."[4] The late Henri Nouwen, in his book *Reaching Out: The Three Movements of the Spiritual,* offered a similar view. It's a wonderful passage to ponder:

> Contemplative reading of the holy scriptures and silent time in the presence of God belong closely together. The word of God draws us into silence; silence makes us attentive to God's word. The word of God penetrates

through the thick of human verbosity to the silent centered of our heart; silence opens in us the space where the word can be heard. Without reading the word, silence becomes stale, and without silence, the word loses its re-creative power. The word leads to silence and silence to the word. The word is born in silence, and silence is the deepest response to the word.[5]

With constant and deliberate practice, silence can transform and lead adults. They can move from a constant struggling act of seeking silence to a continuous, harmonious, peaceful solitude. When this takes place, and as Jack Mezirow often writes, transformative learning takes place. Mezirow suggests that through instrumental tools and communication, adults repeatedly interpret and re-interpret their experiences. Consequently, through reflection, adults are transformed by the "critical reflective process." It's wonderful that adults can ponder their experiences through thoughtful silence and solitude.

The **second practice** is the use of a daily journal. Some may enjoy keeping a journal, while others may find it a difficult task. Journaling is a tool to help people make sense of thoughts and insights. Journaling can be "stream of consciousness" writing. This means one writes words, thoughts, or images without regard to sentence structure or cohesive planning. Others, however, may prefer a more organized and deliberate approach. Research suggests that journaling promotes self-reflection and critical thinking. Unlike our faulty brain memories, written journal notes are a visible, clean-copy reference. In addition, journaling is a tool that stimulates growth.

As suggested, the purpose of the journal is to assist individual growth, reflection, and stimulation. Participants write their weekly journal entries as a self-reflecting stimulant. From time to time, some may choose to share entries during their "talking stick" time. The talking stick is part of the group setting when all participants share their stories and thoughts without any interruption. In some courses, adults use their talking stick opportunity to share some deeply personal struggles. For example, it was a gift when one shared news of their long-time silent struggle and recovery from alcohol addiction.

Some people enjoy journaling, but many find it an effort. For some, it might be a challenge since journaling requires reflection. Thus, they may need guidance or background on how to keep a journal, and specifically, on how to write using their spirit-voice. To help oneself and others, it might be useful for all to consider the following questions when making journal notes:

"At this moment, I am feeling____?"

"At this moment, I feel my spirit leading me to____?"

"At this moment, I feel my spirit is quiet (or noisy) because____?"

"At this moment, is my spirit is full (or empty)?"

"How does this affect me?"

Journaling represents a measured opportunity for participants to use active thinking, active writing, and active reflection, along with passive thinking and passive reflection. Passive thinking and passive reflection are unconscious acts that bring insights to light. Some may say that it's the quiet spirit-voice bursting through active thoughts and offering "fodder to ponder."

The **third individual practice** asks adults to contemplate, consider, and write on the chosen weekly theme. At the end of each group session, the group talks and determines the theme for the next group session. Some individuals chose to use their talking stick time to share insights gleaned from that week's theme.

The Group Experience

The group experience is comprised of **eight practices**. These take place as participants gather for their two-hour weekly session. The sessions should last between six or eight weeks. In postmodernism, adults are likely to commit to this length of a program as opposed to longer programs. However, at the end of the agreed-upon sessions, the group may elect to establish a more long-term group.

During the sessions, the participants sit around a table, so it's easy for all to make notes. Ideally, the number of participants in the group should be six to eight adults. In addition, there is a moderator. The role of the moderator is to help the group stay on-task and to ensure that all participants have opportunities to speak, listen, and share. The moderator acts as the timekeeper, ensuring that the group sticks to the two-hour time commitment.

Some people learn by talking, others by listening, others by observation, and others by practicing and applying insights. One pivotal role of the moderator is to make sure that all find and use their comfortable learning style. The moderator tries to ensure that all participants share equally and are challenged and supported. Sometimes the moderator may nudge some participants to speak less, or others to speak more. At times, the moderator may encourage participants to expand on thoughts or ideas. The moderator doesn't take part in conversations but is a quiet guide who may offer short suggestions! With assistance from the moderator, the participants blend and weave various comfortable and challenging learning styles while supporting the other participants in their comfortable/challenging learning styles.

When the participants gather for their weekly group session, the moderator begins with a period of silence. This **first practice** lasts between two and five minutes. It begins with the moderator leading the group in slow, deep breathing. Next, the moderator leads a short meditative centering exercise. This is the **second practice** of the group experience. The participants close their eyes, and the moderator selects opening comments for the group to focus on. Speaking slowly, quietly, and with a moderate pace, the moderator provides various illustrations, such as:

"Imagine you are near water. Is it a pond, a lake, a stream or an ocean?" Pause.

"What is your spirit-voice saying to you?"

"Is the water still, or moving? Is the water light or dark?" Pause.

"What is your spirit-voice to you?"

"Do you touch the water? If so, why? If not, why not?" Pause.

Like the first practice, this practice lasts between two to five minutes. Each week the format varies, offering different and unique perspectives. At the end of this exercise, the participants may make notes or be silent while others write. Experience shows that most participants take two or three minutes to write comments on how the guided meditation spoke to them. Participants transcribe notes in their workbooks. Sometimes participants use these notes during the talking stick time.

The **third practice** is the talking stick time. A talking stick is an ancient practice used to control conversations. It serves as an equalizer for those who like to dominate and talk, and those who tend to be quiet. This practice makes sure that everyone has an equal voice. The exercise begins when the moderator puts the talking stick in the middle of the table. The participants self-select the order in which they take their turn to talk. When one holds the stick, others are respectfully silent. Thus, everyone shares without interruption. Besides being an equalizer, this practice also empowers participants to share in a safe setting, and possibly share some deeply personal, pressing issues. The sharing time that follows is a time for all to be receptive to the spirit of another. As with all other practices of *Spirituality and Learning*, the deeply personal sharing asks all participants to uphold confidentiality. The talking stick time is also an ideal time for all to consider images such as:

"My spirit-voice is helping me understand (or learn)____."

"My spirit-voice is challenging me to consider____."

While each participant takes their turn with the talking stick, the other participants are silent yet encouraged to make notes. This leads to the **fourth practice** of the group time. If there are five people in the group, and you are talking with the stick, you're undertaking practice number three while the other four are engaged in practice number four. In practice four, one may choose to write questions they would like to ask other participants once the session is completed. In addition, participants stimulated by the thoughts or images of others may discover insights that speak to them; for example, one may ask, "Person 3, I heard you say that____. Can you clarify what that means?" In this practice, each stimulates the others and, in turn, gleans further insights. In our postmodern world that values and promotes competition, confrontation, and consumerism, this practice seeks cooperation and collaboration.

Once every participant has talked during the stick time, the group moves to the **fifth practice,** that of sharing. This "table sharing" encourages participants to share thoughts from their daily journal, reflections from the topic chosen from the previous week, images that occurred to them during the guided meditation, or reactions that developed during the talking stick session. It builds upon everything that took place in the individual's week and the group experiences of that week. Likewise, insights from previous experiences might consciously or unconsciously find their way into the conversation.

The role of the moderator during the table sharing is to offer limited supportive guidance. The moderator is a reflective observer. In addition, the moderator deeply listens to what the adults are saying without the need to talk. As such, the moderator can hear emerging thoughts and, at an opportune moment, quietly offer an insight or overview for all to consider. In addition, the moderator makes sure that no one dominates or controls the conversation.

During the table sharing conversations, it's natural and realistic in postmodernism for participants to share images under the broad title "This is what I think." Thus, the participants are offering opinions. To avoid the natural human practice to dominate or correct others, the participants, need to consider moving from making statements, or offering opinions, to asking questions or seeking clarification. Thus, the conversation shifts from talking modes to listening modes. In other words, instead of thinking of what one is going to say next, the participants become adept at deeper levels, to hear what others are saying.

Person A to Person B: "Did I hear you say___?"

Person B to Person E: "That was interesting. Can you add to that idea?"

Active listening is hard work. In postmodernism, we tend to hear but not listen. By trying to explore questions, we become more adept at avoiding the common trap of anecdotal sharing. Without a doubt, anecdotal sharing will take place, since it's natural, but unless deftly contained by the moderator, it could overwhelm the session and sidetrack the participants from deeper conversations. All participants and the moderator need to monitor their comments and be aware: "Is this comment pertinent, or is it an unnecessary story?" By active listening and the taking of notes, and "forced" quiet when others are talking, we avoid the postmodern dilemma often referred to by Stephen R. Covey, said, "Most people do not listen with the intent to understand; they listen with the intent to reply."

At some point, the moderator calls for a short break. The purpose of the break, the **sixth practice,** is two-fold. First, it allows a restroom break. Second, it allows the participants a short time to decompress and reflect on what is taking place. The short break allows the participants to step back from intense conversations and gives time and opportunity for other perspectives and views to arise. In turn, the mind unconsciously uses this time to shift and sort through emotions and information. In other words, while everyone is one "pause," the brain, heart, and spirit still work at sorting, analyzing, and considering presented images.

Following the break, the conversation resumes. In the **seventh practice,** the moderator gently seeks to help the group discover themes and thoughts they might explore. The moderator seeks to assist everyone to find and use his or her spirit-voice. By the end of the two-hour session, with some limited guidance from the moderator, the group agrees on the next weekly topic. The role of the moderator is to guide and not to set direction. Sometimes selecting one theme is difficult since several themes may be at the forefront. However, it's essential that the group collectively select one theme. The chosen theme is the topic that the participants reflect upon through the next week. It's noteworthy that at the end of the first session of the first group using this format, the chosen topic was loneliness! By selecting this topic, the group showed much trust. Most of the members knew each other before this program. Nevertheless, either among strangers or known fellow church members, stating that loneliness is an issue says much about our postmodern society. Furthermore, this reinforces and confirms how endemic loneliness is in our culture.

The two-hour session ends with the **eighth practice** of the group time— prayer. This prayer evokes quietness. The leader pulls together the thoughts of the group time and holds them in prayer. In turn, it helps prepare people for the week ahead. It seems appropriate that since *Spirituality and Learning* begins with silence that it ends with silence and prayer (or a commentary to a Higher Power) that brings closure.

Spirituality and Learning helps participants in challenging ways. It serves to help all flourish in building and maintaining relationships with others. It challenges participants to explore their relationship with the Godhead, or a "Higher Power." *Spirituality and Learning* serves to help participants explore the hardest relationship of all—that of embracing oneself and discovering, in part, "Who am I?"

Throughout the centuries, countless theologians, philosophers, sociologists, psychologists, and others have explored and commented on the journey inward. Sadly, much suggests that many people never truly attempt to explore or embrace this journey. Some begin the journey but abandon it because of the lack of quick answers or insights. Others discover the "dark night of the soul," as well noted by John of the Cross (1542–1591), become anxious or nervous, and walk away, perhaps because they may be finding facets of their lives they don't want to face, or they feel ill-equipped to address. Perhaps postmodern "Me-ism" and shallowness have muted or greatly reduced the ability to truly enter in and come out.

Conclusion

In recent decades, spirituality has received much academic attention. For example, Schools of Education, Business, and Medicine, and many other forums, feel called to explore this often hidden or unspoken element of people's lives. The bulk of this new research often centers on college students! A recent article exploring the spirituality of college students describes the intention of *Spirituality and Learning*:

> When college students write or are asked about spirituality, they consistently describe it as a journey or quest that takes them inward into the unknown, unexamined regions of their inner lives. It is a journey of introspection and reflection that students sometimes take alone and at other times in the company of others. When asked about the object or purpose of their spiritual journeys, college students often describe it as an inward search for purpose, meaning fulfillment, depth, wholeness, and authenticity. They describe a journey of discovery that is, in the end, not only about understanding themselves in a deeper

and more authentic way but also about discovering their purpose and destiny in life and how these connect to what they believe is sacred and transcendent.[6]

I hope that *Spirituality and Learning* can help to provide adults the opportunity to cultivate their spiritual path, to add depth to their spirit-voice, and to learn to walk more fully with others, with God or a Higher Power, and with oneself. Fourth-century bishop, writer, and theologian Gregory of Nyssia, taking a phrase and image from Philippians 3:13 and identifying the need for people to reach inward and act outward, wrote that people need to affirm their *epektasis*. In modern English, we translate this as "stretching forward," "straining forward," or "perpetual progress." Therefore, *Spirituality and Learning* is an opportunity for adults to strain forward by looking inward, by being re-crafted, by discovering and affirming spirit-voices, and for all to build bridges from who one is to who one may become!

The Structure of Spirituality and Learning

Individual Experience
Daily Silence, which, in time, will hopefully lead to solitude
Daily Journal
Weekly Reflection
Group Experience—six or eight two-hour sessions
Silence with Slow Breathing Exercise
Centering Exercise
Talking Stick and Journaling
Round Table Sharing
Short Break
Continued Sharing and Theme Development
Closing Prayer

APPENDIX B

A PARTIAL LIST OF TOPICS THAT EXAMINE SPIRITUALITY IN POSTMODERNISM

addictions
adolescents
adult learning theory
aging
agriculture
architecture
business chaplains
Celtic postmodernism
children
civic engagement
college—accounting
college—business programs
college—financial programs
college—management
college—medical degrees
college—organizational
behavior degrees
college—sociology
programs
college—teaching degrees
colleges/universities—
in general
colleges/ universities—
student development
clothing fashion
corporate America

culture, race
cyberspace
dance
dementia
development in Christianity
disabilities
ecology
educating clergy
ego development
existentialism
emotional learning
experiential education
faith and art
feminism
future theology
gay men
Gestalt therapy
homelessness
holistic learning
holistic research
human development
interdisciplinary research
journalism
landscape planning
law
leadership

learning compassion
learning styles
liberation research (women)
life-long learning
literature
martial arts
mindfulness
medicine—emergency
room practices
medicine—health
disabilities
medicine—neurology
medicine—obesity research
medicine—pediatrics
medicine—psychological
medicine—psychiatric
medicine—weight
management
mothering
music
mysticism
nature
nursing
paradigm shifts in
Christianity
personality research

phenomenology
philosophy
philosophy human values
policing
politics
postmodernism
psychology
psychotherapy
PTSD depression research
qualitative research
quantitative research
reflective practices

reflexive postmodern
society
religion
religion's relationship
research practices
Romanticism
schoolteacher, practices
schoolteachers, theory
secular context
secular world shifts
social activism
sociology
spiritual intelligence

stages of the soul
suicide prevention behavior
technological society
tourism
transformative learning
trends in research
visual arts
workplace
workplace research
water
workplace theory
yoga

110 topics—For some examples of these topics, look in Zsolnai, L., Flanagan, B. (eds.). (2019). *The Routledge International Handbook of Spirituality in Society and the Professions*. Abingdon-on Thames: Routledge International.

APPENDIX C

SOME TOOLS AND MODELS USED TO "MEASURE" SPIRITUALITY

Research Year	Title	Short Title	Author(s)
2018	Measuring Spirituality and Religiosity in Clinical Settings		Austin, P., Macdonald, J., MacLeod, R. "Measuring Spirituality and Religiosity in Clinical Settings: A Scoping Review of Available Instruments." *Religions*, 9, 70.
2002	The Ironson–Wood Spirituality/ Religiosity Index		Bekelman et al. 2010; Ironson et al. 2002; Mistretta et al. 2017
2017			Black, F., Boyle, A., Bredart, A., Costantini, J., Guo, M.E., et al. "The International Phase 4 Validation Study of the EORTC QLQ-SWB32: A Stand-alone Measure of Spiritual Well-being for People Receiving Palliative Care for Cancer." *European Journal of Cancer Care* (England)
2012	Spiritual Needs Inventory		Buck, H. G., McMillan, S. C. "A Psychometric Analysis of the Spiritual Needs Inventory in Informal Caregivers of Patients with Cancer in Hospice Home Care." *Oncology Nursing Forum* 39: E332–9.

2008	BENEFIT Through spirituality/ religiosity scale		Bussing and Koenig 2008; Xue et al. 2016
2013	Spiritual Needs Questionnaire		Bussing, A., Xiao F., Zhai, Wen B. Peng, and Chang Q. Ling. "Psychosocial and Spiritual Needs of Patients with Chronic Diseases: Validation of the Chinese Version of the Spiritual Needs Questionnaire." *Journal of Integrative Medicine* 11: 106–15.
2008	BENEFIT Scale		Bussing, A., Koenig, H. G. "The BENEFIT through Spirituality/Religiosity Scale—A 6-item Measure for Use in Health Outcome Studies." *The International Journal of Psychiatry in Medicine* 38: 493–506.
2010	SpREUK		Büssing, A., Balzat, H.J., Heusser, P. "Spiritual Needs of Patients with Chronic Pain Diseases and Cancer—Validation of the Spiritual Needs Questionnaire." *European Journal of Medical Research* 15: 266–73.
2015	WHOQOL-SRPB		Camargos, M. G., Paiva, C. E., Barroso, E. M., Carneseca, E. C., & Paiva, B. S. "Understanding the Differences Between Oncology Patients and Oncology Health Professionals Concerning Spirituality/ Religiosity: A Cross-Sectional Study." *Medicine*, 94(47)
2017	The Religious Belief Scale		Chiang, Y., Hsiang-chun L., Tsung-lan. C., Chin-yen. H., Hsiao, Y. "Psychometric Testing of a Religious Belief Scale." *The Journal of Nursing Research: JNR* 25: 419–28.
2009	Brief Multidimensional Measure of Religion and Spirituality		Curcio et al. 2015; Johnstone et al. 2009

2004	The Spirituality Index of Well-being	SIWB	Daaleman, T. P., Frey, B. B. "The Spirituality Index of Well-being: A New Instrument for Health-Related Quality-of-Life Research." *Annals of family medicine,* 2(5), 499–503.
2005	The Spirituality Scale		Delaney, C. "The Spirituality Scale: Development and Psychometric Testing of a Holistic Instrument to Assess the Human Spiritual Dimension." *Journal of Holistic Nursing,* 23(2), 145–167.
1988			Elkins D.N., Hedstrom L.J., Hughes L.L., Leaf J.A., Saunders, C. "Toward a Humanistic Phenomenological Spirituality. Definition, Description, and Measurement." *Journal of Humanistic Psychology.* 28:5–18
1983			Ellison, C.W. "Spiritual Well-being: Conceptualization and Measurement." Journal of Psychology and Theology. 11:330–340.
2013	Advance Cancer Patients' Distress Scale		Fischbeck, S., Maier, B.O., Reinholz, U., Nehring, C., Schwab, R., Manfred E. Beutel. "Assessing Somatic, Psychosocial, and Spiritual Distress of Patients with Advanced Cancer: Development of the Advanced Cancer Patients' Distress Scale." *The American Journal of Hospice & Palliative Care* 30: 339–46.
1999			Fisher, J. "Developing a Spiritual Health and Life-Orientation Measure for Secondary School Students." Paper presented at Research with a Regional/ Rural Focus: proceedings of the University of Ballarat inaugural annual conference, Mt. Helen: Victoria 15th October, 57–63
2010			Fisher, J. "Development and Application of a Spiritual Well-being Questionnaire Called SHALOM." *Religions,* 1: 105–121.

2016			Fisher, J. "Selecting the Best Version of SHALOM to Assess Spiritual Well-being." *Religions* 2016, 7(5), 45
2014	The Spiritual Distress Assessment Tool	SDAT	Gherghina, V., Cindea, I., Popescu, R., Balcan, A. "Spiritual Distress Assessment Tool a Valid Instrument for Elderly Patients in the Perioperative Period: 18AP3-." *European Journal of Anaesthesiology* 31: 267
2003	Spiritual Well-being Questionnaire	SWBQ	Gomez R., Fisher J.W. "Domains of Spiritual Well-being and Development and Validation of the Spiritual Well-being Questionnaire." *Personality and Individual Differences.* 2003;35:1975–1991.
1998	Spiritual Involvement and Beliefs Scale	SIBS-R	Hatch R.L., Burg, M.A., Naberhaus, D.S., Hellmich, L.K. "The Spiritual Involvement and Beliefs Scale. Development and Testing of a New Instrument." *Journal of Family Practice.* 46:476–486.
2017			Hoots, V. "Conceptualizing and Measurement of Spirituality: Towards the Development of a Nontheistic Spirituality Measure for Use in Health Related Fields." Master's thesis, East Tennessee State University.
1992			Howden, J. W. "Development and Psychometric Characteristics of the Spirituality Assessment Scale." Ann Arbor: Texas Woman's University, UMI Dissertation Services.
2002	The Ironson– Woods Spirituality/ Religiosity Index		Ironson, G., Solomon, G.F., Balbin, E.G., O'Cleirigh, C., George, A., Kumar, M., Larson, D., Woods, T.E. "The Ironson-Woods Spirituality/Religiousness Index Is Associated with Long Survival, Health Behaviors, Less Distress, and Low Cortisol in People with HIV/AIDS." *Annals of Behavioral Medicine: A Publication of the Society of Behavioral Medicine* 24: 34–48.

2009	The Brief Multidimensional Measure of Religiousness/ Spirituality	BMMRS	Johnstone, B., Yoon, D.P., Franklin, K.L. *et al.* "Re-conceptualizing the Factor Structure of the Brief Multidimensional Measure of Religiousness/Spirituality." *Journal of Religious Health* 48, 146
1989	The Spirituality and Spiritual Care Rating Scale		Kaczorowski, J.M.,1989
1989	The Spiritual Well-Being Scale		Kaczorowski J. M., *The Hospice Journal*, 5(3–4):105-16.
2008	Daily Spiritual Experience Scale		Kimura et al. 2012; Oji et al. 2017; Steinhauser et al. 2008
2012	The Daily Spiritual Experience Scale	DSES	Kimura, M., de Oliveira, A.L., Mishima, L.S., Underwood, L.G., 2012. "Cultural Adaptation and Validation of the Underwood's Daily Spiritual Experience Scale—Brazilian Version." *Revista da Escola de Enfermagem da U S P* 46: 99–106.
2017	The QRFPC-25		Kouloulias, V., Kokakis, J., Kelekis, N., Kouvaris, J. "A New Questionnaire (QRFPC25) Regarding the Religiosity and Spirituality in People with Life-Threatening Disease: Reliability and Validity in a Population of Cancer Patients Undergoing Radiotherapy." *Journal of Religion and Health* 56: 1137–54.
2009	Brief Serenity Scale		Kreitzer, M. J., Cynthia R. Gross, On A. Waleekhachonloet, Maryanne Reilly-Spong, and Marcia Byrd. "The Brief Serenity Scale: A Psychometric Analysis of a Measure of Spirituality and Well-being." *Journal of Holistic Nursing* 27: 7–16.
2010	The Spiritual Distress Scale		Ku, Ya L., Shih M. Kuo, and Ching Y. Yao. "Establishing the Validity of a Spiritual Distress Scale for Cancer Patients Hospitalized in Southern Taiwan." *International Journal of Palliative Nursing* 16: 134–38.

2000			MacDonald, D. A. "Spirituality: Description, Measurement, and Relation to the Five Factor Model of Personality." *Journal of Personality*, 68, 153–197.
1998	Index of Core Spiritual Experience		McBride et al. 1998; VandeCreek et al. 1995
1998	The Brief Pictorial Instrument for Assessing Spirituality		McBride, J. L., Pilkington, L., Arthur, G. "Development of Brief Pictorial Instruments for Assessing Spirituality in Primary Care." *The Journal of Ambulatory care Management* 21: 53–61
2002	The Spirituality and Spiritual Care Rating Scale		McSherry, W., Draper, P., Kendrick, D. "The Construct Validity of a Rating Scale Designed to Assess Spirituality and Spiritual Care." *International Journal of Nursing Studies* 39: 723–34.
2012	Spiritual Distress Assessment Tool	SDAT	Monod, S., Martin, E., Spencer, E.B., Rochat, E., Bula, C. "Validation of the Spiritual Distress Assessment Tool in Older Hospitalized Patients." *BMC Geriatrics* 12: 13.
2006	WHOQOL Spirituality, Religion, and Personal Beliefs	WHOQOL SRPB	O'Connell, K.A., Saxena S., Underwood L. "A Cross-Cultural Study of Spirituality, Religion, and Personal Beliefs as Components of Quality of Life." *Social Science and Medicine*. 2006;62: 1486–1497.
2014	The Functional Assessment of Chronic Illness Therapy— Spiritual Well-being	FACIT-Sp	Peterman, A. H., Fitchett, G., Brady, M. J., Hernandez, L., Cella, D., 2002. "Measuring Spiritual Well-being in People with Cancer: The Functional Assessment of Chronic Illness Therapy—Spiritual Well-being Scale." (FACIT-Sp). *Annals of Behavioral Medicine* 24: 49–58.
1999	Spiritual Transcendence Scale	STS	Piedmont, R.L. "Does Spirituality Represent the Sixth Factor of Personality? Spiritual Transcendence and the Five-Factor Model." *Journal of Personality*. 67:985–1013.

2005			Rican, P., Janosova, P. "Spirituality: Its Psychological Operationalization Via Measurement of Individual differences: A Czech Perspective." *Studia Psychologica.* 2005;47:157–165.
2002	The Daily Spiritual Experience Scale* the website **dsescale.org** states there are 400 studies using this model.	DSES	Underwood L.G., Teresi J.A., (2002). "The Daily Spiritual Experience Scale: Development, Theoretical Description, Reliability, Exploratory Factor Analysis, and Preliminary Construct Validity Using Health-Related Data." *Annals of Behavioral Medicine.* Winter; 24(1):22–33
2009	Spiritual Care Competence Scale		Van Leeuwen et al. 2009
1995	The Index of Core Spiritual Experience	INSPIRIT	VandeCreek, L., Ayres, S., Bassham, M. "Using INSPIRIT to Conduct Spiritual Assessments." *Journal of Pastoral Care* 49: 83–89
2017	EORTIC QLC-SWB32		Vivat, Bella, Teresa E. Young, J. Winstanley, J.I. Arraras, K. Black, F. Boyle, A. Bredart, A. Costantini, J. Guo, M.E. Irarrazaval, and et al. "The International Phase 4 Validation Study of the EORTC QLQ-SWB32: A Stand-alone Measure of Spiritual Well-being for People Receiving Palliative Care for Cancer." *European Journal of Cancer Care (England)* 26.

APPENDIX D

SOME TOOLS AND MODELS USED TO "MEASURE" MINDFULNESS

Some Early Publications	Title	Abbrev.	Authors
1990	Mindfulness Based Stress Reduction	MBSR	Kabat-Zinn, J. (1990). *Full Catastrophe Living (Revised Edition 2013): Using the Wisdom of Your Body and Mind to Face Stress, Pain, and Illness.* New York. Bantam Books.
1987	Dialectical Behavioral Therapy	DBT	Linehan, M. (1997). "Dialectical Behavior Therapy (DBT) for Borderline Personality Disorder." *The Journal of BDT*, March, 1, 1997, (8) 1.
	Mindfulness Based Cognitive Therapy	MBCT	Segal, Z., Teasdale, J., Williams, M. (2002). *Mindfulness-Based Cognitive Therapy for Depression.* New York: Guilford Press.
1994	Acceptance and Commitment Therapy	ACT	Hayes, S.C., Strosahl, K.D., Wilson, K. G. (2003). *Acceptance and Commitment Therapy: An Experiential Approach to Behavior Change.* New York: Guildford Press.
2003		fMRI	Libert, B. (2003). "Can Conscious Experience Affect Brain Activity?" *Journal of Consciousness Studies*, 10.2., 24–28.

2003	Mindfulness-Based Interventions	2MBI	Baer R.A. (2003). "Mindfulness Training as a Clinical Intervention: A Conceptual and Empirical Review." *Clinical Psychology: Science and Practice.* 2003; 10(2):125–143.
2003	Mindful Attention Awareness Scale	MAAS	Brown, K. W., Ryan, R. M. (2003). "The Benefits of Being Present: Mindfulness and Its Role in Psychological Well-Being." *Journal of Personality and Social Psychology,* (84), 822–848.
	Five Facet Mindfulness Questionnaire	FFMQ	Baer, R.A., Smith, G.T., Hopkins J., Krietemeyer J., Toney L. (2006). "Using Self-Report Assessment Methods to Explore Facets of Mindfulness." *Assessment.* Mar; 13(1):27–45.
2006	Toronto Mindfulness Scale	TMS	Lau, M. Bishop, S., Segal, Z., Buis, T., Anderson, N., Carlson, L., Shapiro, S., Carmody, J., Abbey, S., Devins, G. (2006). "The Toronto Mindfulness Scale: Development and Validation." *Journal of Clinical Psychology.* 62. 1445–67.
2006	Freiburg Mindfulness Inventory	FMI	Walach, H., Buchheld, N., Buttenmüller, V., Kleinknecht, N., Schmidt, S. (2006). Measuring Mindfulness—The Freiburg Mindfulness Inventory Personality and Individual Differences, 40: 1543-1555.
2007	Wheel of Awareness		Siegel, D.J. (2007). *The Mindful Brain: Reflection and Attunement in the Cultivation of Well-being.* New York: W.W. Norton & Company.
2007	Cognitive and Affective Mindfulness Scale – Revised	CAMS-R	Feldman G., Hayes A., Kumar S., Greeson J., Laurenceau J.P. (2007). "Mindfulness and Emotion Regulation: The Development and Initial Validation of the Cognitive and Affective Mindfulness Scale-Revised (CAMS-R)." *Journal of Psychopathology and Behavioral Assessment,* 29(3), 177–190.

2012	Langer Mindfulness Scale		Pirson, M., Langer, E. J., Bodner, Todd, E., Zilcha, S. (2012). "The Development and Validation of the Langer Mindfulness Scale—Enabling a Socio-Cognitive Perspective of Mindfulness in Organizational Contexts" (October 8, 2012). Fordham University Schools of Business Research Paper.
2007	Solloway Mindfulness Survey		Solloway, S. G., Fisher, Jr., W. P. (2007). "Mindfulness Practice: A Rasch Variable Construct Innovation." *Journal of Applied Measurement*, 8, 359–372.
2004	Kentucky Inventory of Mindfulness Skills		Baer R.A., Smith G.T., Allen K.B. (2004). "Assessment of Mindfulness by Self-Report: The Kentucky Inventory of Mindfulness Skills." *Assessment*. 2004 Sep; 11(3):191–206.
1980	Automatic Thoughts Questionnaire		Hollon, S. D., Kendall, P. C. (1980). "Cognitive Self-Statements in Depression: Development of an Automatic Thoughts Questionnaire." *Cognitive Therapy and Research*, 4, 383–395.
2013	State Mindfulness Scale		Tanay, G., Bernstein, A. (2013). "State Mindfulness Scale (SMS): Development and Initial Validation." *Psychological Assessment*, 25, 1286–1299.
2008	Philadelphia Mindfulness Scale		Cardaciotto, L., Herbert, J. D., Forman, E. M., Moitra, E., & Farrow, V. (2008). "The Assessment of Present-Moment Awareness and Acceptance: The Philadelphia Mindfulness Scale." *Assessment*, 15, 204–223.

APPENDIX E

MINDFULNESS IN EDUCATION
RESEARCH HIGHLIGHTS

An Short List of Studies of Mindfulness in Education

Mindfulness and Students

Barnes, V. A., Treiber, F. A., and Davis, H. (2001). "Impact of Transcendental Meditation on Cardiovascular Function at Rest and During Acute Stress in Adolescents with High Normal Blood Pressure." *Journal of Psychosomatic Research.* 51, 597–605.

Barnes, V. A., Bauza, L. B., and Treiber, F. A. (2003). "Impact of Stress Reduction on Negative School Behavior in Adolescents." *Health and Quality of Life Outcomes.* 1(10).

Beauchemin, J., Hutchins, T. L., and Patterson, F. (2008). Mindfulness Meditation May Lessen Anxiety, Promote Social Skills, and Improve Academic Performance among Adolescents with Learning Disabilities." *Complementary Health Practice Review.* 13, 34–45.

Birdee, G. S., Yeh, G. Y., Wayne, P. M., Phillips, R. S., Davis, R. B., and Gardiner, P. (2009). "Clinical Applications of Yoga for the Pediatric Population: A Systematic Review." *Academic Pediatrics.* 9, 212–220.

Biegel, G. M., Brown, K. W., Shapiro, S. L., and Schubert, C. M. (2009). "Mindfulness-based Stress Reduction for the Treatment of Adolescent Psychiatric Outpatients: A Randomized Clinical Trial." *Journal of Consulting and Clinical Psychology.* 77, 855–866.

Bluth, K., Campo, R. A., Pruteanu-Malinici, S., Reams, A., Mullarkey, M., and Broderick, P. C. (2015). "A School-Based Mindfulness Pilot Study for Ethnically Diverse At-risk Adolescents." *Mindfulness.* doi: 10.1007/ s12671-014-0376-1.

Broderick, P. C. and Metz, S. (2009). "Learning to BREATHE: A Pilot Trial of a Mindfulness Curriculum for Adolescents." *Advances in School Mental Health Promotion.* 2(1), 35–46.

Carei, T. R., Fyfe-Johnson, A. L., Breuner, C. C., and Brown, M. A. (2010). "Randomized Controlled Clinical Trial of Yoga in the Treatment of Eating Disorders." *Journal of Adolescent Health.* 46, 346–351.

Davidson, R. J., Dunne, J., Eccles, J. S., Engle, A., Greenberg, M., Jennings, P., and Vago, D. (2012). "Contemplative Practices and Mental Training: Prospects for American Education." *Child Development Perspectives.* 6(2), 146–153.

Felver, J. C., Frank, J. L., and McEachern, A. D. (2014). "Effectiveness, Acceptability, and Feasibility of the Soles of the Feet Mindfulness-Based Intervention with Elementary School Students." *Mindfulness.* 5(5), 589–597.

Flook, L., Goldberg, S. B., Pinger, L., and Davidson, R. J. (2015). "Promoting Prosocial Behavior and Self-Regulatory Skills in Preschool Children through a Mindfulness-Based Kindness Curriculum." *Developmental Psychology.* 51(1), 44–51.

Flook, L., Smalley, S. L., Kitil, M. J., Galla, B. M., Kaiser-Greenland, S., Locke, J., and Kasari, C. (2010). "Effects of Mindful Awareness Practices on Executive Functions in Elementary School Children." *Journal of Applied School Psychology.* 26(1), 70–95.

Galantino, M. L., Galbavy, R., and Quinn, L. (2008). Therapeutic effects of yoga for children: A systematic review of the literature. *Pediatric Physical Therapy, 20,* 66–80.

Greenberg, M. T. and Harris, A. R. (2012). Nurturing mindfulness in children and youth: Current state of research. *Child Development Perspectives, 6*(2), 161-166.

Gregoski, M. J., Barnes, V. A., Tingen, M. S., Harshfield, G. A., and Treiber, F. A. (2010). "Breathing Awareness Meditation and LifeSkills Training Programs Influence upon Ambulatory Blood Pressure and Sodium Excretion among African American Adolescents." *Journal of Adolescent Health.* 48, 59–64.

Harrison, L. J., Manocha, R., and Rubia, K. (2004). "Sahaja Yoga Meditation as a Family Treatment Programme for Children with Attention Deficit-Hyperactivity Disorder." *Clinical Child Psychology and Psychiatry.* 9, 479–497.

Jensen, P. and Kenny, D. (2004). "The Effects of Yoga on the Attention and Behavior of Boys with Attention-Deficit/Hyperactivity Disorder (ADHD)." *Journal of Attention Disorders.* 7, 205–216.

Lawlor, M. S., Schonert-Reichl, K. A., Gadermann, A. M., and Zumbo, B. D. (2012). "A Validation Study of the Mindful Attention Awareness Scale Adapted for Children." *Mindfulness.* 1–12.

Mendelson, T., Greenberg, M. T., Dariotis, J. K., Gould, L. F., Rhoades, B. L., and Leaf, P. J. (2010). "Feasibility and Preliminary Outcomes of a School-Based Mindfulness Intervention for Urban Youth." *Journal of Abnormal Child Psychology.* 38(7), 985–994.

Napoli, M., Krech, P. R., and Holley, L. C. (2005). "Mindfulness Training for Elementary School Students: The Attention Academy." *Journal of Applied School Psychology.* 21(1), 99–125.

Oberle, E., Schonert-Reichl, K. A., Lawlor, M. S., and Thomson, K. C. (2012). "Mindfulness and Inhibitory Control in Early Adolescence." *Journal of Early Adolescence.* 32(4), 565–588.

Raes, F., Griffith, J. W., Van der Gucht, K., and Williams, J. M. G. (2014). "School-based Prevention and Reduction of Depression in Adolescents: A Cluster-Randomized Controlled Trial of a Mindfulness Group Program." *Mindfulness.* 5(5), 477–486.

Razza, R. A., Bergen-Cico, D., and Raymond, K. (2013). "Enhancing Preschoolers' Self-Regulation Via Mindful Yoga." *Journal of Child and Family Studies.* 1062–1024.

Schonert-Reichl, K. A. and Lawlor, M. S. (2010). "The Effects of a Mindfulness-Based Education Program on Pre- and Early Adolescents' Well-being and Social and Emotional Competence." *Mindfulness.* 1(3), 137–151.

Schonert-Reichl, K. A., Oberle, E., Lawlor, M. S., Abbott, D., Thomson, K., Oberlander, T. F., and Diamond, A. (2015). Enhancing Cognitive and Social–Emotional Development through a Simple-to-Administer Mindfulness-Based School Program for Elementary School Children: A Randomized Controlled Trial." *Developmental Psychology.* 51(1), 52–66.

Semple, R. J., Lee, J., Rosa, D., and Miller, L. F. (2010). "A Randomized Trial of Mindfulness-Based Cognitive Therapy for Children: Promoting Mindful Attention to Enhance Social-Emotional Resiliency in Children." *Journal of Child and Family Studies.* 19(2), 218–229.

Semple, R. J., Reid, E. F. G., and Miller, L. (2005). "Treating Anxiety with Mindfulness: An Open Trial of Mindfulness Training for Anxious Children." *Journal of Cognitive Psychotherapy.* 19, 379–392.

Tang, Y., Yang, L., Leve, L. D., and Harold, G. T. (2012). "Improving Executive Function and Its Neurobiological Mechanisms through a Mindfulness-Based Intervention: Advances within the Field of Developmental Neuroscience." *Child Development Perspectives.* 6(4), 361–366.

Thompson M. and Gauntlett-Gilbert J. (2008). "Mindfulness with Children and Adolescents: Effective Clinical Application." *Clinical Child Psychology and Psychiatry.* 13, 395–407.

Van der Oord, S., Bogels, S. M., and Peijnenburg, D. (2012). "The Effectiveness of Mindfulness Training for Children with ADHD and Mindful Parenting for their Parents." *Journal of Child and Family Studies.* 21(1), 139–147.

Zelazo, P. D. and Lyons, K. E. (2012). "The Potential Benefits of Mindfulness Training in Early Childhood: A Developmental Social Cognitive Neuroscience Perspective." *Child Development Perspectives.* 6(2), 154–160.

Zenner, C., Herrnleben-Kurz, S., and Walach, H. (2014). "Mindfulness-Based Interventions in Schools—A Systematic Review and Meta-Analysis." *Frontiers in Psychology.* 5, 603.

Zoogman, S., Goldberg, S. B., Hoyt, W. T., and Miller, L. (2014). "Mindfulness Interventions with Youth: A Meta-Analysis." *Mindfulness.* 6(2), 290–302.

Mindfulness and teachers

Flook, L., Goldberg, S. B., Pinger, L., Bonus, K., and Davidson, R. J. (2013). "Mindfulness for Teachers: A Pilot Study to Assess Effects on Stress, Burnout, and Teaching Efficacy." *Mind, Brian, and Education.* 7(3), 182–195.

Frank, J. L., Reibel, D., Broderick, P., Cantrell, T., and Metz, S. (2015). "The Effectiveness of Mindfulness-Based Stress Reduction on Educator Stress and Well-being: Results from a Pilot Study." *Mindfulness.* 6(2), 208–216.

Jennings, P. A., Frank, J. L., Snowberg, K. E., Coccia, M. A., and Greenberg, M. T. (2013). "Improving Classroom Learning Environments by Cultivating Awareness and Resilience in Education (CARE): Results of a Randomized Controlled Trial." *School Psychology Quarterly.* Advance online publication. doi: 10.1037/spq0000035.

Jennings, P. A., Snowberg, K. E., Coccia, M. A., and Greenberg, M. T. (2011). "Improving Classroom Learning Environments by Cultivating Awareness and Resilience in Education (CARE): Results of Two Pilot Studies." *Journal of Classroom Interactions.* 46, 27–48.

Roeser, R. W., Schonert-Reichl, K. A., Jha, A., Cullen, M., Wallace, L., Wilensky, R., Oberle, E., Thomson, K., Taylor, C., and Harrison, J. (2013, April 29). "Mindfulness Training and Reductions in Teacher Stress and Burnout: Results From Two Randomized, Waitlist-Control Field Trials." *Journal of Educational Psychology.* doi: 10.1037/a0032093.

Roeser, R.W., Skinner, E., Beers, J., and Jennings, P.A. (2012). "Mindfulness Training and Teachers' Professional Development: An Emerging Area of Research and Practice." *Child Development Perspectives.* 6, 167–173.

Singh, N. N., Lancioni, G. E., Winton, A. S., Karazsia, B. T., and Singh, J. (2013). "Mindfulness Training for Teachers Changes the Behavior of their Preschool Students." *Research in Human Development.* 10(3), 211–233.

Mindfulness and Administrators

Wells, C. M. (2013). "Principals Responding to Constant Pressure: Finding a Source of Stress Management." *NASSP Bulletin*, 0192636513504453.

Campbell, E. (2014). "Mindfulness in Education Research Highlights: An Annotated Bibliography of Studies of Mindfulness in Education." Published on-line September 16, 2014. https://greatergood.berkeley.edu/article/item/mindfulness_in_education_research_highlights Retrieved March 12 2020.

NOTES

Introduction

[1] Hamm, R. (2007). *Recreating the Church: Leadership For The Post-Modern Age*. St. Louis: MO. Chalice Press. 8.

[2] Bowman, J.P. and Klopping, I. (1999). "Bandstands, Bandwidth, and Business Communication: Technology and the Sanctity of Writing." Retrieved June 30, 2009.

http://journals.sagepub.com/doi/ pdf/10.1177/108056999906200108.

[3] Chamberlain, P (2020). "Knowledge Is Not Everything." *Design for Health*. 4:1, 1–3. Retrieved March 1, 2021.

https://www.tandfonline.com/doi/pdf/10.1080/24735132.2020.1731203?need Access=true.

[4] Detweiler, C. (2013). *iGods: How Technology Shapes Our Spiritual and Social Lives*. Grand Rapids, MI: Brazos Press, Baker Publishing. 127.

[5] Groen, J. and Jacob, J. (2006). "Spiritual Transformation in a Secular Context: A Qualitative Research Study of Transformative Learning in Higher Education." *International Journal of Teaching and Learning in Higher Education*. 18(2), 76.

[6] Groen, J. (2008). "Paradoxical Tensions in Creating a Teaching and Learning Space within a Graduate Education Course on Spirituality." *Teaching in Higher Education*. 13(2), 193.

Shirley, C. M. (2009). "The Role of Spirituality in the Practice of Transformational

Technical College Leaders." Doctoral Dissertation, University of Georgia. Retrieved April 12, 2010. https://getd.libs.uga.edu/pdfs/shirley_charity_m_200908_edd/shirley_charity_m_200908_edd.pdf. p. 38–39.

7 Tacey, D. (2004). *The Spirituality Revolution: The Emergence of Contemporary Spirituality.* New York: Routledge. 208.

8 Heelas, P. (2008). *Spiritualities of Life: New Age Romanticism, and Consumptive Capitalism.* Oxford: Wiley-Blackwell. 67.

Chapter One
Postmodernism and Western Society

1 Harari, Y. N. (2018). *21 Lessons for the 21st Century.* New York. Signet-Random House.

2 https://quoteinvestigator.com/2013/11/30/tv-gum/

3 Benner, D. G. (2011). *Soulful Spirituality: Becoming Fully Alive and Deeply Human.* Grand Rapids, MI: Brazos Press. 148.

4 Karasu, T. B. (1999). "Spiritual Psychotherapy. " (Special Article). *American Journal of Psychotherapy.* 53: 143-161. 160.

5 Levitin, D. J. (2014). *The Organized Mind: Thinking Straight in the Age of Information Overload.* New York: Dutton-Penguin Group. 96.

6 Brown, B. (2012). *Daring Greatly: How the Courage to Be Vulnerable Transforms the Way We Live, Love and Parent and Lead.* New York: Gotham-Penguin Books. 139–140.

7 https://www.tvfanatic.com/quotes/we-need-to-widen-our-circle-i-have-a-very-wide-circle-i-have/. Retrieved June 27, 2018.

8 Smith, R. S. (2005). *Truth and the New Kind of Christian: The Emerging Effects of Postmodernism in the Church.* Wheaton, IL: Crossway Books. 121.

9 Groen, J. (2008). "Paradoxical Tensions in Creating a Teaching and Learning Space within a Graduate Education Course on Spirituality." *Teaching in Higher Education.* 13(2), 195.

[10]   Brown, L. C. (2008). "Role of Spirituality in Adult Learning Contexts." Doctoral Dissertation, University of Georgia. Retrieved, April 11, 2010.

https://getd.libs.uga.edu/pdfs/brown_laura_c_200812_phd/brown_laura_c_200812_phd.pdf. 2. Citing Robert K.C. Forman (2004). *Grassroots Spirituality: What It Is, Why It Is Here, Where Is It Going?* Charlottesville, VA: Imprint Academic.

[11]   Holt, B. P. (2005). *Thirsty for God: A Brief History of Christian Spirituality.* Minneapolis, MN: Augsburg Fortress Publishers. 46.

[12]   Myers, D., Hope College, Michigan. Quoted in Mark, C. W. (1995). *Spiritual Intelligence (SQ): The Symbiotic Relationship Between Spirit and the Brain: Insights into the Postmodern Journey of Spirituality and Holistic Health.* Bloomington, IN: AuthorHouse. 97.

[13]   Vogel, L. (2000). "Reckoning with the Spiritual Lives of Adult Educators." In L.M. English and M.A. Gillen. *Addressing the Spiritual Dimensions of Adult Learning: What Educators Can Do: New Directions for Adult and Continuing Education.* San Francisco, CA: Jossey-Bass. 19–20.

[14]   Kurzweil, R. (1999). *The Age of Spiritual Machine: When Computers Exceed Human Intelligence.* New York: Penguin Books. 20, 21, 130.

[15]   Colvin, G. (2015). *Humans Are Underrated: What High Achievers Know That Brilliant Machines Never Will.* New York: Portfolio/Penguin. 30.

[16]   Detweiler, C. (2013). *iGods: How Technology Shapes Our Spiritual and Social Lives.* Grand Rapids, MI: Brazos Press, Baker Publishing. 3.

[17]   Carr, N. (2010). *The Shallows: What the Internet Is Doing to Our Brains.* New York: W.W. Norton. 108, 111.

[18]   "Is the Internet Destroying Our Attention Span?" Posted by Nicole Plumridge on August 1, 2013. http://psychminds.com/is-the-internet-destroying-our-attentions-span/.

[19]   Twenge, J. M. and Campbell, W. K. (2010). *The Narcissism Epidemic: Living in an Age of Uncertainty.* New York: Atria Paperback. 259–260.

[20]   Detweiler, C. (2013). op. cit. 126.

21   Besecke, K. (2014). *You Can't Put God in a Box: Thoughtful Spirituality in the Rational Age*. New York: Oxford University Press. 130–131.

22   Slater, P. (2009). *The Chrysalis Effect: The Metamorphosis of Global Culture*. Portland, OR: Sussex Academic Press. 7–8.

Chapter Two
Postmodernism and Western Christianity

1   Bass, D. B. (2012). *Christianity after Religion: The End of Church and the Birth of a New Spiritual Awakening*. New York: HarperOne. 4–5.

2   Dornauer, J. (2015). *Beyond Resistance: The Institutional Church Meets the Postmodern World*. Chicago: Exploration Press. 110–111.

3   Carr, N. (2010). *The Shallows: What the Internet Is Doing to Our Brains*. New York: W.W. Norton. 108.

4   Heelas, P., Woodhead, L., Seel, B., and Szerszynski, B. (2005). *The Spiritual Revolution: Why Religion Is Giving Way to Spirituality* (Religion and Spirituality in the Modern World). New York: Wiley-Blackwell. 2, 5.

5   Herrick, J. A. (2004). *The Making of the New Spirituality: The Eclipse of the Western Religious Tradition*. Downers Grove, IL: IVP. 53.

6   Bass, D. (2012). op. cit. 69–70.

7   Dornauer, J. (2015). op. cit. 21–22.

8   Taylor, P. (2014). *The Next America: Boomers, Millennials, and the Looming Generational Showdown*. New York: PublicAffairs. 114. copyright © 9781610393508. Reprinted by permission of PublicAffairs, an imprint of Hachette Book Group, Inc.

9   Hammett, E. H. (2005). *Spiritual Leadership in a Secular Age: Building Bridges Instead of Barriers* (TCP Leadership Series). Duluth, GA: Chalice Press. 7.

10   Dornauer, J. (2015). op. cit. 110–111

11   Twenge, J. M., Campbell, W. K. (2010). *The Narcissism Epidemic: Living in an Age of Uncertainty*. New York: Atria Paperback. 249.

12   Mercadante, L. (2014). *Belief without Borders: Inside the Minds of the Spiritual but Not Religious*. Oxford: Oxford University Press. 3.

13   Miller, C. K. (1989). *Boomer Spirituality: Seven Values for the Second Half of Life*. Nashville, TN: Discipleship Resources. 130.

14   Twenge, J. M. and Campbell, W. K. (2010). op. cit. p. 249.

15   Bregman, R. (2019). *Humankind: A Hopeful History* (E. Manton and E. Moore, Trans.). London: Bloomsbury Publishing. 14.

16   Van den Heuvel, A. H. (1967). *The Humiliation of the Church*. Philadelphia: Westminster Press. 11.

17   Taylor, P. (2014). *The Next America: Boomers, Millennials, and the Looming Generational Showdown*. New York: PublicAffairs. 4.

18   Veith, G. E. Jr. (1994). *Postmodern Times: A Guide to Contemporary Thought and Culture*. Wheaton, IL: Crossway Books. 211.

19   Ibid. 227–228.

20   Ashbrook, R. T. (2009). *Mansions of the Heart: Exploring the Seven Stages of Spiritual Growth*. San Francisco, CA: Jossey-Bass. 44–45.

Fenwick, T., English, L., and Parson, J. (2001). "Dimensions of Spirituality: A Framework for Adult Educators." Presented at the Canadian Association for the Study of Adult Education, Laval University, Quebec. 80.

Packard, J. (2015). *Church Refugees: Sociologists Reveal Why People Are DONE with Church but Not their Faith*. Loveland, CO: group.com. 28.

21   Indick, W. (2015). *Digital God: How Technology Will Reshape Spirituality*. Jefferson, NC: McFarland Publishing. 35

22   Ibid. 158.

23   Lyon, D. (2000). *Jesus in Disneyland: Religion in Postmodern Times*. Malden, MA: Polity Press/Blackwell Publishing. 22, 34–35, 40, 42–43.

24   Packard, J. (2015). op. cit. 28.

25   Bibby, R. (2017). *Resilient Gods: Being Pro-Religious, Low Religious, or No Religious in Canada*. Vancouver, BC: UBC Press. 29.

      Streib, H. and Hood, R. (2011). "Spirituality" as Privatized Experience-Oriented Religion:

      Empirical and Conceptual Perspectives. *Implicit Religion*. 433-453.

26   Bibby, R. (2017). op cit. 21, 23, 25, 29.

27   Dumestre, M. (1997). *A Church at Risk: The Challenge of Spiritually Hungry Adults*. New York: Crossroad Publishing. 7–8.

Chapter Three
Postmodernism and Western Spirituality

1   Jones, L. (2005). "What Does Spirituality in Education Mean? Stumbling Toward Wholeness." *Journal of College and Character*. 6(7), 1–7.

      http://www.collegevalues.org/pdfs/spirit%20in%20ed.%20jones%20 formatted%20final%202.pdf. 3.

2   Newell, J. P. (2002). *Echo of the Soul: The Sacredness of the Human Body*. Harrisburg, PA: Morehouse Publishing. xiii.

3   "Spirituality in Higher Education: A National Study of College Student's Search for Meaning and Purpose." (2003, July 21). *UCLA Launches Study on Spirituality National Study to track College Student's Spiritual Growth* [Press release]. http://www.spirituality.ucla.edu/news/Spirituality_2003-07-21.pdf.

4   Montgomery-Goodnough, A. and Gallagher, S. J. (2007). "Review of Research on Spiritual and Religious Formation in Higher Education." Proceedings of the Sixth Annual College of Education Research Conference: Urban and International Education Section. 60–65.

      Nash, R. J. and Bradley, D. L. (2007). "Moral Conversation: A Theoretical Framework for Talking about Spirituality on College Campuses." In B. W. Speck and S. L. Hoppe (eds.). *Searching for Spirituality in Higher Education*. 137–154. New York: Peter Lang.

Rogers, J. (2006). "Role-Modeling Authenticity in Higher Education, Spirituality in Higher Education: A National Study of College Student's Search for Meaning and Purpose." 3(1) 1–5.

Small, J. L. (2008). "College Students Religious Affiliation and Spiritual Identity:

A Qualitative Study." Doctoral Dissertation, University of Michigan. Retrieved April 5, 2010. http://sz0029.wc.mail.comcast.net/service/home/~/Small-%20PhD.pdf?auth=co&loc=en_US&id= 119702&part=2.

Cady, D. M. (2007). "Spirituality and Student Development." In B. W. Speck and S. L. Hoppe (eds.). *Searching for Spirituality in Higher Education*. 97–110. New York: Peter Lang.

Hoppe, S. L. (2005) "Spirituality and Leadership." In S. Hoppe (ed). *Spirituality in Higher Education*. 83–92. San Francisco, CA: Jossey-Bass.

Hoppe, S. L. (2007). "Spirituality in Higher Education Leadership." In B. W. Speck and S. L. Hoppe (eds.). *Searching for Spirituality in Higher Education*. 111–136. New York: Peter Lang.

5   Astin, A. W., Astin, H. S., and Lindholm, J. A. (2010). *Cultivating the Spirit: How College Can Enhance Students' Lives*. San Francisco, CA: Jossey-Bass. 2–3.

6   Ibid. 157.

7   Lauzon, A. C. (2001). "The Challenges of Spirituality in the Everyday Practice of the Adult Educator." *Adult Learning,* xi.

8   Groen, J. (2008). "Moving in from the Fringes of the Academy: Spirituality as an Emerging Focus in the Canadian Professional Faculties of Business, Education and Social Work." Draft Article. 9.

English, L. M. and Tisdell, E. J. (2010). "Spirituality and Adult Education." In C.E. Kasworm, A. D. Rose, and J. M. Ross- Gordon (eds.). *Handbook of Adult and Continuing Education*. San Francisco, CA: Jossey-Bass. 285-286.

9   Rossiter, G. (2014). "A Perspective on Spiritual Education in Australian Schools: The Emergence of Non-Religious Personal Development Approaches." In J.

Watson, M. de Souza, and A. Trousdale. *Global Perspectives on Spirituality and Education*. New York: Routledge. 141.

Rossiter. G. (2010). "Perspective on contemporary spirituality: implications for religious education in Catholic schools. *International Studies in Catholic Education*. 129–147.

[10] English, L. M., Fenwick, T. J., and Parsons, J. (2005). "Interrogating Our Practices of Integrating Spirituality into Workplace Education." *Australian Journal of Adult Education*, 45(1). 81.

[11] Jakonen, J. P. (2008). "Beyond Postmodern Spirituality: Ken Wilbur and the Integral Approach." In T. Ahback (ed.) *Papers Read at Postmodern Spirituality*. Abo, Finland. 98.

Westrup, J. (1998). "Invisibility? Spiritual Values and Adult Education." *Australian Journal of Adult and Community Education*. 38 (2) July 1998. 106.

[12] Benefiel, M., Fry, L. W., and Geigle, D. (2014). "Spirituality and Religion in the Workplace: History, Theory, and Research." *Journal of Religion and Spirituality* 6(3), 175.

[13] Neal, J. (2017) "Workplace Spirituality Annotated Bibliography."

https://www.academia.edu/32013953/WORKPLACE_SPIRITUALITY_ANNOTATED_BIBLIOGRAPHY_Compiled.

[14] Allison, A. M. W. and Broadus, P. R. B. (2009). "Spirituality Then and Now: Our Journey through Higher Education as Women of Faith." In K. G. Hendrix and J. D. Hamlet (eds.). *As the Spirit Moves Us: New Directions for Teaching and Learning*, # 120. 77–86. San Francisco, CA: Jossey-Bass.

Astin, A. W. (2004). "Why Spirituality Deserves a Central Place in Higher Education." *Spirituality in Higher Education Newsletter*. UCLA. 1–12.

Astin, H. S. and Astin, A. W. (2009). "Does Spirituality Have a Place in Higher Education?: A Response." *Religion & Education*. 36(2), 124–129. Summer, University of Northern Iowa.

Astin, A. W., Astin, H. S., and Lindholm, J. A. (2010). *Cultivating the Spirit: How College Can Enhance Students' Lives*. San Francisco, CA: Jossey-Bass.

Best, R. (2015). "Spirituality, Faith and Education: Some Reflections from a UK Perspective. In J. Watson, M. de Souza, and A. Trousdale. *Perspectives on Spirituality and Education*. New York: Routledge. 5-20.

Bone, J. (2014). "Spirituality and Early Childhood Education in New Zealand and Australia: Past, Present and Future." In J. Watson, M. de Souza, and A. Trousdale. *Global Perspectives on Spirituality and Education*. New York: Routledge. 116–128.

Campbell, R. C. (2014). "The Role of Service Learning in Developing Spirituality and Transforming Students." Dissertation submitted in partial fulfillment of the requirements for the degree of Doctor of Education: The University of Memphis, May 2014.

Campbell, K. P. (2010). "Transformative Learning and Spirituality: A Heuristic Inquiry into the Experience of Spiritual Learning." Unpublished doctoral dissertation. Capalla University.

Chang, H. and Boyd, D. (2011). *Spirituality in Higher Education: Autoethnographies*. Walnut Creek: CA: LeftCoast Press.

Chickering, A. W., Dalton, J. C., and Stamm, L. (2006). *Encouraging Authenticity & Spirituality in Higher Education*. San Francisco, CA: Jossey-Bass.

Dirkx, J. M. (2003). "Nurturing Soul in Adult Learning." In P. Cranton (ed.). *Transformative Learning in Action: Insights from Practice*. San Francisco, CA: Jossey-Bass.

Duerr, M. (2003). "Survey of Transformative and Spiritual Dimensions of Higher Education." *Journal of Transformative Education* 1(3), 177–211. Retrieved April 2, 2010. http://jtd.sagepub.com/content/1/3/177.

Groen, J. and Jacob, J. (2006). "Spiritual Transformation in a Secular Context: A Qualitative Research Study of Transformative Learning in Higher Education." *International Journal of Teaching and Learning in Higher Education*. 75–88.

Hoppe, S. L. and Speck, B. W. (eds.) (2005). *Spirituality in Higher Education*. San Francisco, CA: Jossey-Bass.

Miller, J., Karsten, S., Denton, D., Orr, D., and Kates, I. C. (2005). *Holistic Learning and Spirituality in Education: Breaking New Ground.* Albany, NY: State University of New York.

Miller, J. (2000). *Education and the Soul: Toward a Spiritual Curriculum.* Albany, NY: State University of New York.

Parks, S. D. (2000). *Big Questions, Worthy Dreams: Mentoring Young Adults in Their Search for Meaning, Purpose and Faith.* Jossey-Bass: San Francisco.

[15] Buck, H. G. (2006). "Spirituality: Concept Analysis and Model Development." *Holistic Nursing Practice.* 20(6), 288–92. Retrieved, Sept. 10, 2017. https://pubmed.ncbi.nlm.nih.gov/17099417/

Calderone, S. (2004). "Current Thinking on the Role of Spirituality in Medical Education & Training Spirituality in Higher Education: A National Study of College Student's Search for Meaning and Purpose." Retrieved December 13, 2010. http://www.spirituality.ucla.edu/docs/newsletters/1/Calderone.pdf.

Sawatzky, R. and Pesut, B. (2005). "Attributes of Spiritual Care in Nursing Practice." *Journal of Holistic Nursing,* 23 (1), March, 19–33.

We, L., Liao, Y., and Yeh, D. (2012). "Nursing Student Perceptions of Spirituality and Spiritual Care." *The Journal of Nursing Research.* 20 (3) September, 219–226.

[16] Sachs, W. L. and Bos, M. S. (2016). *Fragmented Lives: Finding Faith in an Age of Uncertainty.* Harrisburg, PA: Morehouse Publishing. 16.

Bregman, L. (2012). "Spiritual Definitions: A Moving Target." In M. Fowler, J. D. Martin III, and J. L. Hochheimer (eds.). *Spirituality: Theory, Praxis and Pedagogy.* Oxford, UK: Inter-Disciplinary Press. 4.

[17] Taylor, P. (2014). *The Next America: Boomers, Millennials, and the Looming Generational Showdown.* New York: PublicAffairs. 143.

[18] Besecke, K. (2014). *You Can't Put God in a Box: Thoughtful Spirituality in the Rational Age.* New York: Oxford University Press. 39.

[19] Lambert, L, III. (2009). *Spirituality Inc.: Religion in the American Workplace.* New York: New York University Press. 169.

Conder, T. (2006). *The Church in Transition: The Journey of Existing Churches into the Emerging Culture.* Grand Rapids, MI: Zondervan. 111.

Smith, R. S. (2005). *Truth and the New Kind of Christian: The Emerging Effects of Postmodernism in the Church.* Wheaton, IL: Crossway Books. 67–69.

20   English, L. M., Fenwick, T. J., Parsons, J. (2005). Interrogating our practices of integrating spirituality into workplace education. *Australian Journal of Adult Education*, 45(1) April, 7 to 28. 23–24.

21   Milojević, I. (2005). "Critical Spirituality as a Resource for Fostering Critical Pedagogy." *Journal of Futures Studies.* 9(3), February 1 to 16. Retrieved April 18, 2010. http://www.jfs.tku.edu.tw/9-3/A01.pdf. 10.

22   Pillow, W. (2012). *Spirituality Beyond Science and Religion.* Bloomington, IN: iUniverse., 7.

23   Stamm, L. (2006). "The Influence of Religion and Spirituality in Shaping American Higher Education." In A. W. Chickering, J. C. Dalton, and L. Stamm. *Encouraging Authenticity & Spirituality in Higher Education.* San Francisco, CA: Jossey-Bass. 69.

24   Wright, A. (2000). *Spirituality and Education (Master Classes in Education Series).* London: Routledge. Quoting, Davie, G. (1994). *Religion in Britain Since 1945.* Oxford: Wiley-Blackwell. 55.

25   Voas, D. and Crockett, A. (2005). "Religion in Britain: Neither Believing nor Belonging." *Sociology.* 39(1), 25.

26   Öğretici, Y. Z. (2018). "An Exploration of Subjective-Life of Spirituality and Its Impact. Education Science." *Educ. Sci.* 2018, 8(4), 212. https://doi.org/10.3390/educsci8040212. Reprinted in *Education Science Special Edition*, "There is a Crack in Everything." 174.

27   English, L. M. and Gillen, M. A., (2000). "Addressing the Spiritual Dimensions of Adult Learning: What Educators Can Do." *New Directions for Adult and Continuing Education.* San Francisco, CA: Jossey-Bass. 1.

28   Gallagher, E. V. (2009). "Spirituality in Higher Education?" Caveat Emptor. *Religion & Education*, 36(2) Summer, University of Northern Iowa. 71.

29   Fitch, F. E., Fitzgerald, J., Himchak, M. V., and Pisani, E. (2009). "The Quest for Meaning: Teaching Spirituality in Communications, Social Work, Nursing, and Leadership." *Religion and Education*. 36 (3) Fall: University of Northern Iowa. 2.

30   Dumestre, M. (1997). *A Church at Risk: The Challenge of Spiritually Hungry Adults*. New York: Crossroad Publishing. 10.

31   Hood, G. K. (2006). "The Notion of Spirituality in Adult and Higher Education." *Higher Education Perspectives*. 2(1), 172. Quoting, Elkins, D. N., Hedstrom, L.J., Hughes, L.L., Leaf, J. A., and Saunders, C. (1988). "Towards a Humanistic-Phenomenological Spirituality: Definition, Description, and Measurement." *Journal of Humanistic Psychology*. 28(4) Fall, 10.

32   English, L. M., and Gillen, M. A. (2000). op. cit. 1.

33   Ibid. p. 1.

34   A Listing of Some Resources to Explore *Education-Early Childhood Education*

Bone, J. (2014). "Spirituality and Early Childhood Education in New Zealand and Australia: Past, Present and Future." In J. Watson, M. de Souza, and A. Trousdale. *Global Perspectives on Spirituality and Education*. New York: Routledge. 116–128.

Mayes, C. (2001). "Cultivating Spirituality Reflectivity in Teachers." *Teacher Education Quarterly*, 28(2), 5–22. Retrieved September 14, 2009.

http://www.teqjournal.org/backvols /2001/ 28_2/ v28n202.pdf.

Higher Education

Astin, A. W. (2004). "Why Spirituality Deserves a Central Place in Higher Education." *Spirituality in Higher Education Newsletter*. UCLA. April 2004, 1(1), 1–12.

Astin, H. S. and Astin, A. W. (2009). "Does Spirituality Have a Place in Higher Education?: A Response." *Religion & Education*. 36(2), 124–129. Summer, University of Northern Iowa.

Astin, A.W., Astin, H. S., and Lindholm, J.A. (2010). *Cultivating the Spirit: How College Can Enhance Students' Lives*. San Francisco, CA: Jossey-Bass.

Brown, L. C. (2008). "Role of Spirituality in Adult Learning Contexts." Doctoral Dissertation, University of Georgia. Retrieved April 11, 2011.

https://getd.libs.uga.edu/pdfs/brown_laura_c_200812_phd/brown_laura_c_200812_phd.pdf.

Chickering, A. W., Dalton, J. C., and Stamm, L. (2006). *Encouraging Authenticity & Spirituality in Higher Education*. San Francisco, CA: Jossey-Bass.

Dalton, J. C. (2006). "The Place and Spirituality in the Mission and Work of College Student Affairs." In A.W. Chickering, J. C. Dalton, and L. Stamm. *Encouraging Authenticity & Spirituality in Higher Education*. San Francisco, CA: Jossey-Bass. 145-164.

Glazer, S. (ed.). (1999). *The Heart of Spirituality: Spirituality in Education*. New York: Jeremy P. Tarcher.

Groen, J. (2008). "Paradoxical Tensions in Creating a Teaching and Learning Space within a Graduate Education Course on Spirituality." *Teaching in Higher Education*, 13(2), 193–204.

Hood, G. K. (2006). "The Notion of Spirituality in Adult and Higher Education." *Higher Education Perspectives*. 2(1), 166–179.

Hoppe, S. L. and Speck, B. W. (eds.) (2005). *Spirituality in Higher Education*. San Francisco, CA: Jossey-Bass.

Milacci, F. (2003). "A Step Towards Faith: The Limitations of Spirituality in Adult Education Practice." Doctoral Dissertation, Penn State University. Retrieved May 13, 2010. http://digitalcommons.liberty.edu/cgi/viewcontent.cgi?article=1001&context=fac_dis.

Montgomery-Goodnough, A., and Gallagher, S. J. (2007). "Review of Research on Spiritual and Religious Formation in Higher Education." Proceedings of the Sixth Annual College of Education Research Conference: Urban and International Education Section. 60–65.

Speck, B. W. and Hoope, S. L. (eds.) (2007). *Searching for Spirituality in Higher Education*. New York: Peter Lang.

Tisdell, E. (2003). "From Research to Practice: Toward a Spiritually Grounded and Culturally Relevant Pedagogy." Pennsylvania Adult and Continuing Education Research Conference. 132–138.

Vogel, L. (2000). "Reckoning with the Spiritual Lives of Adult Educators." In L.M. English and M.A. Gillen. *Addressing the Spiritual Dimensions of Adult Learning: What Educators Can Do: New Directions for Adult and Continuing Education.* San Francisco, CA: Jossey-Bass. 17–28.

Sociology

Brown, B. (2015). *Rising Strong: The Reckoning, the Rumble, the Revolution.* New York: Spiegal & Grau.

Butot, M. (2007). "Reframing Spirituality, Reconceptualizing Change: Possibilities for Critical Social Work." In J. Coates, J. R. Graham, B. Swartzentruber, and B. Ouellette. *Spirituality and Social Work: Selected Canadian Readings.* Toronto: Canadian Scholars' Press Inc. 143–159.

Coates, J., Graham, J. R., Swartzentruber, B., and Ouellette, B. (eds). (2007.) *Spirituality and Social Work: Selected Canadian Readings.* Toronto: Canadian Scholars' Press Inc.

George, L. K., Larson, D. B., Koenig, H. G., and McCullough, M. E. (2000). "Spirituality and

Health: What We Know, What We Need to Know." *Journal of Social and Clinical Psychology.* 19(1), 102–116.

Lauzon, A. C. (2005). "Spirituality and Adult Education: An Emergent Perspective." Paper presented to the 4th Conference on Spirituality and Social Work. London, Ontario, May 26–May 28.

Psychology

Hill, P. C. (2005). "Measurement in the Psychology of Religion and Spirituality: Current Status and Evaluation." In R.F. Paloutzian and C. L. Park (eds.). *Handbook of Psychology of Religion and Spirituality* (First Edition). New York: Guildford Press. 43–61.

Paloutzian, R. F., and Park, C. L. (eds.) (2005). *Handbook of Psychology of Religion and* Spirituality (First Edition). New York: Guildford Press.

Business and Finance

Groen, J. (2008). "Moving in from the Fringes of the Academy: Spirituality as an Emerging Focus in the Canadian Professional Faculties of Business, Education and Social Work." Draft Article. 1–29.

Hocking, D. E., Myers, M. D., and Cairns, S. (2008). "Toward a Model for the Use of Spirituality in Teaching Accounting." *Journal of Academic and Business Ethics.* (1) January. Retrieved April 20, 2010. http://www.aabri.com/manuscripts/08019.pdfve.

Medical

Balboni, M. J., Puchalski, C. M., and Peteet, J. R. (2014). "The Relationship between Medicine, Spirituality and Religion: Three Models for Integration." *Journal of Religious Health.* 1586–1598. Published on-line, June 12, 2014. Retrieved February 2, 2015.

Calderone, S. (2004). "Current Thinking on the Role of Spirituality in Medical Education & Training Spirituality in Higher Education: A National Study of College Students' Search for Meaning and Purpose." Retrieved December 13, 2010.

http://www.spirituality.ucla.edu/docs/newsletters/1/Calderone.pdf.

Canadian Nurses Association (2010). "WHO definition of Health to Include Spiritual Well-being." Annual Meeting Resolution, 2005. Retrieved February 6, 2011.http://www.cna-nurses.ca/CNA/about/meetings/ resolutions_2005/resolutions_08_e.aspx.

Koenig, H. G. (2010). "Spirituality and Mental Health." *International Journal of Applied Psychoanalytic Studies.* 7(2), 116–122.

Loboprabhu, S. and Lomax, J. (2010). "The Role of Spirituality in Medical School and Psychiatry Residency Education." *International Journal of Applied Psychoanalytic Studies.* 7(2), 180–192.

McBride, J. L. (2011). "The Missing Component in the Spirituality and Medicine Literature: Reflections." *Annals of Behavioral Science and Medical Education*. Vol. 17. No. 1, 7–9. Retrieved January 24, 2015.

Workplace

Groen, J. (2002). "The Experiences and Practice of Adult Educators in Addressing Spirituality within the Workplace: An Empirical Study." In J. M. Pettitt and R. P. Francis (eds.). Proceedings of the 43rd Annual Adult Education Research Conference North Carolina State University. 134–140.

Lakes, R. D. (2000). "Spirituality, Work, and Education: The Wholistic Approach." *Journal of Vocational Education Research*. 25(2).

Marques, J. F. (2006). "Removing the Blinders: A Phenomenological Study of U.S. Based MBA Students' Perception of Spirituality in the Workplace." *Journal of American Academy of Business*. Cambridge. 8(1), 55–61.

Neal, J. (2017). "Workplace Spirituality Annotated Bibliography."

https://www.academia.edu/32013953/WORKPLACE_SPIRITUALITY_ ANNOTATED_BIBLIOGRAPHY_Compiled.

Oliveira, A. (2004). "The Place of Spirituality in Organizational Theory. *Electronic Journal of Business Ethics and Organization*. 9(2). Retrieved August 16, 2010. http://ejbo.jyu.fi/pdf/ejbo_vol9_no2_pages_17-21.pdf.

Sendjaya, S. (2007). "Conceptualizing and Measuring Spiritual Leadership in Organizations." *International Journal of Business and Information*. 2 (1), 104–126.

Overview of Many Topics

Rinallo, D., Scott, L., and Maclaran, P. (2012). "Introduction: Unravelling Complexities at the Commercial/Spiritual Interface." In D. Rinallo, L. Scott, and P. Maclaran (eds.). *Consumption and Spirituality*. Routledge Interpretive Marketing Research. New York: Routledge-Taylor and Francis Group. 1–25.

Chapter Four
Spiritual But Not Religious

[1]   Hunter, G. G. III (1992). *How To Reach Secular People.* Nashville, TN: Abingdon. 29.

[2]   Dumestre, M. (1997). *A Church at Risk: The Challenge of Spiritually Hungry Adults.* New York: Crossroad Publishing. 6.

[3]   Harari, Y. N. (2018). *21 Lessons for the 21st Century.* New York: Signal-Random House. 47.

[4]   Besecke, K. (2014). *You Can't Put God in a Box: Thoughtful Spirituality in the Rational Age.* New York: Oxford University Press. 39.

[5]   Bass, D. (2012). *Christianity after Religion: The End of Church and the Birth of a New Spiritual Awakening.* New York: HarperOne. 46.

[6]   Taylor, P. (2014). *The Next America: Boomers, Millennials, and the Looming Generational Showdown.* New York: PublicAffairs. 130–131.

[7]   Ibid. 131.

[8]   Barna, G. (1991). *User Friendly Churches: What Christians need to Know about the Churches People Love to Go To.* Ventura, CA: Regal Books. 25.

[9]   Wong, Y. R. and Vinsky, J. (2008). "Speaking from the Margins: A Critical Reflection of the 'Spiritual-but-not-Religious' Discourse in Social Work." *British Journal of Social Work,* 39. Retrieved February 6, 2011. 1353–1354. http://www.tandfonline.com/toc/wspi20/12/4.

[10] Shahjahan, R. A. (2010). "Toward a Spiritual Praxis: The Role of Spirituality Among Faculty of Color Teaching for Social Justice." *The Review for Higher Education.* 33(4), 476–477.

[11] https://www.nydailynews.com/sports/baseball/yankees/eternity-mets-yankees-article-1.356918. Retrieved March 25, 2021.

https://www.reliableplant.com/Read/5877/going,-gone-baseball-fans,-se-caskets-are-to-die-for. Retrieved March 25, 2021.

12   Heelas, P., Woodhead, L., Seel, B., and Szerszynski, B. (2005). *The Spiritual Revolution: Why Religion is Giving Way to Spirituality (Religion and Spirituality in the Modern World)*. New York: Wiley-Blackwell. 2.

13   Drescher, E. (2016). *Choosing our Religion: The Spiritual Loves of America's Nones*. New York: Oxford University Press. 45.

14   Gabhart, E. A. (2015). "The Spiritual but Not Religious: Who Are They, and Who Is More Likely to Be One?" (thesis). University of North Texas. 42.

      Fuller, R. C. (2001). *Spiritual but Not Religious: Understanding Unchurched America*. Oxford: Oxford University Press. 5.

      Barna Group (2017). "Meet the Spiritual but Not Religious." Retrieved April 6, 2017. https://www.barna.com/research/meet-spiritual-not-religious.

15   Edgell, P. (2009). "Faith and Spirituality among Emerging Adults." In T. Clydesdale (ed.) *Who Are Emerging Adults? Essay Forum, Changing Sea: the Changing Spirituality of Emerging Adults Project*. The Institute for Policy and Research and Catholic Studies. 1.

16   Drescher, E. (2016). op. cit. 67.

17   Tickle, P. (2008). *The Great Emergence: How Christianity Is Changing and Why*. Grand Rapids, MI: Baker Books. 97.

18   Bibby, R. (2011). *Beyond the Gods & Back: Religion's Demise and Rise and Why It Matters*. Toronto: ProjectCanada Books. 34–35.

19   Vaill, P. (1989). *Managing as a Performing Art: New Ideas of a World of Chaotic Change*. San Francisco, CA: Jossey-Bass Publishers. 2, 29.

20   Bibby, R. (1987) *Fragmented Gods: The Poverty and Potential of Religion in Canada*. Toronto: Irwin Publishing. 62–85.

21   Dalton, J. (2006). "The Place of Spirituality in the Mission and Work of College Student Affairs." In Chickering, A. W., Dalton, J. C., and Stamm, L. (2006). *Encouraging Authenticity & Spirituality in Higher Education*. San Francisco, CA: Jossey-Bass. 154–155.

22   Bass, D. B. (2012). *Christianity after Religion: The End of Church and the Birth of a New Spiritual Awakening*. New York: HarperOne. 69–70.

23   Vaillant, G. (2009). *Spiritual Evolution: How We Are Wired for Faith, Hope and Love*. New York: Broadway Books. 187–188.

24   Zinnbauer, B. J., Pargament, K. I., Cole, B., Rye, M. S., Butter, E. M., Belavich, T. G., Hipp, K. M., Scott, A.B., and Kadar, J.L. (1997). "Religion and Spirituality: Unfuzzying the Fuzzy." *Journal for Scientific Study of Religion*. 36(4). Retrieved May 19, 2012.

     http://www.psychology.hku.hk/ftbcstudies/refbase/docs/zinnbauer/1997/34_Zinnbaue retal1997.pdf. 549, 562.

25   Fuller, R. C. (2001). *Spiritual but Not Religious: Understanding Unchurched America*. Oxford: Oxford University Press. 99–100.

26   Bass, D. (2012). op. cit. 63.

27   Bass, D. (2012). op cit. 66.

28   Barna Group (2017). op cit. 4.

29   Drescher, E. (2016). op. cit. 18–19.

30   Gabhart, E. A. (2015). op cit. 26, 33.

     Lipka, M. and Gecewicz, C. (2017). "More Americans Now Say They're Spiritual but Not Religious." *Pew Research Center: FactTank*. (September 6, 2017). Retrieved, January 6, 2020. https://www.pewresearch.org/fact-tank/2017/09/06/more-americans-now-say-they're-spiritual-but-not-religious/ - http://pewrsr.ch/2xP0Y8w. 6.

31   Gabhart, E. A. (2015). op cit. 33, 35.

32   Lipka, M. and Gecewicz, C. (2017). op cit. 6.

33   Gabhart, E. A. (2015). op cit. 25, 28.

34   Lipka, M. and Gecewicz, C. (2017). op. cit. 6.

35   Drescher, E. (2016). op cit. 20.

36   Lipka, M. and Gecewicz, C. (2017). op. cit. 4.

37 Drescher, E. (2016). op. cit. 20.

38 Lipka, M. and Gecewicz, C. (2017). op cit. 6.

39 Gabhart, E. A. (2015). op. cit. 41–42.

40 Bibby, R. (2017). *Resilient Gods: Being Pro-Religious, Low Religious, or No Religious in Canada*. Vancouver, BC: UBC Press. 152.

41 Ibid. 150.

42 Ibid. 152.

43 Lipka, M. and Gecewicz, C. (2017). op cit. 6.

44 Bibby, R. (2017). op. cit. 166.

45 Kilgore, D. (2011). "Toward a Postmodern Pedagogy." In S. B. Merriam and A. P. Grace. (eds.) *The Jossey-Bass Reader on Contemporary Issues in Adult Education*. San Francisco, CA: Jossey-Bass. NOOK Book. May 15, 2011. 420.

46 Veith, G.E. Jr. (1994). *Postmodern Times: A Guide to Contemporary Thought and Culture*. Wheaton, IL: Crossway Books. 118.

47 O'Murchu, D. (1997). *Reclaiming Spirituality*. New York: Crossroads Books. 23–24

48 Twenge, J. M. and Campbell, W. K. (2010). *The Narcissism Epidemic: Living in an Age of Uncertainty*. New York: Atria Paperback. 307.

49 Bibby, R. (2011). *Beyond the Gods & Back: Religion's Demise and Rise and Why It Matters*. Toronto: ProjectCanada Books. 127–128.

50 Bibby, (2011). op. cit. 129.

51 Fuller, R. C. (2001). *Spiritual but Not Religious: Understanding Unchurched America*. Oxford: Oxford University Press. 99–100.

52 Heelas, P., Woodhead, L., Seel, B., and Szerszynski, B. (2005). op. cit. 1.

53 Drescher, E. (2016). op cit. 51.

[54]   Drescher, E. (2016). op. cit. 118.

[55]   English, L. M., Fenwick, T. J., and Parsons, J. (2005). "Interrogating Our Practices of Integrating Spirituality into Workplace Education." *Australian Journal of Adult Education.* 45(1) April, 8–9.

Brown, L. C. (2008). "Role of Spirituality in Adult Learning Contexts." Doctoral Dissertation, University of Georgia.

https://getd.libs.uga.edu/pdfs/brown_laura_c_200812_phd/ brown_laura_ c_200812_phd.pdf. April 11, 2010. 145.

Tisdell, E. (2003). *Exploring Spirituality and Culture in Adult and Higher Education.* San Francisco, CA: Jossey-Bass. 190–191.

Campbell, K. P. (2010). "Transformative Learning and Spirituality: A Heuristic Inquiry into the Experience of Spiritual Learning." Requirements for the Degree Doctor of Philosophy, Capella University (March 2010). 48.

[56]   Barna Group. (2017). "Meet the Spiritual but Not Religious." Retrieved April 6, 2017.https://www.barna.com/research/meet-spiritual-not-religious. 6.

[57]   Barna Group. (2017). op. cit. 7.

[58]   Stamm, L. (2006). "The Influence of Religion and Spirituality in Shaping American Higher Education." In A. W. Chickering, J. C. Dalton, and L. Stamm. *Encouraging Authenticity & Spirituality in Higher Education.* San Francisco, CA: Jossey-Bass. 69.

Stamm, L. (2006). The Dynamics of Spirituality and the Religious Experience. In A. W. Chickering, J. C. Dalton, L. Stamm. Encouraging Authenticity & Spirituality in Higher Education. (pp. 37-65). San Francisco: Jossey-Bass. 49.

Lyon, D. (2000). *Jesus in Disneyland: Religion in Postmodern Times.* Malden, MA: Polity Press/Blackwell Publishing. 88.

Hill, P. C., Paragment, K. I., Hood, R. W. Jr., McCullough, M. E. Swyers, J. P., Larson, D. B., and Zinnbauer, B. J. (2000). "Conceptualizing Religion and Spirituality: Points of Commonality, Points of Departure." *Journal for the Theory of Social Behavior.* 30:1, 61.

59   Bibby, R. (2011). *Beyond the Gods & Back: Religion's Demise and Rise and Why It Matters.* Toronto: ProjectCanada Books. 127–128.

60   Lambert, L, III. (2009). *Spirituality Inc.: Religion in the American Workplace.* New York: New York University Press. 168–169.

61   Brookfield, S. D. (1987). *Developing Critical Thinkers: Challenging Adults to Explore Alternative Ways of Thinking and Acting.* San Francisco, CA: Jossey-Bass. 170–171.

62   Kinzer, M. (1981). "Christian Identity in Social Change in Technological Society." In P. Williamson and K. Perrotta (eds.). *Christianity Confronts Modernity: A Theological and Pastoral Inquiry by Protestant Evangelicals and Roman Catholics.* Ann Arbor, MI: Servant Books. 1.

63   Barna Group (2020). "Signs of Decline and Hope Among Key Metrics of Faith." Retrieved March 5, 2020. https://www.barna.com/research/changing-state-of-the-church.

64   Tacey, D. (2004). *The Spirituality Revolution: The Emergence of Contemporary Spirituality.* New York: Routledge. 4.

65   Hume, E. (2016). *Door to Door: The Magnificent, Maddening, Mysterious World of Transportation.* New York: HarperCollins. 26.

66   Friedman, T. L. (2007*). The World Is Flat: A Brief History of the Twenty-First Century. (Revised Edition).* New York: Picador/Farrar, Straus and Giroux. 160.

67   Carrette, J., King, R. (2005) *Selling Spirituality: The Silent Takeover of Religion.* New York: Routledge. 128.

Chapter Five
Spirituality and the Brain

1   Culliford, L. (2002). "Spiritual Values and Skills Are Increasingly Recognized as Necessary Aspects of Clinical Care. *British Medical Journal.* Dec 21, 2002. 325(7378), 1434–1435.

Culliford, L. (2005). *Healing from Within: Spirituality and Mental Health.* Self-published. Retrieved, April 6, 2014. http://www.miepvideos.org/Healing%20From%20within.pdf.

Culliford, L. (2010). *The Psychology of Spirituality: An Introduction*. London: Jessica Kingsley Publishers.

Culliford, L. (2014). "The Meaning of Life Diagrams: A Framework for a Developmental

Path from Birth to Spiritual Maturity." *Journal for the Study of Spirituality*. 4(1) (May), 31–44.

2   Thompson, C. (2010). *Anatomy of the Soul: Surprising Connections between Neuroscience and Spiritual Practices That Can Transform Your Life and Relationships*. Carol Stream, IL: Tyndale Momentum

3   Carr, N. (2010). *The Shallows: What the Internet is doing to our Brains*. New York: W.W. Norton.

4   Nelson, K. (2010). *The Spiritual Doorway in the Brain: A Neurologist's Search for the God Experience*. New York: Dutton.

5   Vaillant, G. (2008). *Spiritual Evolution: A Scientific Defense of Faith*. New York: Broadway Books.

Vaillant, G. (2009). *Spiritual Evolution: How we are Wired for Faith, Hope and Love*. New York: Broadway Books.

6   Alper, M. (2006). *The "God" Part of the Brain: A Scientific Interpretation of Human Spirituality and God*. Napperville, IL: Sourcebooks Inc. 94, 96–97.

7   Alper, M. (2006). *The "God" Part of the Brain: A Scientific Interpretation of Human Spirituality and God*. Napperville, IL: Sourcebooks Inc.

Carr, N. (2010). *The Shallows: What the Internet Is Doing to our Brains*. New York: W.W. Norton.

Culliford, L. (2010). *The Psychology of Spirituality: An Introduction*. London: Jessica Kingsley Publishers.

Jennings, T. R. (2013). *The God-Shaped Brain: How Changing Your View of God Transform Your Life*. Downers Grove, IL: IVP Press.

Mark, C. W. (1995). *Spiritual Intelligence (SQ): The Symbiotic Relationship Between Spirit and the Brain: Insights Into the Postmodern Journey of Spirituality and Holistic Health*. Bloomington, IN: AuthorHouse.

Mark, C. W. (2010). *Spiritual Intelligence and the Neuroplastic Brain: A Contextual Interpretation of Modern History.* Bloomington, IN: AuthorHouse.

Nelson, K. (2010). *The Spiritual Doorway in the Brain: A Neurologist's Search for the God Experience.* New York: Dutton.

Newberg, A. (2010). *How God Changes Your Brain: Breakthrough Findings from a Leading Neuroscientist.* New York: Ballantine Books.

Pillow, W. (2012). *Spirituality Beyond Science and Religion.* Bloomington, IN: iUniverse.

Thompson, C. (2010). *Anatomy of the Soul: Surprising Connections between Neuroscience and Spiritual Practices That Can Transform Your Life and Relationships.* Carol Stream, IL: Tyndale Momentum.

Tiger, L. and McGuire, M. (2010). *God's Brain.* Amherst, New York: Prometheus Books.

Vaillant, G. (2008). *Spiritual Evolution: A Scientific Defense of Faith.* New York: Broadway Books.

Vaillant, G. (2009). *Spiritual Evolution: How We Are Wired for Faith, Hope and Love.* New York: Broadway Books.

[8] Carr, N. (2010). op cit. 86.

[9] Carr, N. (2010). op cit. 109, 143.

[10] Carr, N. (2010). op cit. 196.

[11] Levitin, D. J. (2014). *The Organized Mind: Thinking Straight in the Age of Information Overload.* New York: Dutton-Penguin Group. 130–131.

[12] Asghar, J. and Shahzad, K. (2015). "The Rewiring of the Human Brain: A Critique of Cyber-Culture and Its Effects on Our Thinking Abilities." *Journal of the Institute of Social Sciences.* 2 (2), 20–21.

[13] King, K. P. (2010). "Informal Learning in a Virtual Era." In C. E. Kasworm, A. D. Rose, and J. M. Ross-Gordon (eds.). *Handbook of Adult and Continuing Education.* San Francisco, CA: Jossey-Bass. 421.

Asghar, J. and Shahzad, K. (2015). op. cit. 17.

[14] Levitin, D.J. (2014). op. cit. 5.

[15] Borg, J., André, B., Soderstrom, H., and Farde, L. (2003). "The Serotonin System and Spiritual Experiences." *American Journal of Psychiatry*. 160 11, 1965–1969.

Fenwick, P. (2003). "The Neuroscience of Spirituality." Retrieved March 30, 2020.

https://www.semanticscholar.org/paper/The-Neuroscience-of-Spirituality-Fenwick/d226bf72bc581dde62393b2d64416ca3386e7774

Fenwick, P. (2011). "The Neuroscience of Spirituality." Retrieved March 30, 2020.

https://www.rcpsych.ac.uk/docs/default-source/members/sigs/spirituality-spsig/spirituality-special-interest-group-publications-peter-fenwick-the-neuroscience-of-spirituality.pdf?sfvrsn=f5f9fed8_2.

Kurup, R. K. and Kurup, P. A. (2002). "Hypothalamic Digoxin Hemisphere Chemical Dominance and Spirituality." *International Journal of Neuroscience*. 397–407.

Mohandas, E. (2008). "Neurology of Spirituality." *Mens Sana Monographs*. Jan–Dec. 6(1), 63–80.

[16] Sayadmansour, A. (2014). "Neurotheology: The Relationship between Brain and Religion." *Iran Journal of Neurology*. 13 (1), 52.

[17] Kyriacou, D., (2018). "Are We Wired for Spirituality? An Investigation into the Claims of Neurotheology." *HTS Teologiese Studies/Theological Studies*. 74(3), 4973. https://doi.org/10.4102/hts.v74i3.4973. 2.

[18] 1. Ibid. 9–10.

[19] Newberg, A. (2010). *How God Changes Your Brain: Breakthrough Findings from a Leading Neuroscientist*. New York: Ballantine Books. 5–6.

[20] Ibid. 46–47.

21 Ibid. 56.

22 Ibid. 155–157.

23 Ibid. 151–165.

24 Vaillant, G. (2009). *Spiritual Evolution: How We Are Wired for Faith, Hope and Love*. New York: Broadway Books. 22.

Vaillant, G. (2008). *Spiritual Evolution: A Scientific Defense of Faith*. New York: Broadway Books. 22.

25 Vaillant, G. (2009). op. cit. 24.

26 Valliant, G. (2008). op. cit. 187–188.

27 McHargue, M. (2016). *Finding God in the Waves: How I Lost My Faith and Found It Again Through Science*. New York: Convergent. 55–59.

28 Ibid. 59.

29 Ibid. 59.

30 Hull, J. (1985). *What Prevents Christian Adults from Learning?* London: SCM Press. 37.

31 McHargue, M. (2016). op. cit. 119.

32 Milacci, F. (2003). *A Step Towards Faith: The Limitations of Spirituality in Adult Education Practice*. Doctoral Dissertation, Penn State University. Retrieved May 13, 2010. http://citeseerx.ist.psu.edu/viewdoc/download?doi=10.1.1.1014.9377&rep=rep1&type=pdf. 100.

33 McLaren, B. (2011). *Naked Spirituality: A Life with God in 12 Simple Words*. New York, NY: HarperOne. 163.

34 Palmer, P. J. (2010). "Toward a Philosophy of Integrative Education." In P. J. Palmer, A. Zajonc, M. Scribner, and M. Nepo. *The Heart of Higher Education: A Call to Renewal Transforming The Academy through Collegial Conversations*. San Francisco, CA: Jossey-Bass. 29.

35   Alper, M. (2006). *The "God" Part of the Brain: A Scientific Interpretation of Human Spirituality and God.* Napperville, IL: Sourcebooks Inc. 96–97.

36   Tisdell, E. (2003). *Exploring Spirituality and Culture in Adult and Higher Education.* San Francisco, CA: Jossey-Bass. 48.

37   Culliford, L. (2010). op.cit. 19.

38   Tiger, L., McGuire, M. (2010). *God's Brain.* Amherst: New York: Prometheus Books. 11.

39   Ibid. 20.

40   Newberg, A., et al. (2017). "Effect of a One-Week Spiritual Retreat on Dopamine and Serotonin Transporter Binding: A Preliminary Study. *Religion, Brain & Behavior.* 10.1080/2153599X.2016.1267035. 2.

41   Ibid. 2.

42   Ibid. 2.

43   Ibid. 7.

44   Ibid. 11.

Chapter Six
Spirituality and Mindfulness

1   Lazaridou, A. and Pentaris, P. (2016). "Mindfulness and Spirituality: Therapeutic Perspectives." *Person-Centered & Experiential Psychotherapies.* 15:3. Retrieved December 27, 2019. DOI: 10.1080/14779757.2016.1180634. 12–13.

2   Falb, M. D. and Paragament, K. I. (2012). "Relational Mindfulness, Spirituality, and the Therapeutic Bond." *Asian Journal of Psychiatry.* 5, 351.

3   Hyland, T. (2015). "On the Contemporary Applications of Mindfulness: Some Implications for Education." *Journal of Philosophy of Education.* 49 (2), 171.

4   Lazaridou, A., Pentaris, P. (2016). op. cit. 5.

5   Burrows, L. (2013). "Spirituality at Work: The Contribution of Mindfulness to Personal and Workforce Development." In Roger Harris and Tom Short (eds.). *Workforce Development Perspectives and Issues.* Australia: Springer/ Kluwer. 2013. Retrieved February 3, 2015.

https://www.academia.edu/4547163/Spirituality_at_work- the_contribution_ of_mindfulness_to_personal_and_workforce_development. 2.

6   Twenge, J. M. and Campbell, W. K. (2010*). The Narcissism Epidemic: Living in an Age of Uncertainty.* New York: Atria Paperback. 284.

7   Hyland, T. (2015). op cit. 170.

Lazaridou, A. and Pentaris, P. (2016). op. cit. 3.

8   Hyland, T. (2015). op cit. 170–186.

9   Burrows, L. (2013). op. cit. 2.

10   Hyland, T. (2015). op cit. 178.

11   Lazaridou, A. and Pentaris, P. (2016). op. cit. 3.

12   Lazaridou, A. and Pentaris, P. (2016). op. cit. 4.

Hyland, T. (2018). *Philosophy, Science and Mindfulness: Exploring the Links between Eastern and Western Traditions.* Beau Bassin, Mauritius: Scholars' Press. 34.

13   Lazaridou, A. and Pentaris, P. (2016). op. cit. 6.

Hyland, T. (2015). op cit. 171.

14   *Workplace*

Aikens, K. A., Astin, J., Pelletier, K. R., Levanovich, K., Baase, C., Park, Y. Y., and Bondnar, C. M. (2014). "Mindfulness Goes to Work: Impact of an On-Line Workplace Intervention." *JOEM, Journal of Occupational and Environmental Medicine.* 13–4531.

Burrows, L. (2013). "Spirituality at Work: The Contribution of Mindfulness to Personal and Workforce Development." In Roger Harris and Tom Short (eds.). *Workforce Development Perspectives and Issues*. Australia: Springer/ Kluwer. 2013. Retrieved February 3, 2015.

https://www.academia.edu/4547163/Spirituality_at_work-the_contribution_ of_mindfulness_to_personal_and_workforce_development.

Relationships

Barnes, S., Brown, K. W., Krusemark, E., Campbell, W. K., and Rogge, R. D. (2007). "The Role of Mindfulness in Romanic Relationship Satisfaction and Responses to Relationship Stress." *Journal of Marital and Family Therapy*. 33 (4), 482–500.

Falb, M. D. and Paragament, K. I. (2012). "Relational Mindfulness, Spirituality, and the Therapeutic Bond. *Asian Journal of Psychiatry*, 5, 351–354.

Educational

Ager, K., Albrecht, N. J., and Cohen, M. (2015). "Mindfulness in Schools Research Project: Exploring Students' Perspectives of Mindfulness." *Psychology*, 6, 896–914.

Hyland, T. (2015). "On the Contemporary Applications of Mindfulness: Some Implications for Education." *Journal of Philosophy of Education*. 49 (2), 170–186.

[15] Ager, K., Albrecht, N. J., and Cohen, M. (2015). "Mindfulness in Schools Research Project: Exploring Students' Perspectives of Mindfulness." *Psychology*, 6, 897.

[16] Ibid. 912.

[17] Broderick, P. C. and Metz, S. (2009). "Learning to BREATHE: A Pilot Trial of a Mindfulness Curriculum for Adolescents." *Advances in School Mental Health Promotion*. 2(1), 35–46.

[18] Broderick, P. C. (2009). op. cit. 36.

[19] Agar, K. (2015). op. cit. 900.

[20] Beauchemin, J., Hutchins, T. L., and Patterson, F. (2008). "Mindfulness Meditation May Lessen Anxiety, Promote Social Skills, and Improve Academic Performance among Adolescents with Learning Disabilities." *Complementary Health Practice Review*. 13, 34–45.

Erbe, R. and Lohrmann, D. (2015). "Mindfulness Meditation for Adolescent Stress and Well-being: A Systematic Review of the Literature with Implications for School Health Programs." *The Health Educator*. 47 (2), 12.

Broderick, P. C. and Metz, S. (2009). "Learning to BREATHE: A Pilot Trial of a Mindfulness Curriculum for Adolescents." *Advances in School Mental Health Promotion*. 2(1), 35–46.

Ager, K., (2015). op. cit. 896–914.

[21] Albrecht, N. J. (2016). "Teachers Teaching Mindfulness with Children: An Interpretative Phenomenological Analysis." PhD. Thesis. School of Education, Humanities and Law, Flinders University Adelaide, Australia. 282–283.

[22] Beauchemin, J., Hutchins, T. L., and Patterson, F. (2008). "Mindfulness Meditation May Lessen Anxiety, Promote Social Skills, and Improve Academic Performance among Adolescents with Learning Disabilities." *Complementary Health Practice Review*. 13, 43.

[23] Jennings, P., Lantieri, L., and Roeser, R.W. (2012). "Supporting Educational Goals through Cultivating Mindfulness: Approaches for Teachers and Students." In P. M. Brown, M.W. Corrigan, and A. Higgins-D'Alessandro (eds.). *Handbook of Prosocial Education*. Lanham, MD: Rowan & Littlefield. 371–397.

Albrecht, N., Bucu, A., and Ager, K. (2018). "Rome Wasn't Built in a Day: School Counsellors' Perspectives of Teaching Children Mindfulness." *Australian Counselling Research Journal*. 12 (1), 3–17.

[24] Hyland, T. (2017). McDonaldizing Spirituality: Mindfulness, Education and Consumerism, *Journal of Transformative Education*, DOI: 10.1177/1541344617696972, Retrieved March 15, 2020, 1, 5.

[25] Ibid, 3.

[26] Ibid. 28.

Chapter Seven
Spirituality: Loneliness Versus Solitude,
Stillness, Surrender, and Serenity

1   Caird, J. K., Johnston, K. A., Willness, C. R., Asbridged, M., and Steel. P. (2014). "A Meta-analysis of the Effects of Texting on Driving." *Accident Analysis & Prevention.* 71, October 2014, 311–318. https://www.sciencedirect. com/science/article/pii/S000145751400178X.

2   Chittister, J. (1992). *The Rule of Benedict: Spirituality for the 21ˢᵗ Century.* New York: Crossroad. 195–196.

3   Kanungo, R. N. and Mendonca, M. (1994). "What Leaders Cannot Do Without: The Spiritual Dimensions of Leadership." In Jay A. Conger. *Discovering the Spirituality in Leadership.* San Francisco, CA: Jossey-Bass. 190–191.

4   Hendrix, K. G. (2009). "The Spirit That Strengthens Me: Merging the 'Life of the Mind' with 'Life in the Spirit.'" In K. G. Hendrix and J. D. Hamlet (eds.). *As the Spirit Moves Us: New Directions for Teaching and Learning,* # 120. San Francisco, CA: Jossey-Bass. 73.

5   McLaren, B. (2011). *Naked Spirituality: A Life with God in 12 Simple Words.* New York, NY: HarperOne. 223.

6   Wheatley, M. (2002). "The Work of the Servant-Leader." In L. Spears and M. Lawrence. *Focus on Leadership-Servant-Leadership for the 21ˢᵗ Century.* New York: John Wiley and Co. 350.

7   Palmer, P. (1990). *The Active Life: A Spirituality of Work, Creativity, and Caring.* San Francisco, CA: Jossey-Bass. 2.

8   Smith, R. S. (2005). *Truth and the New Kind of Christian: The Emerging Effects of Postmodernism in the Church.* Wheaton, IL: Crossway Books. 82–83.

9   Nouwen, H. (1976). *Reaching Out; The Three Movements of the Spiritual Life.* Glasgow: William Collins and Sons. 19.

10 Beres, L. (2006). "A Reflective Journey: Spirituality and Postmodern Practice." *Currents: New Scholarship in the Human Service.* University of Calgary 3(1).

    http://www.ucalgary.ca/currents/files/currents/v3n1_beres.pdf.

11   Carrette, J., King, R. (2005). *Selling Spirituality: The Silent Takeover of Religion*. New York: Routledge. 42.

12   Campbell, E. (1995). *Silence and Solitude: Inspirations for Meditation and Spiritual Growth*. New York: Harper Collins. 15.

13   Benner, D. G. (2012). *Spirituality and the Awakening Self: The Sacred Journey of Transformation*. Grand Rapids, MI: Brazos Press. 164.

14   Remen, R. N. (1999). "Educating for Mission, Meaning and Compassion." In S. Glazer (ed.). *The Heart of Spirituality: Spirituality in Education*. New York: Jeremy P. Tarcher. 37.

15   English, L. M., Fenwick, T. J., and Parsons, J. (2005). "Interrogating Our Practices of Integrating Spirituality into Workplace Education." *Australian Journal of Adult Education*. 45(1) April 7 to 28, 30.

16   Shea, J. (2005). *Finding God Again*. Washington, D.C.: Rowan and Littlefield. 155.

17   May, G. (1991). *The Awakened Heart: Opening Yourself to the Love You Need*. New York: HarperOne. 46.

18   Fox, M. (2006). A *New Reformation Creation Spirituality and the Transformation of Christianity*. Rochester, VT: Inner Traditions. 101.

19   Holt, B. P. (2005). *Thirsty for God: A Brief History of Christian Spirituality*. Minneapolis, MN: Augsburg Fortress Publishers. 153.

20   Kurtz, E. and White, W. L. (2015). "Recovery Spirituality." *Religions* 6. file:///C:/Users/David%20Robson/Desktop/S%20and%20L/religions-06-00058.pdf. 65, 68, 70.

21   Rohr, R. (2015). *What the Mystics Know: Seven Pathways to Your Deeper Self*. New York: Crossways Publishing Inc. 35.

22   Iyer, P. (2014). *The Art of Stillness*. New York: Ted Books. 41.

23   Brown, B. (2010). *The Gifts of Imperfection: Let Go of Who You Think You're Suppose to Be and Embrace Who You Are—Your Guide to a Wholehearted Life*. Center City, MN: Hazelton Pub. 108.

24   Brown, B. (2012). *Daring Greatly: How the Courage to Be Vulnerable Transforms the Way We Live, Love and Parent and Lead.* New York: Gotham-Penguin Books. 137.

Chapter Eight
Spirituality and Education

1   Remen, R. N. (1999). "Educating for Mission, Meaning and Compassion." In S. Glazer (ed.). *The Heart of Spirituality: Spirituality in Education.* New York: Jeremy P. Tarcher. 35.

2   McLennan, S. (2005). "Doorways to Spirituality for Students: A Chaplain's View." *Journal of College and Character.* (7)2. http://www.collegevalues.org/ pdfs/ doorways%20to%20spirituality%20mclennan%20formatted%20final. pdf. 7.

Tisdell, E. (2008). "Spirituality and Adult Learning." In S.B. Merriam (ed.). *Third Update on Adult Learning Theory: New Directions for Teaching and Learning,* # 119. San Francisco, CA: Jossey-Bass. Nook Book, October 15, 2011. 37.

3   Groen, J. (2008). "Paradoxical Tensions in Creating a Teaching and Learning Space within a Graduate Education Course on Spirituality." *Teaching in Higher Education.* 13(2), 193.

Kasworm, C. E., Rose, D., and Ross-Gordon, J. M. (2010). "Conclusion: Looking Back, Looking Forward." In C. E. Kasworm, A. D. Rose, and J. M. Ross- Gordon (eds.). *Handbook of Adult and Continuing Education.* San Francisco, CA: Jossey-Bass. 443.

4   Apps, J. W. (1994). *Leadership for the Emerging Age: Transforming Practice in Adult and Continuing Education.* San Francisco, CA: Jossey-Bass. 175.

5   Holtschneider, D. (2006). "All the Questions: Spirituality in the University." *Journal of College and Character.* 8(1). November. Retrieved September 14, 2009. http://www.collegevalues.org/pdfs/Holtschneider.pdf. 2–3.

6   Coles, R. (1990). *The Spiritual Lives of Children.* Boston, MA: Houghton Mifflin Company. 15.

7   Ibid. 169.

8   Ibid. 295.

9   Ibid. 300–301.

10   Wright, A. (2000). *Spirituality and Education (Master Classes in Education Series).* London: Routledge. 41.

11   Dillen, A. (2015). "The Complex Flavour of Children's Spirituality in Flanders: Fostering an Open Catholic Spirituality." In J. Watson, M. de Souza, and A. Trousdale. *Global Perspectives on Spirituality and Education.* New York: Routledge. 53.

12   de Sousa, M. (2017). "The Complex Reasons for Missing Spirituality, Democracy and Education." Graduate School of Education and Counseling at Lewis and Clark, Portland, Oregon. 25, (1), 3.

13   Watson, J, de Souza, M., and Trousdale, A. (2014). "Global Perspectives and Context for Spirituality in Education." In J. Watson, M. de Souza, A. Trousdale, (2015). *Global Perspectives on Spirituality and Education.* New York: Routledge. xii–xiii, 297.

14   Best, R. (2015). "Spirituality, Faith and Education: Some Reflections from a UK Perspective." In J. Watson, M. de Souza, and A. Trousdale. *Perspectives on Spirituality and Education.* New York: Routledge. 10.

15   Ibid. 12.

16   Trousdale, A. (2014). "Pluralism and Polarity: Spirituality and Education in the United States." In J. Watson, M. de Souza, and A. Trousdale. *Global Perspectives on Spirituality and Education.* New York: Routledge. 244.

17   de Sousa, M. (2017). op. cit. 3.

18   Miller, J. (2000). *Education and the Soul: Toward a Spiritual Curriculum.* Albany: State University of New York. 140.

19   Ibid. 143.

20   King, P. E. and Boyatzis, C. J. (2015). "Religious and Spiritual Development." In R. M. Lerner (ed.). *Handbook of Child Psychology and Development Science.* Volume 3. New York: John Wiley and Sons. 992, 1012.

Minor, C. V. (2012). *Promoting Spiritual Well-being: A Quasi- Experimental Test of Hay and Nye's Theory of Children's Spirituality.* (Unpublished Doctoral Dissertation). Northcentral University, Prescott Valley, AZ. 72.

21 Robson, D. (2019). *The Intelligence Trap: Why Smart People Make Dumb Mistakes.* New York: W.W. Norton. 202.

22 Norman, J. O. and Renehan, C. (2014). "The Custody of Spiritual Education in Ireland." In J. Watson, M. de Souza, and A. Trousdale. *Global Perspectives on Spirituality and Education.* New York: Routledge. 37–38.

23 Dallaire, M. (2014). "Spirituality in Canadian Education." In J. Watson, M. de Souza, and A. Trousdale. *Global Perspectives on Spirituality and Education.* New York: Routledge. 230.

24 Minor, C. V. (2012). op cit. 59.

25 Campbell, L. (2007). "Art, Spirituality, and Teaching." In B.W. Speck and S.L. Hoppe (eds.). *Searching for Spirituality in Higher Education.* New York: Peter Lang. 163.

26 Vogel, L. (2000). "Reckoning with the Spiritual Lives of Adult Educators." In L.M. English and M.A. Gillen. *Addressing the Spiritual Dimensions of Adult Learning: What Educators Can Do: New Directions for Adult and Continuing Education.* San Francisco, CA: Jossey-Bass. 19.

27 Miller, op. cit. 121.

28 Mayes, C. (2001). "Cultivating Spirituality Reflectivity in Teachers." *Teacher Education Quarterly,* 28(2). Retrieved September 14, 2009.

http://www.teqjournal.org/backvols /2001/ 28_2/ v28n202.pdf. 9, 10.

29 Minor, C. V. (2012). op. cit. 68.

30 Ibid. 26.

31 Alberini-Emmett, G. and Plischke, M. (1993). "Reading in Health Education." In M. Dupis and L. H. Merchant (eds.). *Reading Across the Curriculum: A Research Report for Teachers.* ERIC Clearinghouse on Reading and Communication Skills, Bloomington, IN. 106.

[32]   Kessler, R. (2005). "Nourishing Adolescents' Spirituality." In J. P. Miller, S. Karsten, D.

Denton, D. Orr, and I. C. Kates (eds.). *Holistic Learning and Spirituality in Education.* Albany, NY: State University of New York. 103.

[33]   Hendrix, K. G. (2009). "The Spirit That Strengthens Me: The 'Life of the Mind' With: Life in the Spirit." In K. G. Hendrix and J. D. Hamlet (eds.). *As the Spirit Moves Us: New Directions for Teaching and Learning,* #120. San Francisco, CA: Jossey-Bass. 73.

[34]   Wilson, L. O. (2005). "Listening to Ancient Voices: Reaching Hearts and Souls through Benchmarks and Rites of Passage Experiences in School." In J. P. Miller, S. Karsten, D. Denton, D. Orr, and I. C. Kates (eds.). *Holistic Learning and Spirituality in Education.* Albany, NY: State University of New York. 172.

[35]   Rossiter. G. (2010). "Perspective on Contemporary Spirituality: Implications for Religious Education in Catholic Schools." *International Studies in Catholic Education.* 2:2, 130.

[36]   Ibid. 130.

[37]   Ibid. 131.

[38]   Ibid. 140–141.

[39]   King, P. E. and Boyatzis, C. J. (2015). "Religious and Spiritual Development." In R. M. Lerner (ed.). *Handbook of Child Psychology and development Science.* Volume 3, 990–1014. New York: John Wiley and Sons.

[40]   Ibid. 996.

[41]   Ibid. 1014.

[42]   Ibid. 989, 998.

[43]   Ibid. 999.

[44]   Ibid. 992.

[45]   Barry, C. N., Nelson, L., Davarya, S., and Urry, S. (2010). "Religiosity and Spirituality during the Transition to Adulthood." *International Journal of*

Behavioral Development, 34:311-324. Published online, 1 April 2010. DOI: 10.1177/0165025409350964. 316.

46   Ibid. 315.

47   Ibid. 320.

48   Kessler, R. (2005). op. cit. 102.

49   Ibid. 103–104.

50   Schiller, S. A. (2005). "Contemplating Great Things in Soul and Place." In J. P. Miller, S. Karsten, D. Denton, D. Orr, and I. C. Kates, (eds.). *Holistic Learning and Spirituality in Education*. Albany, NY: State University of New York. 163.

51   Parks, S. D. (2000). *Big Questions, Worthy Dreams: Mentoring Young Adults in Their Search for Meaning, Purpose and Faith*. San Francisco, CA: Jossey-Bass. 145–146.

52   Braskamp, L. (2007). "Three 'Central' Questions Worth Asking." *Journal of College and Character*. 9:1, DOI:10.2202/1940-1639.1101 https://www.tandfonline.com/doi/pdf/10.2202/1940-1639.1101. 3.

53   Lindholm, J. (2007). "Spirituality in the Academy: Reinventing Our Live and the Lives of Our Students." *About Campus*. September–October. Published online in Wiley InterScience, www.interscience.wiley.com).DOI: 10.1002/abc.218 © 2007 Wiley Periodicals, Inc. 3–4.

Stamm, L. (2006). "The Influence of Religion and Spirituality in Shaping American Higher Education." In A. W. Chickering, J. C. Dalton, and L. Stamm. *Encouraging Authenticity & Spirituality in Higher Education*. San Francisco, CA: Jossey-Bass. 86–87.

54   Braskamp, L. (2007). 1.

55   Parks, S. D. (2008). "Leadership, Spirituality, and the College as a Mentoring Environment." *Journal of College and Character*. 10(2). http://www.collegevalues.org /pdfs/Parks.pdf. 4.

56   Lindholm, J. (2007). op. cit. 10.

57 Speck, B. W. and Hoope, S. L. (eds.). (2007). "Spirituality in Applied Disciplines." *Searching for Spirituality in Higher Education.* New York: Peter Lang. 103–104.

58 Dalton, J. C. (2006). "Our Orientation." In A. W. Chickering, J. C. Dalton, and L. Stamm. *Encouraging Authenticity & Spirituality in Higher Education.* San Francisco, CA: Jossey-Bass. 18.

59 Dalton, J. C., Eberhart, D., Bracken, J., and Echols, K. (2006). "Inward Journeys: Forms and Patterns of College Student Spirituality." *Journal of College & Character.* 7(8), 2.

60 Lindholm, J. A. (2006). "The 'Interior' Lives of American College Students: Preliminary Findings from a National Study." In J. L. Heft (ed.). *Passing on the Faith: Transforming Traditions for the Next Generation of Jews, Christians, and Muslims.* New York, NY: Fordham University Press. 75.

61 Love, P. and Talbot D. (1999). "Defining Spiritual Development: A Missing Consideration for Student Affairs." *NASPA Journal.* 37(1), Fall 1999, 363.

62 "Spirituality in Higher Education: A National Study of College Student's Search for Meaning and Purpose: (2003, July 21)." *UCLA Launches Study on Spirituality National Study to track College Student's Spiritual Growth* [Press release]. http://www.spirituality.ucla.edu/news/Spirituality_2003-07-21.pdf.

63 Jablonski, M. (2005). "Hidden Wholeness: Spiritual Leadership." *Journal of College and Character.* 6(8). http://www.collegevalues.org/pdfs/ Hidden%20 Wholeness%20part%20I%20formatted%20final.pdf. 3.

64 Hood, G. K. (2006). "The Notion of Spirituality in Adult and Higher Education." *Higher Education Perspectives.* 2(1), 169.

65 Love, P. and Talbot D. (1999). op. cit. 362.

66 Dalton, J.C. (2006). "Integrating Spirit and Community in Higher Education." In A.W. Chickering, J.C. Dalton, and L. Stamm. *Encouraging Authenticity & Spirituality in Higher Education.* San Francisco, CA: Jossey-Bass. 169.

67 Glazer, S. (ed.). (1999). *The Heart of Spirituality: Spirituality in Education.* New York: Jeremy P. Tarcher. 135.

Moore, T. (2005). "Education for the Soul." In J. P. Miller, S. Karsten, D. Denton, D. Orr, and I. C. Kates (eds.). *Holistic Learning and Spirituality in Education.* Albany, NY: State University of New York. 15.

Mezirow, J. (1991). *Transformative Dimensions of Adult Learning.* San Francisco, CA: Jossey- Bass. 224.

[68] Jones, L. (2005). "What does Spirituality in Education Mean? Stumbling Toward Wholeness." *Journal of College and Character.* 6(7). http://www. collegevalues.org/pdfs/sirit%20in%20ed.%20jones%20formatted%20 final%202.pdf. 1.

[69] Jones, L. (2005). op. cit. 5.

[70] Westrup, J. (1998). "Invisibility? Spiritual Values and Adult Education." *Australian Journal of Adult and Community Education.* 38 (2) July 1998, 109.

Chapter Nine
The Future of Spirituality

[1] Ashton K. (2015). *How to Fly a Horse: The Secret History of Creation, Invention, and Discovery.* New York: Anchor Books. 7.

[2] https://www.brandwatch.com/blog/youtube-stats/. Retrieved January 3, 2021.

[3] Friedman, T. L. (2007*). The World Is Flat: A Brief History of the Twenty-First Century. (Revised Edition).* New York: Picador/Farrar, Straus and Giroux. 520–521.

[4] https://www.plasticsurgery.org/news/blog/why-are-millennials-getting-botox-and-fillers-in-their-twenties. November 17, 2017. Retrieved January 18, 2021.

[5] Veith, G. E. Jr. (1994). *Postmodern Times: A Guide to Contemporary Thought and Culture.* Wheaton, IL: Crossway Books. 178.

[6] Levitin, D. J. (2014). *The Organized Mind: Thinking Straight in the Age of Information Overload.* New York: Dutton-Penguin Group. 6.

[7] Schwartz, C. A. (1999). *Paradigm Shift in the Church: How Natural Church Development Can Transform Theological Thinking.* St. Charles, IL: ChurchSmart Resources. 7.

8   Martin, M. L. (2013). *Spirituality, Medical Science and Health: The Spiritual Effects of a Sense of Entitlement in the Ministry of Healing in the Christian Church.* Unpublished doctoral dissertation, University of South Africa. 108.

9   Rohr, R. (2013). *Immortal Diamond: Searching for Our True Self.* San Francisco, CA: Jossey-Bass. 29.

10   Miller, D. (2003). *Blue Like Jazz: Nonreligious Thoughts on Christian Spirituality.* Nashville, TN: Thomas Nelson. 192.

        Shea, J. (2005). *Finding God Again.* Washington, D.C.: Rowan and Littlefield. 133.

11   Rohr, R. (2013). op. cit. xxiii–xxiv.

12   Carrette, J. and King, R. (2005). *Selling Spirituality: The Silent Takeover of Religion.* New York: Routledge. 77.

13   Rohr, R. (2015). *What the Mystics Know: Seven Pathways to Your Deeper Self.* New York: Crossways Publishing Inc. 39.

14   Veith, G. E. (1994). op. cit. 100.

15   Hamm, R. L. (2007). *Recreating the Church: Leadership for the Postmodern Age.* St. Louis, MO: Chalice Press. 54–55.

16   Bennett, E. E. and Bell, A. A. (2010). "Paradox and Promise in the Knowledge Society." In C. E. Kasworm, A. D. Rose, and J. M. Ross-Gordon (eds.). *Handbook of Adult and Continuing Education.* San Francisco, CA: Jossey-Bass. 415.

17   Tolle, E. (2003). *Stillness Speaks.* Novato, CA: New World Library. 9.

18   Tisdell, E.J. (2014). "Research as Transformative Learning: A Longitudinal Study of Spirituality, Cultural Identity, and Unfolding Wisdom in the Lives of US Educators." In J. Watson, M. de Souza, and A. Trousdale. *Global Perspectives on Spirituality and Education.* New York: Routledge. 278.

19   Fischer, E. (2013). "Writing and Telling Healing the Pain of Disconnection." In C.B. Dillard and C.L. E. Okpalaoka. *Engaging Culture, Race and Spirituality: New Visions (Counterpoints: Studies in the Postmodern Theory of Education).* New York: Peter Lang International. 55.

20   Nouwen, H. (1976). *Reaching Out: The Three Movements of the Spiritual Life.* Glasgow: William Collins and Sons. 36.

21   Harris P. (ed.) (1998). *Silence and Stillness in Every Season: Daily Readings with John Main.* New York: Continuum. 216.

22   Vella, J. (2000). "A Spirited Epistemology: Honoring the Adult Learner as Subject." In English, L. M. and Gillen, M.A. *Addressing the Spiritual Dimensions of Adult Learning: What Educators Can Do: New Directions for Adult and Continuing Education.* 85, Spring, San Francisco, CA: Jossey-Bass. 25.

23   MacKeracher, D. (2004*). Making Sense of Adult Learning* (2nd Ed.). Toronto: University of Toronto Press. 175.

24   Harari, Y. N. (2018). *21 Lessons for the 21st Century.* New York: Signal-Random House. 214.

25   Fleming, J. J. (2005). "The Role of Spirituality in the Practice of Adult Education Leaders." Doctoral Dissertation, University of Georgia. Retrieved July 12, 2009. http://www.coe.uga.edu/p.97.

26   Newell, J. P. (2002). *Echo of the Soul: The Sacredness of the Human Body.* Harrisburg, PA: Morehouse Publishing. 28–29, 30.

27   Chittister, J. (1992). *The Rule of Benedict: Spirituality for the 21st Century.* New York: Crossroad. 77.

28   Chittister (1992). op. cit. 99.

29   L'Engle, M. (1980). *Walking on Water: Reflections on Faith and Art.* New York: Farrar, Straus and Giroux. 69.

30   Steffan, M. C. (2010). *Mystery in Life: Learning from Our Spirituality.* Bloomington, IN: Westbow Press. Nook Book, May 5, 2011. 135.

31   Rogers, J. (2006). "Role-Modeling Authenticity in Higher Education, Spirituality in Higher Education." *A National Study of College Student's Search for Meaning and Purpose.* 3(1), 3.

32   Cannon, M. E. (2013). *Just Spirituality: How Faith Practices Fuel Social Action.* Downers Grove, IL: IVP Books. 23.

[33]   Hoppe, S. L., (2005). "Spirituality and Leadership." In S. Hoppe (ed.). *Spirituality in Higher Education*. San Francisco, CA: Jossey-Bass. 89–90.

[34]   Chittister, J. (1992). op. cit. 87, 88, 97–98.

[35]   Carr, N. (2010). *The Shallows: What the Internet Is Doing to Our Brains*. New York: W.W. Norton. 42.

[36]   Twenge, J. M. and Campbell, W. K. (2010*). The Narcissism Epidemic: Living in an Age of Uncertainty*. New York: Atria Paperback. 282–283.

[37]   Miller, D. (2003). *Blue Like Jazz: Nonreligious Thoughts on Christian Spirituality*. Nashville, TN: Thomas Nelson. 181.

[38]   Veith, G. E. (1994). op. cit. 118–119.

[39]   Vaillant, G. (2008). *Spiritual Evolution: A Scientific Defense of Faith*. New York: Broadway Books. 170.

[40]   Raschke, C. (2004*). The Next Reformation: Why Evangelicals Must Embrace Postmodernity*. Grand Rapids, MI: Baker Academic. 172.

[41]   Vaillant, G. (2009). *Spiritual Evolution: How We Are Wired for Faith, Hope and Love*. New York: Broadway Books. 16.

[42]   Wilkins, S. (2013). "The Gospel Meet American Culture." *Catalyst: Contemporary Evangelical Perspectives for United Methodist Seminarians*. April 1, 2013. Retrieved May 31, 2016. http://www.catalystresources.org/the-gospel-meets-american-culture. 3–4.

[43]   Veith, G.E. Jr. (1994). *Postmodern Times: A Guide to Contemporary Thought and Culture*. Wheaton, IL: Crossway Books. 144.

       Alper, M. (2006). *The "God" Part of the Brain: A Scientific Interpretation of Human Spirituality and God*. Napperville, IL: Sourcebooks Inc. 240–241.

[44]   Vaillant, G. (2008). op.cit. 8.

[45]   Palmer, P. (1990). *The Active Life: A Spirituality of Work, Creativity, and Caring*. San Francisco, CA: Jossey-Bass. 156.

46   Stuart-Buttle, R. (2013) *Virtual Theology, Faith and Adult Education: An Interruptive Pedagogy*: Newcastle upon Tyne, England: Cambridge Scholars Publishing. 109.

47   Cady, D. M. (2007). "Spirituality and Student Development." In B. W. Speck and S. L. Hoppe (eds.). *Searching for Spirituality in Higher Education*. New York: Peter Lang. 98.

48   Steffan, M.C. (2010). op. cit. 96–97.

49   Waaijman, K. (2007). "Spirituality—A Multifaceted Phenomenon." *Studies in Spirituality*. 17, 21.

50   Martin, M. L. (2013). op. cit. 31.

51   Chittister, J. (1992). op. cit. 21–22.

52   Boa, K. (2001). *Conformed to His Image: Biblical and Practical Approaches to Spiritual Formation*: Grand Rapids, MI: Zondervan. 87.

53   Tisdell, E. (2008). "Spirituality and Adult Learning." In S.B. Merriam (ed.). *Third Update on Adult Learning Theory: New Directions for Teaching and Learning*, # 119. San Francisco, CA: Jossey-Bass. Nook Book, October 15, 2011. 39.

54   McLaren, B. (2011). *Naked Spirituality: A Life with God in 12 Simple Words*. New York, NY: HarperOne. 223.

     Iyer, P. (2014). *The Art of Stillness*. New York: Ted Books. 53.

55   http://www.classicmoviehub.com/quotes/film/the-music-man-1962/page/2/

56   Brown, L. C. (2008). "Role of Spirituality in Adult Learning Contexts." Doctoral Dissertation, University of Georgia. https://getd.libs.uga.edu/pdfs/brown_laura_c_200812_phd/ brown_laura_c_200812_phd.pdf, April 11, 2010. 2–3.

57   Veith, G.E. Jr. (1994). *Postmodern Times: A Guide to Contemporary Thought and Culture*. Wheaton, IL: Crossway Books. 84–85.

58   Mizock, L., Chandrika U.M., & Russinova, Z. (2012). "Spiritual and Religious Issues in Psychotherapy with Schizophrenia: Cultural Implications and Implementation." *Religions* 2012, 3, doi:10.3390/rel3010082, Retrieved, December 4, 2014. 84.

59   Watson, J, de Souza, M., and Trousdale, A. (2014). "Global Perspectives and Context for Spirituality in Education." In J. Watson, M. de Souza, A. Trousdale, (2015). *Global Perspectives on Spirituality and Education.* New York: Routledge. 312.

60   Raschke, C. (2004*). The Next Reformation: Why Evangelicals Must Embrace Postmodernity.* Grand Rapids, MI: Baker Academic. 25–26, 178.

61   Veith, G.E. Jr. (1994). *Postmodern Times: A Guide to Contemporary Thought and Culture.* Wheaton, IL: Crossway Books. 211.

62   Hamm, R. L. (2007). *Recreating the Church: Leadership for the Postmodern Age.* St. Louis, MO: Chalice Press. 28.

63   Hunter, G. G., III (1992). *How To Reach Secular People.* Nashville: Abingdon Press. 30.

64   Hawkins, T. R. (1997). *The Learning Congregation: A New Vision of Leadership.* Louisville, KY: Westminster John Knox Press. 5.

65   Friedman, T. L. (2007). *The World Is Flat: A Brief History of the Twenty-First Century.* (revised edition). New York: Picador/Farrar, Straus and Giroux. 233, 240–242, 249.

66   Bregman, R. (2019). *Humankind: A Hopeful History* (E. Manton, E. Moore, trans.). London: Bloomsbury Publishing. 383.

67   Harari, Y. (2018). op. cit. 270.

68   Raschke, C. (2004*).* op. cit. 154.

69   Smith, R. S. (2005). *Truth and the New Kind of Christian: The Emerging Effects of Postmodernism in the Church.* Wheaton, IL: Crossway Books. 57.

70   Brown, B. (2012). *Daring Greatly: How the Courage to Be Vulnerable Transforms the Way We Live, Love, Parent, and Lead.* New York: Gotham Books. 104.

71   Thompson, C. (2010). *Anatomy of the Soul: Surprising Connections between Neuroscienceand Spiritual Practices That Can Transform Your Life and Relationships*. Carol Stream, IL: Tyndale Momentum. 23.

72   Harris P. (ed.) (1998*). Silence and Stillness in Every Season: Daily Readings with John Main*. New York. Continuum. 216.

73   MacKeracher, D. (2004). *Making Sense of Adult Learning* (2nd ed.) Toronto: University of Toronto Press. 175.

74   Vogel, L. (2000). "Reckoning with the Spiritual Lives of Adult Educators." In L. M. English and M. A. Gillen. *Addressing the Spiritual Dimensions of Adult Learning: What Educators Can Do: New Directions for Adult and Continuing Education*. San Francisco, CA: Jossey-Bass. 25.

     Palmer, P (1990). *The Active Life: A Spirituality of Work, Creativity, and Caring*. San Francisco, CA: Jossey-Bass. 23.

75   Wright, A. (2000). *Spirituality and Education (Master Classes in Education Series)*. London: Routledge. 9.

76   Tacey, D. (2004). *The Spirituality Revolution: The Emergence of Contemporary Spirituality*. New York: Routledge. 121–122.

77   Rinallo, D., Scott, L., and Maclaran, P. (2012). "Introduction: Unravelling Complexities at the Commercial/Spiritual Interface." In D. Rinallo, L. Scott, and P. Maclaran (eds.). *Consumption and Spirituality* (1–25). Routledge Interpretive Marketing Research. New York: Routledge-Taylor and Francis Group.

78   Alper, M. (2006). *The "God" Part of the Brain: A Scientific Interpretation of Human Spirituality and God*. Napperville, IL: Sourcebooks Inc. 241.

79   Fromm, E. (1976). *To Have or To Be?*. New York: Continuum. 57.

Appendix A
A Practical Model of "Spirituality and Learning:"
Rooted in Adult Learning Principles

[1]   Tacey, D. (2004). *The Spirituality Revolution: The Emergence of Contemporary Spirituality.* New York: Routledge. 38.

[2]   http://pluk.org/centraldirectory/Adult%20learning%20styles/online.rit.edu-Characteristics_of_Adult_Learners.pdfhttp://online.rit.edu/faculty/teaching_strategies/adult_learners.cfm. Retrieved November 18, 2012.

[3]   Ferrer, J. N. (2011). "Participatory Spirituality and Transpersonal Theory: A Ten-Year Retrospective." *The Journal of Transpersonal Psychology.* 43(1), 4.

[4]   Palmer, P. (1993). *To Know as We Are Known: Education as a Spirituality Journey.* New York: HarperOne. 121.

[5]   Nouwen, H. (1976). *Reaching Out: The Three Movements of the Spiritual Life.* Glasgow: William Collins and Sons. 125.

[6]   Dalton, J. C., Eberhart, D., Bracken, J. and Echols, K. (2006). "Inward Journeys: Forms and Patterns of College Student Spirituality." *Journal of College & Character.* 7(8), 2.

BIBLIOGRAPHY

Ager, K., Albrecht, N. J., and Cohen, M. (2015). "Mindfulness in Schools Research Project: Exploring Students' Perspectives of Mindfulness." *Psychology*, 6, 896–914.

Aikens, K. A., Astin, J. Pelletier, K. R., Levanovich, K., Baase, C., Park, and Y.Y., Bondnar, C. M. (2014). "Mindfulness Goes to Work: Impact of an On-Line Workplace Intervention." *JOEM, Journal of Occupational and Environmental Medicine*, 13–4531.

Alberini-Emmett, and, G., Plischke, M. (1993). "Reading in Health Education." In M. Dupis, L.H. Merchant (eds.). *Reading Across the Curriculum: A Research Report for Teachers*. ERIC Clearinghouse on Reading and Communication Skills, Bloomington, IN.

Albrecht, N. J. (2016). *Teachers Teaching Mindfulness with Children: An Interpretative Phenomenological Analysis*. PhD. Thesis. School of Education, Humanities and Law, Flinders University Adelaide, Australia.

Albrecht, N., Bucu, A., and Ager, K. (2018). "Rome Wasn't Built in a Day: School Counsellors' Perspectives of Teaching Children Mindfulness." *Australian Counselling Research Journal*. 12 (1). 3–17.

Allison, A. M. W., and Broadus, P. R. B. (2009). "Spirituality Then and Now: Our Journey through Higher Education as Women of Faith." In K. G. Hendrix, and J. D. Hamlet (eds.). *As the Spirit Moves Us: New Directions for Teaching and Learning*. # 120 (77–86). San Francisco: Jossey-Bass.

Alper, M. (2006). *The "God" Part of the Brain: A Scientific Interpretation of Human Spirituality and God.* Napperville, IL: Sourcebooks Inc.

Apps, J. W. (1994). *Leadership for the Emerging Age: Transforming Practice in Adult and Continuing Education.* San Francisco: Jossey-Bass.

Asghar, J., and Shahzad, K. (2015). "The Rewiring of the Human Brain: A Critique of Cyber-Culture and its Effects on Our Thinking Abilities." *Journal of the Institute of Social Sciences.* 2 (2) 13–23.

Ashbrook, R. T. (2009). *Mansions of the Heart: Exploring the Seven Stages of Spiritual Growth.* San Francisco: Jossey-Bass.

Ashton K. (2015). *How to Fly a Horse: The Secret History of Creation, Invention, and Discovery.* New York: Anchor Books.

Astin, A. W. (2004). "Why Spirituality Deserves a Central Place in Higher Education." *Spirituality in Higher Education Newsletter.* UCLA. April 2004, 1(1) 1–12.

Astin, A.W., and Astin, H.S. (2009). "Does Spirituality Have a Place in Higher Education?: A Response." *Religion & Education.* 36(2) (124–129). Summer, University of Northern Iowa.

Astin, A. W., Astin, H. S., and Lindholm, J. A. (2010). *Cultivating the Spirit: How College Can Enhance Students' Lives.* San Francisco: Jossey-Bass.

Balboni, M. J., Puchalski, C. M., Peteet, J. R. (2014). "The Relationship between Medicine, Spirituality and Religion: Three Models for Integration." *Journal of Religious Health.* 1586-1598. Published on-line, June 12, 2014, Retrieved February 2, 2015.

Barna, G. (1991). *User Friendly Churches: What Christians Need to Know about the Churches People Love to Go To.* Ventura, CA: Regal Books.

Barna Group (2017). "Meet the Spiritual but Not Religious." Retrieved April 6, 2017. https://www.barna.com/research/meet-spiritual-not-religious.

Barna Group (2018). https://www.barna.com/research/friends-loneliness/? utm_source =Barna+Update+List&utm_campaign=9dae118275-EMAIL_CAMPAIGN_2018_07_10_11_32_COPY_01&utm_medium= email&utm_term=0_8560a0e52e-9dae118275-172047133&mc_ cid=9dae118275&mc_eid=f1e482a4e1

Barna Group (2020). "Signs of Decline and Hope Among Key Metrics of Faith." Retrieved March 5, 2020. https://www.barna.com/research/ changing-state-of-the-church.

Barnes, S., Brown, K.W., Krusemark, E., Campbell, W. K., and Rogge, R. D. (2007). "The Role of Mindfulness in Romanic Relationship Satisfaction and Responses to Relationship Stress." *Journal of Marital and Family Therapy*. 33 (40), 482–500.

Barry, C. N., Nelson, L., Davarya, S., and Urry, S. (2010). "Religiosity and Spirituality During the Transition to Adulthood." *International Journal of Behavioral Development*. 34:311–324. Published online, April 1, 2010. DOI: 10.1177/0165025409350964.

Bass, D. (2012). *Christianity After Religion: The End of Church and the Birth of a New Spiritual Awakening*. New York: HarperOne.

Beauchemin, J., Hutchins, T. L., and Patterson, F. (2008). "Mindfulness Meditation May Lessen Anxiety, Promote Social Skills, and Improve Academic Performance among Adolescents with Learning Disabilities." *Complementary Health Practice Review*. 13, 34–45.

Benefiel, M., Fry, L.W., and Geigle, D. (2014). "Spirituality and Religion in the Workplace: History, Theory, and Research. *Journal of Religion and Spirituality* 6(3), 175.

Benner, D. G. (2011). *Soulful Spirituality: Becoming Fully Alive and Deeply Human*. Grand Rapids, MI: Brazos Press.

Benner, D. G. (2012). *Spirituality and the Awakening Self: The Sacred Journey of Transformation*. Grand Rapids, MI: Brazos Press.

Bennett, E. E., and Bell, A. A. (2010). "Paradox and Promise in the Knowledge Society." In C. E. Kasworm, A. D. Rose, and J. M. Ross-Gordon (eds.) *Handbook of Adult and Continuing Education.* (411-420). San Francisco: Jossey-Bass.

Beres, L. (2006). "A Reflective Journey: Spirituality and Postmodern Practice." *Currents: New Scholarship in the Human Service.* University of Calgary 3(1). http://www.ucalgary.ca/currents/files/currents/v3n1_beres.pdf.

Best, R. (2015). "Spirituality, Faith and Education: Some Reflections from a UK Perspective." In J. Watson, M. de Souza, and A. Trousdale. *Perspectives on Spirituality and Education.* (5–20). New York: Routledge.

Besecke, K. (2014) *You Can't Put God in a Box: Thoughtful Spirituality in the Rational Age.* New York: Oxford University Press.

Bibby, R. (2011). *Beyond the Gods & Back: Religion's Demise and Rise and Why It Matters:* Toronto: ProjectCanada Books.

Bibby, R. (1987) *Fragmented Gods: The Poverty and Potential of Religion in Canada.* Toronto: Irwin Publishing.

Bibby, R. (2017). *Resilient Gods: Being Pro-Religious, Low Religious, or No Religious in Canada.* Vancouver, BC: UBC Press.

Boa, K. (2001). *Conformed to His Image: Biblical and Practical Approaches to Spiritual Formation:* Grand Rapids, MI: Zondervan

Bone, J. (2014). "Spirituality and Early Childhood Education in New Zealand and Australia: Past, Present and Future." In J. Watson, M. de Souza, and A. Trousdale *Global Perspectives on Spirituality and Education.* (116–128). New York: Routledge.

Borg, J., André, B., Soderstrom, H., and Farde, L. (2003). "The Serotonin System and Spiritual Experiences." *American Journal of Psychiatry.* 160, 11, 1965–1969.

Bowman, J. P., and Klopping, I. (1999). "Bandstands, Bandwidth, and Business Communication: Technology and the Sanctity of Writing." Retrieved June 30, 2009. http://journals.sagepub.com/doi/pdf/10.1177/108056999906200108.

Brandwatch. (2020).https://www.brandwatch.com/blog/youtube-stats/Feb. 21, 2020, retrieved January 3, 2021.

Braskamp, L. (2007). "Three 'Central' Questions Worth Asking. *Journal of College and Character.* 9:1, DOI:10.2202/1940-1639.1101 https://www.tandfonline.com/doi/pdf/10.2202/1940-1639.1101.

Bregman, L. (2012). "Spiritual Definitions: A Moving Target." In M. Fowler, J.D. Martin III, and J.L. Hochheimer, (eds.) *Spirituality: Theory, Praxis and Pedagogy.* (3–10). Oxford, UK: Inter-Disciplinary Press.

Bregman, R. (2019). *Humankind: A Hopeful History* (E. Manton, E. Moore, Trans.). London: Bloomsbury Publishing.

Broderick, P. C., and Metz, S. (2009). "Learning to BREATHE: A Pilot Trial of a Mindfulness Curriculum for Adolescents." *Advances in School Mental Health Promotion.* 2(1), 35–46.

Brookfield, S. D. (1987). *Developing Critical Thinkers: Challenging Adults to Explore Alternative Ways of Thinking and Acting.* San Francisco: Jossey-Bass.

Brown, B. (2010). *The Gifts of Imperfection: Let Go of Who You Think You're Suppose to Be and Embrace Who You Are—Your Guide to a Wholehearted Life.* Center City, MN: Hazelton Pub.

Brown, B. (2012) *Daring Greatly: How the Courage to Be Vulnerable Transforms the Way We Live, Love, Parent, and Lead.* New York: Gotham Books.

Brown, B. (2015) *Rising Strong: The Reckoning, the Rumble, the Revolution.* New York: Spiegal & Grau.

Brown, L. C. (2008). "Role of Spirituality in Adult Learning Contexts." Doctoral Dissertation, University of Georgia. Retrieved April 11, 2010. https://getd.libs.uga.edu/pdfs/brown_laura_c_200812_phd/brown_laura_c_200812_phd.pdf.

Buck, H. G. (2006). "Spirituality: Concept Analysis and Model Development." *Holistic Nursing Practice.* 20(6):288–92. Retrieved September 10, 2017. https://pubmed.ncbi.nlm.nih.gov/17099417/

Burrows, L. (2013). "Spirituality at Work: The Contribution of Mindfulness to Personal and Workforce Development." In Roger Harris and Tom Short (eds.) *Workforce Development Perspectives and Issues.* Australia: Springer/Kluwer. 2013. Retrieved February 3, 2015. https://www.academia.edu/4547163/Spirituality_at_work-_the_contribution_of_mindfulness_to_personal_and_workforce_development.

Butot, M. (2007). "Reframing Spirituality, Reconceptualizing Change: Possibilities for Critical Social Work." In J. Coates, J. R. Graham, B. Swartzentruber, and B. Ouellette. *Spirituality and Social Work: Selected Canadian Readings.* (143–159). Toronto: Canadian Scholars' Press Inc.

Cady, D. M. (2007). "Spirituality and Student Development." In B. W. Speck, S. L. Hoppe (eds.). *Searching for Spirituality in Higher Education.* (97–110). New York: Peter Lang.

Caird, J. K., Johnston, K. A., Willness, C. R., Asbridged, M., and Steel. P. (2014). "A Meta-Analysis of the Effects of Texting on Driving." *Accident Analysis & Prevention.* 71, October 2014. 311–318. https://www.sciencedirect.com/science/article/pii/S000145751400178X.

Calderone, S. (2004). "Current Thinking on the Role of Spirituality in Medical Education & Training Spirituality in Higher Education: A National Study of College Student's Search for Meaning and Purpose." Retrieved December 13, 2010. http://www.spirituality.ucla.edu/docs/newsletters/1/Calderone.pdf.

Campbell, E. (1995). *Silence and Solitude: Inspirations for Meditation and Spiritual Growth.* New York: Harper Collins.

Campbell, E. (2014). "Mindfulness in Education Research Highlights: An Annotated Bibliography of Studies of Mindfulness in Education." *Greater Good Magazine.* Published by the Greater Good Science Center at UC Berkeley. Published online September 16, 2014. Retrieved March 12, 2020. https://greatergood.berkeley.edu/article/item/mindfulness_in_education_research_hig hlights.

Campbell, K. P. (2010). *Transformative Learning and Spirituality: A Heuristic Inquiry into the Experience of Spiritual Learning.* Unpublished doctoral dissertation. Capalla University.

Campbell, L. (2007). "Art, Spirituality, and Teaching." In B.W. Speck, and S.L. Hoppe (eds.). *Searching for Spirituality in Higher Education.* (157–166). New York: Peter Lang.

Campbell, R. C. (2014). *The Role of Service Learning in Developing Spirituality and Transforming Students:* Dissertation submitted in partial fulfillment of the requirements for the degree of Doctor of Education: The University of Memphis, May 2014.

Canadian Nurses Association (2010). "WHO definition of Health to Include Spiritual Well-being." Annual Meeting Resolution—2005. Retrieved February 6, 2011. http://www.cna-nurses.ca/CNA/about/meetings/ resolutions_2005/resolutions_08_e.aspx.

Cannon, M. E. (2013). *Just Spirituality: How Faith Practices Fuel Social Action.* Downers Grove, IL: IVP Books.

Carr, N. (2010). *The Shallows: What the Internet Is doing to Our Brains.* New York: W.W. Norton.

Carrette, J., King, R. (2005). *Selling Spirituality: The Silent Takeover of Religion.* New York: Routledge.

Chamberlain, P. (2020). "Knowledge is not Everything." *Design for Health*, 4:1, 1–3. https://www.tandfonline.com/doi/pdf/10.1080/24735132. 2020.1731203?needAccess=true. retrieved March 1, 2021.

Chang, H., Boyd, D. (2011). *Spirituality in Higher Education: Autoethnographies.* Walnut Creek: CA: LeftCoast Press.

Chickering, A. W., Dalton, J. C., and Stamm, L. (2006). *Encouraging Authenticity & Spirituality in Higher Education.* San Francisco: Jossey-Bass.

Chickering, A. (2006). "Strengthening Spirituality and Civic Engagement in Higher Education." *Journal of College & Character.* 8(1) Retrieved from http://www.collegevalues.org/ pdfs/Chickering%20 remarks.pdf.

Chittister, J. (1992). *The Rule of Benedict: Spirituality for the 21st Century.* New York: Crossroad. http://www.classicmoviehub.com/quotes/ film/the-music-man-1962/page/2/ retrieved February 13, 2020.

Coates, J., Graham, J.R., Swartzentruber, B., and Ouellette, B. (eds.). (2007.) *Spirituality and Social Work: Selected Canadian Readings.* Toronto: Canadian Scholars' Press Inc.

Conder, T. (2006). *The Church in Transition: The Journey of Existing Churches into the Emerging Culture.* Grand Rapids, MI, Zondervan.

Coles, R. (1990). *The Spiritual Lives of Children.* Boston: Houghton Mifflin Company.

Colvin, G. (2015). *Humans Are Underrated: What High Achievers Know That Brilliant Machines Never Will.* New York: Portfolio/Penguin.

Conger, J. A. (1994). *Spirit at Work: Discovering the Spirituality in Leadership.* San Francisco: Jossey-Bass.

Culliford, L. (2002). "Spiritual Values and Skills Are Increasingly Recognized as Necessary Aspects of Clinical Care. *British Medical Journal*. December 21, 2002; 325(7378): 1434–1435.

Culliford, L. (2005). *Healing from Within: Spirituality and Mental Health*. Self-published. Retrieved April 6, 2014. http://www.miepvideos. org/Healing%20From%20within.pdf.

Culliford, L. (2010). *The Psychology of Spirituality: An Introduction*. London: Jessica Kingsley Publishers.

Dallaire, M. (2014). "Spirituality in Canadian Education." In J. Watson, M. de Souza, and A. Trousdale. *Global Perspectives on Spirituality and Education*. (221–232). New York: Routledge.

Dalton, J. C. (2006). "Our Orientation." In A. W. Chickering, J. C. Dalton, and L. Stamm. *Encouraging Authenticity & Spirituality in Higher Education*. (16–19). San Francisco: Jossey-Bass.

Dalton, J. C. (2006). "The Place and Spirituality in the Mission and Work of College Student Affairs." In A.W. Chickering, J. C. Dalton, and L. Stamm. *Encouraging Authenticity & Spirituality in Higher Education*. (145–164). San Francisco: Jossey-Bass.

Dalton, J.C. (2006). "Integrating Spirit and Community in Higher Education." In A.W. Chickering, J.C. Dalton, and L. Stamm. *Encouraging Authenticity & Spirituality in Higher Education*. (165–185). San Francisco: Jossey-Bass.

Dalton, J. C., Eberhart, D., Bracken, J., and Echols, K. (2006). "Inward Journeys: Forms and Patterns of College Student Spirituality." *Journal of College & Character*. 7(8) 1–22.

Davie, G. (1994). *Religion in Britain Since 1945*. Oxford: Wiley-Blackwell. de Sousa, M. (2017). "The Complex Reasons for Missing Spirituality." *Democracy and Education*. Graduate School of Education and Counseling at Lewis and Clark, Portland, Oregon. 25, (1), 1–7.

Detweiler, C. (2013). *iGods: How Technology Shapes Our Spiritual and Social Lives.* Grand Rapids, MI., Brazos Press, Baker Publishing.

Dillen, A. (2015). "The Complex Flavour of Children's Spirituality in Flanders: Fostering an Open Catholic Spirituality." In J. Watson, M. de Souza, and A. Trousdale. *Global Perspectives on Spirituality and Education.* (45–57). New York: Routledge.

Dirkx, J. M. (2003). "Nurturing Soul in Adult Learning." In P. Cranton (ed.). *Transformative Learning in Action: Insights from Practice.* San Francisco: Jossey-Bass.

Dornauer, J. (2015). *Beyond Resistance: The Institutional Church Meets the Postmodern World.* Chicago: Exploration Press.

Drescher, E. (2016). *Choosing our Religion: The Spiritual Loves of America's Nones.* New York: Oxford University Press.

Duerr, M. (2003). "Survey of Transformative and Spiritual Dimensions of Higher Education." *Journal of Transformative Education.* 1(3) 177–211. Retrieved April 2, 2010. http://jtd.sagepub.com/content/1/3/177.

Dumestre, M. (1997). *A Church at Risk: The Challenge of Spiritually Hungry Adults.* New York: Crossroad Publishing.

Elkins, D. N., Hedstrom, L. J., Hughes, L. L., Leaf, J. A., and Saunders, C. (1988). "Towards a Humanistic-Phenomenological Spirituality: Definition, Description, and Measurement." *Journal of Humanistic Psychology.* 28(4) Fall, 6–18.

English, L. M., and Gillen, M. A., (2000). "Addressing the Spiritual Dimensions of Adult Learning: What Educators Can Do." *New Directions for Adult and Continuing Education.* San Francisco: Jossey-Bass.

English, L. M., Fenwick, T. J., and Parsons, J. (2005). "Interrogating Our Practices of Integrating Spirituality into Workplace Education." *Australian Journal of Adult Education.* 45(1) April, 7–28.

English, L. M., Tisdell, and E. J. (2010). "Spirituality and Adult Education." In C.E. Kasworm, A. D. Rose, and J. M. Ross- Gordon (eds.) *Handbook of Adult and Continuing Education.* (285– 294). San Francisco: Jossey-Bass.

Erbe, R., and Lohrmann, D. (2015). "Mindfulness Meditation for Adolescent Stress and Well-being: A Systematic Review of the Literature with Implications for School Health Programs." *The Health Educator.* 47. (2). 12–19.

Falb, M. D., and Paragament, K. I. (2012). "Relational Mindfulness, Spirituality, and the Therapeutic Bond." *Asian Journal of Psychiatry.* 5, 351–354.

Fenwick, P. (2003). "The Neuroscience of Spirituality." Retrieved March 30, 2020. https://www.semanticscholar.org/paper/The-Neuroscience-of-Spirituality-Fenwick/d226bf72bc581dde62 393b2d64416ca3386e7774.

Fenwick, P. (2011). "The Neuroscience of Spirituality." Retrieved March 30, 2020. https://www.rcpsych.ac.uk/docs/default-source/members/ sigs/spirituality-spsig/spirituality-special-interest-group-pub lications-peter-fenwick-the-neuroscience-of-spirituality. pdf?sfvrsn=f5f9fed8_2.

Fenwick, T., English, L., and Parson, J. (2001). "Dimensions of Spirituality: A Framework for Adult Educators." Presented at the Canadian Association for the Study of Adult Education, Laval University, Quebec, 78–85.

Ferrer, J. N. (2011). "Participatory Spirituality and Transpersonal Theory: A Ten-Year Retrospective." *The Journal of Transpersonal Psychology.* 43(1) 1–34.

Fischer, E. (2013). "Writing and Telling Healing the Pain of Disconnection." In C.B. Dillard and C.L.E. Okpalaoka. *Engaging Culture, Race and*

Spirituality: New Visions (Counterpoints: Studies in the Postmodern Theory of Education). (42–57). New York: Peter Lang International.

Fitch, F. E., Fitzgerald, J., Himchak, M. V., and Pisani, E. (2009). "The Quest for Meaning: Teaching Spirituality in Communications, Social Work, Nursing, and Leadership." *Religion and Education.* 36 (3) Fall: University of Northern Iowa.

Fleming, J. J. (2005). "The Role of Spirituality in the Practice of Adult Education Leaders." Doctoral Dissertation, University of Georgia. Retrieved July 12, 2009. http://www.coe.uga.edu/.

Fox, M. (1979). *A Spirituality Named Compassion: Uniting Mystical Awareness with Social Justice.* Minneapolis, MN, Winston Press.

Fox, M. (2006). A *New Reformation Creation Spirituality and the Transformation of Christianity.* Rochester, Vermont: Inner Traditions.

Friedman, T. L. (2007). *The World is Flat: A Brief History of the Twenty-First Century.* (Revised Edition). New York: Picador/Farrar, Straus and Giroux.

Fromm, E. (1976). *To Have or To Be?.* New York: Continuum.

Fuller, R. C. (2001). *Spiritual but Not Religious: Understanding Unchurched America.* Oxford: Oxford University Press.

Gabhart, E. A. (2015). *The Spiritual But Not Religious: Who Are They, and Who Is More Likely to Be One?* (Unpublished Master's Thesis). University of North Texas.

Gallagher, E. V. (2009). "Spirituality in Higher Education?" Caveat Emptor. *Religion & Education*, 36(2) Summer, University of Northern Iowa, 68-87.

George, L. K., Larson, D. B., Koenig, H. G., and McCullough, M. E. (2000). "Spirituality and Health: What We Know, What We Need to Know." *Journal of Social and Clinical Psychology.* 19(1), 102–116.

Glazer, S. (ed.). (1999). *The Heart of Spirituality: Spirituality in Education.* New York: Jeremy P. Tarcher.

Groen, J. (2002). "The Experiences and Practice of Adult Educators in Addressing Spirituality within the Workplace: An Empirical Study. In J. M. Pettitt and R. P. Francis (eds.). *Proceedings of the 43rd Annual Adult Education Research Conference* (134–140). North Carolina State University.

Groen, J. and Jacob, J. (2006). "Spiritual Transformation in a Secular Context: A Qualitative Research Study of Transformative Learning in Higher Education." *International Journal of Teaching and Learning in Higher Education.* 18(2), 75–88.

Groen, J. (2008). "Moving in from the Fringes of the Academy: Spirituality as an Emerging Focus in the Canadian Professional Faculties of Business, Education and Social Work." Draft Article. 1–29.

Groen, J. (2008). "Paradoxical Tensions in Creating a Teaching and Learning Space within a Graduate Education Course on Spirituality." *Teaching in Higher Education*, 13(2)193– 204.

Hamm, R. (2007). *Recreating the Church: Leadership For The Post-Modern Age.* St. Louis: MO. Chalice Press.

Hammett, E. H. (2005). *Spiritual Leadership in a Secular Age: Building Bridges Instead of Barriers (TCP Leadership Series).* Duluth, GA: Chalice Press.

Harari, Y. N. (2018). *21 Lessons for the 21st Century.* New York: Signet-Random House.

Harris P. (ed.) (1998). *Silence and Stillness in Every Season: Daily Readings with John Main.* New York: Continuum.

Hawkins, T. R. (1997). *The Learning Congregation: A New Vision of Leadership.* Louisville, KY: Westminster John Knox Press.

Hendrix, K. G. and Hamlet, J. D. (eds.). (2009). *As the Spirit Moves Us: New Directions for Teaching and Learning,* # 120. San Francisco: Jossey-Bass.

Hendrix, K. G. (2009). "The Spirit That Strengthens Me: Merging the "Life of the Mind" with "Life in the Spirit." In K. G. Hendrix and J. D. Hamlet (eds.). *As the Spirit Moves Us: New Directions for Teaching and Learning,* # 120. San Francisco: Jossey-Bass.

Heelas, P., Woodhead, L., Seel, B., and Szerszynski, B. (2005). *The Spiritual Revolution: Why Religion Is Giving Way to Spirituality (Religion and Spirituality in the Modern World).* New York: Wiley - Blackwell.

Heelas, P. (2008). *Spiritualities of Life: New Age Romanticism, and Consumptive Capitalism.* Oxford: Wiley-Blackwell.

Hill, P. C., Paragment, K. I., Hood, R. W. Jr., McCullough, M. E. Swyers, J. P., Larson, D. B., and Zinnbauer, B.J. (2000). "Conceptualizing Religion and Spirituality: Points of Commonality, Points of Departure." *Journal for the Theory of Social Behavior.* 30:1.

Hill, P. C. (2005). "Measurement in the Psychology of Religion and Spirituality: Current Status and Evaluation." In R.F. Paloutzian and C. L. Park (eds.). *Handbook of Psychology of Religion and Spirituality (First Edition).* (43–61). New York: Guildford Press.

Hocking, D. E., Myers, M. D., and Cairns, S. (2008). "Toward a Model for the Use of Spirituality in Teaching Accounting." *Journal of Academic and Business Ethics.* (1) January. Retrieved April 20, 2010. http://www.aabri.com/manuscripts/08019.pdfve.

Holt, B. P. (2005). *Thirsty for God: A Brief History of Christian Spirituality.* Minneapolis, MN. Augsburg Fortress Publishers.

Holtschneider, D. (2006). "All the Questions: Spirituality in the University." *Journal of College and Character,* 8(1). November. Retrieved September 14, 2009. http://www.collegevalues.org/pdfs/Holtschneider.pdf. 2–3.

Hood, G. K. (2006). "The Notion of Spirituality in Adult and Higher Education." *Higher Education Perspectives*. 2(1), 166–179.

Hoppe, S. L. and Speck, B. W. (eds.) (2005). *Spirituality in Higher Education*. San Francisco: Jossey- Bass.

Hoppe, S. L. (2005). "Spirituality and Leadership." In S. Hoppe and B.W. Speck (eds.). *Spirituality in Higher Education*. (83–92). San Francisco: Jossey-Bass.

Hoppe, S. L. (2007). "Spirituality in Higher Education Leadership." In B. W. Speck and S. L. Hoppe (eds.). *Searching for Spirituality in Higher Education*. (111–136). New York: Peter Lang.

http://pluk.org/centraldirectory/Adult%20learning%20styles/online.rit. edu- Characteristics_of_Adult_Learners.pdf http://online.rit. edu/faculty/teaching_strategies/adult_learners.cfm. Retrieved November 18, 2012.

https://quoteinvestigator.com/2013/11/30/tv-gum/. Retrieved March 1, 2021.

Hull, J. (1985). *What Prevents Christian Adults from Learning?* London: SCM Press.

Hume, E. (2016). *Door to Door: The Magnificent, Maddening, Mysterious World of Transportation*. New York: HarperCollins.

Hunter, G. G., III. (1992). *How To Reach Secular People*. Nashville: Abingdon Press.

Hyland, T. (2015). "On The Contemporary Applications of Mindfulness: Some Implications for Education." *Journal of Philosophy of Education*. 49 (2). 170–186.

Hyland, T. (2017). McDonaldizing Spirituality: Mindfulness, Education and Consumerism, *Journal of Transformative Education*, DOI: 10.1177/1541344617696972, https://www.academia.edu/31891168/

Mc_Donaldizing_Spirituality_Mindfulness_Educa tion_and_ Consumerism. Retrieved March 15, 2020.

Hyland, T. (2018). *Philosophy, Science and Mindfulness: Exploring the Links between Eastern and Western Traditions*. Beau Bassin, Mauritius: Scholars' Press.

Indick, W. (2015). *Digital God: How Technology Will Reshape Spirituality*. Jefferson, NC: McFarland Publishing.

"Is the Internet Destroying Our Attention Span?" Posted by Nicole Plumridge on Aug. 1, 2013, http://psychminds.com/is-the-interne t-destroying-our-attentions-span/.

Iyer, P. (2014). *The Art of Stillness*. New York: Ted Books.

Jablonski, M. (2005). "Hidden Wholeness: Spiritual Leadership." *Journal of College and Character*. 6(8), 1–6. Retrieved from http://www. collegevalues.org/pdfs/ Hidden%20Wholeness%20part%20I%20 formatted%20final.pdf. 3.

Jakonen, J. P. (2008). "Beyond Postmodern Spirituality: Ken Wilbur and the Integral Approach." In T. Ahback, (ed.) Papers read at Postmodern Spirituality, Abo, Finland, 11–13 June 2008. 92–109.

Jennings, P., Lantieri, L., and Roeser, R.W. (2012). "Supporting Educational Goals through Cultivating Mindfulness: Approaches for Teachers and Students." In P. M. Brown, M. W. Corrigan, and A. Higgins-D'Alessandro (eds.) *Handbook of Prosocial Education*. Lanham, MD: Rowan & Littlefield. 371–397.

Jones, L. (2005). "What Does Spirituality in Education Mean? Stumbling Toward Wholeness." *Journal of College and Character*. 6(7), 1–7. Retrieved September 14, 2009. http://www.collegevalues.org/pdfs/ spirit%20in%20ed.%20jones%20formatted%2 0final%202.pdf.

Kanungo, R. N. and Mendonca, M. (1994). "What Leaders Cannot Do Without: The Spiritual Dimensions of Leadership." In Jay A.

Conger. *Discovering the Spirituality in Leadership*. (162–198). San Francisco: Jossey-Bass.

Karasu, T. B. (1999). "Spiritual Psychotherapy." (Special Article). *American Journal of Psychotherapy*. 53: 143–161.

Kasworm, C. E., Rose, D., and Ross-Gordon, J. M. (2010). "Conclusion: Looking Back, Looking Forward." In C. E. Kasworm, A. D. Rose, and J. M. Ross- Gordon (eds.) *Handbook of Adult and Continuing Education*. (441–452). San Francisco: Jossey-Bass.

Kessler, R. (2005). "Nourishing Adolescents' Spirituality." In J. P. Miller, S. Karsten, D. Denton, D. Orr, and I. C. Kates (eds.). *Holistic Learning and Spirituality in Education*. (101–107). Albany: State University of New York.

Kilgore, D. (2011). "Toward a Postmodern Pedagogy." In S. B. Merriam and A. P. Grace. (eds.) *The Jossey-Bass Reader on Contemporary Issues in Adult Education*. (416–424). San Francisco: Jossey-Bass. NOOK Book. May 15, 2011

King, K. P. (2010). "Informal Learning in a Virtual Era." In C. E. Kasworm, A. D. Rose, and J. M. Ross- Gordon (eds.) *Handbook of Adult and Continuing Education*. (421–430). San Francisco: Jossey-Bass.

King, P. E. and Boyatzis, C. J. (2015). "Religious and Spiritual Development." In R.M. Lerner (ed.) *Handbook of Child Psychology and Development Science*. Volume 3, 990–1014. New York: John Wiley and Sons.

Kinzer, M. (1981). "Christian Identity in Social Change in Technological Society." In P. Williamson and K. Perrotta (eds.). *Christianity Confronts Modernity: A Theological and Pastoral Inquiry by Protestant Evangelicals and Roman Catholics*. Ann Arbor, MI: Servant Books.

Koenig, H. G. (2010). "Spirituality and Mental Health." *International Journal of Applied Psychoanalytic Studies*. 7(2), 116–122.

Kurtz, E. and White, W. L. (2015). "Recovery Spirituality." *Religions.* 6, 58–81. file: C:/Users/David%20Robson/Desktop/S%20and%20L/religions-06-00058.pdf.

Kurup, R. K. and Kurup, P. A. (2002). "Hypothalamic Digoxin Hemisphere Chemical Dominance and Spirituality." *International Journal of Neuroscience.* 397–407.

Kurzweil, R. (1999). *The Age of Spiritual Machine: When Computers Exceed Human Intelligence.* New York: Penguin Books.

Kyriacou, D., (2018). "Are We Wired for Spirituality? An Investigation into the Claims of Neurotheology." *HTS Teologiese Studies/Theological Studies.* 74(3), 4973. https://doi.org/10.4102/hts.v74i3.4973.

L'Engle, M. (1980). *Walking on Water: Reflections on Faith and Art.* New York: Farrar, Straus and Giroux.

Lakes, R. D. (2000). "Spirituality, Work, and Education: The Wholistic Approach." *Journal of Vocational Education Research,* 25(2).

Lambert, L, III. (2009). *Spirituality Inc.: Religion in the American Workplace.* New York: New York University Press.

Lauzon, A. C. (2001). "The Challenges of Spirituality in the Everyday Practice of the Adult Educator." *Adult Learning.* 12(3) 4–7.

Lauzon, A. C. (2005). "Spirituality and Adult Education: An Emergent Perspective." Paper presented to the 4th Conference on Spirituality and Social Work, London, Ontario, May 26–May 28.

Lazaridou, A. and Pentaris, P. (2016). "Mindfulness and Spirituality: Therapeutic Perspectives." *Person-Centered & Experiential Psychotherapies.* 15:3, 235–244. Retrieved December 27, 2019. DOI: 10.1080/14779757.2016.1180634.

Levitin, D. J. (2014). *The Organized Mind: Thinking Straight in the Age of Information Overload.* New York: Dutton-Penguin Group.

Lindholm, J. A. (2006). "The 'Interior' Lives of American College Students: Preliminary Findings from a National Study." In J. L. Heft, (ed.). *Passing on the Faith: Transforming Traditions for the Next Generation of Jews, Christians, and Muslims.* (75–102). New York, NY: Fordham University Press.

Lindholm, J. (2007). "Spirituality in the Academy: Reinventing our Live and the Lives of our Students." *About Campus.* September–October. Published online in Wiley InterScience www.interscience.wiley.com).DOI: 10.1002/abc.218.

Lipka, M. and Gecewicz, C. (2017). "More Americans Now Say They're Spiritual but Not Religious." *Pew Research Center: Fact Tank* (September 6, 2017). Retrieved January 6, 2020. https://www.pewresearch.org/fact-tank/2017/09/06/more-americans-now-say-they're-spiritual-but-not-religious/ - http://pewrsr.ch/2xP0Y8w.

Loboprabhu, S., Lomax, J. (2010). "The Role of Spirituality in Medical School and Psychiatry Residency Education." *International Journal of Applied Psychoanalytic Studies.* 7(2), 180–192.

Love, P. and Talbot, D. (1999). "Defining Spiritual Development: A Missing Consideration for Student Affairs." *NASPA Journal.* 37(1), Fall 1999.

Lyon, D. (2000). *Jesus in Disneyland: Religion in Postmodern Times.* Malden MA: Polity Press/Blackwell Publishing.

MacKeracher, D. (2004*). Making Sense of Adult Learning (2ⁿᵈ Ed.)* Toronto: University of Toronto Press.

Marques, J. F. (2006). "Removing the Blinders: A Phenomenological Study of U.S. Based MBA Students' Perception of Spirituality in the Workplace." *Journal of American Academy of Business.* Cambridge, 8(1), 55–61.

Mark, C. W. (1995). *Spiritual Intelligence (SQ): The Symbiotic Relationship Between Spirit and the Brain: Insights Into the Postmodern Journey of Spirituality and Holistic Health.* Bloomington, IN: AuthorHouse.

Martin, M. L. (2013). *Spirituality, Medical Science and Health: The Spiritual Effects of a Sense of Entitlement in the Ministry of Healing in the Christian Church.* Unpublished doctoral dissertation, University of South Africa.

May, G. (1991). *The Awakened Heart: Opening Yourself to the Love You Need.* New York: HarperOne.

Mayes, C. (2001). "Cultivating Spirituality Reflectivity in Teachers." *Teacher Education Quarterly.* 28(2), 5–22. Retrieved September 14, 2009. http://www.teqjournal.org/backvols /2001/ 28_2/ v28n202.pdf.

McBride, J. L. (2011). "The Missing Component in the Spirituality and Medicine Literature: Reflections." *Annals of Behavioral Science and Medical Education.* Vol. 17. No. 1, 7–9. Retrieved January 24, 2015. https://link.springer.com/article/10.1007/BF03355141.

McHargue, M. (2016). *Finding God in the Waves: How I Lost My Faith and Found It Again Through Science.* New York: Convergent

McLaren, B. (2011). *Naked Spirituality: A Life with God in 12 Simple Words.* New York, NY: HarperOne.

McLennan, S. (2005). "Doorways to Spirituality for Students: A Chaplain's View." *Journal of College and Character.* (7)2. http://www. collegevalues.org/pdfs/ doorways%20to%20spirituality%20 mclennan%20formatted%20final.pdf.

Mercadante, L. (2014). *Belief without Borders: Inside the Minds of the Spiritual but Not Religious.* Oxford: Oxford University Press.

Milacci, F. (2003). "A Step Towards Faith: The Limitations of Spirituality in Adult Education Practice." Doctoral Dissertation, Penn State University. Retrieved May 13, 2010. http://citeseerx.ist.psu.edu/ viewdoc/download?doi=10.1.1.1014.9377&rep=rep1&type =pdf/

Miller, C. K. (1989). *Boomer Spirituality Seven Values for the Second Half of Life.* Nashville: Discipleship Resources.

Miller, D. (2003). *Blue Like Jazz: Nonreligious Thoughts on Christian Spirituality.* Nashville, TN: Thomas Nelson.

Miller, J., Karsten, S., Denton, D., Orr, D., and Kates, I. C. (2005). *Holistic Learning and Spirituality in Education: Breaking New Ground.* Albany: State University of New York.

Miller, J. (2000). *Education and the Soul: Toward a Spiritual Curriculum.* Albany: State University of New York.

Milojević, I. (2005). "Critical Spirituality as a Resource for Fostering Critical Pedagogy." *Journal of Futures Studies.* 9(3), February 1–16. Retrieved April 18, 2010. http://www.jfs.tku.edu.tw/9-3/A01.pdf. 10.

Minor, C. V. (2012). *Promoting Spiritual Well-being: A Quasi- Experimental Test of Hay and Nye's Theory of Children's Spirituality.* (Unpublished Doctoral Dissertation). Prescott Valley, AZ: Northcentral University.

Mizock, L., Chandrika U. M., and Russinova, Z. (2012). "Spiritual and Religious Issues in Psychotherapy with Schizophrenia: Cultural Implications and Implementation." *Religions.* 2012, 3, 82–98. doi:10.3390/rel3010082. Retrieved, December 4, 2014.

Mohandas, E. (2008). "Neurology of Spirituality." *Mens Sana Monographs.* Jan–Dec. 6(1), 63–80.

Montgomery-Goodnough, A. and Gallagher, S. J. (2007). *Review of Research on Spiritual and Religious Formation in Higher Education. Proceedings of the Sixth Annual College of Education Research Conference: Urban and International Education Section.* 60–65.

Moore, T. (2005). "Education for the Soul." In J. P. Miller, S. Karsten, D. Denton, D. Orr, and I. C. Kates (eds.). *Holistic Learning and Spirituality in Education.* (9–15). Albany, NY: State University of New York.

Nash, R. J. and Bradley, D. L. (2007). "Moral Conversation: A Theoretical Framework for Talking about Spirituality on College Campuses."

In B. W. Speck and S. L. Hoppe (eds.). *Searching for Spirituality in Higher Education*. (137–154). New York: Peter Lang.

Neal, J. (2017). "Workplace Spirituality Annotated Bibliography." https://www.academia.edu/32013953/WORKPLACE_SPIRITUALITY_ANNOTATED_BIBLIO GRAPHY_Compiled.

Nelson, K. (2010). *The Spiritual Doorway in the Brain: A Neurologist's Search for the God Experience*. New York: Dutton.

Newberg, A. (2010). *How God Changes Your Brain: Breakthrough Findings from a Leading Neuroscientist*. New York: Ballantine Books.

Newberg, A., et al. (2017). "Effect of a One-Week Spiritual Retreat on Dopamine and Serotonin Transporter Binding: A Preliminary Study." *Religion, Brain & Behavior*. 1–14. 10.1080/2153599X.2016.1267035.

Newell, J. P. (2002). *Echo of the Soul: The Sacredness of the Human Body*. Harrisburg, PA: Morehouse Publishing.

Norman, J. O. and Renehan, C. (2014). "The Custody of Spiritual Education in Ireland." In J. Watson, M. de Souza, and A. Trousdale. *Global Perspectives on Spirituality and Education*. (33–44). New York: Routledge.

Nouwen, H. (1976). *Reaching Out: The Three Movements of the Spiritual Life*. Glasgow: William Collins and Sons.

Öğretici, Y. Z. (2018). "An Exploration of Subjective-Life of Spirituality and Its Impact." *Education Science*. Educ. Sci. 2018, 8(4), 212. https://doi.org/10.3390/educsci8040212. Reprinted in *Education Science Special Edition, There Is a Crack in Everything*.170–181.

Ó Murchú, D. (1997). *Reclaiming Spirituality*. New York: New York. Crossroads Books.

Oliveira, A. (2004). "The Place of Spirituality in Organizational Theory." *Electronic Journal of Business Ethics and Organization*.

9(2). Retrieved August 16, 2010. http://ejbo.jyu.fi/pdf/ejbo_vol9_no2_pages_17-21.pdf.

Packard, J. (2015). *Church Refugees: Sociologists reveal why people are DONE with church but not their faith.* Loveland, CO: group.com.

Palmer, P. (1990). *The Active Life: A Spirituality of Work, Creativity, and Caring.* San Francisco: Jossey-Bass.

Palmer, P. (1993). *To Know as We are Known: Education as a Spirituality Journey.* New York: HarperOne.

Palmer, P. J. (2010). "Toward a Philosophy of Integrative Education." In P.J. Palmer, A. Zajonc, M. Scribner, AND M. Nepo. *The Heart of Higher Education: A Call to Renewal Transforming The Academy through Collegial Conversations.* (19–33). San Francisco: Jossey-Bass.

Paloutzian, R. F., Park, C. L. (eds.) (2005). *Handbook of Psychology of Religion and Spirituality (First Edition).* New York: Guildford Press.

Parks, S. D. (2000). *Big Questions, Worthy Dreams: Mentoring Young Adults in Their Search for Meaning, Purpose and Faith.* Jossey-Bass: San Francisco.

Parks, S. D. (2008). "Leadership, Spirituality, and the College as a Mentoring Environment." *Journal of College and Character.* 10(2). http://www.collegevalues.org /pdfs/Parks.pdf.

Pillow, W. (2012). *Spirituality Beyond Science and Religion.* Bloomington, IN: iUniverse.

plasticsurgery.org/news/blog/why-are-millennials-getting-botox-and-fillers-in-their-twenties, November 17, 2017. Retrieved January 18, 2021.

Plumridge, N. (2013). "Is the Internet Destroying Our Attention Span? Posted by Nicole Plumridge on August 1, 2013. http://psychminds.com/is-the-internet-destroying-our-attention-span/.

Putnam, R. D. (2021). *The Upswing: How America Came Together a Century Ago and How We Can Do It Again.* New York: Simon and Schuster.

Raschke, C. (2004*). The Next Reformation: Why Evangelicals Must Embrace Postmodernity.* Grand Rapids, MI: Baker Academic.

Remen, R. N. (1999). "Educating for Mission, Meaning and Compassion." In S. Glazer (ed.). *The Heart of Spirituality: Spirituality in Education.* (33–49). New York: Jeremy P. Tarcher.

Rinallo, D., Scott and L., Maclaran, P. (2012). "Introduction: Unravelling Complexities at the Commercial/Spiritual Interface." In D. Rinallo, L. Scott, and P. Maclaran (eds.). *Consumption and Spirituality.* (1–25). Routledge Interpretive Marketing Research. New York: Routledge-Taylor and Francis Group.

Robson, D. (2019). *The Intelligence Trap: Why Smart People Make Dumb Mistakes.* New York. W.W. Norton.

Rogers, J. (2006). "Role-Modeling Authenticity in Higher Education, Spirituality in Higher Education." *A National Study of College Student's Search for Meaning and Purpose.* 3(1) 1–5.

Rohr, R. (2013). *Immortal Diamond: Searching for Our True Self.* San Francisco: Jossey-Bass.

Rohr, R. (2015). *What the Mystics Know: Seven Pathways to Your Deeper Self.* New York: Crossways Publishing Inc.

Rossiter. G. (2010). "Perspective on Contemporary Spirituality: Implications for Religious Education in Catholic Schools. *International Studies in Catholic Education.* 2:2, 129–147.

Rossitier, G. (2014). "A Perspective on Spiritual Education in Australian Schools: The Emergence of Non-Religious Personal Development Approaches." In J. Watson, M. de Souza and A. Trousdale. *Global Perspectives on Spirituality and Education.* (140–152). New York: Routledge.

Sachs, W. L. and Bos, M. S. (2016). *Fragmented Lives: Finding Faith in an Age of Uncertainty*: Harrisburg, PA: Morehouse Publishing.

Sawatzky, R. and Pesut, B. (2005). "Attributes of Spiritual Care in Nursing Practice." *Journal of Holistic Nursing.* 23 (1), March, 19–33.

Sayadmansour, A. (2014). "Neurotheology: The relationship between Brain and Religion." *Iran Journal of Neurology.* 13 (1), 52–55.

Schiller, S. A. (2005). "Contemplating Great Things in Soul and Place." In J. P. Miller, S. Karsten, D. Denton, D. Orr, and I. C. Kates (eds.). *Holistic Learning and Spirituality in Education.* (161–166). Albany: State University of New York.

Sendjaya, S. (2007). "Conceptualizing and Measuring Spiritual Leadership in Organizations." *International Journal of Business and Information.* 2 (1), 104–126.

Shahjahan, R. A. (2010). "Toward a Spiritual Praxis: The Role of Spirituality Among Faculty of Color Teaching for Social Justice." *The Review for Higher Education.* 33(4), 473–512.

Shea, J. (2005). *Finding God Again.* Washington, D.C.: Rowan and Littlefield

Shirley, C. M. (2009). "The Role of Spirituality in the Practice of Transformational Technical College Leaders." Doctoral Dissertation, University of Georgia. Retrieved April 12, 2010. https://getd.libs.uga.edu/pdfs/shirley_charity_m_200908_edd/shirley_charity_m_2009 08_edd.pdf.

Slater, P. (2008). *The Chrysalis Effect: The Metamorphosis of Global Culture.* Portland: OR: Sussex Academic Press.

Small, J. L. (2008). "College Students' Religious Affiliation and Spiritual Identity: A Qualitative Study." Doctoral Dissertation, University of Michigan. Retrieved April 5, 2010. http://sz0029.wc.mail.comcast.net/service/home/~/Small-%20PhD.pdf?auth=co&loc=en_US&id= 119702&part=2.

Smith, R. S. (2005). *Truth and the New Kind of Christian: The Emerging Effects of Postmodernism in the Church.* Wheaton, Il.: Crossway Books.

Speck, B. W. and Hoope, S. L. (eds.) (2007). *Searching for Spirituality in Higher Education.* New York: Peter Lang.

"Spirituality in Higher Education: A National Study of College Student's Search for Meaning and Purpose: (2003, July 21)." *UCLA Launches Study on Spirituality National Study to track College Student's Spiritual Growth* [Press release]. http://www. spirituality.ucla.edu/ news/Spirituality_2003-07-21.pdf.

Stamm, L. (2006). "The Influence of Religion and Spirituality in Shaping American Higher Education." In A. W. Chickering, J. C. Dalton, and L. Stamm. *Encouraging Authenticity & Spirituality in Higher Education.* (66–91). San Francisco: Jossey-Bass.

Schwartz, C. A. (1999). *Paradigm Shift in the Church: How Natural Church Development Can Transform Theological Thinking.* St. Charles, IL: ChurchSmart Resources.

Steffan, M. C. (2010). *Mystery in Life: Learning from Our Spirituality.* Bloomington, IN: Westbow Press. Nook Book, May 5, 2011.

Streib, H. and Hood, R. (2011). "'Spirituality' as Privatized Experience-Oriented Religion: Empirical and Conceptual Perspectives." *Implicit Religion.* 14 (4), 433–453.

Stuart-Buttle, R. (2013). *Virtual Theology, Faith and Adult Education: An Interruptive Pedagogy.* Newcastle upon Tyne, UK: Cambridge Scholars Publishing.

Tacey, D. (2004). *The Spirituality Revolution: The Emergence of Contemporary Spirituality.* New York: Routledge.

Taylor, P. (2014). *The Next America: Boomers, Millennials, and the Looming Generational Showdown.* New York: PublicAffairs.

Thompson, C. (2010). *Anatomy of the Soul: Surprising Connections between Neuroscience and Spiritual Practices That Can Transform Your Life and Relationships*. Carol Stream, IL: Tyndale Momentum.

Tickle, P. (2008). *The Great Emergence: How Christianity is Changing and Why*. Grand Rapids, MI: Baker Books.

Tiger, L. and McGuire, M. (2010). *God's Brain*. Amherst: New York: Prometheus Books.

Tisdell, E. (2003). "From Research to Practice: Toward a Spiritually Grounded and Culturally Relevant Pedagogy." Pennsylvania Adult and Continuing Education Research Conference. 132–138.

Tisdell, E. (2003). *Exploring Spirituality and Culture in Adult and Higher Education*. San Francisco: Jossey-Bass.

Tisdell, E. (2008). "Spirituality and Adult Learning." In S.B. Merriam (ed.) *Third Update on Adult Learning Theory: New Directions for Teaching and Learning*, # 119. (36–46). San Francisco: Jossey-Bass. Nook Book, October 15, 2011.

Tisdell, E. J. (2014). "Research as Transformative Learning: A Longitudinal Study of Spirituality, Cultural Identity, and Unfolding Wisdom in the Lives of US Educators." In J. Watson, M. de Souza, and A. Trousdale. *Global Perspectives on Spirituality and Education*. (270–281). New York: Routledge.

Tolle, E. (2003). *Stillness Speaks*. Novato, CA: New World Library.

Trousdale, A. (2014). "Pluralism and Polarity: Spirituality and Education in the United States." In J. Watson, M. de Souza, and A. Trousdale. *Global Perspectives on Spirituality and Education*. (233–246). New York: Routledge.

Twenge, J. M. and Campbell, W. K. (2010). *The Narcissism Epidemic: Living in an Age of Uncertainty*. New York: Atria Paperback.

Vaill, P. (1989). *Managing as a Performing Art: New Ideas of a World of Chaotic Change*. San Francisco: Jossey-Bass Publishers.

Vaillant, G. (2008). *Spiritual Evolution: A Scientific Defense of Faith*. New York: Broadway Books.

Vaillant, G. (2009). *Spiritual Evolution: How We Are Wired for Faith, Hope and Love*. New York: Broadway Books.

Van den Heuvel, A. H. (1967). *The Humiliation of the Church*. Philadelphia: Westminster Press.

Veith, G.E. Jr. (1994). *Postmodern Times: A Guide to Contemporary Thought and Culture*. Wheaton, Ill: Crossway Books.

Vella, J. (2000). "A Spirited Epistemology: Honoring the Adult Learner as Subject." In L.M. English and M.A. Gillen. "Addressing the Spiritual Dimensions of Adult Learning." *What Educators Can Do: New Directions for Adult and Continuing Education*. 85, Spring, (7–16). San Francisco: Jossey-Bass.

Voas, D., and Crockett, A. (2005). "Religion in Britain: Neither Believing nor Belonging." *Sociology*. 39(1), 11–28.

Vogel, L. (2000). "Reckoning with the Spiritual Lives of Adult Educators." In L.M. English and M.A. Gillen. *Addressing the Spiritual Dimensions of Adult Learning: What Educators Can Do: New Directions for Adult and Continuing Education*. (17–28). San Francisco: Jossey-Bass.

Waaijman, K. (2007). "Spirituality—A Multifaceted Phenomenon." *Studies in Spirituality*. 17, 1–113.

Watson, J, de Souza, M., and Trousdale, A. (2014). "Preface." *Global Perspectives on Spirituality and Education*. (xi–xiii). New York: Routledge.

Watson, J, de Souza, M., and Trousdale, A. (2014). « Global Perspectives and Context for Spirituality in Education." In J. Watson, M. de Souza, and A. Trousdale. (2015). *Global Perspectives on Spirituality and Education*. (294–314). New York: Routledge.

We, L., Liao, Y., and Yeh, D. (2012). "Nursing Student Perceptions of Spirituality and Spiritual Care." *The Journal of Nursing Research*. 20 (3) September, 219–226.

Westrup, J. (1998). "Invisibility? Spiritual Values and Adult Education." *Australian Journal of Adult and Community Education*. 38 (2) July 1998, 106–110.

Wheatley, M. (2002). "The Work of the Servant-Leader." In L. Spears and M. Lawrence. *Focus on Leadership-Servant-Leadership for the 21st Century*. (349–362). New York: John Wiley and Co.

Wilkins, S. (2013). "The Gospel Meet American Culture." *Catalyst: Contemporary Evangelical Perspectives for United Methodist Seminarians*. April 1, 2013. Retrieved May 31, 2016. http://www. catalystresources.org/the-gospel-meets-american-culture.

Wilson, L. O. (2005). "Listening to Ancient Voices: Reaching Hearts and Souls through Benchmarks and Rites of Passage Experiences in School." In J. P. Miller, S. Karsten, D. Denton, D. Orr, and I. C. Kates (eds.). *Holistic Learning and Spirituality in Education*. (167–177). Albany: State University of New York.

Wong, Y. R., Vinsky, J. (2009). "Speaking from the Margins: A Critical Reflection of the 'Spiritual-but-not-Religious' Discourse in Social Work." *British Journal of Social Work*, (39) 7, (1343–1359). Retrieved February 6, 2011. http://www.tandfonline.com/toc/wspi20/12/4.

Wright, A. (2000). *Spirituality and Education (Master Classes in Education Series)*. London: Routledge.

www.tvfanatic.com/quotes/we-need-to-widen-our-circle-i-have-a-very-wide-circle-i-have/. Retrieved June 27, 2018.

Zinnbauer, B. J., Pargament, K. I., Cole, B., Rye, M. S., Butter, E. M., Belavich, T. G., Hipp, K. M., Scott, A.B., and Kadar, J.L. (1997). "Religion and Spirituality: Unfuzzying the Fuzzy." *Journal for Scientific Study of Religion.* 36(4) 59–564. Retrieved May 19, 2012. http://www.psychology.hku.hk/ftbcstudies/refbase/docs/zinnbauer/1997/34_Zinnbauer_etal1997.pdf.

Zsolnai, L. and Flanagan, B. (eds.) (2019). *The Routledge International Handbook of Spirituality in Society and the Professions.* Abingdon-on Thames, UK: Routledge International.

ABOUT THE AUTHOR

After completing his undergraduate degree at the University of Toronto in his hometown, David Robson entered seminary. In 1981, he graduated with his M. Div. from the College of Emmanuel and St. Chad in Saskatoon, Saskatchewan. Consequently, he was ordained as a deacon and priest in the Anglican Church of Canada. David spent the first half of his ordained parish ministry in his native Ontario. In these years, he completed both a Th.M. on police stress, an M.Ed. on pre-marriage education at Queen's University, Kingston, and undertook additional clinical training. This was accomplished while fully engaged in parish ministry. Many early mornings made this possible! (ditto for this book). He spent much in time in communities as a police, fire, and hospital chaplain. In addition, he served as a volunteer fire fighter.

In 1999, he became the Rector of St. Paul's Episcopal Church in Philipsburg, Pennsylvania* and the Chapel of the Good Shepherd in Hawk Run. At this time, he completed his D. Min. in educating clergy in local settings. In 2005, while remaining in the Diocese of Central Pennsylvania, he accepted the call as the Rector of St. Andrew's in the city of York, where he remained until his retirement. David is an Honorary Canon of St. Stephen's Cathedral, Harrisburg. Today, he assists at Christ Church Anglican, Belleville, where he began his ordained ministry and met his wife, Lynn. Their son, John, and family live nearby.

This book clearly shows his love of reading and reflection! He enjoys gardening because it soothes the spirit and cannot be tackled quickly!

---

* This is reported to be the first church in the USA to make modern use of electric lights. However, the DC current proved very noisy, and the lights were removed two years after installation. This was long before David arrived.

Made in the USA
Las Vegas, NV
19 January 2022

41818946R00213